SECOND EDITION

FOR THE RECORD

THE UNITED FRUIT COMPANY'S SIXTY-SIX YEARS IN GUATEMALA

BY DIANE K. STANLEY

EDITORIAL ANTIGUA S.A.

Copyright © 2000 by Joan Acosta

All rights reserved,
including the right of reproduction
in whole or in part in any form.

Published by:
EDITORIAL ANTIGUA S.A.
Guatemala City, Guatemala

Originally published 1994 in Guatemala
by Diane K. Stanley
Copyright © 1994 Diane K. Stanley

ISBN 99922-722-0-1

Printed in Guatemala

Editorial Antigua S.A.
3 Avenida 0-50 Zona 2
Guatemala City, Guatemala
www.macaw.com

To all those employees –
especially my mother and father –
who worked for *La Frutera*.

Introduction to the Second Edition

Since it was first published seven years ago, Diane K. Stanley's *For the Record: The United Fruit Company's Sixty-Six Years in Guatemala* remains a classic study of the United Fruit Company and of the decisive events which led to the overthrow of the Jacobo Arbenz government in 1954. In deflating the "black legend" of United Fruit, her book opens the door to a fresh interpretation of 20th-century Guatemalan history and to a more clear understanding of the challenges the country faces in the 21st century.

A few note-worthy events have occurred since *For the Record* was first published, including the signing of a Peace Accord between the government and URNG guerrillas on December 29, 1996. The Peace Accord brought an end to 36 years of armed conflict in Guatemala and has placed the country on the path to greater institutional and social stability. While the peace agreement has brought other positive changes, such as a more professional civilian police force, many of the government's commitments remain unfulfilled, despite the ongoing presence of a United Nations mission to verify compliance with the Accord.

Other events that have occurred since Diane Stanley published her book include the concession of Guatemala's railroad to a U.S. company, the Railroad Development Corporation (RDC) of Pittsburgh, Pennsylvania, in June 1997. By 1995, less than thirty percent of Guatemala's rails were estimated to be in good working condition and the government had definitively stopped train service. That same year, FEGUA's wooden terminal station in Guatemala City mysteriously burned, destroying evidence about IRCA properties that had been transferred to the government along with the railroad. On winning the 1997 bid for a 50-year concession, RDC president Henry Posner said, "This is the most difficult prospect I have ever seen. To my knowledge the rehabilitation of a railroad system that has been completely shut down has never been tried before anywhere in the world." Despite the gloomy forecast, RDC invested approximately $5 million to restore the Puerto Barrios to Guatemala City line in 1999 and began transporting freight in December that same year. Trains now run daily in Guatemala and RDC expects to haul more than 80,000 tons of cargo in 2001.

The Quiriguá Hospital, donated by United Fruit to the Guatemalan government in the early 1970s, serves as a training center for rural health technicians, and is currently being renovated and enlarged with assistance from the Japanese government.

In November 2000, Chiquita Brands International, United Fruit's successor, became the first global banana producer to obtain certification from the Rainforest Alliance's Better Banana Project, meeting environmental and social standards for growing the fruit on 127 company-owned farms in Colombia, Costa Rica, Honduras, Panama and Guatemala. Criteria for certification included wildlife, soil and wetlands conservation measures, strictly-managed use of agrichemicals and integrated waste management systems. Certified bananas now account for two-thirds of Chiquita's shipments to the U.S. and ninety percent of those to Europe.

Chiquita also reported severe financial problems in 2000, with losses of nearly $54 million in the third quarter of the year, due to world-wide overproduction of bananas and the rebuilding of its Honduran plantations, wiped out by Hurricane Mitch in 1998.

A few small changes in the text, mostly typographical, have been made in the second edition and new photos have been included from the extensive photographic collection at the Centro de Investigaciones Regionales de MesoAmerica (CIRMA). The publisher thanks Tomás Chitic, Rosie Conde and Valia Garzón Diaz, of Fototeca Guatemala at CIRMA, for their kind assistance in locating photographs. The assistance of Joan Acosta and Miguel Bello in proofreading the book is also gratefully acknowledged.

Contents

Introduction to the Second Edition	i
Preface	v
Acknowledgements	vii

1. The Historical Setting — 1
- Changing Export Crops and Political Stability — 4
- German Coffee Planters Become a Commanding Force — 5
- Indian Laborers: Foundation of Guatemala's Coffee Economy — 10
- Justo Rufino Barrios and the Coffee Boom — 12
- Railroads Arrive — 13

2. A Major Merger and a Major Railroad — 20
- Boston Fruit Joins Forces with a Railroading Genius — 24
- Estrada Cabrera and the Railroad to the Atlantic — 26
- The Disputed Line to El Salvador — 35

3. The Origins of United Fruit's "Black Legend" — 40
- Banana Lands Bring Guatemala and Honduras Close to War — 45
- United Fruit Moves to the Pacific Coast — 47
- The Company Finds a Friend in a Cruel Dictator — 49
- The Compañía Agrícola Reneges on its 1930 Contract — 53
- UFCO Becomes a Majority Stockholder in the Railroad — 55
- The IRCA: Target of Innumerable Criticisms — 60
- UFCO's Telecommunications Operations — 63
- The Great White Fleet Monopolizes Atlantic Coast Shipping — 64
- Analyzing UFCO's "Black Legend" — 66

4. Banana Production and its Personnel — 70
- The Organization of a Banana Division — 79
- UFCO Personnel Policies — 82
- Farm Overseers: On the Cutting Edge of Banana Production — 86
- Jungle-Edge Working Conditions — 88

5. Social Life and Social Concerns — 97
- Salaries and Commissary Privileges — 102
- Medical Care: A Constant, Critical Need — 105
- UFCO's Distinctive Housing Facilities — 110
- Addressing Educational Needs — 116
- An Agricultural School Serving the Americas — 120
- Helping to Preserve Guatemala's Heritage — 123

6. The U.S. and United Fruit Confront the Guatemalan "Time Machine" — 130
The October 20 Revolution and the "White Candidate" — 132
Labor Unions: Sustenance of the Revolution — 136
U.S.-Guatemala Relations Deteriorate — 141
Arana's Murder: Immediate and Long-term Implications — 143
"An Agrarian Reform is of Capital Importance" — 147
Guatemala's Most Historic Law is Promulgated — 152

7. Protecting UFCO's Interests or Excising a Communist Beachhead? — 160
UFCO Mounts an Effective Media Campaign — 163
John Foster Dulles vs. Guatemala — 164
A U.S. Policy Based on Vested Interests? — 169
"If They Gave a Gold Piece for Every Banana" — 171
More than a Barracks Revolt — 173
United Fruit's Role in the Coup — 179
Reasons for Intervention Still in Dispute — 181
The Clock Turns Back — 184
The Arbenz Legacy — 187

8. New Management Precipitates UFCO's Departure — 190
New Management Implements Needed Changes — 192
La Frutera Abandons its South Coast Plantations — 194
Eli Black's AMK Corporation Buys Out United Fruit — 197
United Brands Sells Bananera to Del Monte — 199

9. Evaluating Sixty-Six Years of Operations — 201
United Fruit's Impact on the Guatemalan Economy — 215
La Frutera's Legacy — 220

Epilogue — 226
Transformations in the Banana Industry — 228
Chiquita Banana Returns to Guatemala — 233
Chiquita Brands International Today — 234
The Railroad: Obsolete, Inefficient and Subsidized — 237

Chapter Notes — 239

Bibliography — 274

Maps
Route of the IRCA's Guatemalan Operations — 19
Distribution of Guatemala's Crop Lands (1960) — 159

Preface

Few American companies operating in Latin America have been more consistently criticized than the United Fruit Company. Incorporated in New Jersey in 1899, the Boston-based banana company at one time owned or leased approximately 3.5 million acres in Guatemala, Honduras, Costa Rica, Nicaragua, Panama, Cuba, Jamaica, the Dominican Republic, Colombia and Ecuador. In its peak years, during the 1930s, United Fruit employed upwards of 100,000 persons, more than 90 percent of whom were Latin Americans. Nowhere has the Company been more castigated than in Guatemala, where it began its operations in 1906, and sold its last holdings to the Del Monte Corporation in 1972. Historians, economists, journalists, politicians, lawyers and others — both American and Guatemalan — have written extensively about the United Fruit Company, usually in disparaging terms. In the 1950s, even Miguel Angel Asturias, Guatemala's Nobel Prize-winning novelist, wrote a bitter trilogy censuring the Company.

Most of the literature, particularly books and articles written by Guatemalans who participated in the revolutionary "ten years of spring" which the country experienced between 1944 and 1954, was published thirty to forty years ago. In the interim, the unremitting violence that has afflicted Guatemala for the last three decades — some of which has been directed at scholars, regardless of their ideological persuasions — has made Guatemalan historians extremely reluctant to analyze the ten years of the Arévalo/Arbenz administrations or that of succeeding governments. There is, therefore, a notable dearth of books by Guatemalan scholars who might have written more objectively about this convoluted period of their country's history.

Nearly all recent histories of Guatemala by North American scholars, however, continue to exploit the establishment's prevailing views of the United Fruit Company (today's Chiquita Brands International). These historians repeat the same negative assertions — many of which are untrue or have been distorted. As a result, a "black legend" has evolved that holds UFCO responsible for a long list of nefarious practices, chief of which are a constant, reprehensible interference in the nation's politics, the ruthless exploitation of its workers, and the extraction of millions of dollars in profits, while contributing virtually nothing to Guatemala's development.

Having been born at a United Fruit Company hospital on Guatemala's north coast and lived for several years in the division headquarters for its south coast plantations, I have always found it curious that so many scholars have consistently repeated the same accusations about UFCO's Guatemala operations. It is even more intriguing that virtually no historians have sought to verify whether most of the oft-repeated charges are, in fact, valid. This book, which does not pretend to be an academic treatise, puts on the record essentially all of the criticisms that have been published about the United Fruit Company's tenure in Guatemala. While some of the allegations are certainly valid, it is also apparent that many others are completely erroneous — as only a few authors have thus far pointed out. Not surprisingly, U.S. scholars have largely dismissed these writers as "apologists."

Most accounts about the banana company have also failed to describe the significant contribution that United Fruit made to Guatemala's human and economic development. In addition to providing employment to tens of thousands of workers and paying them the nation's best rural wages, the Company also offered its employees excellent medical care, rent-free housing, and six years of free schooling for countless children. By clearing and draining thousands of acres of jungle that are today among the country's most productive farm lands, United Fruit converted Guatemala into a major banana producer, thereby ending the country's unhealthy dependence on its exports of coffee. The Company's pioneering work in eliminating malaria and other tropical diseases early in the twentieth century also demonstrated that Guatemala's sparsely inhabited coastal areas offered rich, previously unexploited agricultural zones. Ultimately, the taxes and salaries that the United Fruit Company paid, and the millions of dollars of foreign exchange earnings that it annually generated, impacted in an important way on Guatemala's economy.

The book also examines the frequently repeated charge that the United States engineered the 1954 coup against the government of President Jacobo Arbenz Guzmán in order to regain the land Guatemala had expropriated from the United Fruit Company. Although UFCO was certainly instrumental in orchestrating an effective media campaign against the Arbenz government, it is clear that the Eisenhower administration was intent on ousting what it considered to be a Communist beachhead that threatened U.S. national security. Spurred on by John Foster Dulles, his vehemently anti-Communist secretary of state, President Eisenhower would have moved to depose Arbenz even if the United Fruit Company had never operated in Guatemala.

Finally, the book provides little-known information about the enormous effort that was required to establish immense banana plantations in the midst of isolated jungles, where health concerns and the oppressive heat were constant, debilitating factors. While United Fruit's complex and efficient division of labor was undoubtedly instrumental in transforming huge wilderness areas into productive farm lands, it was the employees — Guatemalan, North American and European — whose hard work made possible the conquest of Guatemala's disease-ridden coastal areas. In doing so, those rugged individuals and their families were forced to cope with the extreme isolation and overwhelming tedium that characterized life on a banana plantation. That they were able to do this, particularly early in the twentieth century, is a remarkable feat that has been little understood or recognized.

Acknowledgements

While I very much value the encouragement that many friends — both in the United States and Guatemala — gave me while I was involved in this project, special thanks are due to Stephen R. Elliott, the director of the Centro de Investigaciones Regionales de Mesoamérica (CIRMA), located in Antigua, Guatemala. Mr. Elliott and his staff provided unfailing assistance with some of the more technical aspects of the preparation of my manuscript. I was also permitted to use CIRMA's excellent library facilities and assigned a comfortable cubicle in which to undertake much of my research.

I am particularly indebted to those banana executives who shared their knowledge and experiences with me. Gerald K. Brunelle, general manager of Del Monte's Guatemala operations, was singularly cooperative, inviting me to visit Bananera and subsequently sharing information on many aspects of today's banana industry. The general manager of the Compañía

Bananera Guatemalteca Independiente, Mario Mena, afforded me valuable facts about the country's second-largest banana company and its current association with Chiquita Brands International, the successor to the United Fruit Company. In La Lima, Honduras, Roberto Turnbull, assistant to the general manager for one of Chiquita Brands's flagship operations, was extremely knowledgeable about all aspects of banana production in the 1990s. William S. Swinford, the general manager of Dole's Honduran plantations at La Ceiba, furnished ample facts on the current operations of an enterprise (the Standard Fruit and Steamship Company) that was once the United Fruit's chief competitor. Finally in Honduras, Dr. Simón E. Malo, then-director of the Escuela Agrícola Panamericana, introduced me to many aspects of an outstanding agricultural school founded by the United Fruit Company in 1942.

More personal recollections of life on a UFCO division were provided through a number of interviews with former employees or their children which Mr. Brunelle and his Bananera staff arranged. These included Dr. Francisco Alvarez, Benjamín Carol Cardoza, César Castillo Barajas, Laura de la Vega, Carlos Haroldo Gomar, Aura Marina Meza de Dardón and Adán Solís.

In Antigua, I was pleased to be able to interview Drs. Edwin M. Shook and E. Croft Long, who contributed, respectively, to the section on the United Fruit Company's restoration of the Maya ruins at Zaculeu and the medical advances undertaken by Dr. Neil P. Macphail, long-time medical director of UFCO's Quiriguá Hospital.

I was extremely gratified that former President Juan José Arévalo, who died in October, 1990, at the age of eighty-six, graciously gave of his time to respond to a number of written questions I submitted to him in April, 1989.

Special thanks are due particularly to those United Fruit Company veterans who, through letters and occasional telephone calls, shared experiences that often had transpired more than fifty years ago. They included Lazarus S. Greenberg, Ted A. Holcombe, John R. Silver, Ike M. Smith, and my uncle, Max P. Campbell. Mr. Silver was uncommonly helpful in clearly recalling distant events that had taken place in Bananera and Tiquisate. All of these gentlemen, now in their 80s, provided unique, little-known information about the United Fruit Company's long years in Guatemala.

Finally, enormous thanks to my sister, Joan E. Acosta, my twin, David W. Stanley, and my brother-in-law, David A. Porter. The later, whose photographs are included in the book, was also most helpful in sharing some of his computer mastery in the preparation of my manuscript. Numerous excellent suggestions for changes in the text were made by my sister and brother, who were unusually supportive and helpful throughout the preparation of this work. Their assistance will be forever appreciated.

-1-

The Historical Setting

oaring twenty-five feet above the closely-cropped grass, the intricately-carved stone monuments are the most colossal stelae the Maya ever sculpted. The mysterious obelisks, which resemble giant, oval tombstones, are compelling testimony to the industry of the pre-Columbian Indians who, more than a thousand years ago, established an imposing city-state at Quiriguá, deep in the jungles of Guatemala's north coast.[1] About a mile from the National Park at Quiriguá, and a few hundred yards from what was once the best hospital in Guatemala, lies a small graveyard where cows trample paths in the exuberant growth of tropical vines and bushes. A sharp machete is required to chop away the thick foliage covering dozens of tombstones, many of them moss encrusted. The twentieth century headstones bear such names as Macphail, Ellerby, Arnold and Turton. They attest to another group who helped to build a very different empire on the same lands the Maya once farmed.

Approximately 300 miles to the west, on the sweltering Pacific coast, an overgrown section of the cemetery in Tiquisate contains nearly twenty distinctive, white cement tombs. All but one of the brass plaques with the names of the deceased have been stolen. Those engraved in stone reveal the names of Watkins, Daniels, Norton and Hamilton. The pioneering Americans and Europeans who are buried at Quiriguá and Tiquisate were among the hundreds of workers and their families who began arriving in Guatemala in 1906 to establish what would become the country's largest agricultural enterprise: the banana plantations of the United Fruit Company.

The first employees of the company found a country that was as exotic, picturesque and primitive as any in Latin America. Covering 42,052 square miles, the Republic of Guatemala is about the size of Pennsylvania. But its towering volcanoes, cool highland plateaus, steamy coastal plains and even a miniature semi-desert provide far greater geographic diversity than any state in the U.S. A giant relief map, located in a park in Guatemala City, graphically reveals the country's most striking characteristic: a chain of thirty-seven volcanoes which begins at the Mexican border in the northwestern part of the country and extends 180 miles south to the boundary with El Salvador. Many of the majestic peaks are smoothly conical and rise upwards of 12,000 feet; several are still active and continually puff luminous white smoke.

Southern Guatemala contains the nation's best agricultural land: the Pacific coastal plain, approximately 150 miles long and twenty to forty miles wide. Sloping from the highlands to the Pacific Ocean, the area can be divided into two bands. The upper piedmont, ranging in altitude from 2,000 to 3,500 feet, is volcanic in origin, and contains some of the most fertile soils in the tropics. This is Guatemala's coffee belt, where the country's major export crop is grown. The lower piedmont, which extends to the Pacific Ocean, is more level, and the hot, often humid climate is debilitating. This area is also extremely fertile, although some sections lack water, especially during the dry season. From 1936 to 1964, the United Fruit Company's south coast subsidiary, the Compañía Agrícola de Guatemala, produced millions of stems of bananas in this torrid region, but today the lower piedmont is used primarily to raise sugar cane, soy beans, sesame and cattle.

On the approximately seventy miles that constitute Guatemala's Atlantic seaboard is the department of Izabal, an area nestled between Honduras on the south and Belize to the north. The Motagua River, on which the Maya located Quiriguá, drains a long, fertile valley before emptying into the Atlantic south of Puerto Barrios. It was in this jungled, swamp-filled area where the United Fruit first began operations in 1906, and where Del Monte today utilizes the same land to grow thousands of acres of bananas. Located on one of the finest deep-water harbors in Central America, Puerto Barrios was for many years Guatemala's principal seaport and the facility from which all of United Fruit's bananas were shipped.

Like all tropical regions, Guatemala enjoys two seasons. The wet or rainy season, which Guatemalans call their "winter," extends from May to October; its torrential downpours often cause extensive flooding and landslides. The dry season, or "summer," when grass and low-growing vegetation become brown and dusty, stretches from October to May. Nevertheless, rainfall varies substantially from one area to another. In Quiriguá, for example, it rains approximately ninety-seven inches per year; in Escuintla, on the Pacific coast, annual rainfall averages seventy-two inches; and in the northeastern city of Cobán, where Guatemalans claim it rains thirteen months a year, the annual rainfall is an impressive 101 inches.[2]

It is not known whether malaria and other deadly tropical diseases plagued Guatemala's lowland areas before the Spanish conquistadors appeared. By the time they arrived in 1524, however, the bulk of Guatemala's Indian population was scattered throughout the central highlands. During the colonial period the Spaniards demonstrated little interest in exploiting the colony's coastal areas and, once independent of Spain, Guatemalans evidenced scant enthusiasm for developing the lowlands. As the writer Frederick Upham Adams noted in 1914, "like all other Central American countries, Guatemala had neglected and ignored its Caribbean lowlands. To the mass of the people of Guatemala, who lived in the highlands, the coasts were dreaded. They were the feared sections of the *tierras calientes*, the fever-stricken hot lands."[3]

Convinced that European immigration could assist in the development of Guatemala's north coast, President Mariano Gálvez (1831-1838) actively encouraged European colonization. The first colonization program, sponsored by London's Eastern Coast Company, brought 225 British colonists to Guatemala in 1836. The Guatemalan government generously provided the settlers with 14,000 acres, located in the department of Izabal, near where the Polochic River empties into Lake Izabal. But the site, which they named New Liverpool, hardly resembled "the earthly paradise" the company had glowingly described in its promotional propaganda. As a result, the community was soon abandoned.[4]

Four years later, the same company attempted to establish another settlement, named Abbotsville, not far from the ill-fated New Liverpool. But, again, with no help from the Guatemalan government and little from the London-based company, the colony of sixty-eight hardy individuals soon found they were no match for the diseases, oppressive heat and hardships of the isolated locale. By 1844, Abbotsville had ceased to exist. A final, major attempt at European colonization was made in 1842, when the government contracted a Belgian company to establish a modern port at Santo Tomás, the site of the present-day port of Santo Tomás de Castilla, not far from Puerto Barrios. The experience of those 1,000 colonists, however, was similar to the unfortunate individuals who settled New Liverpool and Abbotsville. Those who did not succumb were eventually moved to the interior of the country or returned to Europe.

These early experiments to settle foreigners on Guatemala's disease-ridden north coast, where, early in the twentieth century, the United Fruit Company would successfully develop immense banana plantations, provide dramatic evidence of the difficulty inherent in establishing healthy, productive, self-sustaining communities in the midst of remote tropical wilderness areas. It is clear that even in this century only an affluent, well-organized enterprise, with ample experience in tropical agricultural procedures, would be capable of turning swampy, unhealthy areas into enormous, remunerative farms.

CHANGING EXPORT CROPS
AND POLITICAL STABILITY

About the same time that immigration schemes were failing, significant changes were taking place in Guatemala's economy. During the colonial period, cacao, exported to Mexico, and indigo, which found markets in Peru and Mexico, represented the colony's most important commercial crops. By the middle of the nineteenth century, the dyestuff cochineal — in heavy demand by textile factories in England and France — had become Guatemala's leading export. After 1857, however, when chemical dyes were invented, cochineal was no longer a viable export crop. Thus, the collapse of the cochineal market forced the country to look for new sources of export revenues. The solution was found in what is still Guatemala's leading export crop: coffee.

The emergence of coffee as a dynamic cash crop coincided with the first sustained political stability Guatemala had known since its independence in 1821. That the country was able to enjoy nearly twenty-six years of relative peace was due almost entirely to Rafael Carrera, an illiterate peasant leader who, in 1838, at age twenty-three, amassed a force of 12,000 Indians and successfully overthrew the Liberal presidency of Dr. Mariano Gálvez. Although Carrera did not become president until 1840, he ruled Guatemala until his death in 1865.

During the Gálvez administration, prizes were awarded to the first farmer who could harvest one hundred quintals of coffee. (One quintal equals 101.4 pounds). The Carrera government also actively encouraged the raising of coffee. Articles were published with instructions on how to raise the crop; a model coffee farm was established; free seedlings were provided, and the central government frequently ordered officials in numerous departments to increase coffee growing within their jurisdiction.

The lengthy, complicated methods required to grow and process coffee had far-reaching consequences for Guatemala. One of the most significant brought a dominance of foreigners among the earliest coffee growers. Because the nascent coffee *fincas* (farms) required capital outlays, which could not be recovered for at least four years, during which the coffee trees matured, many prospective Guatemalan coffee growers were unable to obtain scarce and costly credit to establish their farms. Moreover, as the Guatemalan economist Valentín Solórzano has noted, "the backward mentality of the Guatemalan *criollos* [individuals of Spanish ancestry born in the New World] did not allow for investments in anything but commerce or cattle." [5]

GERMAN COFFEE PLANTERS BECOME A COMMANDING FORCE

Numerous foreigners, more easily able to obtain credit abroad, quickly saw the future profitability of the new crop. Thus, Colombian, French, Spanish and Belgian immigrants soon established large *fincas* on the higher Pacific piedmont and in the highlands. The largest and most important group of foreigners was the Germans, who began arriving in significant numbers in the 1870s. Many of them settled in the cool, humid area around Cobán, in the northeastern department of Alta Verapaz, where their coffee was shipped down the Polochic River to the Lake Izabal-Río Dulce water system and then embarked on ships from the port of Livingston. In the late 1880s, German interests were also largely responsible for the construction of a 30-mile railroad that freighted coffee from near Cobán to a village not far from Lake Izabal, where a German-dominated steamship company then transported the beans to Livingston. Loaded onto German ships, the coffee sailed directly to Hamburg or Bremen.

There were several reasons why large numbers of Germans migrated to Guatemala. In Hamburg, where Guatemala's mountain-grown coffee was highly regarded, numerous companies were formed to establish coffee plantations in various parts of the country. These enterprises recruited Germans to administer their farms. Similarly, the growing number of German commercial firms in Guatemala gave preference in hiring to their own countrymen, whom they contracted in Germany. The two principal reasons Germans immigrated to Guatemala were the generous terms offered by successive Liberal governments, and the attractive concessions negotiated by the German empire for its citizens.

Taking power in 1871, the Liberals commenced Guatemala's "reform period" — and a series of presidents fully committed to increasing the nation's coffee production. The confiscation of Roman Catholic Church properties under President Justo Rufino Barrios (1873-1885), provided the government with extensive and valuable lands that would soon be made available to coffee growers. For example, by 1883, nearly one million acres had been virtually given away to 373 new or established farms. Averaging 2,642 acres per farm, such vast extensions were sufficient to plant well over a million coffee trees on each *finca*.[6] Barrios, know as *El Reformador*, also provided land for cattle and bananas, which he offered for as little as fifty *pesos* (the equivalent of one dollar) per *caballería* (109.8 acres.)[7]

Although much of the land sold or given away during the Barrios government consisted of unused tracts, former church properties or state-owned land, thousands of acres were taken from the communal land owned by the Maya. Dispossessing them of their farms was a calculated move designed to create rural unemployment and thus force the Indians to work on the coffee *fincas*. As one scholar has pointed out, "the key to the independence of the village Indians was their communal land. While they retained this, and the political and social institutions to protect it, an individual member had little incentive to labor for low wages on someone else's coffee plantation."[8]

The availability of enormous tracts of fertile, inexpensive land and cheap labor were among the most attractive inducements that Guatemala offered to prospective foreign coffee growers. What made the country particularly appealing to Germans was an unusual treaty negotiated in 1887 by Werner von Bergen, the adroit German minister in Guatemala. The treaty assured complete government protection to all German citizens and their properties during the ten years that the document was in force. Germans were free to reside and travel anywhere in the country; they were at liberty to rent or purchase land, shops and warehouses; their freedom of religion was assured, and young men were exempt from Guatemala's military service. Moreover, German citizenship was guaranteed to the legitimate children born of German citizens in Guatemala.[9]

The 1887 treaty was undoubtedly responsible for the second large wave of German immigrants that began arriving in the early 1890s. The sizable sums of German capital subsequently invested in commercial and agricultural enterprises were also a result of the treaty. By 1897, when there were nearly 1,000 Germans resident in Guatemala, they owned forty firms, worth the equivalent of nearly $5 million. Nearly fifty Germans or German companies owned more than 680,000 acres of coffee farms valued at approximately $16 million. The extensive lands they held represented an impressive 2.14 percent of the entire country.[10] Understandably, an extension of the treaty was a constant concern for Germans living in Guatemala, as well as the German foreign office in Berlin. Skillful German diplomats, however, were successful in extending the treaty seven times, until it finally expired in 1915.

That the German coffee growers were extraordinarily efficient is readily apparent in comparing their production with that of other *finqueros* (farmers). At the end of the century, the 200,000 quintals of coffee that they annually produced represented one-third of Guatemala's total production, and an astonishing 1.3 percent of the total world production of the bean.[11] Their productivity can best be illustrated by figures obtained by the U.S. Department of Commerce in 1914:[12]

Nationality	Number of plantations	Production in quintals	Average yield in quintals
Guatemalans	1,657	525,356	317
Germans	170	358,353	2,170
Others*	252	133,167	528
*Including Americans	16	19,285	1,205

What accounts for the phenomenal success of the German coffee growers? Guatemala's Regina Wagner notes that it was not simply greater capitalization. More importantly, the Germans possessed attributes that made them excellent administrators: discipline, tenacity, hard work and the ability to marshal all their resources in the building of a solid, efficient and proud enterprise.[13] Like other foreign planters, the Germans also used new and effective techniques to control the plagues and diseases that affect coffee trees; they were among the first to fertilize their crops, and they employed rational methods of organization on their plantations.[14] Most significant of all, the Germans were "hands-on" administrators who usually lived year-round on their farms, closely supervising all aspects of the daily operations. Guatemalan *finqueros*, on the other hand, often preferred to live in the capital, only occasionally visiting their plantations, and delegating the day-to-day management to hired administrators.[15]

Another scholar assesses the success of German coffee growers in somewhat different terms:

in comparison with the rest of the indigenous landed aristocracy, which had to compete for its place in the market, the Germans established a well integrated, vertical monopoly with direct access to privately owned German banks, transport facilities for the shipping of the product to the European and North American markets, and ownership of the product retailing and distribution. The Germans formed a tight, cohesive subculture... Their entrepreneurial ability advanced them to a position of politico-economic predominance which was maintained even during the depression when the price and amount of coffee exported dropped drastically . . . The Germans were the single most influential and powerful politico-economic group between 1918 and 1936.[16]

The Guatemalan historian J.C. Cambranes also acknowledges that the Germans were adept at using their own and Berlin's significant power in obtaining their objectives. He cites a case in 1906 where the Guatemalan army entered one of the *fincas* owned by Erwin Paul Dieseldorff and summarily "enlisted" several of his workers as recruits. As one of the most prominent Germans in the country, Dieseldorff immediately asked the influential director of the Banco Colombiano in Guatemala City to intercede with higher authorities.

Based on documents that we have discovered, if the pressure exerted by Dieseldorff had not been successful, he most assuredly would have directed himself to the president, either personally or through the representative of the German empire in Guatemala. If this had not produced the desired results, there is no doubt the problem would have been transferred to Berlin where a German war ship would have been dispatched to visit our coast as evidence of German power and proof that the empire supported the demands of its citizens.[17]

By the end of the last century German entrepreneurs were obviously making an enormous contribution to Guatemala's coffee industry and to its growing domestic commerce. For Guatemalans, however, there was a significant trade-off to the presence of a large foreign colony that exerted immense economic and political influence on the small nation's affairs. Not only did the Germans possess extensive tracts of some of the country's most fertile land, they also enjoyed unique and generous concessions not extended to other immigrants. In addition, many German *finqueros* benefited from the services of a largely German-owned railroad, directly profiting from the distribution and retailing of much of the coffee they produced. Ultimately, there was the inescapable reality that Guatemala's German residents were backed by a powerful European empire not adverse to protecting its citizens through diplomatic arm twisting or, if necessary, "gun boat diplomacy." Thus, a relatively large, affluent and extremely influential group of foreigners was well entrenched in Guatemala when the United Fruit Company began its operations there in 1906.

INDIAN LABORERS: FOUNDATION OF GUATEMALA'S COFFEE ECONOMY

Foreign and native *caficultores* (coffee farmers) could never have prospered in Guatemala without the abundant and cheap labor provided by thousands of Indians. Commencing with the colonial period, the Maya provided a seemingly limitless work force for the Spaniards, who regarded them as idolatrous barbarians whose customs debased human nature. Nor did the Maya fare any better after Guatemala's independence from Spain, for the *criollos* and *ladinos* (individuals of mixed Spanish and Indian blood) continued the cruel exploitation of the indigenous peoples.

By the mid 1870s, however, it became apparent that the coffee growers' ever-increasing manpower needs were not being fully met. President Justo Rufino Barrios thus began issuing a series of decrees designed to address the urgent problem. In 1876, a new law ordered *jefes políticos* (the administrative chiefs of each of the country's twenty-two departments) to provide fifty to 100 able-bodied men from villages within their jurisdictions whenever plantation owners required laborers. The Indians were expected to work at least two weeks until they were relieved by the next group of recruits. Another important decree, the law against vagrancy, was promulgated in 1878 and allowed the police to arrest persons who "did not habitually work." The punishment for vagrancy was forty days of work in public institutions "or elsewhere." [18]

It was left to Justo Rufino Barrios's nephew, President José María Reyna Barrios, to enact the last important nineteenth century law regarding Indian labor. Under the guise of protecting rural workers, the government promulgated the 1894 *Reglamento del Servicio de Trabajadores Agrícolas* (Regulation on Landworkers' Services), which obliged every able-bodied worker to carry a booklet attesting to his integrity, his level of productivity and whether he was indebted to any *finquero*. An individual who was unable to produce an up-to-date booklet was regarded as a "vagrant" and immediately fined and sent to a plantation. He remained there until he was able to work off the fine.

For the Indians, life on the farms was appallingly primitive. They lived in crowded, miserable, one-room huts, usually constructed of bamboo walls with roofs of thatched palm leaves (*manaca*) and floors made of packed soil. In the rainy season, torrential rains often turned these damp floors to mud. There was, of course, neither electricity nor potable running water; consequently, women carried water from nearby rivers in heavy earthenware jugs. Clothes were washed in the nearest river. Women and children also spent long hours each day searching for and hauling home firewood, essential for cooking. Corn, black beans, chile, tortillas and *pozol* (a drink produced from toasted cornmeal) made up the Indians' monotonous and meager diet. Plantation owners generally did not provide rations of corn or beans to their laborers, allowing them, instead, to farm small plots of land.

On most *fincas* the men worked from 6 AM until 5 or 5:30 PM. At day's end, the foreman read off a list of what each worker had accomplished: the number of pounds of coffee picked, the amount of land cleared, coffee trees planted or pruned, and many other duties. These figures were used to calculate the worker's salary, which he received each week or every fifteen days.[19] At the turn of the century, wages in the highlands ranged from 2 to 4 cents a day. On the Pacific coast, where there was more competition for labor, workers received the equivalent of 10 cents a day.[20]

There were several reasons why the Indians were treated so unjustly. First, there was an historical precedent. Since the conquest, most Spaniards, who regarded the Maya as lazy and deceitful, had dealt harshly with the indigenous peoples. Plantation owners in the latter part of the nineteenth century had inherited these views, and clearly still shared many of them. A second factor, in a country where coffee growers continually complained about a paucity of laborers, was economic. The difficulties in obtaining workers meant that those laborers who were available should be made to work as hard as possible. Finally, most *finqueros*, politicians, intellectuals and the higher strata of Guatemalan society genuinely believed the Indians had degenerated to an abysmal decadence that made them inferior to many other races.[21]

JUSTO RUFINO BARRIOS AND THE COFFEE BOOM

Many of the members of today's affluent classes trace their wealth to the twelve-year regime of President Justo Rufino Barrios. Indeed, *El Reformador* himself accumulated a vast fortune unequalled in the country.[22] The coffee bonanza that Guatemala enjoyed during the last three decades of the nineteenth century was made possible by a combination of factors, many of them due to Barrios's efforts — and a number of which have had a lasting effect on the country.

Convinced that coffee constituted the engine for Guatemala's development, the dictator provided innumerable incentives for its production. One of the most significant measures was the huge tracts of land that the government granted or sold for risible prices and which the new owners soon converted into coffee plantations. (In many instances, however, only a portion of the land was put into production and much of it — then and today — remained idle.) In fact, one historian estimates that between 1870 and 1920, an astonishing 2,470,000 acres of land previously classified as state, church or Indian communal lands were acquired by aspiring planters.[23]

But Guatemala's coffee boom would not have been possible had it not been for the millions of American and European consumers who began exerting an enormous demand for the aromatic drink. Between 1850 and 1857, world production of the bean totaled 647 million pounds; twenty years later, the figure had risen an impressive 57 percent to over one billion pounds of coffee.[24] During this period, when African coffees were not yet competing with Latin American coffees, Guatemala achieved its highest share of world production: 76,780,200 pounds or 3.7 percent of the world's production of the bean during the 1895-1899 period.[25] As Edelberto Torres Rivas, one of Guatemala's most distinguished historians, has noted, however, Central America's production of coffee would increase during the twentieth century, but its share of the world market would decrease. Thus, the golden era of coffee production in Guatemala corresponded to the last thirty years of the nineteenth century, ending approximately at the beginning of this century.[26]

With Guatemala having quintupled its production of coffee between 1871 and 1884, transportation of the bulky export crop became a vital necessity for the country. The few cart roads available when the Liberals came to power had undergone little improvement or even maintenance since the colonial period. As one scholar has observed, the inadequate roads "delayed shipments, immobilized capital, and raised export expenses, hampering Guatemala's ability to compete internationally." [27]

Another significant obstacle to the growth of coffee exports was the country's deficient ports. The issue was further complicated by Guatemala's geography. Because the coffee belt faces the Pacific Ocean, it was, in one sense, more economical for the beans to be exported from nearby Pacific ports. But Guatemala's principal markets lay in Europe or on the southern or eastern coast of the United States. Consequently, exports from Guatemala's Pacific coast were required to "go south to go north." Coffee and other products had to be shipped to Panama and then transported by rail across the isthmus to the Atlantic Ocean. The rough handling and long delays caused by this inefficient system frustrated exporters. Moreover, the rates charged were prohibitively high. At one point, exasperated Guatemalan merchants even contracted the German Kosmos line for an "all-water" route which took their goods to Europe via the Straits of Magellan.[28]

Still another geographic factor regarding the Pacific ports is that nowhere on the coast is there a protected, deep-water harbor. The huge waves that pound the black, volcanic beaches required ships loading or unloading at San José to anchor three-fourths of a mile off-shore. Passengers and goods were then loaded onto lighters, which ferried them to a steel pier. On the Atlantic, the port of Livingston presented similar difficulties for the shipping of high-bulk commodities such as coffee.

RAILROADS ARRIVE

Although there was an obvious need for improved port facilities, successive Liberal governments determined that the country's paramount requirement was a more effective domestic transportation system. Aware of the successful railroad building programs already completed or underway in the United States and Europe, President Barrios envisioned a railroad system that would link the Pacific and Atlantic oceans, thus providing coffee growers with fast, efficient transportation to either coast. *El Reformador* probably knew that although the initial costs of building a railroad are considerably higher than constructing roads, rail lines transport bulky cargoes more efficiently. Moreover, Guatemala's broken terrain and six months of heavy rains make railroads — once constructed — less expensive to maintain.

Reflecting the importance of linking coffee-producing areas to port facilities, the first railroad was constructed on the south coast between the town of Escuintla, a regional coffee center, and San José, then the busiest port in the country. To construct the thirty miles of track, the government awarded a concession in 1877 to two Americans, William Nanne and Louis Schlesinger, who represented California capitalists. They completed the line in three years.

In 1880, Nanne was awarded another concession, this one to complete the railroad from Escuintla to Guatemala City. When it was inaugurated on July 19, 1884, General Barrios's forty-ninth birthday, the exuberant "Reformer," decked out as a stoker, rode into the capital in the cab of the steam-powered locomotive. When the first train ever seen in Guatemala City chugged into the station, Barrios leaped to the ground and "gave free play to his emotion and satisfaction." [29]

In 1881, a new concession was granted to J.H. Lyman, D.P. Fenner and J.B. Bunting, representing a California company, to construct a short rail line between the coffee-producing area around the town of Retalhuleu and the Pacific port of Champerico.

The railroad-building concessions that the Liberals awarded also invariably included large tracts of land — not unlike those granted by the U.S. government, which awarded 180 million acres of land to seventy railroad companies during the last century.[30] In Guatemala, the government awarded William Nanne 164,700 acres in the department of Izabal; 109,800 acres in the northeastern part of the country were bestowed in the concession for the Retalhuleu-Champerico railroad; a 1902 contract to build a line on the Pacific coast between Coatepeque and Caballo Blanco was good for 54,900 acres; and the contractor for the railroad between Coatepeque and Ayutla (now called Tecún Umán) received 10,980 acres.[31]

But if "an outlet through the north was the fondest hope of the farmers and of all Guatemalans," the country would have to wait twenty-four long years before a railroad from Puerto Barrios to Guatemala City was finally completed in 1908.[32] Overriding greed, engineering difficulties, financial reverses, corruption, fraud, Liberal naivete and high construction costs all played a part in the lengthy building of the 197-mile railroad. Finally, as in most of Central America, banana plantations would provide the incentive for completing the track.

The first efforts to build the line began early in the 1880s when the Barrios government attempted to interest Guatemalan or foreign investors in the project. But few entrepreneurs responded. A subsequent survey undertaken by Guatemala's Ministry of Development explained the investors' wariness. Unlike the short sections of railroads on the Pacific coast, which were comparatively inexpensive to build and provided attractive, short-run profits, the railroad to the Atlantic confronted numerous unknowns. Principal among them was whether the railroad could be operated at a profit. Because it would traverse the thinly populated, underdeveloped departments of Izabal and Zacapa, there was some question as to who the railroad would serve. Besides, Livingston's inefficient facilities still constituted the only port on the Atlantic, and there was no assurance that Pacific coast coffee growers would divert their exports to the Atlantic. Even if they did, large amounts of coffee were only exported during a few months of the year.

There was also far more formidable terrain to cope with. The area near the Atlantic and much of the land along the banks of the Motagua River were waterlogged and swampy, covered with dense jungle and infested with poisonous snakes, malaria-bearing mosquitoes and wild animals. It was a pestilential, sweltering region, with at least six months of heavy, daily rains — conditions most foreign engineers were unfamiliar with. Once past the swamps and jungles, the last sixty-one miles would require outstanding engineering and substantial funding to cross the deep ravines and high mountains east of Guatemala City.

The initial effort, begun by President Barrios in 1883, was a clever plan, which, had it been successful, would have permitted Guatemalans to finance the construction of the railroad — and thus own the utility. By requiring all persons earning more than eight pesos a month to buy "subscriptions" of four pesos a year over a decade, Barrios hoped to raise 120 million pesos (a little more than $1 million).[33] Although collection of the "subscriptions" met with widespread resistance, the government determined it had sufficient funds on hand by May, 1884 to sign a contract with Cornie & Company of Knoxville, Tennessee. Their line was to begin at the newly inaugurated Atlantic port of Puerto Barrios, on the Gulf of Amatique, and extend westward sixty-two miles. Two other contracts were quickly let to American companies for the construction of short stretches of railroad that would link with Cornie & Company's line.

For its part, the government agreed to provide the contractors with 2,000 workers. But Guatemala's Indians, well aware of the steamy, unhealthy conditions prevailing on the north coast, could not be enticed — even with promises of one-peso-a-day wages. And President Barrios, fearing the dragooning of Indians might disrupt the manpower needs of the *finca* owners, refused to conscript the highlanders. The solution was found in a premise dear to the Liberals, who continued to believe that the Indians' "clogged blood" could be "bleached out" by the immigration of foreigners. Plots of nearly thirty acres would be offered to all immigrant laborers who worked a year or more on the railroad. With this added stimulus, American contractors began recruiting workers in the United States.

In the fall of 1884, hundreds of Americans disembarked in Puerto Barrios to work on the railroad. Unfortunately, there were two major problems with their recruitment. Many of the workers, described as "jailbirds from all the Mississippi Valley," and "pretty tough cattle to handle," were clearly not suited for the extremely hard work, under unhealthy, primitive conditions, that prevailed in the "vegetable hell" of Guatemala's north coast. Equally important, the contractors had made no provisions for the health of their workers. Until December 1884, no doctor had even been employed, and the only "hospital" was a crude, open, leaf-covered shed.[34]

Work on the railroad came to a halt early the next year when funds for its construction were used to prepare militarily for President Barrios's hope to unite all of Central America — by force, if necessary. When *El Reformador* was killed in April, 1885, while leading his forces into El Salvador, the funds remaining for the construction of the line "disappeared into the pockets of fleeing politicians." [35] During the next seven years, eight agreements were signed for the construction of the railroad, but none of the companies was able to fulfill its contract. Finally, in 1892, shortly after General José María Reyna Barrios assumed the presidency, a concession was awarded to Sylvanus Miller, an American, to build the railroad from Puerto Barrios to Tenedores, approximately twenty-five miles. The contract was fulfilled that same year.

The efficient Mr. Miller was subsequently rewarded with three more contracts. By 1896, using workers brought in from the United States, Mexico and numerous Caribbean countries, Miller had pushed the narrow-gauge track an additional eighty miles to the town of Zacapa. The twenty-mile stretch from Zacapa to the tiny village of El Rancho was completed while Reyna Barrios was still president. For the next four years, several individuals (two were American and one was Guatemalan) were granted a concession — and government subsidies — to operate the line between Puerto Barrios and El Rancho. As U.S. historian J. Fred Rippy observes, however, "It was all too evident that it was being operated at a large annual loss for the Guatemalan government." [36]

In 1900, after Martin Roberts, the American who owned the concession to operate the railroad, died in California, the Estrada Cabrera government took over the line. It soon negotiated a contract, however, with the Central American Improvement Company, a New Jersey corporation dominated by a man who would eventually become well known in Guatemala: Minor C. Keith. The Improvement Company undertook to repair the old line and agreed to complete the railroad from El Rancho to the capital within three years. In compensation, the company would receive the right to operate the line for ten years and would be granted large tracts of land. In addition, when the railroad to the capital was completed, the government would award Keith and his associates with bonds worth four million gold pesos.

Making needed repairs on the old line, the Improvement Company operated the railroad for nearly three years. Washouts were frequent, however, and the costs of repairs extremely high. Moreover, the old railroad was in wretched condition. In July, 1901, an American engineer reported that "the track is very poor. The rails are heavy for a narrow gauge road, but the track is badly out of line. The ties are of mahogany, rosewood and ebony, but even ebony lasts only two years. The train runs about ten miles an hour and makes long stops." [37] Not surprisingly, the company gave up its concession on October 29, 1903 — without having completed the track from El Rancho to the capital. Thus, nineteen years after the first concession had been let, the railroad to the Atlantic stretched only 136 miles and stopped at El Rancho, located at 900 feet above sea level. The most difficult stretch was still to come: sixty-one miles over the continental divide, traversing deep gorges, and climbing or tunneling through rugged mountains before reaching Guatemala City's mile-high location.

As Guatemala entered the twentieth century, it was apparent that the nation had made tremendous gains in developing a viable cash crop that provided far more export earnings than had cacao, indigo or cochineal. The new industry, however, exerted profound and often adverse effects on the country's indigenous peoples who not only lost immense tracts of their communal lands, but were also forced to work on newly-established coffee plantations. Furthermore, the country's economy had become dangerously vulnerable to unstable world coffee prices, particularly as Brazil's production of the bean soared during the last decade of the 1800s. At the turn of the century, therefore, it was abundantly clear that Guatemala urgently needed to diversify its monoculture economy.

It was a Boston-based banana company that would help break the country's unhealthy dependence on one export crop. Moreover, by investing millions of dollars to develop giant banana plantations on Guatemala's north coast, the United Fruit Company would also make possible President Barrios's dream of a coast-to-coast railroad system.

THE HISTORICAL SETTING

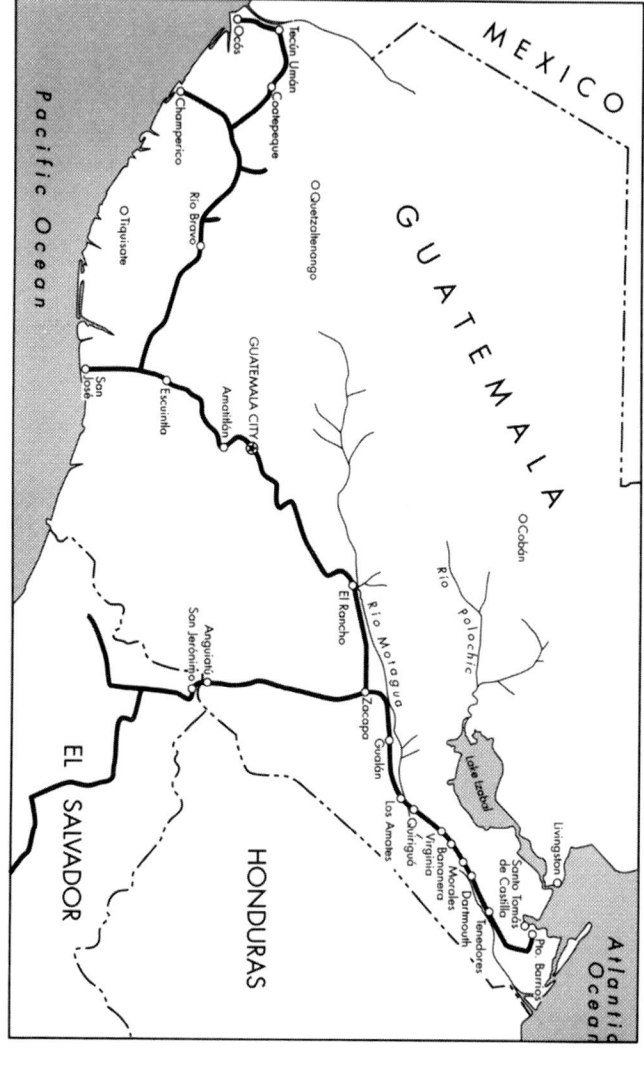

ROUTE OF THE IRCA'S GUATEMALA OPERATIONS

The International Railways of Central America traversed Guatemala from east to west and El Salvador from north to south. The 375 miles of track between Puerto Barrios and Tecún Umán included 143 stations, requiring stops "at every village larger than a cluster of huts." Most of the stations shown above were related to the construction of the railroad or important to the United Fruit Company's operations.

19

- 2 -
A Major Merger and a Major Railroad

he movements of the fruit-cutting crew at the foot of the banana plant, which looked like a green cross, resembled Jews with ladders and lances trying to lower a green Christ converted into a stem that descended, among arms and ropes, and was carefully received . . . then transported in small cars to receive sacramental baths and soon wrapped in a bag with special padding.[1]

The United Fruit Company's sixty-six-year pursuit of Guatemala's "green Christ" brought about far-reaching economic, political and social changes that still exert an impact on the country. How could a company whose 1955 gross sales were less than those of Macy's department store play such a decisive role in the history of Guatemala?[2]

The answer begins 124 years ago in Port Antonio, Jamaica, where Captain Lorenzo Dow Baker, a Cape Cod skipper, purchased 160 stems of green bananas for a shilling (approximately 20 cents) a stem. When his schooner arrived in Jersey City ten days later, he quickly sold the ripe cargo for $2 a stem. The following year, in 1871, Baker again visited Port Antonio and bought 400 stems of the perishable fruit, which he later sold in Boston — the first large cargo of bananas marketed in that city.

Although bananas were little known in the United States when Baker began selling them, the unfamiliar tropical fruit soon found quick acceptance.[3] At the Philadelphia Centennial Exposition of American Independence in 1876, bananas wrapped in tinfoil were sold to curious customers for 10 cents apiece. If, however, there were handsome profits to be made in the brisk sale of bananas, the business was also risky.

Since the banana is not edible if allowed to ripen on the plant, it must be cut green, usually ripening within two weeks of being harvested. Thus, sailing ships, which could be delayed by calms, headwinds or tropical storms, had to make port before the fruit had spoiled. If the stems had been roughly handled, the bananas would be bruised and unattractive. And since the delicate fruit cannot withstand cold weather, it was not possible to ship bananas to Boston during the winter, when they would be exposed to freezing temperatures.

Nevertheless, Captain Baker soon learned that two out of three cargoes of Jamaican bananas usually reached Boston in good condition. Moreover, the profits on a single shipload of the fruit were so high that they more than offset the one out of three cargoes that arrived with unsalable bananas. Before long, Baker began marketing his fruit to Andrew W. Preston, a young man who worked for Seaverns & Company, a local produce firm, and in 1877 the canny Yankee moved to Port Antonio, where he established the L.D. Baker Company, General Shipping. Although the company bought and sold on commission such tropical products as pineapples, coconuts, oranges and spices, its main objective was to purchase as many bananas as the island could produce. Within a year, Baker had contracted for all the bananas that Jamaican growers were producing on approximately 2,000 acres.

In the meantime, Andrew Preston, "who conceived of banana growing and marketing as a great industry — as a chain from the field to the consumer," was quietly seeking out potential investors in a banana company.[4] Working closely with Captain Baker, Preston was able to interest eight New Englanders in investing a total of $15,000 to establish the Boston Fruit Company. The year was 1885 — the same year that Guatemala's *El Reformador*, principal architect in developing another great agricultural industry, met an untimely death.

The Boston Fruit Company's modest launching included ten partners, eight of whom contributed $1,500 and received one share in the company. However, Captain Jesse H. Freeman, a friend of Baker's, invested $1,875 in the new company and his one and one-fourth shares commanded the presidency of the fledgling enterprise. Preston, whose $750 investment represented "the best part of a year's income," received one-half a share, and was named manager of the Boston office.[5] With characteristic Yankee frugality, all the partners agreed that during the first five years, no dividends were to be paid; instead, all earnings would be plowed back into the company.

If the Boston Fruit Company was the first banana company established in that city, it was by no means the first in the country. At least sixty other companies or individuals were selling the fruit from ports throughout the eastern seaboard. Due to its proximity to Central America and its mild winters, permitting year round handling of the fruit, New Orleans had become the "banana capital of the world." In the Mississippi Valley, New York, Philadelphia and other east coast ports, the banana trade was highly competitive — and precarious. The same year that the Boston Fruit Company was founded, at least six companies, considerably larger than the Massachusetts firm, went bankrupt.

At that time, there were two principal reasons the banana trade was a risky enterprise. Since the fruit was transported on sailing vessels, with holds that were unrefrigerated, ships frequently arrived with a cargo of rotten bananas.[6] Although the story may be apocryphal, the writer Charles Morrow Wilson describes a certain Captain Slumpy Gus who neared a U.S. port with a schooner loaded with ripe bananas. Also aboard was a crew member the captain suspected had contacted yellow fever. Knowing U.S. port authorities would quarantine the ship for several days, during which the bananas would spoil, Captain Gus simply threw the sick man overboard — and successfully sold his cargo.[7]

If unpredictable schedules were a problem, banana importers also faced a chaotic situation when good quality fruit did make it to the United States. "Ports deluged with the fruit for a few days would have none at all the following week, and one port often would be flooded with fruit while ports nearby would have less than a dozen bunches."[8] Not surprisingly, the brokers or jobbers who purchased the fruit at dockside took full advantage of this buyer's market. It was not uncommon for them to wait until the perishable cargo was almost spoiled before they would acquire the fruit for minimal sums. However, with Andrew Preston assuring the sale of bananas that Captain Baker was shipping from Jamaica, the Boston Fruit Company immediately prospered. During its first year of operation, the company sold approximately 150,000 stems of bananas, and tripled its sales the following year. Within two years, the initial $15,000 investment had grown an impressive 1,300 percent, with cash resources standing at $200,000.[9]

Since there was no obligation to pay dividends to its ten shareholders, the Boston Fruit Company moved quickly to put its earnings to work. In Jamaica, Captain Baker bought the company's first banana plantations: four farms totalling 1,300 acres, and estimated to produce at least 150,000 stems of fruit annually. Arguing that speed at sea would mean increased profits, Preston convinced his partners of the need to own a steamship. Accordingly, the company purchased for $65,000 the *Marmion*, 200 feet long (considered large in 1888) and able to stow and deck 20,000 stems of bananas.

Before long, Boston Fruit leased two new steamships similar in size to the *Marmion*, but able to sail at twelve and a half knots, the fastest ships then operating in the Caribbean. Since Preston had virtually saturated the banana market in Boston, the new twin ships were soon invading Philadelphia and Baltimore with Jamaican bananas. Significantly, the "Boston Twins," as the ships were dubbed, also provided quarters for half a dozen passengers — presaging the thousands of American tourists the United Fruit Company would eventually transport to Guatemala aboard the ships of its Great White Fleet.

By 1890, five years after Boston Fruit was founded, it was the most successful banana company in the country.[10] There were larger firms in the trade, but none could point to Boston Fruit's spectacular profits: the original investment had grown to $531,000 — a capital gain of approximately 3,600 percent.[11] Formally incorporated under the laws of Massachusetts in 1890, the Boston-based company soon embarked on a quest for new banana markets. With Boston Fruit subscribing half the capitalization, banana companies were rapidly founded in Baltimore, Philadelphia and New York. In addition, it acquired shares in three New York-based banana companies, including the Banes Fruit Company, which raised and shipped fruit from Banes, Cuba to New York City. By 1905, however, after it had become apparent that Cuba's climate was not appropriate for large scale banana production, the Company began raising sugarcane on its Cuban properties.

Another significant innovation was the founding, in 1898, of the Fruit Dispatch Company, dedicated to the distribution and sales of Boston Fruit's bananas to inland markets throughout the United States. The need for such an organization was obvious: five American ports were receiving 95 percent of all bananas imported into the country, and customers in those same port cities accounted for 80 percent of the nation's consumption of the yellow fruit. But those consumers represented a scant 16 percent of the buying public in the United States.[12]

While Boston Fruit's domestic operations were growing and becoming more efficient, Preston realized the company's future was uncertain without a steady, diversified supply of bananas. Although the company was raising the golden fruit in Cuba and Santo Domingo, most of its bananas were still being produced in Jamaica. When devastating hurricanes swept across that island in 1898, destroying five times as many bananas as Captain Baker had been able to export, it was clear the Boston Fruit Company urgently required new areas of production. The company's pressing need was met by a giant in the banana business: Minor C. Keith, who owned, leased or held concessions for more than 200,000 acres of land in Central America and Colombia.

BOSTON FRUIT JOINS FORCES
WITH A RAILROADING GENIUS

Curiously, it was railroads, rather than bananas, that first brought the Brooklyn-born Keith to the isthmus. His maternal uncle was Henry Meiggs, an adventuresome jack-of-all-trades, who gained fame as a railroad builder in Chile and Peru. Moreover, the Meiggs Railways in Peru earned half a billion dollars over a twenty year period by transporting guano for an immensely profitable fertilizer industry that Meiggs established.[13] Thus, Minor Keith observed early on that his Uncle Henry became wealthy not as a builder of railroads but as an astute entrepreneur who knew how to put his rail lines to productive use.

In 1870, when President Tomás Guardia of Costa Rica wanted a railroad constructed from the Atlantic coast to San José, the capital, he turned to the renowned Mr. Meiggs. Although Meiggs had never been to Costa Rica and had no experience building railroads through swamps and tropical jungles, he agreed to take on the project in return for more than 800,000 acres of land. To oversee the work, Meiggs called upon his nephew, Henry Meiggs Keith, then twenty-three. Minor Keith, a year younger, decided to join his brother and was given the job of administering the camp's mess hall. The building of the railroad from what is today Puerto Limón to San José is a dramatic, twenty-year saga in which thousands of workers died, including three of Minor Keith's brothers.[14] As a result, Minor Keith took on the monumental task of completing Costa Rica's railroad to the Atlantic.

Financing for the costly line was always problematic. Thus, as the railroad slowly pushed inland, Keith began to search for a paying cargo that would assist in funding its completion. When he learned that two American brothers in Panama were growing bananas along the Panama Railway tracks and successfully exporting them to New York, Keith began raising the fruit near Puerto Limón. By 1878, he was selling small quantities of Costa Rican bananas in New Orleans. Within seven years, his Tropical Trading and Transport Company, chartered in London, was exporting more than half a million stems of bananas from Costa Rica.[15]

In time, Keith expanded his holdings: 10,000 acres of jungle lands near Bluefields, Nicaragua; another 10,000 near the Almirante Bay on Panama's Atlantic coast; and 15,000 acres around Santa Marta, Colombia. By 1890, Keith, who shipped nearly all of his bananas to New Orleans and Mobile, had become the world's largest producer of bananas. Four years later, in an effort to tap into new markets, the banana magnate approached the country's most successful banana-selling company. The result was an agreement authorizing Boston Fruit to sell north of Cape Hatteras all bananas grown and exported by Keith's Colombia Land Company, Ltd. and his Tropical Trading and Transport Company.

In 1898, the same year Boston Fruit's Jamaica plantations suffered devastating hurricane losses, Keith experienced two severe financial crises. First, a New York investment banking firm that had extended short-term loans to Tropical Trading and Transport Company went bankrupt, leaving Keith to pay off about $1.5 million. Later in the year, the principal New Orleans distributor of Keith's bananas, also declared bankruptcy. Since Keith was a partner in the company, he lost over $1 million in the insolvent organization. If Minor Keith was in compelling need of capital, the prosperous Boston Fruit Company had a critical need for new banana-producing lands. A merger of the two organizations seemed imminent when Keith traveled to Boston late in 1898.

On March 30, 1899, the *Boston Journal* published a brief article, datelined Trenton, New Jersey, reporting the incorporation of the United Fruit Company.[16] Although the twelve-line article did not state which companies or individuals were involved in the incorporation, the new company represented a merger of the Boston Fruit Company and Minor Keith's Tropical Trading and Transport Company, his Colombia Land Company, Ltd. and his Snyder Banana Company. Keith traded the shares of his three companies for a total of $3.9 million in United Fruit Company stocks. Boston Fruit received United Fruit Company stock worth $5.1 million.[17]

The new company, which had an authorized capital of $20 million, now owned or leased 212,394 acres of land in Central America, the Caribbean and Colombia. Approximately 62,000 acres of its holdings were actually in production. The Company also owned 112 miles of railroad, representing, for the most part, Keith's Costa Rican efforts. In addition, United Fruit owned eleven steamships, ranging in size from 600 to 1,000 tons, supplemented by twelve to thirty ships which it rented or chartered. Within one year of its creation, nearly $11.3 million of the United Fruit Company's shares had been subscribed by the public.[18]

From its founding, the former Boston Fruit Company controlled the new organization — a fact reflected in the distribution of its officers. Andrew Preston was named president and director; Minor Keith became the Company's first vice president; and Captain Lorenzo Baker became tropical manager, the same position he had held with the Boston Fruit Company.[19] These men also reflected the three components of the new company that would exert powerful and diverse influences on Guatemala: the country's largest agricultural enterprise; the eventual ownership of Guatemala's railroad system and principal Atlantic port; and the domination of the nation's maritime shipping by UFCO's Great White Fleet.

ESTRADA CABRERA AND THE RAILROAD TO THE ATLANTIC

If 1898 represented a turning point for both the Boston Fruit Company and Minor Keith, the year also witnessed historic changes in Guatemala. In February, President José María Reyna Barrios, who had brought the country to financial ruin, was mysteriously assassinated when he returned one evening from the theater. The first designate to the presidency was a forty-one-year-old lawyer serving as Reyna Barrios's Minister of Government and Justice: Manuel Estrada Cabrera. Destined to be one of the most cruel, sinister and paranoid tyrants ever to rule Guatemala, Estrada Cabrera (1898-1920) was duly elected president late in 1898.[20]

Estrada Cabrera, whose twenty-two-year regime is described in Miguel Angel Asturias's masterful novel, *El Señor Presidente*, was the man whose government the United Fruit Company had to deal with during its first nineteen years in Guatemala. Numerous U.S. authors have frequently quoted — and left unchallenged — a glib comment about the Estrada Cabrera government made by Thomas P. McCann, a former employee of the United Fruit Company. In his tendentious, often inaccurate book, *An American Company, The Tragedy of United Fruit*, McCann states "at the time we entered Central America, Guatemala's government was the region's weakest, most corrupt and most pliable. In short, the country offered an 'ideal investment climate.'"[21]

Considering that Estrada Cabrera's tyranny endured far longer than that of any of his Central American counterparts, it is difficult to understand how McCann could characterize the Guatemalan dictator as "weak" or "pliable." In fact, Dana G. Munro's comprehensive 1918 survey of the five Central American states found that Estrada Cabrera's military despotism was "more absolute than any other on the isthmus."[22] And in an area of the world where presidents are usually unscrupulous, there is no proof that Estrada Cabrera was any more corrupt than any of his contemporaries.

During Estrada Cabrera's long dictatorship, his government signed one contract with the United Fruit Company and two major contracts with railroads that Minor Keith would build.[23] Since a large part of UFCO's "black legend" (*leyenda negra*) in Guatemala stems from its association with Keith's railroad, and the various contracts both companies signed with Estrada Cabrera, it is worth studying the documents in some detail.

The 1901 contract that United Fruit signed with the Guatemalan government obligated the Company to carry mail between Puerto Barrios and New Orleans, as well as nine other Central American ports. For this service, the government paid $30,000 a year. More importantly, United Fruit was permitted to purchase bananas from independent growers and export them from Puerto Barrios to the United States. In fact, Torres Rivas explains that the Guatemalan government negotiated the contract on behalf of north coast banana growers because of their pressing need for a regular shipping service between Puerto Barrios and New Orleans. As a result, the new "secure market" multiplied banana cultivation, according to another Guatemalan historian.[24]

Nevertheless, one of UFCO's harshest antagonists finds astounding attributes in the 1901 contract. Manuel Galich, who served as the first Minister of Foreign Relations during the presidency of Jacobo Arbenz Guzmán (1951-1954), claims that in exchange for $30,000 a year, the Company gained "the transfer, although dissembled by ambiguous terms, of land along the Motagua River; the ruin of independent banana growers; control of the railroads and the wharf at Puerto Barrios and, in sum, the economic conquest of an extensive and rich area, and the ad-hoc trampoline to achieve total control of our economy, with all the [corresponding] financial and political corollaries."[25] Another Guatemalan, Alfonso Bauer Paiz, charges that the shipping contract was merely a "sheep skin covering the wolf." While providing no documentation to support his metaphorical allegation, Bauer Paiz claims that United Fruit was simply waiting for Keith's 1904 contract to award him extensive grants of land which UFCO would then utilize to establish banana plantations.[26]

Similarly, another author maintains the Company used the 1901 contract as a means to "consolidate itself on the Atlantic coast," subsequently growing bananas "illegally" in the Motagua Valley.[27] As detailed in the following chapter, the facts do not bear out this contention. Indeed, even Rafael Piedra-Santa Arandi, an acknowledged critic of *La Frutera*, as the Company is known in Guatemala, admits that it is "exaggerated" to claim that the 1901 contract permitted UFCO's north coast consolidation.[28]

Three years after the United Fruit Company signed its first contract with Guatemala, a contract was signed between Percival Farquhar, representing Minor Keith, and the Estrada Cabrera government. The 1904 document committed Keith to the construction of the final, difficult and costly sixty-one miles that would take the railroad from El Rancho to Guatemala City. Historian Mario Monteforte Toledo maintains that the only reason Estrada Cabrera granted the concession was to obtain the U.S. government's recognition of his 1904 re-election.[29] Regina Wagner, however, reveals — and conclusively documents — that Estrada Cabrera, concerned because most of the Pacific coast railroads were in the hands of Americans, wanted German capitalists to complete and subsequently own and operate the railroad to the Atlantic. For various reasons, however, German entrepreneurs were not interested in the risky venture.[30]

It can be asked why Minor Keith, whose Central American Improvement Company had not been able to complete the railroad to the Atlantic, would once again take on such an arduous challenge. The answer can be found in Keith's persistent, ambitious — and somewhat quixotic — dream of uniting Mexico, and thus the United States, with a trans-isthmian railroad stretching from Guatemala's Mexican border through Central America to Panama.[31] The first span of this bold plan would link Guatemala's Pacific and Atlantic lines to a branch from the latter which would extend to the border with El Salvador. There, the line would join a railroad that Keith would build from the Guatemalan border south to Cutuco on the Gulf of Fonseca, a body of water which El Salvador shares with both Honduras and Nicaragua. He presumably envisioned continuing the line through southern Honduras, and then traversing both Nicaragua and Costa Rica to finally link the railroad with Panama.

To dedicate all of his time and efforts to this project, Keith disposed of most of his shares in the United Fruit Company soon after the new organization was formed. This action not only allowed him to liquidate his numerous debts, but also gave him the freedom to revert to his first love: the building of railroads. Although Henry Meiggs's nephew may have been an impractical railroading visionary, he was an astute businessman. Keith knew from his experiences in Costa Rica and with the Central American Improvement Company that Guatemala's Atlantic railroad would not be economically viable unless it transported far more freight than it was then carrying. The solution would be the same one he had successfully pioneered in building Costa Rica's Atlantic railroad: the freighting of bananas. Therefore, before signing the 1904 contract, Keith received Andrew Preston's assurances that the United Fruit Company would establish banana plantations along the railroad line in the Motagua Valley.[32]

Joined by Sir William Van Horne, the builder of the Canadian Pacific, Keith formed the Guatemala Railway Company in 1904. One of the company's most important stockholders was Thomas H. Hubbard, who owned Guatemala's Central Railway, the line from Guatemala City to San José, which Keith and Van Horne purchased in 1912, thereby changing the name of the line from the Guatemala Railway Company to the International Railways of Central America (IRCA). (By 1912, Hubbard owned all of Guatemala's Pacific coast lines). Virtually every one of the United Fruit Company's detractors has maintained that UFCO owned the Guatemala Railway Company, later known as the IRCA. For example, Oscar de León Aragón, a prominent Guatemalan attorney who has written one of the most extensive studies of the railroad's two contracts with the Estrada Cabrera government, erroneously maintains that the United Fruit Company was the sole owner of the railroad. The author comes to this conclusion merely because Keith was one of the founders and the vice president of the United Fruit Company.[33]

Another analysis of the relationship between the two companies was provided in 1935 by Charles David Kepner, Jr. and Jay Henry Soothill in their highly critical study of the United Fruit Company, *The Banana Empire: A Case Study of Economic Imperialism.* Noting that Keith was the "common ancestor" of both the railroad and the fruit company, the authors observe that "throughout the history of these two companies they have been kept close together by interlocking directorates. Besides Keith, the late Andrew W. Preston, former president of the United Fruit Company, and Bradley W. Palmer, chairman of its executive committee, have been members of the boards of directors of the IRCA." Kepner and Soothill reveal, however, that the railroad was also jointly owned by Henry Schroeder and Company, United Fruit and some British interests.[34]

Nevertheless, in his 1968 study of the United Fruit Company, U.S. economist Richard Allen LaBarge quotes UFCO's comptroller as stating in 1955 that

> the IRCA board of nine members is and always has been independently constituted, all of whom, except for one, the United Fruit Company nominee, have no affiliation with or owe no allegiance to the United Fruit Company. This situation has existed ever since we acquired the stock and . . . we have meticulously kept it that way so that both internally in Guatemala and externally in the United States, England and elsewhere it could never be held that the Company dominated the board to the advantage of the Company over its competitors.[35]

The question of ownership of the railroad and how its initial funding was obtained is perhaps best left to Keith, who, in a letter to the Guatemalan Ministry of Development, dated May 21, 1921, asserted that the railroad to the Atlantic "was constructed with personal funds provided by Sir William Van Horne, General Hubbard and Minor C. Keith, investing from their own funds more than $7 million to comply with the obligations contracted with the government of the republic . . . because it was not possible to find bankers who would buy its bonds due to the government's poor credit rating." [36]

Incorporating the new company in New Jersey, the three entrepreneurs subsequently took $10 million in preferred stock which they later used to raise one million British pounds in order to purchase Hubbard's Central Railroad. Nevertheless, the United Fruit Company — already planning to begin operations in Guatemala — recognized the need for a solvent, well-run railroad that could transport its bananas from plantations along the Motagua River to Puerto Barrios. As a result, UFCO soon purchased 17 percent of the shares of the Guatemala Railway Company.[37] Although the United Fruit Company would become a majority stock holder in the railroad in 1936, discussed in Chapter 3, UFCO's initial purchase of 17 percent of the shares of the new enterprise hardly constituted ownership.

Within the four years stipulated in the 1904 contract, Keith's superb engineers had constructed innumerable tunnels, several cuts through solid rock, and seventy bridges, one of them across a ravine 244 feet deep, to make possible a railroad that climbed 4,000 feet in just sixty-one miles. When the railroad was officially inaugurated on January 19, 1908, the government termed the line "one of the most glorious triumphs which [Guatemalans] . . . have been able to win in arduous and constant work for the fatherland." [38] Solórzano, however, puts a different slant on the accomplishment.

> *Eight years of the twentieth century had to pass before Guatemalans could possess what had been dreamed of since colonial times: a route to the north sea for the export of our products; but in reality, it was not as gratifying as the dreams held by the leaders of [our] independence, the men of the 1830s or of the Reform. The railroad was not ours; we had been incapable, because of the dishonesty, ambition and ignorance of our leaders, of completing the work, which had always been within the realm of the possible for our nation.*[39]

Undoubtedly Solórzano is correct in asserting the country could have financed the last sixty-one miles of the Atlantic railroad. It is questionable, however, whether the line could have been operated profitably. The government undoubtedly would have been forced to provide large, annual subsidies to the railroad had not the United Fruit Company soon made massive use of the line. Keith calculated that shipments of millions of stems of bananas would keep his railroad profitable. Initially, he was proven right, but by the mid-1930s, when UFCO's north coast banana productions had been severely affected by Panama disease, a deadly root fungus, and Guatemala's exports and imports had plummeted because of the worldwide depression, the railroad was virtually bankrupt. As a consequence, the United Fruit Company, totally dependent on the line to transport its bananas, moved to rescue the ailing railroad (*see Chapter 3*).

Opponents of the IRCA usually provide a long list of the concessions Keith "extracted" from the Estrada Cabrera government. Left unsaid, however, is that virtually all of the concessions were similar to those awarded previous railroad builders. For example, Canadian historian Jim Handy writes that "Cabrera was more than generous to the new Guatemalan Railway Company . . . 100-foot right of way across most of the country; 4,600 *caballerías* [505,080 acres] of land; a monopoly on rail transport to the Caribbean; free use of material such as stone and lumber on all public land along the railway; exemption from most taxes for ninety-nine years, and the right to control water that encroached on railway lands."[40]

But nearly all these concessions — with a few variations — were standard in the approximately twenty contracts the Guatemalan government began letting to railroad builders as early as 1877. As noted previously, large tracts of land were invariably awarded to the contractors. In fact, a prominent Guatemalan attorney stated in 1920 that the government had awarded a total of 5,100 *caballerías*, or 559,000 acres, in railroad concessions.[41] Nevertheless, Handy exaggerates when he states that 4,600 *caballerías* were given to the Guatemalan Railway Company. Article VI of the contract awards the company 1,500 *caballerías* (164,700 acres) in an area called "Los Andes," near the Motagua River.[42]

Handy also asserts that the railroad's accounts could not be inspected by the government, when the contract states the government did indeed retain this right and, in fact, the company was required to provide Spanish-language versions of its accounts. The same author notes that the most important aspect of the contract was the stipulation that the company was to exercise "the sole and exclusive government on the railway and never be subject to the intervention of the government." Nonetheless, as Keith was to learn a few years later, in a dictatorship this kind of proviso could be disregarded. Thus, in 1913, the minister of government declared that for reasons of "security and public order," trains that were not regularly scheduled had to receive the prior permission of the minister of development before they could be dispatched.[43]

Several new elements, however, were incorporated into the 1904 contract. Critics have noted that Keith was awarded ownership of the 136 miles of track that already had been laid between Puerto Barrios and El Rancho. It would have made little sense, however, for the Guatemala Railway Company to own and operate only the sixty-one miles of track it would construct between El Rancho and Guatemala City. Moreover, at least three previous contracts in the late 1890s had already made the same concession.

To the future dismay of many Guatemalans, the 1904 contract also awarded the company the wharf at Puerto Barrios — valued at

$25,000 — and fifty-one acres of land in that marshy, unhealthy village. Few historians have bothered to point out, however, that the railroad was responsible for making the new town of Puerto Barrios liveable. In a comprehensive contract the Guatemala Railway Company signed with the Estrada Cabrera government in August 1908, the former agreed to complete a long list of sanitation projects designed to reduce the area's high incidence of malaria. In addition, the railroad committed itself to constructing a large water tank which would provide potable water to the customs house, the port authorities, the only hotel in the town and six other locations within Puerto Barrios. In 1917, the government belatedly acknowledged, in a formal accord signed by Estrada Cabrera, that the railroad had complied with the 1908 contract. And only in 1921 — thirteen years after Keith had completed the railroad to the Atlantic — did President Carlos Herrera (1920-1921) formally acknowledge that the 1904 contract had been fulfilled.[44]

That the government granted the Guatemala Railway Company ownership of the wharf at Puerto Barrios was not exceptional.[45] On the Pacific coast, the San José facility had been owned and operated by one individual since 1866.[46] Also on the Pacific coast, the 1896 contract for the construction of a railroad between Coatepeque and the port of Ocós permitted the railroad builders to merge their company with the owners of the port facility. Thus, the railroad both owned and operated the port at Ocós.[47]

The two most onerous and novel provisions of the contract concerned the disposition of the railroad and the resolution of conflicts. All previous contracts stated that at the expiration of the concession, usually ninety-nine years, the line would revert — at no cost — to the government of Guatemala. Inexplicably, the 1904 contract permitted the company to sell to the government, in the year 2003, the railroad, all its rolling stock and facilities "for the value it has at that time."[48] Also unusual was the stipulation regarding "doubts" that might arise between the government and the contractors in the fulfillment of the agreement. Previous contracts stated that when disputes arose, there could be no recourse to diplomatic channels. Instead, arbiters for both sides would be named and their findings would be considered definitive. The 1904 contract contained similar language, but allowed the company to resort to diplomatic procedures after all other mechanisms had been exhausted.

Another significant but little noted concession was designed to give "all possible protection" to the nation's agriculture. Thus, agricultural products, with the exception of coffee, were to be free of export taxes for a period of thirty-five years. This concession, and the two described above, can only be explained as a measure of the government's critical need to complete the long-delayed railroad.

THE DISPUTED LINE TO EL SALVADOR

Undoubtedly one of the most inaccurate and often incomplete accounts of Keith's Central American activities concerns his dogged efforts to build a rail spur from the town of Zacapa, in eastern Guatemala, to Anguiatú on the border with El Salvador.

Within a month after the line to the Atlantic was inaugurated, Frederick Williamson, representing the Guatemala Railway Company, signed an agreement for the construction of seventy-seven miles of track between Zacapa and the village of Anguiatú. Known as the Méndez-Williamson contract, the 1908 document committed the company to completing the line within four years. The Estrada Cabrera government, for its part, agreed to pay $7,500 for every kilometer of track laid, and promised to provide 3,500 workers for the duration of the construction.

As it became clear to Keith and his associates, however, that the government was not complying with the commitments the latter had acquired in the 1904 contract, Keith delayed construction of the line to El Salvador. One of Keith's principal concerns was the government's failure to make the agreed-upon yearly payments to the railroad — a 5 percent annual interest over a fifteen-year period for its $4.5 million costs of construction. Notwithstanding the government's failure to make "guaranteed" payments to the company for the construction of the line to the Atlantic, the railroad steadfastly complied with the clause in the 1908 contract requiring monthly fines if the railroad to El Salvador were not completed within the stipulated four years. Thus, by 1921, when the contract was finally annulled, the railroad had paid — and the government had accepted — fines amounting to $54,000.[49] Moreover, even by

1921, thirteen years after the line to the Atlantic had been completed, the government still had not provided the IRCA with legal titles attesting to the railroad's right-of-way for all segments of its Atlantic coast railroad. Nor had titles been provided for all of the fifty-one acres of land ceded in Puerto Barrios.[50]

Ultimately, after years of acrimonious debate and no solution to its difficulties with the Estrada Cabrera government, the railroad's management sought the assistance of the U.S. government. Major General George W. Davis, a former governor of the Panama Canal Zone, was thus dispatched to Guatemala in 1914 to attempt to mediate a solution. The issues were not resolved, however, and the contract was finally annulled in 1921 by President Carlos Herrera, who replaced Estrada Cabrera after the latter was forced to resign in 1920. Curiously, Bauer Paiz, de León Aragón, Monteforte Toledo and other Guatemalan critics of the IRCA do not explain why the railroad did not comply with its 1908 contract. Nor do any of these authors even mention General Davis's visit to Guatemala or the outstanding debt that the Estrada Cabrera government owed the railroad. Piedra-Santa Arandi, author of a long article on the railroad, blithely asserts that "other investigators" will have to determine why the 1908 contract was not fulfilled.[51]

Despite the 1921 annulment of the Méndez-Williamson contract, however, the tenacious Keith was not to be dissuaded. By this time he was somewhat nearer to his dream of an intercontinental railroad: his $3.5 million purchase of all the railroads on Guatemala's south coast provided the International Railways of Central America with 375 miles of track. Thus, the narrow-gauge line stretched from the Mexican border to within eighty miles of the boundary with El Salvador. (By 1920, the International Railways of Central America estimated that it had cost approximately $12.6 million to construct all of Guatemala's railroads).[52] In El Salvador, Keith had already completed a 156-mile steel line from the company's deep water port of Cutuco to San Salvador, and work was under way to build a railroad from the Salvadoran capital to San Jerónimo, across from the Guatemalan border town of Anguiatú.

President Herrera, a supporter of Central American unification, was a well regarded but ineffectual leader who, like many subsequent Guatemalan presidents, did not command the loyalty of all elements of the army. As a result, after only twenty months in office, a triumvirate of generals, led by General José María Orellana, presented the president with numerous demands, including the installation of a cabinet dominated by the army and the abolishment of both the Supreme Court and the Congress. Refusing to comply with such outrageous demands, Herrera resigned in December 1921. The first designate to the presidency was General Orellana (1921-1926) who was elected president the following February, thus commencing twenty-three continuous years of governments headed by four army generals.

Several Guatemalan historians, including Monteforte Toledo, have maintained that the United States surreptitiously backed Herrera's overthrow because he had cancelled Keith's concession and had refused to allow the Electric Bond and Share Company, a U.S. firm, to secure control of the country's largest, German-owned electrical company. In fact, as U.S. historian Joseph A. Pitti points out, diplomatic dispatches from the American Legation in Guatemala made clear that the U.S. government was "dismayed by the December barracks revolt . . . The American minister in Guatemala, Benton McMillin, regarded the coup as motivated by 'personal political ambitions' and 'as very unfortunate for Guatemala.'" [53]

Nevertheless, once Orellana was elected president, the U.S. Legation advised the general that his government would not receive Washington's official recognition until written assurances were provided that the issue of Keith's contract and that of the Electric Bond and Share Company were resolved. Orellana obligingly provided such a document, but the IRCA's new contract, which had to be approved by the Legislative Assembly, was twice remitted back to the president for revisions. The new agreement, which differed in several important aspects from the 1908 contract, was finally approved in May 1923.

One of the most significant changes stipulated that all of the IRCA's lines would revert to the government — at no cost — after eighty-six years. This, of course, would include the railroad to the Atlantic, thereby rescinding the much criticized clause in the 1904 contract. Few detractors of the railroad have bothered to note this important fact, however. Nor did the new concession permit disputes to be taken to the American Legation in Guatemala City or directly to the State Department in

Washington.

Keith also agreed to donate to the government half of all the profits earned in operating the Zacapa-Anguiatú line, and gave back to the state 109,800 acres of the 164,700 he had been granted through the 1904 contract — a fact also unremarked by most of the IRCA's critics. Although the Guatemalan government no longer committed itself to providing 3,500 workers for the project, the railroad did not seek an increase in construction costs. As in the annulled 1908 contract, the new agreement stated that the government would pay $7,500 per kilometer of rail laid. Since the line would extend for 113 kilometers or seventy-seven miles, the government was thus required to pay $847,500 for the construction of the spur to El Salvador. In exchange, the contract required the Guatemalan government to reimburse the railroad the sum of $1,475,000. Detractors of the contract maintain that this sum, plus the subsidies to be paid for each kilometer, meant that the government paid many times over for the line to El Salvador. The facts are otherwise, although several historians have chosen to overlook them.

To begin with, the figure of $1,475,000 is approximately what Guatemala owed the IRCA by 1923. In fact, General Davis advised the Department of State in 1914 that the railroad had an outstanding claim on the Guatemalan government in the amount of $1,250,000.[54] In an accord signed by President Herrera in 1920, he acknowledged that his government owed the IRCA the equivalent of $1,454,182.[55] This sum included bills for government freight and passenger fares, subsidies for the operation of various Pacific coast lines, and the payments the Estrada Cabrera government had guaranteed Keith for his construction of the El Rancho-Guatemala City line. Herrera thus paid the IRCA the dollar equivalent of approximately $500,000 and agreed to repay the remainder of the debt in three annual installments of $323,151.[56] Neither de León Aragón nor Bauer Paiz mention this fact, while Handy erroneously asserts that the claim was denied by all Guatemalan governments until 1936 when President Jorge Ubico (1931-1944) "cancelled" the debt by paying the railroad the equivalent of $400,000.[57]

The fact is that by 1927, the commitment President Herrera had made had not fully liquidated the government's debt to the railroad, with interest having accrued on the unpaid balance. In addition, because subsequent governments had failed to pay for new expenses incurred, Guatemala owed the railroad the quetzal equivalent of $2,515,008. To pay off the obligation, President Lázaro Chacón (1926-1930) agreed to issue government bonds, known as the "Bonds of the Republic of 1927," paying interest, in dollars, of 8 percent annually over a twenty-year period.[58] Bauer Paiz and de León Aragón, both vehement critics of the railroad, utterly fail to mention the bond issue.

Nevertheless, by 1936 the government still owed the railroad $1,832,937. The IRCA's management, undoubtedly weary of the long drawn out matter, then made substantial concessions. It turned over to the government bonds and coupons of the 1927 issue at a face value of $883,000, plus $17,660 in certificates corresponding to the half-payment of the coupon of November 1933. The railroad also cancelled $84,417 in claims for interest from April 1933, to April 22, 1936, and cancelled its claim of $844,860 for the construction of the line to El Salvador.[59] In exchange, the government of President Jorge Ubico paid the IRCA the equivalent of $400,000.[60] Providing no source for his allegation, Bauer Paiz claims that the railroad received more than $1 million in cash, plus $7,500 for each kilometer of the railroad to El Salvador.[61] The IRCA did, however, rescind two clauses in the 1923 contract: payment to the government of half its annual profits on the line to El Salvador, and the government's right to examine the company's books.[62]

Thus, rather than the $2 million that some historians claim the steel line to El Salvador cost the Guatemalan people, the government expended less than one-fourth that amount. The controversial railroad was finally inaugurated on December 30, 1929, but Minor Keith never lived to see its completion — or the realization of a trans-isthmian line stretching from Guatemala to Panama.[63] He died in June of 1929 at the age of eighty-one.

The Origins of United Fruit's "Black Legend"

We took the least desirable land along the river bottoms, for which there was no other commercial use than the raising of bananas. In nearly every instance this land was shunned as unhealthy, swarming as it was with mosquitoes.[1]

This 1929 statement by Victor M. Cutter, president of the United Fruit Company, aptly describes the jungle-ridden, malaria-infested lands which UFCO began cultivating in 1906 on Guatemala's north coast.

In the Motagua Valley, these "least desirable" tracts were characterized by many of the agricultural requirements essential for raising bananas, which thrive in well-watered, well-drained, non-acidic soil with less than 40 percent clay content. Because banana plants produce throughout the year, they need an equitably distributed annual rainfall of seventy-five to 100 inches — 1.5 inches of water each week; otherwise, irrigation is required. Irrigation systems, however, were not necessary on most of UFCO's north coast plantations because of plentiful and frequent rains throughout the year.

The United Fruit Company made its first purchase of land in 1904 when it bought 3,831 acres of jungle near Quiriguá and laid out its first plantation: an experimental tract of 1,250 acres of bananas.[2] When it became apparent that the valley's fertile soil was eminently well suited for raising bananas, the Company made extensive purchases of land in 1906 and 1907. The following year it increased its plantings to 5,080 acres. By 1913, UFCO had purchased 126,189 acres of land, of which 27,122 acres were dedicated to the cultivation of bananas. United Fruit's annual report for that year places the cost of the Guatemala development at $3.8 million. UFCO had invested more money in Costa Rica, Panama and Colombia, but Guatemala, with banana exports valued at $825,670, stood third in the production of bananas.[3]

Some authors have contended that the United Fruit Company operated illegally in Guatemala until 1924, when it rented public lands from the government along the Motagua River. In fact, like many foreign coffee growers, UFCO initially sought no government concessions and, like other foreign companies or individuals, it legally purchased and registered the properties it acquired. In addition, United Fruit apparently had access to approximately 50,000 acres of the land that Keith had been awarded by the Guatemalan government for his railroading efforts.

Another allegation, one that is extensively treated in Miguel Angel Asturias's fictional trilogy on the United Fruit Company, concerns the displacement of peasants (*campesinos*), particularly on the Atlantic coast, whose farms were purchased by the banana company early in the twentieth century. Although none of UFCO's critics has stated how many peasants lost their farms, Galich accuses the Company of having acquired three-fourths of the land around seven villages in the Motagua Valley.[4] Since United Fruit legally purchased its properties, however, it can be assumed that the subsistence farmers affected by the Company's acquisitions were adequately compensated for the sale of their parcels. Galich further criticizes the Company for having dispossessed *campesinos* of their farms along the Motagua River after the Guatemalan government leased approximately sixty miles of land to UFCO in 1924. But the 1924 contract states that the "national lands" that were being leased would not include cultivated land and would be "measured and marked by a Guatemalan engineer named by the government."[5]

One of the principal reasons the United Fruit Company leased additional land on Guatemala's north coast was because of an alarming development that began affecting all of the Company's Central American banana plantations early in the twentieth century. A deadly fungus disease, which first made significant inroads in 1903 at UFCO's Bocas del Toro division in Panama, began to plague the banana lands. Originally termed "banana wilt" or "banana blight," the fungus infection soon became known as "Panama disease" because of the devastation it caused at Bocas del Toro.

Within seven years, the Company was forced to abandon 15,000 acres of plantations on Panama's Atlantic coast. Eventually, nearly 50,000 acres of banana lands in the Bocas region were lost to Panama disease, causing United Fruit to cease all production in that area.[6] By 1915 the disease, which usually made its devastating appearance within ten years of the planting of new banana lands, had invaded Costa Rica, Honduras and Guatemala. Spread by wind, by water and by the moving of infected soil particles on shoes, on clothing or on animals, the virulent fungus enters the banana plant through its root stalk. After the lower leaves wither and break off, newer leaves at the top of the plant also turn a dull yellow. Infected plants do not produce exportable bananas. Another critical factor was the variety of banana which the United Fruit Company produced. Known as the Gros Michel, this type of banana was particularly susceptible to Panama disease.

Although UFCO conducted intensive research to discover methods of combating the disease, fungicides that were developed proved prohibitively expensive. In the late 1930s, the Company began experimenting in Honduras with a procedure known as "flood fallowing," whereby infected fields were submerged under water for six to eighteen months. Because the fungus requires continuous supplies of oxygen in order to survive, the huge artificial lakes were partially successful in eliminating the disease. Within five years, however, Panama disease usually reappeared in the fields that had been flooded, requiring the re-inundation of the same fields. Not only were the results of this procedure less than satisfactory, the dyking of thousands of acres, the subsequent required deep discing of the land, and the laborious replanting of banana rhizomes were all costly measures. Moreover, flood fallowing was not possible in areas where the bedrock is porous, a condition that prevails on Guatemala's south coast, where the United Fruit Company established plantations in 1936.[7]

While UFCO sometimes converted the diseased fields to producing crops unaffected by the fungus, it often simply abandoned the infested fields and established new ones. Thus, by 1950, the United Fruit Company had been forced to discontinue banana cultivation on about 900,000 acres of land throughout the isthmus, with Panama disease the chief reason for abandonment or shifts to other crops.[8] The continuous moving of banana cultivation to virgin acreage required that extensive tracts of land be held in reserve. This requisite was largely responsible for the huge land holdings that United Fruit acquired and held in reserve in Guatemala and elsewhere in Central America.

The United Fruit Company's 1924 rental agreement, which covered a twenty-five year period and could be renewed, stipulated that the Company would pay the Guatemalan government an annual rent of $6,000 dollars. In addition, UFCO agreed to pay a 1 cent tax on each stem of bananas it exported, and $12 for each mahogany or cedar tree exported. The Company also obligated itself to transport the country's international mail on its banana ships at no cost to the government.[9]

One of the most tendentious, often incorrect accounts of the United Fruit Company's first years in Guatemala can be found in Richard H. Immerman's *The CIA in Guatemala*. The author asserts that because the United Fruit Company initially had no "formal" standing in Guatemala, Keith, under the name of the Agricultural Company of Guatemala, negotiated the 1924 contract with José María Orellana's government in order to obtain legal status for United Fruit. Apart from the fact that the United Fruit Company had signed a formal agreement with the Guatemalan government in 1901, there is no documentation — and Immerman provides none — indicating that Keith's dealings with the Orellana government concerned anything but the construction of the railroad to El Salvador. Immerman's mention of the Agricultural Company of Guatemala (UFCO's south coast subsidiary, the Compañía Agrícola de Guatemala) is also out of context, since it was not until 1930 that the Compañía Agrícola de Guatemala signed a contract with the Guatemalan government. In fact, the subsidiary was not even incorporated in New Jersey until 1928 — two years after Orellana had left office.[10]

De León Aragón charges that the 1 cent tax and the $6,000 rental figure agreed to in the 1924 contract are "simply ridiculous" when compared to the privileges and exemptions that the Company received in return.[11] It is worth noting, nonetheless, that the banana tax clearly abrogated Keith's 1904 contract which stated that no agricultural products — except for coffee — would be taxed during a thirty-five year period. United Fruit, therefore, voluntarily assumed an export tax it was not legally required to pay.

Although an annual rental of $6,000 seems a negligible fee for such extensive properties, LaBarge points out that

> *the rights it [the Company] had acquired with the Guatemalan government appeared almost without value . . . The land acquired was often inaccessible; road and railway transportation with connecting tramway links had to be constructed and rolling stock supplied. Labor efficiency proved to be extremely low. Sanitation was practically nonexistent, and the incidence of disease was high throughout the area. Malaria was endemic; tuberculosis, pneumonia, influenza, intestinal parasites, and venereal diseases were common . . . Firms operating in a developed economy do not face these difficulties, for such 'external economies' as a healthy, educated labor force, sanitation, and transport facilities are already functioning.*[12]

The 1924 contract also permitted the Company to import duty free many articles which de León Aragón maintains had nothing to do with the production of bananas. He cites such items as telegraph and telephone lines, rails, rolling stock, fuel, and all the machinery and materials necessary for the construction and maintenance of its railroads and telephones. To assert that these items had nothing to do with the production of bananas is either disingenuous or demonstrates little understanding of the requirements in operating thousands of acres of banana plantations. In order to transport harvested fruit, it was necessary to build dozens of miles of railroad throughout UFCO's banana farms. Connecting with the IRCA's main line to Puerto Barrios, these spurs were essential in expeditiously moving the highly perishable fruit from the plantations to dockside.

An indispensable element of the entire operation was rapid, reliable communication. Company officials had to know when ships would be arriving in Puerto Barrios in order to advise particular farms of the grade and quantity of fruit desired, and the time for cutting it. Therefore, telephones and telegraphic systems — virtually unknown in the area at that time — were the only methods of assuring the transmission of such vital information.

The contract, which required ratification by the Guatemalan Legislative Assembly, was not approved by that body until 1927. Before ratifying the document, however, the Assembly insisted on an increase in the annual rental fee. The United Fruit Company therefore agreed to an $8,000 a year increment, thus reimbursing the government $14,000 annually for the swamp-filled, malarial jungle land.

BANANA LANDS BRING GUATEMALA AND HONDURAS CLOSE TO WAR

The 1924 rental agreement also gave cause to what British historian Victor Bulmer-Thomas has stated is the "worst charge" that can be made against the United Fruit Company's long presence in Guatemala: a narrowly averted war between Honduras and Guatemala.[13] The origin of the dispute lay in the poorly defined Atlantic coast boundary between the two nations. The wild, sparsely settled region south of the Motagua River, where the two countries border, had been in dispute for nearly a century when it became apparent that the area included prime banana lands.

On the Honduran side, the area was developed by Samuel Zemurray, one of the banana industry's most controversial and colorful pioneers.[14] The son of a poor Bessarabian farmer, Zemurray had immigrated to the United States in 1892, where he soon began profitably selling UFCO bananas in Mobile and New Orleans. By 1905, however, Zemurray determined he wanted his own sources of supply, and the United Fruit Company was not adverse to helping finance the venture. Thus, after Zemurray founded the Hubbard-Zemurray Company, UFCO purchased 60 percent of the common stock issue. But the association did not prove mutually satisfactory, and the United Fruit Company sold its interests two years later. After a plunge in banana prices nearly ruined Zemurray's company in 1911, he reorganized his venture as the Cuyamel Fruit Company and obtained a second rental agreement from the Honduran government. Before long, his company became one of UFCO's fiercest competitors.

The 24,710 acres that Zemurray obtained from the Honduran government were located between his existing cultivations and the Guatemalan border. Like the United Fruit Company, Cuyamel Fruit required railroads to carry bananas from its plantations to a point of embarkation, in this case Puerto Cortés, Honduras. Thus, in 1913, Zemurray requested President Estrada Cabrera's permission to build a railroad thirty miles west of the Honduran town of Cuyamelito in order to ship his bananas to Puerto Cortés. After two years of negotiations, the Guatemalan government denied Zemurray's request. Undeterred, the Cuyamel Fruit Company continued its construction of the railroad, "with the armed protection of the government of Honduras." [15]

By 1918, with no resolution to the simmering border issue, the U.S. Department of State offered its good offices to mediate the dispute. Representatives of both nations were invited to Washington, but the U.S. government's efforts proved unsuccessful, and the dispute flared again following Guatemala's 1924 rental agreement. According to Virgilio Rodríguez Beteta, whom President Lázaro Chacón named Guatemala's minister to Honduras in 1927, there was "a notable difference" in the neutral stance taken by United Fruit, which also owned nearly 90,000 acres of banana plantations in Honduras, and the openly pro-Honduran position adopted by the Cuyamel Fruit Company. Indeed, the diplomat states that Zemurray, "who felt more Honduran than the Honduran people, more papist than the Pope and more anti-Guatemalan than all the Hondurans combined," was the cause of the "present and future misfortunes that weighed upon and threatened the two countries." [16]

Early in 1928, Cuyamel Fruit began building a railroad south of the Motagua River and, according to Rodríguez, originated the rumor that Honduras was mobilizing its troops to protect the construction. Falling into the trap, Guatemala's President Chacón quickly mobilized his army. War between the two neighbors seemed imminent. After Minister Rodríguez telegraphed his president, however, advising that Honduras had not deployed its army and that the Honduran minister of war was, in fact, visiting the Nicaraguan border — nowhere near the disputed area — Chacón withdrew his troops. In addition, Rodríguez received assurances from the Honduran government that Cuyamel's railroad construction would be stopped. The conflict, finally settled by the two governments in 1933, was largely resolved after Zemurray sold his banana company in 1929 for 300,000 shares of United Fruit stock worth $31.5 million. He thus became UFCO's largest single stockholder.[17] In return, United Fruit obtained 35,000 acres of cultivated banana lands in Honduras, Nicaragua and Mexico; fifteen banana ships; the shipping facilities at Puerto Cortés; railroads and equipment — enough to produce and ship more than six million stems of bananas annually.[18]

Ultimately, the near war between the two neighbors cannot be totally attributed to the Cuyamel Fruit Company and its principal rival. In fact, Pitti quotes a 1924 dispatch from the American Legation in Guatemala City which speculated that President Orellana had made the Motagua Valley lands available to the United Fruit Company "in order to enlist United States backing in the border dispute."[19] Perhaps the most evenhanded observation of the near war has been made by Honduran historian Mario R. Argueta: "if the border dispute existed before, absolutely independent of the two North American fruit companies, it was intensified by their rival interests. Nevertheless, it is difficult to determine if the companies were more interested in using the governments to achieve their economic objectives or if the governments used the companies to obtain their political goals."[20]

UNITED FRUIT MOVES TO THE PACIFIC COAST

In 1928, even as United Fruit was involved with the Honduran border dispute, it became embroiled in what was to become its most contentious contract with the government of Guatemala. Because Panama disease was making ruinous inroads into the Company's Atlantic coast plantations, new banana lands were urgently required. And since UFCO was interested in shipping bananas directly to the west coast of the United States, Guatemala's lower Pacific piedmont provided an ideal location for establishing new plantations. There was, however, one major impediment: Guatemala's Pacific coast provided no adequate deepwater port.

In order to commence the development of a south coast operation, the Compañía Agrícola de Guatemala, 100 percent owned by the United Fruit Company, was established in 1928. In that same year, the Company requested permission from the government to construct a modern port near Concepción, on the Pacific coast. The port-building contract that the Compañía Agrícola subsequently obtained does not specify the cost of the facility, but de León Aragón claims that a Company pamphlet circulated at the time estimated the cost to be approximately $25 million.[21] Such a figure, however, is preposterously high. Kenneth Grieb, author of the most detailed biography available on President Jorge Ubico, states that the port could have cost slightly more than $1 million, while May and Plaza assert the pier and the facilities servicing the wharf would have involved expenditures far under $5 million.[22]

Although President Chacón awarded the concession in 1928, the Legislative Assembly refused to ratify it. Some coffee growers and other opponents of the contract argued that the government — and not *La Frutera* — should build a national port on the country's south coast. Nonetheless, at the Company's urging, Chacón again submitted the proposal to the Assembly the following year. "Undoubtedly, the widely held view that inefficiency and corruption permeated the upper ranks of officialdom, as well as that old bugaboo of North American firms — nationalism — fueled the legislature's hostile reception of the United Fruit Company's renewed request for permission to build a Pacific port," Pitti explains.[23]

Once again, the contract was withdrawn from the Assembly floor and submitted for the fourth time in February 1930. Strong nationalistic sentiments — evident throughout Guatemala during the 1920s — and Congressional suspicions that the contract "might line the pockets of a few favored officials," were certainly factors in the lawmakers' unwillingness to ratify the contract. But other considerations were also at work. UFCO's monopoly of the country's banana industry was resented by many in the Assembly, and its relationship with the International Railways of Central America, which monopolized the country's transportation system, was "an alliance, which, although ill-defined, nevertheless appeared to defraud Guatemalans."

The most important reason for the Legislative Assembly's continuing refusal to approve the contract, however, was purely political.

As the effects of the worldwide depression deepened, President Chacón's increasingly inept handling of the economy came under ever harsher criticism in the Congress. The port-building concession, on which so much of Chacón's prestige rested, had become little more than a power struggle between the president and the legislature. Indeed, the American minister, Sheldon Whitehouse, in a dispatch to the State Department, reported that many deputies freely acknowledged that they opposed the contract because "its approval by the Assembly might strengthen the government." [24]

The document still had not been approved by the Congress when President Chacón suffered a debilitating stroke on December 12, 1930, causing him to resign seventeen days later. The controversial contract was finally ratified by the Congress in June 1931, after General Jorge Ubico had been elected president — an election in which critics maintain both the U.S. government and the United Fruit Company played a role.

Immerman's version of this period of Guatemala's and the United Fruit Company's history is also badly skewed. He contends that once President Chacón signed the contract "Zemurray, aware that Chacón was seriously ailing, opted to remain neutral so as not to antagonize any of his potential successors." In fact, Zemurray did not take over the reins of the United Fruit Company until January 1933, three years after President Chacón had died and two years after Ubico was elected president. Like Monteforte Toledo, who insinuates that the United Fruit Company was behind Estrada Cabrera's ascension to power, Immerman also attempts to make a nefarious connection between the banana company and the election of one of Guatemala's most ruthless dictators. "It was more than just a coincidence," Immerman writes, "that Zemurray's rise to power in United Fruit paralleled the inauguration of the Ubico regime." [25]

THE COMPANY FINDS A FRIEND IN A CRUEL DICTATOR

Paradoxically, General Ubico, the man favored by the United Fruit Company in the 1931 presidential elections, was destined to unleash forces in Guatemala which ultimately would prove extremely harmful to *La Frutera*. For the revolution which led to Ubico's 1944 resignation brought about significant, long-overdue reforms that effectively dismantled much of the system that Ubico and his predecessors had forged. Indeed, Kenneth Grieb, Ubico's discerning U.S. biographer, asserts that "the *Caudillo* [chief] made the revolution both possible and necessary." [26]

If Ubico's well-known pro-American stance made him a favorite of U.S. firms, the United States government played a pivotal role in aiding the general's rise to power. After President Chacón was incapacitated, General Manuel Orellana overthrew the provisional government. Acting on the 1923 Treaty of Peace and Amity, which bound isthmian governments to withhold recognition from any regime seizing power by a coup, Minister Whitehouse advised Orellana that the United States would not recognize his government. Once Whitehouse persuaded Orellana to relinquish power, the Legislative Assembly elected José María Reina Andrade as first designate or provisional president. Because the American minister insisted that new elections should be held as soon as possible, nationwide balloting was scheduled for February 6-7, 1931. The abbreviated campaign clearly favored the one well-known politician who was organized, on the scene and eager for the presidency: General Jorge Ubico.

The son of a wealthy coffee *finquero* and prominent politician, Ubico, who was Justo Rufino Barrios's godson, had enjoyed a celebrated military career before serving as Estrada Cabrera's *jefe político* (political chief) in the departments of Alta Verapaz and Retalhuleu. Exceptionally well organized, efficient, honest and hard working, Ubico soon distinguished himself as one of the country's most effective departmental heads. Nevertheless, as Handy has observed, Ubico's term as *jefe político* of Retalhuleu demonstrated "the attributes that would later determine the temper of his years as president: a brutal obsession with stability and a penchant for administrative detail." [27]

There was never any question who would win the 1931 elections: General Ubico ran uncontested. As Pitti has noted, this fact negates the charge that the United Fruit Company "bought" Ubico's election. Furthermore, the historian contends "it is unlikely that even the fruit giant could have imposed Ubico as president if he had faced concerted opposition. But he did not."[28] That the U.S. government's actions made Ubico's election possible is clear. Grieb points out, however, that Washington's intrusive role in Guatemala's affairs was the result of an all-too-frequent fallacy in American diplomacy.

Although Whitehouse was well aware that his actions were facilitating the rise of Ubico, he did not consciously endeavor to aid the general. American policy in this instance was consistent with its stands in other isthmian crises . . . The problem was that the stand was based on general principles, in complete disregard of the local situation . . . The Guatemalan crisis of 1930-1931 illustrates the hazards of applying a general policy hastily, and the dangers of making a seemingly innocent initial commitment from which it is most difficult to withdraw.[29]

Assuming office on February 14, 1931, one of Ubico's first important acts was to obtain legislative approval of the port-building contract initially sought by the Compañía Agrícola in 1928. Several Guatemalan historians have charged that the Company offered to construct the south coast port "as a pretext to legalize its situation on the Pacific coast" or as "bait" to penetrate the area.[30] Even historian Piero Gleijeses, author of the most extensively researched book on Guatemala's "ten years of spring," (1944-1954) erroneously asserts that the contract provided the Compañía Agrícola "a grant of two hundred thousand hectares [494,000 acres] at Tiquisate on the Pacific coast."[31] In fact, the Company's south coast holdings never included more than approximately 297,000 acres — considerably less than the figure Gleijeses uses.

Indeed, the much-disputed contract contains only one concession of land: twenty *manzanas* (thirty-four acres) to establish a town next to the new port. Moreover, there are only three articles in the twenty-six article contract concerning the banana business; all others refer to the construction of a wharf, a rail spur connecting the port with the IRCA's main line, and buildings to accommodate government customs officials. All items imported for the construction of the port, the railroad spur, hospitals and communications systems were exempted from duties — concessions that the Company presumably could have obtained without committing itself to the construction of an expensive new port. In addition, the Compañía Agrícola agreed to a 100 percent increase in the 1 cent a stem export tax it had been paying since 1924.

The contract also stated that at its fifty-year termination, in 1981, "the port, together with the auxiliary works for navigation, the wharves or piers, the lighthouse, the radiotelegraphic station, everything that has been built on the bed or bottom of the Pacific Ocean . . . the ownership of the railroad branch . . . the lands on which the works mentioned in this article . . . will become the property of the state, without compensation of any kind, and free of all encumbrances." [32]

No major concessions of land were included in the contract because the Compañía Agrícola had already purchased properties on the south coast. The 181,878 acres the Company initially acquired had been ceded first to Arthur E. Wallenberg, a naturalized British subject of Swedish descent. Included in his 1923 concession was the right to construct a $100,000 port on the Pacific. "Eccentric and concerned more with holding on to his concession for speculative purposes, Wallenberg did nothing to develop the region," Pitti asserts.[33] Two years later, Wallenberg sold the property to a British firm, which in turn marketed the holdings in 1926 to Guatemala Plantation Limited, a Swedish concern.

It is curious that numerous Guatemalan authors have praised the Swedish company because it began operations on the south coast with no concessions or contract granted by the government. The same authors, however, criticize the United Fruit Company for having "illegally" initiated operations on the Atlantic coast because the Company sought no contract from the Estrada Cabrera government.

Offering no evidence to support his charge, de León Aragón maintains that the Company did everything possible to stop Guatemala Plantation Limited from constructing a Pacific port. Arguing that the Compañía Agrícola realized it would lose "all hope of establishing itself in the south" if it did not move against the Swedish company is somewhat far-fetched since the primeval area was thinly populated and underdeveloped. In fact, as late as 1950, a team from the International Bank for Reconstruction and Development (IBRD) noted that "at present, except for the port of San José and the operations of a United Fruit Company subsidiary at Tiquisate, the region is only sparsely populated."[34] De León Aragón continues his flawed account by stating that the Swedish company sold its properties to the California Guatemala Fruit Corporation in 1928 because the former realized it was "impossible to fight against the United Fruit Company which had more than $25 million and official support."[35]

Since the California Guatemala Fruit Company had no connection with UFCO, it would appear that the Swedish firm also used the property for speculative purposes. Indeed, this practice was continued by the California company when it sold the land for $269,607 to the Nagualate Land Company, a subsidiary of the Compañía Agrícola de Guatemala.[36] Finally, in 1930 the Nagualate Land Company ceded its rights to UFCO's Compañía Agrícola.

With no port from which to embark its fruit, the Company did not immediately undertake banana production in the area. Nor did it consider transporting south coast bananas to Puerto Barrios by rail. Most United Fruit experts doubted bananas could make a bruising, unrefrigerated rail haul of 300 miles — over one of the most heavily-graded railroads in the hemisphere. "No one had yet carried bananas so far under tropical conditions with primitive railroad equipment," La Barge points out.[37] Nevertheless, Henry T. Heyl, manager of the Atlantic coast division, was convinced bananas could withstand such a journey. Trials conducted in August 1936 proved him right; shortly thereafter UFCO moved to establish a new division at Tiquisate, about twenty miles from the Pacific Ocean.

THE COMPANIA AGRICOLA RENEGES ON ITS 1930 CONTRACT

By this time, a paradoxical situation had occurred: the Company, which had fought so tenaciously to obtain the concession for a Pacific port, had decided it no longer wanted to build the facility. The Compañía Agrícola's failure to construct the port and the subsequent long-term consequences constitute one of the major criticisms levelled against UFCO's Guatemala operations. There were, however, several reasons that compelled the Company to abandon its plans for a Pacific port.

In 1928, when the Compañía Agrícola first sought the port-building concession, the United Fruit Company was enjoying record levels of banana production. But as the effects of the 1929 Wall Street crash intensified in the United States, imports of bananas fell steeply: from 65.1 million stems in 1929 to 39.6 million in 1933.[38] In the three years between 1930 and 1933, UFCO's isthmian plantings declined from a total of 190,000 acres to 130,000.[39] Although the Company continued to pay small dividends throughout the depression, the value of its stock plummeted from $105 a share to $10 1/4.[40]

In New Orleans, where UFCO's largest shareholder watched in dismay as the value of his shares declined by almost 90 percent, Sam Zemurray swung into action. In January 1933, he appeared at United Fruit's Boston headquarters and, after a frosty reception from the board of directors, presented enough proxies to make himself "managing director, in charge of operations." Zemurray immediately undertook numerous significant initiatives, chief of which was, according to Bulmer-Thomas, "a deliberate attempt to shift the burden of adjustment to the world depression onto its tropical divisions."[41] This policy led to a 43 percent reduction in UFCO's production and meant that banana prices in the United States declined much less than most other commodities.[42]

Reducing banana production, however, required dismissing employees. Indeed, even before Zemurray assumed the helm, United Fruit's management had decreed two wage reductions, totalling 25 percent, for all UFCO employees. In addition, United Fruit was confronting a new and dangerous development throughout the isthmus. By 1935, the dreaded sigatoka or leaf spot disease was moving unchecked through UFCO's vast banana plantations in Guatemala and Honduras. At the end of the 1930s, the disease had invaded all of the Company's isthmian banana lands, and it was feared that the entire banana industry would be destroyed by the highly contagious, fast-moving disease.

Yellow sigatoka is an air-borne fungus which first destroys the upper leaves of a plant. This, in turn, affects the size of the stems, causing irregular ripening which makes the fruit unsuitable for shipping. In time, UFCO's agronomists developed an expensive but effective method of controlling the virulent fungus. A mixture of copper sulphate, lime and water, which United Fruit called "Bordeaux", was regularly sprayed on the banana leaves by giant, overhead sprinkler systems. Another method of applying the mixture was through the costly construction of hundreds of miles of pipes through which the liquid was pumped. Workers supplied with enormous hoses connected their equipment to the pipes and laboriously hand sprayed an average of five acres of bananas each day.[43] While plants infected with sigatoka are neither cured nor immunized by the Bordeaux mixture, the liquid prohibits the advance of the disease.

Nevertheless, when sigatoka first began ravaging United Fruit's north coast plantations — and there was no known method of combating the fungus — it appeared the Company would have to completely relocate to the Pacific coast. As Grieb points out, "the necessity of financing the expensive and desperate campaign to develop an antidote that would effectively combat sigatoka and the shift of the production to the Pacific zone, caused United Fruit to reconsider the expense involved in constructing the Pacific port. In this situation the cost of shipping the bananas across the isthmus by rail appeared far less imposing than the amount of investment that would be required to construct the new dock.[44]

UFCO BECOMES A MAJORITY STOCKHOLDER IN THE RAILROAD

If the Depression, the emergence of sigatoka and the spreading inroads of Panama disease brought the United Fruit Company to its lowest ebb, the International Railways of Central America, a victim of Guatemala's degenerating economy, was virtually bankrupt. The nation's exports, largely coffee, decreased from a high of $33.9 million in 1927 to only $9.3 million in 1933; imports, which soared to $30.7 million in 1928 had dropped to $7.5 million by 1933.[45] As a result, the railroad's net income declined sharply: from $2.4 million in 1929 to an abysmal $14,000 in 1933.[46]

Since the railroad derived a major portion of its net revenues by transporting coffee and other products from the Pacific coast to Puerto Barrios, the construction of a modern port on the south coast would only have hastened the IRCA's demise. The railroad's leadership therefore urged the Compañía Agrícola to use the IRCA for the cross-country haulage of bananas. The issue undoubtedly posed an onerous dilemma for the Company. If it constructed the Pacific port, the railroad, which transported UFCO's Atlantic coast bananas to Puerto Barrios, would soon fall into bankruptcy. Given the Guatemalan government's critical budget situation, it was impossible for the Ubico regime to purchase, operate and maintain the IRCA's rolling stock and its 445 miles of railroad.[47] And certainly no private investor would be interested in purchasing a virtually bankrupt railroad which might soon lose its most lucrative, long-haul revenues.

Finally, in 1935 the Compañía Agrícola advised the Ubico government that it wished to postpone the construction of a Pacific port. Negotiations were initiated that same year, culminating in a contract signed March 3, 1936, which allowed the Company to "suspend," but not terminate, its obligation to construct a port. The only reason given for the failure to comply with the 1930 contract was a terse sentence stating that "world economic conditions do not permit at present the construction of the port." Bauer Paiz offers a confused and unsubstantiated explanation for United Fruit's actions. He asserts that the Company never intended to build the port and signed the 1930 contract, knowing it would default on its obligations in order to "intimidate certain groups of recalcitrant IRCA shareholders so that they would submit to the pretensions of the banana trust . . . leading to the bankruptcy of the railroad."[48] Similarly, Immerman's explanation that United Fruit "saw no financial gain" in building the port, and that such an "expensive project would have cut deeply into its profits," fails to explain why the Company had fought so persistently to obtain the port-building concession.[49]

The new contract, in effect until June 6, 1981, provided many of the same concessions permitted in the 1930 document. Among them were duty-free exemptions for the construction of a hospital and public health dispensaries to be "put into public service," which the Company "will freely administer and operate." Exemptions were also provided for the installation of a radio station, telephone and telegraphic facilities for its own use and "to place in public service." Furthermore, the Company was allowed to build twenty-five miles of railroad track within its Tiquisate plantations to connect with the International Railways of Central

America. Few of UFCO's critics have noted that the 1936 contract also stated that the railroad, hospitals, dispensaries, radiotelegraph and radiotelephone systems, "buildings, instruments, tools, furnishings and implements used in the respective operation of each of said services...will pass to the state, without cost or remuneration whatsoever and free from all encumbrances at the termination of this contract."

The Compañía Agrícola also returned to the government 35,000 acres of UFCO land on the Atlantic coast "for the establishment of an agricultural colony and whatever other uses the government may deem convenient"; obligated itself to purchase approximately 1.5 million stems of bananas annually from independent, south coast growers — in addition to the two million stems already under contract — and forfeited a $50,000 performance bond it had posted in 1931.[50] Gleijeses implies that the $50,000 was, in effect, the price the Company paid for the 200,000 hectares that he incorrectly maintains were awarded in the 1930 contract.[51]

Of enormous significance to Ubico, the Compañía Agrícola also extended to the government an advance of $1 million against future taxes. The loan, to be repaid at 4 percent over a six-year period, came at a fortuitous moment for the financially strapped regime which had suffered a liquidity crisis the previous year, compelling suspension of its foreign debt payments. As Grieb explains, "the government desperately needed funds, [but] regular financial houses showed little interest in granting further loans. United Fruit constituted the only available source."[52] In his detailed study of the United Fruit Company's contracts, de León Aragón makes no mention whatsoever of the loan, while Bauer Paiz dubiously asserts that the loan was "a lucrative banking operation which any Guatemalan or foreign bank could have satisfied at less burdensome conditions for the country."[53]

A separate contract, also executed March 3, 1936, modified the United Fruit Company's 1924 rental agreement for properties located in the Motagua Valley. Thus, UFCO agreed to a yearly increase of $20,000, bringing the annual rental fee to $34,000. The Company also committed itself to paying an export tax of 1.5 cents per stem, up from the 1 cent-per-stem tax it had been paying since 1924. It further agreed to pay 2 cents per stem from 1949 until the termination of the contract in 1981. While noting that the new tax rates were extremely low, Grieb points out that "they did represent sizeable increases over the existing rates if measured by percentage, and as such probably represented effective use of the government's limited bargaining position at that moment." [54]

Why did Ubico allow the Company to abrogate its contractual obligations? In the first instance, when the Compañía Agrícola initially approached Guatemala's president about a release from its port-building obligation, Ubico was intent on securing the U.S. government's tacit approval for a second term of office. Although the constitution clearly barred incumbents from re-election, Ubico cleverly orchestrated a national plebiscite in May 1935, which gave him a huge mandate to continue his government for another six years — until 1943. Since Washington was opposed to Latin American *continuismo*, the State Department did not approve of Ubico's transparent efforts to retain power, but as the *Caudillo's* U.S. biographer observes, the dictator "clearly outmaneuvered the State Department and compelled a reversal of American policy." [55] Nevertheless, during the months that Ubico was manipulating the U.S. government, he could not afford to be seen as unfriendly to the largest American concern in Guatemala.

According to Grieb, an even more compelling reason for allowing the Compañía Agrícola to renege on its port-building contract was because

> *the Ubico regime recognized that the nation could scarcely afford any interruption in production of its second leading export, and consequently entered the negotiations determined to do everything possible to maintain it, while simultaneously securing additional funds to overcome its own temporary financial difficulties. Although aspiring to the construction of the Pacific port as part of its plan to improve the national transportation system, the port was a minor consideration when cast against the dire prospect of loss of the nation's second leading source of income, which seemed a distinct possibility at the time the negotiations were conducted.*[56]

And because banana prices recovered from the depression more rapidly than coffee, there was a dramatic change in the ratio of income from the two crops, particularly after the south coast plantations came into production. Bananas, therefore, were becoming increasingly important as a source of national income throughout Ubico's tenure. Even in 1931, well before the Compañía Agrícola began production on the south coast, United Fruit employed 4,500 Guatemalan workers; annually spent a total of $5,116,000 in salaries and other expenditures; paid $264,250 in yearly taxes to the Guatemalan government; and purchased $120,400 of Guatemalan products for its commissaries and other operations.

Ten years later, after the Pacific coast plantations came on line, the Company's total payroll increased to 14,135 workers. This figure, when added to the number of individuals servicing *La Frutera's* employees and those individuals who benefited from the Company's purchases within Guatemala, caused the U.S. Embassy to estimate that "at least 25,000 persons in Guatemala owe their livelihood directly to the banana industry."[57] By 1950, this number had increased considerably, despite a reduction in the Company's work force. Employing 11,669 employees, *La Frutera* estimated that approximately 12,000 persons on the north coast and 25,000 individuals on the south coast depended on the United Fruit Company for their livelihood.[58]

While the 1936 contract permitted the Company to construct a Pacific port anytime within the next forty-five years, it was probably apparent to the government and the Guatemalan people that the Compañía Agrícola would not exercise this option. Instead, the Company's fortunes were now irrevocably tied to those of the IRCA. As May and Plaza noted, the new relationship constituted "a major — and perhaps *the* major — source of irritation surrounding the Company's operations in Guatemala."[59]

On September 17, 1936 the IRCA and the Compañía Agrícola signed an agreement providing the latter with 185,000 shares of the IRCA's authorized but unissued common stock, increasing United Fruit's interest in the railroad from 17 percent to 42.6 percent of the total stock. Moreover, the Compañía Agrícola was given the IRCA's new issue of 3.5 percent twenty-year collateral notes with a face value of $1.75 million. In return, UFCO paid the railroad $2.1 million in cash, most of which the IRCA applied toward a first mortgage note due in 1941.[60]

The Compañía Agrícola also agreed not to construct a Pacific port unless both parties found it mutually advantageous.

THE IRCA: TARGET OF INNUMERABLE CRITICISMS

La Frutera's close affiliation with the railroad inevitably linked the Company to numerous negative charges made against the railroad. One of the chief complaints dealt with the IRCA's freight rates. In fact, as early as 1918, Munro noted that the railroad's rates discriminated against north coast users and favored those on the Pacific coast. The rates were set, the author charged, "with a view to giving Puerto Barrios, which is served by the fruit company steamers, every possible advantage over the Pacific coast ports." [61]

If freight rates to the Pacific ports were proportionately higher, it was still more economical for coffee growers to export their product from the two nearby Pacific ports of Champerico or San José. Nevertheless, Kepner and Soothill found that while 81 percent of Guatemala's 1929 coffee exports were produced on plantations closer to the Pacific Ocean than to Puerto Barrios, only 31 percent were shipped via Champerico or San José.[62] It is obvious that south coast clients simply preferred to utilize the Atlantic seaboard because their exports did not have to transit the Panama Canal in order to reach the east coast markets of the United States or Europe.

A number of writers have also criticized the railroad for exacting freight rates that were "among the highest in the world." Even the Guatemalan poet and essayist Carlos Wyld Ospina attacked the IRCA for charging more to transport freight from Puerto Barrios to the capital than it cost to ship goods from England to Puerto Barrios.[63]

The question of IRCA freight rates was extensively examined by a team of experts from the International Bank for Reconstruction and Development, which visited Guatemala in 1950 at the request of the government. Noting that "direct comparisons are seldom valid in matters of this kind," the team concluded that the IRCA's average freight rates "exceed those of many other countries. It is quite possible that they are higher than they should be." [64] Nevertheless, numerous Guatemalan scholars continue to maintain that the IBRD explicitly stated that the IRCA's freight rates were the "highest in the world," whereas the team never made such an assertion.

The IBRD mission did, however, list several reasons for the railroad's elevated freight costs. They found, for example, that "passenger-carrying trains stop at every village that is larger than a cluster of huts. [In the 197-mile trip between Puerto Barrios and Guatemala City, there were sixty station stops. The journey from the capital to the Mexican border, a total of 178 miles, included eighty-three stations — a stop approximately every two miles]. This type of service is very expensive to a railroad and not very remunerative. It can be financed only by charging high passenger rates or by absorbing passenger service losses in the charge for freight movements."

The study also pointed out that the railroad operated over very difficult terrain on a single-track line.

> *The movement of all trains is slowed by the necessity for meeting and passing trains at sidings only. Moreover, as density of traffic rises it also increases the cost of operation because of the greater number of passings required, each involving a loss of time and fuel consumed in stopping, waiting and starting. The need is also increased for the intricate and careful dispatching necessary for hauling heavy two-way traffic on a single track.* [65]

Yet another factor in the IRCA's rate structuring was its need to import practically all of its equipment and supplies, paying transportation and handling charges which increased both its investment and operating costs. Even in 1916, the U.S. Department of Commerce remarked that "the cost of operation is considerable in a country where there is by no means an abundance of either freight or passenger traffic and even the fuel has to be imported.[66]

In comparing the IRCA with railroads in the United States, which assessed freight rates far lower than the former, the IBRD team concluded that there were three principal reasons for the higher ton-mile rates in Guatemala: 1) the absence of effective competition; 2) the lack of any governmental control over IRCA rates, in contrast to the regulatory powers over interstate rail rates vested in the U.S. Interstate Commerce Commission; and 3) the short hauls and heavy grades, causing high costs that were not sufficiently balanced by the more economical, longer hauls on the level or on lighter grades enjoyed by most railroads in the United States.[67]

After 1936, another litigious issue emerged when, according to Bulmer-Thomas, the IRCA "adopted a pricing policy which discriminated blatantly in favor of UFCO's bananas against other goods." [68] While the railroad charged the Compañía Agrícola $90 for every banana car it transported from Río Bravo to Puerto Barrios, the Standard Fruit Company, UFCO's principal competitor, paid $200 per carload of bananas, and coffee shippers were forced to pay $350 for every coffee-filled box car traveling from Escuintla to Puerto Barrios.[69] Nevertheless, LaBarge contends that the differing rates "have never been comparable, for the Compañía Agrícola supplies all of its own rolling stock, in 1955 consisting of forty-one steam locomotives, six diesel locomotives, and 640 banana cars, representing a total of some $5 million." [70] By comparison, the IRCA owned eighty-five steam locomotives, thirteen diesel electric locomotives and 348 banana cars.[71] The UFCO subsidiary also performed services not provided by independent shippers: spotting empty cars and picking up banana-laden cars for delivery in train-load lots to a juncture point where the Compañía Agrícola's tracks joined with those of the IRCA. Although the trains were operated by railroad employees and the equipment moved over IRCA tracks, the rolling stock — and its maintenance — were all supplied by the Compañía Agrícola.

It was left to a U.S. court of law, however, to finally determine whether the equipment and maintenance that the Compañía Agrícola provided to the railroad justified the preferential freight rates. In this complicated, lengthy court case, which began in 1949, a minority of IRCA stockholders sued both the railroad and the United Fruit Company because of the lower freight rates provided to UFCO and its south coast subsidiary. By calculating the additional monies United Fruit would have paid if the IRCA had not provided the Company with special freight rates, the minority stockholders demanded a $20 million settlement. The case was finally resolved in 1963 when the New York State Supreme

Court ruled in favor of the stockholders. The United Fruit Company subsequently paid the railway $5.5 million. After the U.S. Justice Department sued the United Fruit Company in an antitrust suit that began in 1954, the Company agreed to divest itself of all its stock ownership in the IRCA by June 30, 1966.

UFCO'S TELECOMMUNICATIONS OPERATIONS

Although the United Fruit Company's telecommunications operations in Guatemala have not been the subject of extensive criticism, they are often cited as another example of the long reach of The Octopus (*El Pulpo*), as the Company is known in much of Central America. Like railroads and port facilities, communications systems were an essential element in UFCO's expeditious handling of an extraordinarily perishable commodity. Thus, in 1922, in a contract signed between the Orellana government and United Fruit, the latter was permitted to construct and operate a radio station in Puerto Barrios for a period of twenty years. Sufficiently powerful to communicate with the United States, Europe and South America, the station was not authorized to serve the public. Official government messages were, however, sent free of charge.

Four years later, UFCO was authorized to lease the Puerto Barrios radio station to Tropical Radio Telegraph Company, a wholly-owned subsidiary of the United Fruit Company. Founded in 1904 to service the Company's own line of communications, Tropical Radio soon began operating as a regular public utility. Covering a period of sixteen years, the 1926 contract permitted Tropical Radio to operate as a public service and to transmit, receive and deliver messages to all those locations within Guatemala "named by the General Bureau of Telegraphs."[72]

In 1932, not long after General Ubico became president, Tropical Radio received a major concession: the leasing for a five-year period of the government's international radio-telegraphic station. Agreeing to pay five thousand dollars annually for the lease of the facility, the UFCO subsidiary also committed itself to "install, maintain and operate . . . a modern and efficient apparatus for radiotelegraph and radiotelephone communication."[73] Tropical Radio's contract was extended in 1941 and again in 1946, when the company agreed to invest not less than $100,000 to install new equipment and improve its radio-telecommunications service. In 1957, when the contract was extended for nine more years, the communications company also guaranteed to reimburse the government the annual equivalent of at least $25,000.

THE GREAT WHITE FLEET MONOPOLIZES ATLANTIC COAST SHIPPING

If the United Fruit Company's ownership of Tropical Radio has not been the target of undue criticism, its maritime operations have been frequently cited as one of *El Pulpo's* mightiest tentacles. Although UFCO's ships, painted a gleaming white and soon known as the Great White Fleet, carried all of the Guatemalan government's correspondence on its ships at no cost, no president had ever granted the Company a concession for exclusive use of the pier in Puerto Barrios. In effect, however, the Company's banana ships monopolized Guatemala's navigational trade. The matter was further exacerbated because the IRCA owned the wharf in Puerto Barrios and, in 1926, purchased the bankrupt port facility at San Jose for $218,000.[74] Thus the railroad owned and operated the country's two major shipping facilities. In a written interview, former President Juan José Arévalo (1945-1951), asserted that as a consequence of the United Fruit Company's monopoly of the country's maritime commerce, no ship "could touch the coasts of Guatemala without the approval of the UFCO. As a consequence, ships from other places did not arrive at our ports."[75]

Since the IRCA owned the Puerto Barrios wharf, it can be assumed that all ships docking at the facility coordinated their arrivals with the railroad company, but it is exaggerated to contend that "ships from other places did not arrive." For example, Monteforte Toledo points out that 297 (or 57 percent) of 532 ships which arrived at Puerto Barrios in 1953 belonged to United Fruit.[76] Moreover, the wharf at Puerto Barrios did not handle all of the country's commerce. While the facility was clearly Guatemala's busiest harbor, the Pacific ports of Champerico and San José were also active. Using Bank of Guatemala figures, LaBarge found that between 1946-1953, the Puerto Barrios facility handled between 44 to 54 percent of the country's total volume of imports, and between 82 and 93 percent of the country's total exports.[77]

Nevertheless, the extent of United Fruit's control over Guatemala's international commerce gave the Company enormous leverage in its dealings with the government. By threatening to suspend or even partially suspend its shipping operations to and from Guatemala, UFCO had the power to disrupt the nation's economy — a fact bitterly resented by many Guatemalans. And, indeed, the Company did partially curtail its operations on several occasions during the 1940s and early 1950s after striking banana workers or stevedores substantially decreased the amount of fruit available for export.

Critics such as Monteforte Toledo also charge that

> *the combination of the railroad business with that of the wharf and maritime transport within one consortium restricts the international commerce of Guatemala and impedes its diversification of markets and the ability to obtain cheaper shipping . . . [The IRCA's service] is channeled almost exclusively to the banana company, without attending to the needs of the economic development of the country . . . The congestion of goods at the port or at stations is due almost always to an arbitrary policy against specific nationally produced articles or as a means of repression against the government.*[78]

Although the IBRD's mission to Guatemala did not address the issue of the United Fruit Company's monopoly of the country's maritime trade, the team noted that a

> *significant aspect of the situation in Puerto Barrios is, that, to all intents and purposes, the area is under the complete control of the United Fruit Company and the International Railway Company. That control extends over the movement of practically all import and export cargo through the Atlantic areas. In the mission's opinion, notwithstanding a sincere effort on the part of the railway company to render satisfactory service to the public, this condition is unhealthy; it would, of course, be mitigated by control under a public utilities commission and construction of a second pier . . . ownership or control of property in*

FOR THE RECORD

> *Puerto Barrios gives the railway company a virtual monopoly on the construction and operation of piers and on the use of the inshore harbor area. It is inevitable that this situation should give rise to charges of discrimination in rates and services between customers and to complaints of excessive charges against the public . . . Likewise, the heavy use of Puerto Barrios by the United Fruit Company, a large stockholder in the railway company, may justify some complaints as to the slow handling of other cargo, even though it be recognized that the perishable nature of the principal Fruit Company export (bananas) requires that it be accorded prompt handling and therefore given right-of-way over less perishable products.*

Nevertheless, the IBRD team did look into complaints about the movements of goods in Puerto Barrios. After noting that "service by the railway company, both over its pier and in its rail operations, has been excellent despite the many criticisms levelled at it," the experts pointed out there was an "inadequacy of warehousing facilities for the receipt and examination of merchandise by the customs service in both Guatemala City and Puerto Barrios. The system now in use results in congested storage at these points and causes the immobilization of large numbers of railway cars through lack of space into which to unload their cargoes."[79] Based on the IBRD's findings, it is clear, therefore, that the IRCA was not solely responsible for many of the charges that have been levelled against the railroad.

ANALYZING UFCO'S "BLACK LEGEND"

Indeed, close examination of most of the indictments against United Fruit detailed in this chapter demonstrates that there were often complex issues involved that defy facile allegations. The fact that more than fifty years have passed since many of these charges were first aired also permits a more dispassionate examination of UFCO's "black legend." A case in point is the Company's failure to comply with the 1930 contract. It is now obvious that a modern, deep-water port on Guatemala's Pacific coast would not have contributed significantly to the economic development of that area — a fact readily perceived by the IBRD. "Avoid any large investment of public funds for improvement of Pacific ports in the near future," the experts counselled. The Bank based its recommendation on two factors: the reduced cargo movement through the Pacific ports of San José and Champerico, and a study of Guatemala's south coast which revealed the absence of any natural harbor, or even any area where a protected harbor could be constructed without heavy original expenditures.

In the more than forty years since the IBRD made its recommendation, the Guatemalan government has constructed a deep-water port, called Puerto Quetzal, near San José. Completed in 1983, at a cost of approximately $50 million, the 2,625-foot pier is protected by two breakwaters, one of which is nearly three-quarters of a mile long.[80] Nevertheless, this modern port is far less active than Santo Tomás de Castilla, which began operations in 1955 and now handles approximately 70 percent of the nation's international maritime commerce.

Of far more significance to the Guatemalan economy was the inauguration in 1959 of an asphalt-surfaced, all-year highway between Puerto Barrios and Guatemala City. Completion of this highway had been one of the major recommendations made by the IBRD mission. When the team visited Guatemala in 1950, the highway extended only from Guatemala City to Los Amates, near Quiriguá. In fact, the mission expressed bafflement at the government's "inexplicable failure" to complete that portion of the highway located between Los Amates and Puerto Barrios.

When the highway to the Atlantic was finally inaugurated, the IRCA — for the first time in its history — suffered a net loss of $1.1 million. Although its losses declined somewhat during the following two years, by 1962 the railroad was again running annual losses of more than $1 million.[81] Nor was the IRCA ever again able to operate in the black. In 1968, sixty years after Minor Keith's first train arrived in the capital, the Guatemalan government nationalized the railroad, taking over all its rolling stock and properties, including its piers at Puerto Barrios and San José.

From today's vantage, it is clear that the United Fruit Company's decision to renege on its port-building commitment and thus keep the IRCA operational was ultimately far more critical to Guatemala's economic development than was the construction of a Pacific port. The country has enjoyed such a facility for more than ten years, but it is apparent that the nation's exporters and importers overwhelmingly prefer to utilize Guatemala's Atlantic seaboard to expedite their cargos. Nor has the construction of Puerto Quetzal caused any major changes in the overall economic development of the south coast.[82] What *is* obvious is that long before 1959 the country was in critical need of an all-weather highway to the Atlantic which would have effectively broken the IRCA's monopoly on north coast transportation. Such competition would undoubtedly have forced the railroad to lower its freight rates, thereby benefiting the nation's exporters and importers.

Despite all the critical — and largely erroneous — charges that Guatemalan writers, in particular, have formulated against the manner in which United Fruit acquired land on the country's north and south coasts, UFCO must be given credit for transforming vast areas of remote tropical wilderness into rich farm lands. The thousands of acres that it drained and cleared on Guatemala's Atlantic coast are still among the most productive banana lands anywhere in the world — and account for Guatemala's third-most-important agroexport. Similarly, the jungled region of the Pacific coast, converted by *La Frutera* into verdant plantations, opened up a large, new agricultural area that currently produces impressive quantities of export crops.

Although a number of writers have censured the United Fruit Company for its role in the near war with Honduras, at least two factors have often been overlooked. Because United Fruit also owned plantations in Honduras, the Company's stance in the dispute was considerably more conciliatory than that of the Cuyamel Fruit Company, whose holdings were located exclusively in Honduras. It is also clear that the governments of both Guatemala and Honduras pursued their own political agendas in the handling of the long-festering border issue. To assert, therefore, that United Fruit was largely responsible for the tensions between the two neighbors is to misrepresent a complex issue that involved both national and foreign interests.

The United Fruit Company's monopolization of Guatemala's maritime trade and its control of the country's only important means of transportation obviously constituted crucial elements of the nation's infrastructure, permitting the Company to exercise far more influence than most agricultural enterprises might be expected to exert. As noted above, however, the railroad's monopoly of Guatemala's transportation system could have been immediately destroyed if the highway from Guatemala City to Puerto Barrios had been completed long before 1959.

The fact that United Fruit's Great White Fleet dominated Guatemala's shipping was not due to any special government concession, but simply an economic reality. That is, a vital part of UFCO's operations necessitated a fleet of refrigerated ships completely under the Company's control. As a result, the Great White Fleet's vessels readily outnumbered other ships serving Guatemala. Unlike the IRCA's control of Guatemala's transportation system, however, there was little that the Guatemalan government might have done to end UFCO's shipping monopoly if bananas were to continue to rank as a major export crop. There was simply no other company that needed to serve Puerto Barrios several times a week, year in and year out.

- 4 -

Banana Production and its Personnel

Less than four months after General Jorge Ubico assumed the presidency, the compliant legislature ratified the controversial contract permitting the Compañía Agrícola, UFCO's south coast subsidiary, to import duty-free much of the equipment needed to begin operations on Guatemala's Pacific coast. Supervisory personnel for the new division, almost without exception, was provided by experienced employees who were transferred from United Fruit's north coast headquarters at Bananera. In the thirty years since the United Fruit Company had begun planting bananas in the Motagua Valley, agricultural technology had made numerous advances, but establishing a banana division was still an immensely expensive, labor-intensive job.[1]

Both coasts shared many similarities: impervious jungles, unrelenting heat, swarming insects and venomous snakes. Since the Pacific coast is considerably drier than the Motagua Valley, however, draining those fields was not the daunting task it proved to be on the north coast. Numerous sepia-colored photographs, taken by the United Fruit Company during the 1920s, document the enormously difficult preparation of banana plantations on Guatemala's Atlantic coast. Understandably, the photographer seems obsessed with water. There are dozens of scenes of swamps and rivers; huge trees and branches hurled against flooded river banks; washed-out bridges and inundated fields of banana plantations. Several photos illustrate how dikes, canals and bridges were built and how pumps and dredges rehabilitated the land. A cumbersome, steam-operated dragline is often seen in operation as the photographer demonstrates one of the methods used to drain the swamps: twenty-feet-deep ditches that dwarf the workers standing at their raw, muddy edges. One remarkable photograph shows a surveyor, standing almost neck-deep in brackish water, as he peers through a transit at a colleague, who holds a large measuring rod and is also deeply submerged in water.

Before any work began, elaborate surveys of topography, soils and possible sites for railroads and drainage systems were undertaken. In 1906, UFCO established its first headquarters in Guatemala at a site several miles east of Quiriguá. The town, which the Company named Virginia, was located alongside the railroad to the Atlantic, thereby permitting bananas to be rapidly shipped to Puerto Barrios. By 1936, aerial surveys were occasionally used to help engineers lay out the location of Tiquisate, the town which would become the Compañía Agrícola's Pacific coast headquarters. The experts selected a site not far from the village of Río Bravo, a station on the IRCA's south coast line.

After the site of the division headquarters was determined, engineers mapped out the location of the approximately twenty farms which constituted a UFCO division. Workers then began constructing the Company's headquarters, the multi-faceted facility that would subsequently serve as the support unit for the workers who carved out immense banana plantations from the sweltering jungles. The headquarters of a United Fruit Company division was, in effect, a small, self-contained town. Covering an area of approximately 100 acres, the town included a complex of central offices, houses, railroad yards and shops, equipment depots and machine shops, power plants and telephone and telegraph stations. Additionally, there was a large hospital, school, church, dairy, slaughter house, commissary, and usually recreational facilities such as a club house, nine-hole golf course, swimming pool, tennis courts, bowling alley, soccer and baseball fields.

But before such extensive facilities could be built, the most concerted attack ever mounted against Guatemala's pestilent wilderness had to be undertaken. "What the actual attack on the jungle means can hardly be pictured to any one who is not familiar with the dense, dank growth of the tropics. The jungle is a tangled mass . . . impossible to travel ten feet without cutting, so thick are the brush and vines. Even the surveying of these stretches is only for the tropical expert," one writer has commented.[2] The impervious wilderness could only be conquered with a massive assault by machete-wielding workers.[3] On the thinly-populated Atlantic coast, many of the jungle busters were imported from British Honduras (today's Belize) and the West Indies. At Tiquisate, where more *ladino* workers were available, the Company soon contracted hundreds of men to clear the land and build the numerous structures that would serve as Company headquarters. Once the division headquarters was functioning, work immediately began on clearing nearby wilderness areas which would eventually be transformed into thousands of acres of banana farms.

Living conditions for the workers who established the banana farms were extremely primitive. Approximately 200 laborers, usually supervised by at least two North Americans or Europeans, the overseer and a timekeeper, were required to slash out a farm of 800 to 1,000 acres. Mark Trafton, Jr., who worked on the 1928 opening of *La Esperanza*, a United Fruit banana farm on Panama's Pacific coast, describes the facilities of a work camp similar to those on the north coast of Guatemala in the early 1900s.

> *La Esperanza was a clearing along the right-of-way of the future railroad. There were a number of manaca shacks for the overseers, timekeepers, and foremen, a stable with about twenty riding mules, a messhall, a commissary, and a medical dispensary, all palm-thatched. The labor camps for the 200 workers, were located about a mile away, and consisted of two large barracks of poles and thatch which they cut in the jungle. All supplies and building materials arrived once a week on the tractor supply wagon. My manaca shack was a new one. Furnishings were a large folding canvas cot, with a mosquito net, a small folding camp stool, a wooden bench, a galvanized bucket, and a kerosene lamp. I added to those furnishings by acquiring a few empty wooden boxes at the commissary for storage. The shack did have a wooden floor — a few rough hewn planks laid on the bare ground.*
>
> *The mess shack where the overseers and timekeepers took our meals, consisted of a long wooden slab table with benches on both sides and a couple of kerosene lanterns hanging above the table . . . Water was kept*

in some diesel oil drums which had been cleaned out. Some badly chipped china and glassware and an assortment of 'silver,' probably from old Company ships, graced the table . . . There was no refrigeration of any kind so, save for a few tins of imported goodies, everything was 'fresh,' right out of the jungle or nearby rivers.

Some of the delicacies we feasted on almost every day: the highly esteemed flesh of tepescuintle, a large rodent the size of a small pig; wild hogs; wild pigs (peccaries); pigeons; forest deer; chachalaca, pheasant-like birds; crested guan, large turkey-family birds; tinamous, small ground birds; partridges; wood-quail; many varieties of fish and crocodile tail; bushels of tender hearts of palm; fruits such as zapote, caimito, *and of course bananas. Rice and beans, brought in by traders from the interior, were also staples . . . Before each meal in the evening, the dispensarian, 'Doctor' Smith, a black Jamaican, had the power to withhold the single cup of free grog, Gorgona rum, until each diner had downed a couple of ounces of liquid quinine to prevent malaria.*[4]

After clearing away the tangled underbrush, the laborers turned to the digging of drainage ditches, "back-breaking work using long-handled shovels and throwing each heavy shovel full of clay loam, sometimes from a depth of six or seven feet, up and out of the ditch, clearing a berm on the side by at least three feet. The drains had been staked out and the cubication calculated by engineers." [5] (Drainage ditches were essential because banana roots will rot if they are planted below the water table.)[6] In Tiquisate, immense draglines were brought in to excavate long miles of canals which would carry river water to pumping stations used to irrigate the banana farms, providing the equivalent of two inches of rainfall every week during the dry season.[7]

Equipped with diesel engines, each station was capable of pumping 5,000 gallons of water per minute to thirty-six tall towers. During the nearly five hours that each tower was operated, approximately 157,500 gallons of water were applied to the three acres covered by the giant structure.[8] In Tiquisate, ditches were also required for the pipes used in the overhead spraying of Bordeaux to combat sigatoka disease. Pumping stations were installed throughout every farm and thousands of "risers," or towers, which covered a radius of seventeen yards, were erected in order to fine spray the atomized Bordeaux mixture on banana plants every eighteen weeks.[9]

Once the ditches had been excavated, the fields were lined and staked in order to provide regularly-spaced rows of banana plants. Because the banana has no seed, it is propagated from a "bit" or root stock taken from another plant. These bits, which weighed between five and ten pounds, were planted approximately eighteen inches below the surface of the soil at intervals of twelve feet. Nearly 300 rhizomes were planted to an acre. Only after the bits were planted was attention given to felling the giant tropical trees, some more than 150 feet tall. On the Atlantic coast, before chain saws and bulldozers were used, this work was accomplished by axe-swinging choppers who erected a scaffold about ten feet high around each tree "in order to avoid cutting through any more wood than necessary . . . In a jungle clearing it was not uncommon to have five or six chopping crews working simultaneously on big trees."[10]

No effort was made to remove the giant trees from the fields once they had been felled. Within six months, the blistering heat and humidity turned the small wood into mulch, and within two or three years even the huge tree stumps had decayed. "When a tract is planted and the trees felled, the general appearance of the plantation is just a little worse than when it was jungle," one observer wryly noted.[11] As soon as approximately 1,000 acres of bananas were planted, typically less than two years after the initial work of clearing the jungle had begun, the laborers and overseers were transferred to another virgin area to begin the strenuous task of laying out a new farm. By the time the men were relocated to the new wilderness, a railroad spur had been extended to their camp site. Construction crews were then brought in to build the permanent facilities for the employees who would maintain and operate the farm.

Each United Fruit Company farm, which housed approximately 200 workers and their families, was designed as a separate, virtually self-sufficient unit — a miniature replica of the division headquarters. As May and Plaza note, "a checkerboard of roads, ditches, and bridges covers each farm, and all farms are interconnected with roads and narrow-gauge tramways or railroads along which steam, diesel or gasoline powered rolling stock carries in materials, fertilizers, equipment, supplies and work force, and over which the harvested fruit moves out. All are interconnected, too, by power, electric light, and telephone lines. The transport and communications network binds the several farms to the division center." [12] Most camps also contained a school house, health dispensary and commissary. If such facilities were not provided, they were available at another camp, usually less than two miles distant. Often there was a club house. Supervisory personnel, such as the overseer and timekeeper, were provided with single-family houses similar to those in the division headquarters. Additional structures in a camp included sheds, garages and other utilitarian facilities.

Laborers on each new farm were soon put to work. One of their first tasks was to move into the recently-planted fields to replant bits that had not sprouted. Those that had sprouted — usually about a month after being planted — produced a number of shoots (ratoons), and it was necessary to prune the weakest ones from each plant. The most vigorous shoot, called a "daughter," was left intact, thus assuring a new banana-bearing plant once the mature plant, or "mother," produced a stem of fruit.[13] Another essential job was the periodic machete slashing of the exuberant growth of tropical vegetation which soon sprang up in the cleared fields. This process was repeated every three or four months in order to keep the riotous jungle at bay. Once the plants matured, however, their enormous leaves somewhat inhibited the growth of weeds, thereby reducing the frequency of weed control.

Young banana plants first form a leaf stock or stem that gradually lengthens and thickens to form a "trunk" of vascular bundles. The Gros Michel, the variety of banana which UFCO produced for more than fifty years, often reached eighteen to twenty feet in height, with gigantic leaves, eight to twelve feet in length and about two feet broad.[14] Within approximately nine to twelve months, the mature plant would "shoot," producing a curious, purple bud which evolved, within thirteen weeks, into a stem that grew upside down. Each banana plant produced only one stem of bananas, which was composed of "hands" or clusters. These hands grew separately in spirals, each containing from ten to twenty-five individual bananas or "fingers."

Commercially, bananas were classified as ranging from nine to six hands. United Fruit did not export or purchase from independent growers any stems producing fewer than six hands. Because the Gros Michel variety has a very shallow root system and each twenty-five-foot tall plant bore a stem of bananas that often weighed upwards of eighty pounds, it was necessary to prop each stem with one or two bamboo poles to prevent the plant from toppling in light winds. The poles, however, were not effective against the hurricane-force winds that periodically sweep across Guatemala, particularly the south coast. Winds of thirty-five miles per hour could easily mow down hundreds of acres of the top-heavy plants. When such climatic conditions occurred, thousands of acres of banana plants crashed to the ground, causing what United Fruit termed a "blowdown." In order to rehabilitate the flattened fields, machete-swinging workers severed the tallest stalk of each toppled plant near its root system, permitting a new, strong shoot to eventually replace the fallen stalk. Since it required ten months to a year for the affected fields to again begin producing fruit, blowdowns made banana production — especially on the Pacific coast — an extremely risky business for the United Fruit Company.

Banana plantations yield fruit throughout the year, but the mature, although unripe, fruit was harvested on the basis of precise schedules timed to the arrivals of ships at loading ports. Another significant consideration in harvesting was the ship's destination. For example, if the vessel was scheduled for New Orleans, more mature bananas were harvested. If the fruit was being dispatched to more distant ports, such as the east coast of the United States or Europe, "thinner," or a slightly less mature grade of fruit, was selected. The harvesting also had to be carefully coordinated with railroad schedules so that the cut fruit moved with minimal delay to the waiting ship.

Although some aspects of the harvesting of bananas have changed considerably since UFCO's era, the basic procedures have not varied. Banana harvesters still work in teams of two. A "cutter," equipped with a long-handled implement that ends in a sharp, chisel-like head, notches the stalk of the plant just below the banana stem. As the plant bends under the weight of the heavy fruit, a waiting carrier or "backer," with padding on his shoulder, gently receives the stem. Using a machete, the "cutter" then quickly severs the stem from the stalk. Early in the century, the "backer" transported the fruit to a mule, which was later replaced by tractor-pulled, padded trailers. (Today the bananas are hung on aerial tramways and tractor-pulled into packing stations, as described more fully in the epilogue.) Once the trailers were fully loaded, the bananas were hauled to small stations located on railroad spurs.

Before being loaded into the well-ventilated, wooden-slatted railroad cars, the stems were suspended from hooks and dipped at least six times in a weak solution of sodium bisulfate. This dipping not only removed the dried Bordeaux mixture previously sprayed on the banana plants, but it also killed spiders and other insects that might be hidden in the bananas. The stems were then given a second bath of clear water. Once the fruit had dried, a perforated bag of polyethylene plastic was slipped over each stem — a practice UFCO began in 1950 to reduce bruising and scarring of the bananas. Finally, the stems were loaded into waiting railroad cars, the sides of which were padded with semi-circular sections of the stalks of mature banana plants. After the fruit arrived at dock side, it was unloaded and either accepted or rejected for export. The base of each accepted stem was cut with a small knife and painted with a fungicidal paint to prevent stem rot from developing during the voyage. Placed on mechanical conveyor belts, the fruit was loaded into the hold of the ship, refrigerated to a cool fifty-two degrees Fahrenheit to prevent ripening.[15] Within approximately two weeks, the bananas, with a shelf life of two to four days once placed in the produce section of supermarkets, would be for sale throughout the United States.[16]

That the United Fruit Company was able to establish a banana division in the midst of primitive, unhealthful and isolated conditions is quite remarkable. And yet, after Frederick Upham Adams visited Virginia in 1913, he described a place that "is modern in every respect . . . Here are well-equipped railroad shops, an electric lighting and power plant, steam laundry, and up-to-date stores with supplies fresh from the United States and abroad. The residential district contains streets and dwellings which would be a credit to any community, yet all this was a wilderness only a few short years ago." [17]

In the mid-1920s, United Fruit's management decided to move its headquarters to a site approximately thirty miles east of Virginia. According to John R. Silver, who was employed by the Company when it relocated to a town UFCO named Bananera, the move was necessary because new plantations were being established many miles to the east of Virginia. This was the land UFCO had rented from the Guatemalan government under the 1924 contract. "By eliminating the town of Virginia and closing some small facilities at Quiriguá and Bobos, management and all supervisors were brought together in a larger, more modern divisional headquarters, making for a more efficient and economic operation," Silver told the author.[18] Carlos Haroldo Gomar, who began working for the United Fruit Company in 1945, also remarks that "there were fewer problems with flooding around Virginia, but the land was not very well suited for banana growing. The soil's clay content was too high; as a result, good drainage was not possible."[19] Construction of the new town began in 1926; by the end of 1929, Bananera was fully operational.[20]

Photographs documenting the building of the town illustrate an amazing number of structures being erected simultaneously: a three-story-high machine shop, made of tall steel beams, with corrugated iron walls; an imposing lumber shed; an enormous "M and S," or materials and supply building; as well as a steam-powered electrical generating and ice-making plant, constructed of bricks. Concurrent with the construction of these utilitarian facilities was the building of numerous houses. One photograph, grandly captioned "Third Street and Railroad Avenue," illustrates two forlorn rows of thirteen wooden houses, standing in a bleak, raw area with no vegetation whatsoever except for a few coconut trees. In the foreground is a view of a railroad track.[21]

Located next to the village of Morales, Bananera was well positioned at a juncture between the IRCA's Atlantic railroad and more than eighty miles of track, which United Fruit would eventually build. This line — the so-called "belt" — ran parallel to the IRCA's and skirted the Motagua River, connecting nearly all of the Company's banana farms. At Virginia, most of the clapboard houses were dismantled and shipped by rail to Bananera, where they were once again reassembled. Today the tiny village of Virginia, accessible over a rough dirt road branching off the Atlantic highway, is comprised of a few modest houses owned by local farmers. Four cement pilings, on which a UFCO building was once mounted, and a railroad track are about all that remain of the Company's first headquarters in Guatemala.

THE ORGANIZATION OF A BANANA DIVISION

The complicated and costly job of establishing immense banana plantations in the midst of remote tropical jungles required first-rate organization and management. The United Fruit Company developed a remarkably efficient organization that effectively administered every aspect of the diverse activities required to produce and harvest one of the world's most perishable fruits.

Each division was headed by a manager, who, in Guatemala, was accountable to a general manager based in the capital. The latter reported directly to the Boston offices. The divisional manager and his deputy, the assistant manager, supervised a disparate number of activities. A table of organization showed the manager overseeing such dissimilar areas as agriculture, engineering, accounting, law, mechanical, materials and supplies, merchandise, medicine, construction, railroads, transportation, maintenance of ways, hotels, electrical and telephone systems, and even an ice plant.[22] Significantly, the Company did not establish a department of labor relations in each division until 1954.

One of the most vital employees was the superintendent of agriculture who was responsible for the efficient operation of all the farms — upwards of 20,000 acres of banana plantations. The superintendent supervised the two districts, which usually comprised a division, and each district was composed of eight farms. Heading up each district was a district superintendent of agriculture who, in turn, supervised the overseer of each farm in his area of responsibility. Assisted by a timekeeper, the overseer was directly responsible for the entire farm and its labor force of 125 to 200 workers.

Like the division manager, the overseers supervised a number of different operations and were charged with maintaining interminable reports and records: payrolls, fruit estimates, harvest tabulations, overall farm budgets, reports on the school, work contracts, accounts of acreage and livestock, requisition slips, hospital records, condition of bridges and irrigation systems, weather reports and an individual account for every worker on the farm. Much of this material was incorporated into reports maintained at the division headquarters where detailed files were kept on the grade, quality and quantity of bananas harvested at each farm. This information was essential in estimating future quotas and upcoming schedules for harvesting the fruit.

Another key individual was the chief of the engineering department. With his staff of assistants and clerks, he directed land surveys, the planning of new farms, drainage and irrigation programs, bridge and road construction, electrical and communications systems, water-supply installations, the building of levees and numerous other construction projects. A large mechanical department was indispensable to assuring that a huge, dissimilar inventory of equipment was maintained and kept operational. Skilled mechanics were required to work on everything from steam locomotives to tractors, engines, trucks, draglines, automobiles, pumps, motorcars and even domestic appliances. Since spare parts were often not immediately available, the machine shops became adept at producing a diverse inventory of needed items in order to keep essential equipment functioning.[23]

In isolated banana divisions, the materials and supplies department, was also vital to the efficient administration of the enterprise. This department stored and distributed thousands of needed articles: farm tools, motor parts, paint, cables, screws, furniture, household appliances, ropes, coffins and hundreds of other items. "M and S" inventories, maintained long before computers were available, ran to hundreds of closely-printed pages.

Largely because there were so few Guatemalans who were trained as engineers, agronomists, mechanics, accountants, doctors or nurses, United Fruit filled most of its higher-ranking positions during the first three decades of the twentieth century with skilled American or European employees. Guatemalan employees were divided into three categories. At the top of the scale were those individuals who worked directly for American supervisors and lived within the Tiquisate or Bananera compounds. Many of these employees were university graduates and worked in administrative positions within the departments of agriculture, engineering, accounting, mechanics and others.

By the early 1940s, however, it was no longer necessary to staff all supervisory positions with personnel from the United States or Europe, since many Guatemalans and other Central American professionals were fully capable of holding such jobs. By 1950, for example, 97.1 percent of the Company's 11,699 employees were Guatemalan.[24] This gradual change in personnel practices not only reflected the increasing professionalism of well-trained Guatemalan university graduates, but also represented a response to UFCO's declining ability to attract American employees to its tropical divisions. As LaBarge commented in 1959, "despite the presence of important fringe benefits, such as lower taxes, free housing, meals and entertainment below cost at the Company clubs, and free transportation to and from North America for a month's paid vacation at home each year, it has proved increasingly difficult to induce capable North Americans to leave the United States and Canada, where good jobs in familiar surroundings are readily available." [25]

The Company's educational facilities were another factor in its inability to attract American employees. Because the schools in Tiquisate and Bananera did not go beyond the eighth grade, employees with high school age children had to send their youngsters to boarding schools in the United States or in Guatemala City. If sent to the U.S., long periods of separation were endured when the children were still in their early teens. After 1950, United Fruit began providing its employees with a yearly educational allowance of $1,000 and free transportation for youths to travel to and from Guatemala and their American school. LaBarge notes, however, that "even this inducement has not stemmed the decline of permanent personnel from North America." [26]

The highest-paid Americans and Guatemalans within each division constituted a very small number of the total work force. For example, in 1956, when the Tiquisate and Bananera divisions employed 9,052 workers, only about 8 percent earned salaries averaging $3,157 a year. The remaining 92 percent of the work force earned an average annual salary of $979.[27]

Semi-skilled workers, who were usually literate, constituted the second category of Guatemalan employees hired by the United Fruit Company. These included mechanics, carpenters, electricians, tractor drivers, chauffeurs, cooks and low-level office workers. Because of the nature of their work, nearly all these employees lived in Company-provided housing located outside of the Bananera or Tiquisate compounds. Most of the semi-skilled workers were paid by the month, and, by 1956, nearly all of them earned the equivalent of $100 or more per month.

The bulk of the work force was composed of unskilled workers, having little or no formal education. These men held unspecialized jobs, such as fruit cutters, maintenance-of-way workers, ditch diggers, banana loaders, machete workers and sigatoka spraymen. Concentrated on the banana farms, this category of worker was paid by the hour or, more often than not, by the job, or *tarea*. In 1956, such employees earned the equivalent of $40 to $50 a month.[28] By comparison, the country's 1956 per capita income was the equivalent of $244 — a scant $20 a month.[29]

UFCO PERSONNEL POLICIES

It is unclear how the United Fruit Company recruited experienced North American or European employees in 1906 to supervise the construction of Virginia and establish the first large-scale banana plantations on Guatemala's north coast. It seems likely that skilled personnel were transferred from the Company's already-established divisions in Costa Rica, Panama, Cuba and Jamaica. As noted above, it was not until after World War II that the United Fruit Company began experiencing difficulties in recruiting Americans to work in the isthmus. Until the mid-1940s — and particularly during the Depression — the Company's competitive salaries and attractive benefits made UFCO's Central American divisions appealing places for adventuresome young men and women. New employees, who had often heard about United Fruit through friends or relatives already with the Company, signed a comprehensive contract before they sailed to their new duties in the tropics. Typical of these contracts was one signed by Kathryn Campbell in June 1930 which assigned her as a comptometer operator in UFCO's Guatemala accounting department, then located in Puerto Barrios. (Two years later the department was moved to the far more pleasant and healthful division headquarters at Bananera.)

After establishing that the Company would pay Campbell a salary of $125 a month, the contract tersely advised that "the Company reserves the right to transfer you at any time to any other division or any other position in its service for which you may be considered qualified." Stating that the Company would provide the new employee with steamship transportation from New York to Puerto Barrios, the contract quickly made clear that

> *return transportation will be for your own account, but after one year's service may be furnished by the Company, in its discretion, provided your services have been satisfactory. In consideration of the Company furnishing south bound transportation, it is agreed that an amount equivalent to the cost thereof will be deducted from your salary in ten equal monthly installments. In the event your services are terminated within twelve months, the amount so deducted will be applied against your return transportation, any unpaid balance to be for your account. In the event your services are not terminated within twelve months, the amount so deducted will be refunded to you. All other traveling expenses, including railway fares, hotel bills, passport fees, landing permits, taxes on tickets, etc. will be paid by you and will not be refunded to you under any circumstances.*

There were, however, some attractive perquisites.

> *Sleeping quarters will be furnished free of charge by the Company, but meals, laundry and other incidentals will be for your own account . . . Six weeks vacation, with free steamship transportation from the tropical division to your nearest home port and return, is usually allowed after the first eighteen months of service . . . Such medical and hospital service as the Company's medical authorities think proper and can render in the tropical division in which you are employed, and where the necessity of such service is contracted in line of duty, will be furnished . . . At present 2 percent of your monthly salary will be deducted for this service.*

The United Fruit Company provided no formal orientation programs that would have introduced new employees to Guatemala's rich history, its diverse geography and complex, multi-racial society. Clearly, this was a serious oversight for individuals being sent to remote tropical outposts, where conditions were often extremely difficult and certainly very different from North America or Europe. Printed on the reverse side of each standard contract, however, was a long essay entitled "suggestions for employees for the tropics." By today's standards, the document is both patronizing and sexist; nonetheless, it makes an attempt to prepare the employee for the vicissitudes of life on an isolated banana division.

> *As a new man, you will doubtless find life in the tropics quite different in many ways from that which you have been leading. Opportunities for social intercourse are necessarily more limited, and you must learn to do without many of the pleasures and recreations to which you have been accustomed. You will soon learn that the romance and excitement so common to literature on the tropics are not often met with outside the pages of novels. Preserve an open mind and accept conditions as you find them, bearing in mind that the first steps in any line of endeavor are apt to be disagreeable and discouraging.*
>
> *Do not fall into the error of thinking that you are pursuing a different course or meeting different conditions from those experienced by anyone before you. There are very few men now employed by the Company in the tropics who have not started out in the same way and gone through experiences similar to those through which you will pass. Tropical operations can only be learned by actual experience. It is, therefore, absolutely essential to your success that you begin at the bottom of the ladder . . .*
>
> *You may hear complaints from both old and new employees to the effect that life in the tropics is dull and offers no diversions; such complaints do not come from the men who are making the most of their opportunities, for any man who is enterprising can find diversion to take the place of the social life, games and other amusements left behind. To anyone who has a liking for nature, the tropics offer an endless source of study and of pleasure. Almost every location has adjacent to it vast areas of jungle, a thorough knowledge of which will go a great way toward fitting you for efficient work.*
>
> *If outdoor excursions offer no attraction, there is time for reading. Some men are apt to consider themselves out of current life and events because they live away from large centers of commercial and political activity. As a matter of fact, there is no reason why a man living in the tropics should not be much better read than if he lived in a large center where his evenings are apt to taken up with trivial and unprofitable*

> *amusements. Books and magazines, as a rule, cost no more in the tropics than elsewhere, and it is strictly up to the individual whether or not he maintains his interest in the affairs of the world and keeps himself informed on the questions of the day.*

United Fruit attempted to impart to its new employees a degree of sensitivity concerning Latin American customs when it advised:

> *... avoid preconceived prejudices about the country and its people. You will find customs strange to you and conditions distinctly different from those in the United States. Do not assume that the American customs are better, and, what is more important, do not voice your assumptions to the people of the country. Remember that they are as loyal to their customs and their country as you are to yours. Instead, learn to appreciate the conditions and customs of the country. The first step in this direction is to learn the Spanish language. The importance of this cannot be overestimated, as without this knowledge you will be unable to understand the people and their customs. Remember that you have chosen to live amongst them for several years to come.*

The list of "suggestions" ends with a few personal admonishments:

> *... do not fall into the common error of thinking because you happen to be away from home and relatives that it does not matter what you do or how you behave. The man who can lose his self-respect and yet retain the respect of others has yet to be born. Remember that you are now an employee of the Company and that whatever you do will be either beneficial or detrimental to the interests of the Company, of which you are a part. Remember that the quarters you are given to live in are for your comfort; treat them as you would your own home. The Company is only too willing to do everything in its power to make you comfortable, happy and contented, but it is only with your cooperation that this end can be accomplished. After you have been located a while and a new man comes, try to help him out as others have helped you. This is the spirit which will help the organization and will assist you in attaining the success you desire.*[30]

FOR THE RECORD

FARM OVERSEERS: ON THE CUTTING EDGE OF BANANA PRODUCTION

It is doubtful that the Company's pontificating provided much solace for many of the young employees, usually bachelors in their twenties, who were assigned to the entry-level positions of overseers or timekeepers on banana farms. These were exhausting, lonely jobs in remote, primitive areas where the heat was a constant, debilitating factor. In his book *Those Wild West Indies*, Edmund S. Whitman, who began his UFCO career in 1921 as a timekeeper in Honduras, described a typical day in the life of an overseer. Excerpts from his account demonstrate the wide range of responsibilities that overseers coped with on a daily basis:

5:00 AM — *Rises and turns out timekeeper, sees that cook, yardman and stockman are on the jobs. Takes rainfall and temperature readings.*

6:00 AM — *His two foremen appear at the office to report that fruit-cutting preliminaries are well underway; all the mules are at the camp, properly equipped with packsaddles and pads, all fruit-cutting gangs have been told exactly how many bunches to harvest, and all of them have seen a model bunch illustrating the proper degree of fullness required for the New York market. Each foreman reports that fruit cars have already been spotted at the various spurs as requested the previous evening. Overseer goes over work sheets preparatory to riding the farm.*

7:00 AM — *Rides the farm, checking cutters as to grade and quantity,*
11:00 *also sees that mules are not overloaded and that freshly-cut bunches are properly loaded into cars. At the same time, he keeps an eye on the status of work under way on which labor will be done during days where there is no fruit cutting: ditch digging, pruning, replanting, bridge and road construction, regrassing pastures and repairing fences, keeping camp grounds in trim. Makes notes to see that certain animals are rebranded, certain fines imposed for sloppy or deceitful work.*

11:00   *Returns to house, issues commissary coupons to contrac-*
12 Noon *tors against their balance on the payroll, issues hospital passes, administers quinine, issues barbed wire, rope and nails for various jobs, settles domestic dispute between laborers and families in his camp. Lunches on okra soup, beef stew, red beans, rice, breadfruit, alligator pears and pineapples (latter two commodities out of his own yard).*

Following lunch and during the most enervating part of the day, Whitman, like all of his employees, rested, but by 2 PM he was again astride his mule overseeing the last of the fruit-cutting operation. Three hours later he returned to his office where a foreman gave him precise details on the number of stems cut by each cutting crew, the number loaded into each car and its spur location. He then telephoned this information to the chief clerk of his district. After a dinner identical to what his cook had served him at lunch, the overseer and timekeeper ended their day sitting on the porch "complaining about heat and gossiping about the Company." By 8 PM the overseer's ten-hour workday was over and he had retired for the night.[31]

Some respite to this tiring routine was provided on weekends, when overseers and timekeepers often rode a motorcar, an automobile mounted on steel railroad wheels which moved on a railroad track, and went into Bananera or Tiquisate to attend a dance at the club, play golf, tennis or baseball and enjoy the Company's swimming pool. Undoubtedly the most important aspect of those weekends was the opportunity to socialize with other American or European employees, thus helping to dispel the loneliness and isolation of life on the banana farms.

As might be expected, the turnover of these jobs was fairly high; in fact, Wilson reports that in the 1920s "fewer than half of the fledgling timekeepers served out their first year, and only about one in five stayed long enough to qualify for promotion." [32] But if an employee was able to endure a year or two on a banana farm, and if he performed well, his chances for advancement within the United Fruit Company were usually good. Indeed, many of the Company's highest ranking officers, both in the tropics and in Boston, began their careers as timekeepers or overseers. The first-hand experience these veterans gained provided the

Company with a corps of well-informed executives who understood every aspect of the production of one of the world's most delicate fruits.

JUNGLE-EDGE WORKING CONDITIONS

Although the banana business did not engender the kind of stress often found on factory assembly lines or in today's hard-driving corporate offices, there were human and social problems that most contemporary companies do not confront. As May and Plaza pointed out, "through necessity, not choice, the Company has become enmeshed in the establishment of company towns with all of their supporting activities, and has undertaken the servicing of far broader communities with land transport, communications, port and shipping services and a variety of other activities designed to meet the exceptionally demanding logistics of its major business. Each of these extraneous activities stretches the normal range of corporation-community relationships." [33]

While it is certainly true that United Fruit's range of responsibilities was far greater than that of most U.S. companies, a number of its management practices, particularly earlier in the century, left much to be desired. This was true for a variety of complex reasons. In the first instance, North American and European employees who arrived in Guatemala during the approximately first four decades of the twentieth century were often imbued with a pronounced sense of Anglo-Saxon superiority, especially as concerned the usually uneducated and poorly-trained Guatemalan laborers they often supervised.

At its most extreme, such condescending views produced comments similar to those of the American writer Eugene Cunningham, who toured Central America in 1920 and subsequently wrote

> ... these people are the slaves of their environment, gripped by a primal apathy that holds young and old alike. They have fertile lands, but rather than scratch the surface and plant seed, they lie in the shade and scratch their empty bellies ... Undoubtedly some part of the heritage of the average Anglo-Saxon is the instinct to clean up a mess wherever found. Always, as we watched these people, there arose in us a vast disgust at the depths of their sloth, which keeps them bedded down in

filthy hovels, ambition-less, future-less. There came the impulse to roll up sleeves and start immediately at the work of reform. Always, too, came the thought, what couldn't the white man's industry and perseverance do with these countries![34]

This kind of arrogance — similar to the attitudes held by many wealthy Guatemalan *finqueros* regarding their Indian workers — often led to an all-too-common stereotype that Guatemalan laborers were "lazy good-for-nothings who were better off being ordered about like animals than directed like men." [35] In fact, LaBarge, who visited all eight of UFCO's isthmian divisions in the 1950s, found that

. . . the grievances which cause the most bitter conflicts are those which reflect upon the worker's status as a human being. These are questions of the treatment which they receive at the hands of the administrators. "No nos respetan" (They don't respect us.) was the sentiment voiced first in every union headquarters I visited, and non-union workers echoed the view. It is unquestionably true that many of the Company's tropical administrators veil their contempt for the common workers all too thinly. Some make no effort at all. The attitude that "these people" are an insensitive, inferior and stupid species for whom the most common courtesies are not requisite probably costs the Company more in strikes, in slowdowns, and in general bad relations and publicity than the entire battle against the banana diseases.[36]

The imperious attitude of many UFCO supervisors, coupled with the fact that, except for a brief period in the 1920s, the Guatemalan government did not permit the establishment of unions until 1944, meant that workers who encountered inequitable, rude administrators had no recourse except to submit to the petty tyrant's treatment or resign their jobs. Another contributing element in the Company's labor relations was the fact that the longer its American and European employees remained in the tropics, the more they lost touch with the reality of growing union strength in the United States and Europe. Thus, after 1944 when unions were permitted in Guatemala, many of the Company's older, high-ranking employees, who had never before confronted organized demands from their workers, strongly disliked and resented having to deal with a powerful new union. The fact that the unions in both Bananera and Tiquisate contained numerous, virulently anti-American Communists, as discussed in *Chapter 7*, further exacerbated United Fruit's management-union relations. And when UFCO's managers compared *La Frutera's* salaries and fringe benefits with those prevailing on most of Guatemala's farms, they had little patience with union demands for higher wages and increased benefits.

Following observations first made by Kepner in 1936, authors such as Schlesinger and Kinzer, Immerman and other American writers have charged that the United Fruit implemented "institutionally racist policies" because "most of the Company's American overseers were from the deep South and brought their racial attitudes with them." [37] This frequently repeated allegation has a curious history. Kepner bases his remarks on a superficial, often inaccurate Master's thesis that was presented by John L. Williams in 1925 at Clark University in Worcester, Massachusetts. Titling his thesis "The Rise of the Banana Industry and its Influence on Caribbean Countries," Williams acknowledges that "a large part of the information regarding the banana industry was gained during the writer's two years in Guatemala, where daily contact with local conditions provided information not found in any printed source."[38] Nowhere in his thesis, however, does Williams state that he worked for the United Fruit Company, yet Immerman describes him as "the overseer of the Bananera plantation" — a position that did not even exist.

Assuming, however, that Williams did hold the position of timekeeper or even overseer on one of United Fruit's north coast banana farms, it is questionable whether his accounts of racial problems on one farm should be extrapolated to make sweeping statements about UFCO's personnel policies. Indeed, Williams inadvertently reveals some of his own prejudices when he states "one very disturbing feature in the relations of blacks and whites was the victory of Jack Johnson, the Negro pugilist, over a white man. This event certainly had its effect on the black race, making them very arrogant, and exhibiting signs of superiority." Admitting that "one of my best friends was murdered by a Jamaican," Williams seems to particularly dislike Jamaican blacks whom he describes as "British subjects . . . who feel that they are equal to any other persons in the world." The allegation that many of UFCO's managers were Southerners, and thus racists, may be based on a facile generalization that Williams made: "the big problem is the Jamaican Negro ... Place this British subject, with his cocky attitude, under the strict eye of a white boss ... from south of the Mason and Dixon line, and trouble forthwith results."

If Williams was in a position of authority, he may well have implemented a policy on his banana farm that numerous authors have been quick to repeat. "To avoid complications," Williams wrote, "a strict color line is drawn. All persons of color must always give the right of way to whites, and remove their hats while talking. A rule also forbids any laborer from entering the front yard of any white man's residence."[39] Silver, however, emphatically denies such policies. He also terms "slanderous" Williams's assertion that Jamaicans were "a big problem," recalling that "most Jamaican blacks were very competent and important supervisors for the Company." The veteran banana man also points out that the Company's somewhat haphazard recruitment system produced a widespread pool of employees from throughout the United States and Europe, with no preference given to hiring Southerners; neither did they predominate.[40]

Jay H. Soothill, who worked for the Company in Costa Rica and Panama during the 1920s and early 1930s, also refuted charges of racism and confirmed the preferential treatment given Jamaican blacks.

> *On the banana farms, in sixteen years I never observed race hatred. Most of the foreigner overseers prefer West Indian Negroes to natives for the reason that they both speak the same language. The overseers see few others during the week than their laborers and they are intimately associated with them in handling the work, day in and day out. I do not mean that they become chummy socially, but that the idea of a difference in color seldom if ever enters their heads; they are both too busy.*[41]

A personnel problem of a different nature developed in the 1940s as Guatemalans began filling the administrative positions that were once held by Americans or Europeans. Laborers often resented the fact that their own countrymen, who enforced UFCO standards of work and

Company policies, now acted as their supervisors, usually taking United Fruit's position and not always that of the workers. Many laborers considered their new Guatemalan supervisors to be *entreguistas* (sold out to the Americans) and little more than traitors to Guatemala.[42] Nevertheless, LaBarge notes that "the ordinary worker's distrust both of the *gringo* administrator and of his *entreguista* cohorts probably reflects the usual differences between management and labor far more than it does national differences, and controls for this observation exist wherever serious labor-management conflicts develop between persons of the same nationality." [43]

There was yet another concern that affected higher-level Guatemalan employees: a salary discrimination that was based on nationality. As Kepner observed, "in Guatemala in 1929, when national stenographers were earning $35 to $50 per month, female stenographers, using English as well as Spanish, $75 to $125, and male stenographers of the same qualifications $150, foreigners holding the same positions were receiving from $200 to $250." [44] That the Company paid its "imported employees" more than it did Guatemalans is, however, understandable. The United Fruit Company's diverse and complex operations required individuals possessing specific skills — skills that were not generally available in Guatemala during the first three or four decades of the twentieth century. In order to attract qualified, English-speaking employees, UFCO set salary scales sufficiently high to induce North Americans and Europeans to leave the comforts of home and live in sweltering, remote jungle communities.

Like employees in many large U.S. companies, United Fruit's workers were extremely conscious of the perquisites that went with increasing advancement within the hierarchy. But the phenomenon was far more extreme and pervasive than such issues as the size, furnishings or location of an office. LaBarge points out that in the highly stratified divisions

> *shoes indicate advancement to the semi-skilled and skilled classes. White shirts, motorcycles, and a membership in the American club are symbols of admission to the lower administration. Regular consumption of imported products from the United States attests to membership in the*

> *higher administrative and managerial classes. Types of housing, of furniture, of schooling, of hospital care, of hotel and dining facilities, and means of remuneration all carry rigid class distinctions far beyond those usually found in the United States.*[45]

Not surprisingly in such a disparate organization, intradepartmental turf battles also plagued the United Fruit Company's operations. And, as in all large organizations, "a few men have acquired division-wide and even Company-wide reputations for obstinacy in their dealings with others. Consciously or unconsciously, they promote existing rifts in order to aggrandize their departments and themselves on the failures of others who must depend on their support." [46] Professional and personal differences were aggravated by another situation most U.S. companies do not encounter: the fact that the highest-level employees lived in a small, claustrophobic compound where frequent personal and social contact was almost inevitable.

Mediating serious personnel problems fell to the manager of the division, but, as Wilson remarked in 1947,

> *though reasonably well chosen, some of the tropical managers persisted in various actions and attitudes that were not invariably enlightened. The home office administration remained considerably in advance of management policies current in some, though not all, of the tropical divisions. In the tropics there remained certain factors of snobbery, discrimination, and jungle-edge bureaucracy that impeded progress and required further remedies. The ratio of citizen employees to Norte Americanos was approximately ten to one, but in some instances native workers were still being retarded in deserved promotions and the social habits in some of the Company towns were not so democratic as they might and should have been.*[47]

Another significant lacuna in the Company's personnel policies was the fact that Spanish was not formally taught to its North American and European employees — despite the Company's contract with each new employee stressing the importance of learning the language. Instead, each individual had to "pick up" the language in a haphazard manner, usually resulting in something called "Spanglish," English words mixed in with ungrammatical Spanish that was often heavily accented and difficult for Spanish speakers to understand. The failure to teach its employees Spanish had two important consequences. It obviously limited the individual's communications with his employees, often causing misunderstandings because of the foreigner's inability to express himself clearly. Moreover, "Spanglish" was a source of frequent amusement, if not disdain, on the part of Guatemalan laborers who sometimes equated the inability to speak their language with a lack of intelligence. Clearly, UFCO's failure to teach its employees Spanish was a disservice to the employee, to the personnel he supervised and, ultimately, to the United Fruit Company itself.

It was a knowledgeable, socially-conscious expert in public relations who, in 1947 after visiting United Fruit divisions in Honduras and Guatemala, identified numerous serious lapses in Company management. Edward Bernays, "a blazing figure in American public relations for four decades," had been hired by Zemurray during World War II after the banana tycoon had begun to realize that the United Fruit Company confronted increasingly serious public relations problems in Central America.[48] After spending a month in Honduras and Guatemala, Bernays later wrote, "I came back greatly impressed both by the efficiencies and inefficiencies of the Company. I was amazed at the Company's accomplishment in transplanting men and materials to a jungle area, and at how effectively it used them in its yellow-gold plantations."

At the same time, however, there was a "glaring omission" in the Company's employment practices: no attention was given to providing new employees with written materials concerning their areas of responsibility. "The only memory the Company had was the collective memory of individuals. The fifty years' experience in growing bananas was learned by trial and error by every new employee. There were no manuals to speed the learning process and transmit knowledge and experience. As for promising young employees, they were given no clear-cut information about the Company, its operations or their future chances of growth."

Zemurray's counsel on public relations also perceived a serious issue that was intensified by the sheer isolation of all of the Company's tropical employees. UFCO executives, he found, were "unaware of the new literature available in their particular field of interest — agriculture, industrial relations or tropical agriculture." Yet another critical subject that Bernays identified was one which Zemurray and other high-ranking officers apparently chose to disregard. Nevertheless, if they had listened to the their astute public relations expert in 1947, UFCO's subsequent labor problems in Guatemala and elsewhere might have been significantly ameliorated. Bernays observed that "the native agricultural workers were treated as human machines rather than as human beings and without regard to their folkways or culture patterns."

Following his Central American visit, Bernays submitted a comprehensive memorandum to Zemurray which provided an extensive list of effective recommendations that would have gone far toward improving the Company's personnel policies. Pointing out a critical need for orientation handbooks and on-the-job booklets, Bernays also suggested establishing libraries with up-to-date materials on tropical agriculture, engineering and other pertinent topics in order to keep executives informed of advances in their own fields. One of the most acute problems was a lack of sustained communication between management and employees, a problem that Bernays believed could be redressed by periodic meetings, letters, memoranda, news bulletins and bulletin boards. In order to improve morale, Bernays suggested awards for merit and urged the Company's managers to plan programs that would further identify employees with the United Fruit Company and its policies. In retrospect, many of the consultant's recommendations seem fairly obvious. He noted, for example, that "wives were criticizing the commissary not for what it carried but for what it did not. A simple consumer survey once a year, asking customers for preferences as to products and brands, might have corrected an ever-present gripe."

Bernays, however, received no reaction to his perspicacious recommendations. As he later wrote, "the people in the tropics were remote from Boston; they produced their banana quotas, and that was what counted. Fruit Company executives in the tropics were tough characters who had come up through the ranks; they were action-related men. What I proposed must have seemed like mollycoddling." [49]

In 1956, nine years after Bernays's perceptive report, the United Fruit Company, which by then had experienced major difficulties with its Central American laborers, issued an eleven-page memorandum that incorporated several of the principles UFCO's counsel on public relations had initially advocated. Dispatched to all divisions managers, the "statement of policy on labor relations" was drafted by Almyr L. Bump, the vice president of tropical operations who had recently been assigned to Boston after ten turbulent years as manager of the Tiquisate division and later as the general manager of all of United Fruit's Guatemala operations.[50] The memorandum, which calls for more conciliatory, compassionate treatment of all employees, seems clearly directed at relations with UFCO's farm laborers.

> *We must sincerely and honestly feel personal concern about the problems that affect the individual worker and his family . . . We must avoid gaining objectives through the weight of our importance or economic power. Instead, we must see to it that all of our supervisors who handle labor think of each worker as a human being; that he acts to safeguard the long-term interests of the Company, which calls for a sincere understanding of the people and of their attitudes, sensitivities and reactions . . . No assignment of functions will achieve our objective unless we understand the point of view of the individuals with whom we are working and try to accord them individual respect and dignity. We cannot tolerate or look down on workers or their union representatives and expect to get cooperation. A system based on fear or domination or a legalistic or technicalistic attitude toward human relations cannot give us what we are seeking.[51]*

Bump's directive, and the fact that by the late 1950s high-ranking Company executives in Central America had learned all too painfully that unions did indeed have the power to cause costly strikes helped contribute to a new, more understanding approach toward United Fruit's banana workers. Equally important, many veteran administrators were being replaced by younger men, whose attitudes toward Central Americans were less overbearing than those of their predecessors and for whom unions were not anathema.

- 5 -
Social Life and Social Concerns

We lived like the rich without being rich. We had golf, tennis, a swimming pool, a bowling alley and a club. The quality of life was very good.[1] These recollections by a Guatemalan formerly employed by the United Fruit Company in Bananera attest to UFCO's success in addressing one of the major personnel problems that the fruit giant confronted throughout the isthmus: the numbing boredom often inherent to small, remote communities.

The need for maintaining extensive recreational facilities for its employees was a major consideration because of the geographic isolation that characterized United Fruit's banana divisions. The variety of stores, restaurants, entertainment facilities, cultural events and other amenities offered by the average metropolitan area were only available in Guatemala City. The mile-high capital also provided another important attribute: a respite from the blistering heat of the coast. Nevertheless, employees and their families in Bananera and Tiquisate seldom journeyed to the capital because of the expenses involved in such trips. Another reason was the discomfort of travel.

Since the highway to the Atlantic was not completed until 1959, Bananera employees who visited Guatemala City before that year were forced to use the railroad — a tiresome trip in unairconditioned coaches, with no dining facilities, that took the better part of a day. The rail trip from Tiquisate to the capital required at least five or six hours and was equally uncomfortable. Although there was an unpaved road from Tiquisate to the capital, a trip to Guatemala City represented an arduous drive of nearly eight hours. In the rainy season, the road was frequently impassable due to washed out bridges and stretches of treacherous mud; during the dry season, a foot or more of thick, blinding dust covered much of the route.

In fact, during most of the years the United Fruit operated in Guatemala, the country's deficient "highway" system, and the fact that the Company did not usually make cars available for travel outside the banana divisions, meant that many *Fruteros* and their families visited little of "the land of eternal spring." By the 1940s the Company had acquired a few small aircraft which were used almost exclusively by the manager and other high-level employees for business trips to the capital and between the two divisions. Approximately ten years later, Aviateca, Guatemala's national airline, began regular service between Tiquisate and the capital.

To compensate for the somewhat claustrophobic living conditions imposed by the isolated banana divisions, the United Fruit Company attempted to provide its laborers with a variety of diversions. On many farms, the Company built club houses which included a dance floor, snack-and-drink facilities and tables for games. Club members usually elected their own officers to administer each facility. At least once a week the clubs were also the site of free movie showings for all laborers and their dependents. During the 1950s, for instance, the Company spent approximately $25,000 annually in the rental and projection of motion pictures for its employees.[2]

UFCO actively sponsored sports programs, helping to organize teams and providing its laborers with uniforms and equipment to play soccer, softball and other games. Soccer games were routinely scheduled between teams from different banana farms. Like the housing the Company provided its laborers, the recreational facilities that UFCO made available were far superior to anything offered by other plantation owners in Guatemala. Even on most farms today, a soccer field is usually all that *finqueros* provide their laborers for after-work diversion.

Whether Guatemalan, North American or European, those individuals and their spouses who lived within the Bananera and Tiquisate compounds usually encountered enormous changes — and sacrifices — when they became employees of the Company. Boredom-fighting facilities were thus especially important for those usually well-educated, cosmopolitan persons. Nearly all of the Guatemalans had been educated and previously employed in the capital. In addition to abandoning the conveniences of Guatemala City, these family-oriented Latins had to forsake their parents and numerous relatives when they moved to United Fruit's remote, virtually inaccessible banana plantations. Guatemalans also had to overcome the disdain, if not fear, that generations of their countrymen had experienced regarding the nation's disease-ridden coastal areas.

Although leaving behind a large, tightly-knit, extended family may not have been as burdensome for most North Americans or Europeans who came to Guatemala, the foreign employees faced adjustments of another nature. They had to cope with an underdeveloped country whose society and culture were very different from anything they had previously experienced. Learning to speak and understand Spanish was imperative, but employees often discovered that fluency in the language did not necessarily prepare them to supervise Guatemalan laborers who were usually poorly trained or educated.[3]

The new, often confusing surroundings were magnified by a feeling of being out of touch with the rest of the world. There were no daily newspapers and, of course, no television. Shortwave radio broadcasts were the only means of learning about developments in the United States and elsewhere. Long distance calls to and from Guatemala were not possible until the mid 1930s, and mail from abroad, transported on UFCO's banana ships, usually took weeks to arrive.

There was, however, one overriding aspect of life on a banana division that all employees — foreign or Guatemalan — had to cope with: the sauna-like temperatures that prevailed year round during much of the day. In the era before air conditioning, only large ceiling or floor fans were available to partially relieve the oven-like heat. In Bananera, humidity levels usually vied throughout most of the year with temperature readings, but on the south coast, humidity readings dropped noticeably during the dry season. Nevertheless, the months from October to May were a dusty, sere period when temperature levels tended to soar even higher.

Despite the enervating climate, Fruit Company employees in Bananera and Tiquisate engaged in a number of activities that helped to overcome the boredom and isolation of life on a banana division. The most thorough documentation of the social and sporting events that characterized life in these two communities can be found in copies of the United Fruit Company's house organ, *Unifruitco*. Initiated in 1925, the magazine was published monthly until the late 1950s when it reverted to a bi-monthly publication. A well-designed, attractive magazine, usually about fifty pages in size, *Unifruitco* was replete with dozens of black and white photographs. Divided into two sections titled "The Tropics" and "The States," the magazine included articles written by volunteer "correspondents" who forwarded their news items to the New York offices where the house organ was published.[4] In the 1950s, articles began appearing in Spanish that were written by some of UFCO's Latin American employees. In addition, the editors usually incorporated into the magazine reports on significant corporate developments within the Company, whether in the United States or in the field.[5]

Often written in a breezy, informal style, *Unifruitco's* articles describe a wide variety of activities within the Tiquisate and Bananera compounds that kept employees and their families occupied. There are reports on parties held for new arrivals or *despedidas* hosted for individuals transferred to other divisions, barbecues, dances at the club, news of children home for the holidays, school Halloween parties, bridal showers, weddings, and many other events. Undoubtedly the most popular sport for men, women and children was golf, and considerable space was given to reporting on tournaments, particularly the annual event featuring the best golfers from both divisions.

A more personal account of life in Tiquisate is afforded by Jean Solovan, a Canadian who arrived at the division in 1946 to work as a stenographer in the manager's office. Solovan, who was thirty-six and single, was initially assigned to share an apartment with a female Guatemalan employee. Upon her arrival, she found her new home contained

> *a big living room furnished with a rattan couch and chairs, and a writing desk. The coffee table had a big bouquet of powerfully scented gardenias. There was also a Frigidaire for cold drinks and drinking water, and an antique telephone for making local calls. [A handle on the telephone had to be cranked in order to reach an operator who then placed the call.] The apartment had two bedrooms at the back with a bathroom in between. The downstairs area was a breezeway and served as a laundry facility.*[6]

Although the new employee was only paid $150 a month, she noted that a modest $30 was deducted from her salary for the three meals she received daily at the club house. Other deductions included 2 percent of her earnings for medical coverage and 4 percent toward a pension plan.

> *Monthly club dues were two dollars, which entitled a member to see two movies a week (U.S. films with Spanish subtitles), attend all social events in the club, use the golf course, tennis court, swimming pool, and library. There was no tax. I had a free, fully furnished apartment . . . Company bedding and towels were taken to the Company laundry for free service.*

Solovan, who subsequently worked in Bananera and two divisions in Panama for a total of sixteen years with the Company, apparently enjoyed her first exposure to the life United Fruit offered its employees.

> *There was no excuse for anyone to be lonesome. Tropical employees worked hard but they also knew how to enjoy good clean fun. Social life here surpassed anything I ever experienced in Edmonton. We had movies, dances, bridge and tea parties, dinner parties, and a pool. Sometimes we made a trip to the Pacific Ocean's warm water with miles of sandy beaches.*
>
> *In the Fruit Company zone, everything was within walking distance, including the golf course where there were many excellent players. A tournament was arranged with employees from Honduras who arrived by air in the Company DC-3. After the pros finished their game,*

many employees were enticed into the act, beginners joined top-notch players. A cart with Guatemalan beer was wheeled around the golf course and a barbecue completed the tournament. Many old friends from other divisions enjoyed getting together again and talked about the good old days working together in other countries. It was like a homecoming.[7]

Life for the employees' children, many of whom had been born at the UFCO hospitals in Quiriguá or Tiquisate, was carefree. "Those were the happiest days of my life," recalls Laura de la Vega, who was born in Tiquisate and lived there until she was nine, when her father was transferred to Bananera. "It was a wholesome atmosphere, with parties for the young people in the homes, dancing to juke box music in the bowling alley, barbecues and many other activities."[8] Acclimatized to the heat, the youths played strenuous games of tennis or basketball, and cooled off in the large Company swimming pool. Like their parents, a number of children also played golf. Birthday parties, usually featuring *piñatas*, were a way of life — and a source of many *Unifruitco* photographs. Attending the movies, shown at the club on Wednesday and Saturday evenings, was a highlight of each week — and provided a glimpse of the "outside world."

SALARIES AND COMMISSARY PRIVILEGES

Although the salaries the United Fruit Company paid its unskilled workers seem extremely low by current U.S. standards, the cost of living was also much lower than today. Moreover, laborers enjoyed numerous important indirect wage subsidies. Even without taking into account the benefits provided by the Company, its most hostile detractors readily acknowledge that the United Fruit always paid its laborers the highest farm wages in the country.[9] Thus, when the author asked former President Juan José Arévalo what had been the United Fruit Company's most notable contribution to Guatemala's economic development, he conceded "we must recognize that the salaries paid by the Company were the highest at that time, and in that form contributed to the development of agriculture."[10]

After noting that the daily wage in many parts of Guatemala was only 5 cents a day during the thirteen years of the Ubico dictatorship, Luis Cardoza y Aragón, apparently referring to United Fruit's farm laborers, points out that by 1949 workers in "unhealthy regions" of the country were earning over 80 cents a day or $288 a year. This minuscule percentage of the country's overall rural work force (10,527 UFCO workers out of a total of 1,092,794 farm laborers) earned twice as much as three-fourths of Guatemala's agricultural workers. That is, 894,872 laborers earned as little as 14 to 40 cents a day, and only 21,056 workers were paid a wage equivalent to United Fruit's farm laborers.[11]

Forty-five years later, the wages paid to most of Guatemala's farm workers have not increased markedly. In 1990, for example, the government decreed a new minimum daily wage for farm laborers that required plantation owners to pay their workers ten quetzales — or the equivalent of only $1.93 a day. A high-ranking union official subsequently complained, however, that many *finqueros* continued paying their laborers the previous daily salary of 4.60 quetzales (less than one dollar) and that "there are no competent authorities to make the *finqueros* comply with the law."[12]

The United Fruit Company's employees also enjoyed another significant benefit that substantially stretched their salaries: the use of Company-operated commissaries that sold many staples at subsidized prices. In the 1946-1954 period, for example, the average price for a pound of corn was the equivalent of 2 cents; black beans sold for 4 cents a pound and milk was priced at 13 cents a quart.[13] Like many U.S. companies that operated in remote areas of Latin America, United Fruit established its commissaries simply because there were no grocery stores or shops of any kind in the remote jungles where the banana farms were originally established. In addition to selling staple food items and UFCO-provided milk and meat, the commissaries sold clothing, shoes, textiles, household items, and many other dry goods — nearly all of which were purchased in Guatemala.

Nonetheless, these facilities have been the target of some criticism. In *Social Aspects of the Banana Industry*, Kepner charges that "in Guatemala it [UFCO] has been advancing a large proportion of the workers' pay through commissary orders in spite of the provision of the labor law that no employer shall withhold more than 10 percent of its workers' wages for advances of any kind previously made to them."[14] Handy is more explicit when he states "as in the coffee *fincas*, workers were kept in debt to the Company through easy credit available in the network of Company stores." Although providing no source for the charge, he adds "indeed, at times the only wages offered were in the form of credit notes to be used at these stores."[15]

One American employee who began working in the Bananera division in 1929 freely acknowledges that commissary credit was provided to the laborers, but recalls the reasons for this practice. Paid monthly, the laborers frequently spent their wages within a week to fifteen days after each pay day, and were thus often destitute by the middle of the month.[16] UFCO was, therefore, forced to provide limited commissary credit to many of its laborers and their dependents in order to tide them over until the next pay day. Nor was it possible for overseers to keep funds on hand in order to advance cash payments to its laborers. "Company farms were located in very isolated and dangerous areas," the former executive recalls. "The farms were connected only by UFCO or IRCA railroads. To pay workers, a traveling paymaster, provided with an armored railroad car and armed Guatemalan soldiers, traveled the railroad lines with cash to pay all workers."[17]

It should also be noted that Company commissaries did not engage in price gouging. On the contrary, once local shops were set up near the commissaries, (particularly the large Tiquisate and Bananera commissaries) competing stores often complained that *La Frutera* undersold the same goods. Monteforte Toledo takes criticism of the commissaries one step further by contending that the UFCO outlets were in a position to "decisively influence" consumer prices throughout the country.[18] It seems unlikely, however, that thirty-six commissaries, almost all of which were located on remote banana farms on Guatemala's south and north coasts, could have exerted such leverage, particularly in Guatemala City.

Another indirect wage subsidy enjoyed by the United Fruit Company's workers was the free use of significant acreage to cultivate crops which they could consume or sell. For example, in 1952, the Company gave its employees on both coasts the use of 3,238 acres, which they utilized to produce 176,000 quintals of corn, 26,800 quintals of black beans, 16,000 quintals of rice and 450,000 stems of plantains.[19]

MEDICAL CARE: A CONSTANT, CRITICAL NEED

Few Guatemalans know that the individual most responsible for the sanitation and medical advances that the United Fruit Company brought to the country's north and south coast banana plantations was also the person most responsible for completing the railroad to the Atlantic: Minor C. Keith. In 1899, Keith convinced Andrew Preston that it was impossible to do business in Central America before overcoming the health problems of the workers. Having lost three brothers during the building of the railroad in Costa Rica, Keith knew from tragic personal experience how dangerous the tropics could be.

By 1898 medical science had established that both yellow fever and malaria are transmitted by particular species of mosquitoes. Thus, on United Fruit plantations in Costa Rica, Panama, Colombia, Jamaica and Cuba an unceasing war was declared on the lethal insects. As Victor M. Cutter, UFCO's pragmatic president, declared in 1929,

> *we early learned that laborers must be kept in good health if our plantations were to be systematically worked... There was no philanthropy in the fact that it was necessary to build up a medical and sanitary service that cost thousands of dollars annually. It was simply good business... As a result of our efforts yellow fever and smallpox have disappeared from our plantations, hookworm is under control, and we are beginning to bring malaria and dysentery under control.[20]*

Adams, who visited the Company's north coast plantations in 1913, observed that because Guatemala represented a new UFCO operation, its managers had benefited from experiences learned in other divisions. As a result, camps for the banana workers were located on high ground, and the entire camp area was provided with effective, year-round drainage. Most houses were screened; large areas of swamp were drained, and stagnant pools and slow-running streams were regularly treated. In addition, grass and low-lying vegetation around the camps and within the Virginia division were kept trimmed; no garbage, tin cans or bottles, which might collect water and provide breeding sites for mosquitoes, were permitted in areas adjacent to the houses.[21]

Extensive sanitary measures, however, were not sufficient to cope with the region's high incidence of malaria and other virulent diseases. In an area where there were no hospitals, one of the Company's most urgent needs was for a modern, well-equipped and well-staffed hospital. In 1908, two years after the Company had initiated its Guatemala operation, a small hospital was completed at Dartmouth, several miles east of Virginia. It was to this somewhat primitive facility that one of the most remarkable men in the annals of Guatemalan medicine arrived to begin a lifetime of service to the people of the Motagua Valley. Dr. Neil P. Macphail, a Scot from Argyllshire, first came to Central America early in the twentieth century when the British government stationed him as a quarantine officer in what is today Belize City. By 1908, however, the doctor had made his way to the United Fruit Company hospital at Dartmouth, where he subsequently oversaw the construction of the new, much larger facility at Quiriguá, inaugurated in 1913.

As director of the new hospital, Macphail administrated what one author describes as "the finest institution of its kind between New Orleans and the progressive capitals of South America." Constructed of steel and concrete, at a cost of approximately $150,000, the two-story structure eventually accommodated up to 250 patients. The 340-foot-long building, configured in the shape of an airplane, included a maternity ward, intensive care unit, convalescent wards, operating theater, and laboratories. The building's "fuselage" included living accommodations for some of the doctors and nurses, a large, modern kitchen, staff dining room, cold storage plant and laundry. A nearby generator met the hospital's electrical needs, including the operation of several elevators. "The whole structure is designed as a unit, and all of its parts are connected by screened corridors, so that attendants may pass from one area to another without possibility of permitting the ingress of mosquitoes and other insects," Adams commented.[22]

Generally regarded as the best medical facility in Guatemala, the hospital — located on a high hill facing the Merendón mountains —

was only about one mile from the Maya ruins of Quiriguá. And because United Fruit operated a small hotel near the hospital, many tourists, who arrived at Puerto Barrios aboard ships of the Great White Fleet, traveled by train to visit the ruins and spend a day or two in Quiriguá. One such visitor in 1933 was Aldous Huxley.

> *At Quiriguá we spent three very pleasant days as the guests of Dr. MacPhail, [sic] the head of the United Fruit Company's hospital. The place was astonishingly beautiful and our host one of the best and most charming men. The doctor's professional reputation stands very high; but it is his kindness and his wisdom that have made of him the universal godfather of Guatemala . . . He is an institution, one of the best in the country.*[23]

The high regard that many Guatemalans felt for the Scottish physician may have been due, in part, to his implementation of a benevolent policy that the United Fruit Company adopted at both its hospitals: the free annual treatment of hundreds of patients who were not employed by the Company. While most of these individuals lived near Tiquisate or Bananera, where there were no hospitals available, many Guatemalans also journeyed from other parts of the country for the excellent, free care that United Fruit's well-trained medical staff provided. As noted in more detail below, during 1950 the two UFCO hospitals treated nearly 3,500 non-employees — or almost as many individuals as it employed in its Bananera division.

In a country where the vast majority of doctors and dentists avoid living in Guatemala's lowland areas and are therefore concentrated in the capital, Neil Macphail was one of the first physicians to dedicate an entire career to practicing medicine in one of Guatemala's most torrid regions. When he died in 1949, while still serving as director of the Quiriguá Hospital, the pioneering doctor had spent forty-one years in the Motagua Valley.[24]

That he and his staff were remarkably successful in saving lives can be seen by the following chart which provides statistics on the numbers and causes of death of United Fruit Company employees between 1919 and 1931:[25]

Cause	Deaths in hospital	Diseases treated in hospital
Malaria	91 (13%)	12,526 (47%)
Diseases of respiratory system	231 (34%)	1,306 (4.9%)
Tuberculosis	63	285
Diseases of nervous system	34	644
Diseases of circulatory system	27	467
Typhoid	24	507
Syphilis	10	813
Total	480	16,548

During the thirteen-year period covered in the above table, the Company's annual work force averaged 3,911 employees, with a death rate that declined from sixteen per 1,000 employees in 1919 to only eight deaths per 1,000 in 1931. These figures are all the more impressive when compared to overall death rates in Guatemala, where 23.2 deaths were recorded for every 1,000 persons during the 1922-1931 period. The death rate in the department of Izabal, where the United Fruit Company was located, was one of the highest in the country: 32.6 per 1,000 inhabitants. The nation's highest death rate, 37.5 per 1,000 Guatemalans, was in the department of Escuintla where, soon after it began operations, the Compañía Agrícola constructed a hospital accommodating 320 patients — the third largest in the country.[26]

An integral part of the Company's medical program was a comprehensive system of health dispensaries, staffed by pharmacists, who visited the workers' camps on an almost daily basis. Trained to treat simple illnesses, the health dispensers were also essential in initially diagnosing infirmities and determining whether the employee or his dependents required hospitalization. This combination of preventive medicine and prompt hospitalization was a significant element in combatting malaria, intestinal and respiratory disorders, and such infectious diseases as typhoid, diphtheria, whooping cough and smallpox. The vital role played by the dispensaries can be observed by comparing the number of sick employees and their dependents who were treated in the dispensaries during 1950 against the number of individuals that required hospitalization:[27]

	Bananera division	Tiquisate division
Total number of employees	4,723	7,292
Number of hospitals	1	1
Number of dispensaries	8	13
Individuals treated in dispensaries	47,513	76,066
Individuals hospitalized	3,622	7,658
Total number of days hospitalized	41,054	102,437
Charity cases	576	2,716
Days hospitalized	5,434	29,430
Cost of treatment	$18,149	$70,143
Total cost of operating hospitals and dispensaries	**$258,639**	**$399,276**

Significant annual expenditures were also made by the United Fruit Company in ongoing sanitation work throughout all housing areas, both on the banana farms and within the two divisions. In 1950, sanitation programs in both divisions cost the Company $197,306 — a figure only slightly less than the Guatemalan government spent for sanitation work throughout the entire country during the same period.[28] As a result of UFCO's ongoing sanitation programs, there were dramatic decreases in the malarial infection rate of its employees: from 21.9 percent in Bananera during 1929 to 0.1 percent in 1954; and from 15.3 percent in Tiquisate during 1938 to 0.3 percent in 1954.

The team of experts from the International Bank of Reconstruction and Development that visited Guatemala in 1950 quickly understood that the United Fruit Company's remarkable success at reducing the incidence of malaria among its employees was of considerable significance to the country's future development. In an article synthesizing much of the IBRD's overall report, George E. Britnell, the head of the team, notes

> *from the practical point of view it is useless to talk of developing agriculture on the Pacific coast without dealing with malaria and public health policies . . . If the threat of malaria were removed, as has been done in the great banana plantations of the United Fruit Company at Tiquisate, numbers of highland Indians might be settled permanently in these regions.*[29]

LaBarge also comments on the IBRD's recommendation that the Guatemalan government needed to intensify its battle against contagious diseases, malaria, intestinal parasites, and unsanitary conditions in general, especially in the tropical lowlands. "Much of the work accomplished on this recommendation has been due exclusively to efforts by the United Fruit Company," he observes.[30]

Even Kepner was forced to admit that

> *the United Fruit Company has received considerable praise for its health work. Much of this praise is deserved; its hospitals are superior to most medical establishments in the Caribbean area and it has greatly reduced tropical diseases. It has done much more for the health of its workers than the governments of Guatemala and Honduras have done for their own people.*[31]

UFCO'S DISTINCTIVE HOUSING FACILITIES

Undoubtedly one of the most significant benefits that *La Frutera* provided all of its employees was rent-free housing in facilities that were singularly alike in appearance throughout the isthmus. Although the sizes of the wooden structures varied, they were nearly always built on cement stilts about eight to twelve feet above the ground. Designed to keep the structures off the humid, often marshy ground and to capture prevailing breezes, United Fruit's distinctive architectural design also provided a cemented area under each house which could be used for a variety of purposes.

In Bananera, the laborers' houses were often trim, three and four multiple units that provided each employee and his dependents with one large room. More often than not, the workers' camps were built in a long line next to the railroad track. By 1936, however, the Company had changed this design; instead, workers' houses in Tiquisate usually consisted of long, multi-unit barracks, each of which housed approximately fifty laborers and their families. Each worker was provided with a unit containing two rooms. Like the houses in Bananera, the homes were built of sawn lumber, but were located around an open rectangle laid out as a soccer field. In both divisions, the roofs of all the buildings were made of corrugated galvanized iron, rendering them watertight against the torrential rains.

The cemented area beneath each unit contained a laundry area and kitchen with a native, brazier-like stove that utilized firewood. In the Tiquisate division, communal toilets and bathing facilities were provided at the rear of each barrack, but indoor sanitation was not provided on the north coast until the early 1940s. According to Benjamín Carol Cardoza, who began work on a UFCO farm in 1940,

> *there were no toilets on my farm. Bodily needs were taken care of in the banana plantations or along the railroad tracks. We bathed in nearby rivers. The Company provided us wells for drinking water, but because of all the minerals in the water, it didn't taste very good and was usually a yellow color. So most of the time we drank water from the Motagua.*[32]

Nor did UFCO's first houses for laborers provide electricity; instead, kerosene lamps were furnished. Carol Cardoza recalls, however, that electricity was available in 1940. "We didn't have light during the day, but it was furnished from 4 PM to 6 AM," he remembers. By the late 1930s, when the Tiquisate division was established, housing for workers usually included electricity, and potable water was provided to every kitchen.

Since indoor sanitation was a novelty to most of the Company's laborers, UFCO found it necessary to maintain sanitary squads which regularly scrubbed and disinfected toilets and bathing facilities in all the laborers' camps. Even today, however, a senior Guatemalan employee in Del Monte's Bananera division maintains that "our workers don't know how to take care of the housing we give them, and they still have very little concept of sanitation." Because of the average Guatemalan worker's limited knowledge of sanitation, UFCO maintenance crews systematically collected all garbage strewn around the laborers' homes and periodically treated the interiors of all houses in an effort to eliminate mosquitoes, cockroaches and other insects.

At Bananera and Tiquisate, where the compounds were surrounded by a high, barbed-wire fence, most of the supervisory and executive personnel lived in single-family structures, each with its own large yard.[33] Hedges of tall hibiscus plants or colorful, well-trimmed crotons often surrounded each yard. Both divisions were filled with a multiplicity of flowering trees, shrubs and an immense variety of tropical trees that produced mangoes, papayas, guavas, coconuts, avocados and many other edible fruits unknown in the United States. Each compound averaged approximately 100 acres and contained between seventy and 120 houses. Bananera, which was smaller, was built around a picturesque lagoon, with several small bridges interconnecting innumerable sidewalks throughout the compound. Located near a large river, Tiquisate's most distinctive feature was a long, wide, grass-filled airfield, which also served as the third hole of the golf course. The airfield divided the number of houses in the compound into two areas roughly comparable in size.

In Tiquisate, the manager, assistant manager and the director of medical services lived in commodious quarters, each of which was constructed on a high hill. Single persons in lower-grade positions were usually provided with small, two-room apartments within a barrack-like "bachelors' quarters." Since these units did not contain kitchens, most unmarried employees took their meals at the Company's club house. The size of the single-family houses, "equal to or in most cases superior to that available to persons of similar income status in the United States," depended on the employee's rank within the organization.[34] UFCO furnished all of these quarters with major appliances, furniture and household effects. The maintenance of each house and its yard was also provided by the Company. In the open, park-like areas that characterized both divisions, dozens of workers kept the grass mowed, trees and bushes trimmed and roads in good repair.[35]

There was a noticeable difference in the housing the United Fruit Company provided for its laborers and that furnished to its supervisory personnel. Historians such as Handy have described the workers' housing as "abysmal; whole families lived in twelve-foot square huts, with inadequate water and sanitary facilities." [36]

While noting that UFCO worker housing "contrasts favorably with many of the ramshackle shanties inhabited by Jamaican immigrants, and their raised wooden floors are more hygienic than the dirt floor of adobe or *manaca* huts," Kepner also criticized the facilities as being "decidedly overcrowded. Entire families occupy single rooms about twelve feet square." [37]

At the same time, however, Kepner acknowledges that "some of these families, accustomed to living in close quarters, increase the congestion by taking in boarders." He also makes another revealing remark. After pointing out that "unlike the cottages of the higher grade employees, the camps of the United Fruit Company's laborers are hardly ever screened," he admits that "Dr. Deeks [chief of United Fruit's medical department] and others have reported that the Company has expended considerable money on screening, without being able to induce workers to use these protections against the menace of the mosquito." [38]

Today it is easy to criticize the housing that the Company provided its laborers, particularly earlier in the twentieth century. There is no doubt that the quarters were rudimentary, crowded and often uncomfortable. Nevertheless, it is useful to put the issue into perspective. In the first place, the housing that the United Fruit Company furnished its workers compared favorably with that provided by other U.S. companies operating throughout Latin America. As historian Mira Wilkins has observed, housing for workers in the 1920s "rarely had indoor toilets or running water . . . Electricity, for lighting, came in practically every case before indoor toilets or running water . . . The homes provided by the corporation for the workers and their families were far superior to anything existing locally." [39]

More pertinent is a comparison between UFCO's housing and that provided by other plantation owners in Guatemala. No *finqueros*, whether Guatemalan or foreign, furnished their workers with housing and sanitary facilities that were in any way comparable to United Fruit's quarters. As Whetten observed in 1961,

the vast majority of the population has housing that is grossly inadequate

> *in terms of modern standards of either health or convenience... Over half the population seven years of age and over live in ranchos, which may be roughly defined as "huts" or "shacks" and certainly represent minimal housing facilities... Most of them [the ranchos] are of inferior construction, have dirt floors and lack sanitary facilities. They usually consist of one room... They seldom have windows, and animals are often kept in the house... Nearly two-thirds (64.2 percent) of the rural inhabitants live in ranchos as compared with 18.9 percent of the urban.*[40]

U.S. journalist Daniel James, who visited the Tiquisate division in the early 1950s, also provides a vivid description of the conditions prevailing in Pueblo Nuevo, the town that had grown up outside the UFCO compound, where small shops and markets serviced *La Frutera's* laborers.

> *One must see for himself, as this writer has, the acute contrast between the way United Fruit workers and other Guatemalans live... In the town of Pueblo Nuevo, for example, the people live in wretched hovels which are extremely overcrowded, lack elementary sanitary facilities, and are located on narrow and dirty streets... The children are forced to play in incredibly dirty surroundings, and are taught in incredibly primitive schools... UFCO's workers live in well-built frame structures of recent construction that possess such facilities as plumbing, electricity and screens. They are raised off the ground so as to keep out as much dust and heat and let in as much air as possible... The surroundings are landscaped and relatively free of trash and garbage... While UFCO's Guatemalan workers live by no means as well as workers in the United States, they are as aristocrats compared with other Guatemalan workers.*[41]

By the 1950s, United Fruit recognized that the rustic barracks it provided its laborers supplied little privacy and generated no sense of community pride.[42] As a result, the Company began providing its Central American laborers with houses first designed and used in Tiquisate. Named the "Guatemala type" or "T-type," these single-family dwellings were constructed directly on the ground, and had cement floors. The living quarters in the front of the building were connected by a roofed breezeway to a structure in the rear which contained a kitchen and a bath. A small fenced yard was provided at the side of each building. The houses, which cost approximately $2,000 apiece, were prefabricated in Tiquisate and could be erected in less than eight hours.

By 1956, UFCO was replacing the old barracks-style housing in Tiquisate at the rate of one single-family house per day. Writing in 1958, May and Plaza noted that replacing the older type of housing for the Company's 60,000 laborers (located in six countries) would require a replacement investment of $90 to $120 million. The authors reported, however, that on those farms where one-family dwellings had been put into service "there has been a significant increase in worker morale and sense of community responsibility." [43]

Decades after the United Fruit Company routinely provided sanitary facilities to its workers, a study prepared in 1980 for the USAID Mission in Guatemala found that of 122 south coast farms (most of them coffee *fincas*, but also plantations dedicated to raising sugar cane and cotton) barely half of them provided latrines for their workers. Potable water was not supplied to the individual homes of workers, although two-thirds of the farms surveyed provided *pilas* (communal basins) for their workers. Nevertheless, only eight farm owners had analyzed the bacteriological content of their water supplies during the previous two years. "Of fifty-four plantation water samples analyzed by AGROSALUD during 1979, only twenty-nine samples were found to be relatively free from contamination." [44]

Even in 1988, only 41 percent of Guatemala's rural population had access to potable water, and less than half the population (48 percent) had the use of sanitary facilities.[45] Moreover, it is estimated that 80 percent of the country's approximately 10 million inhabitants live in crowded one-room shacks or huts where the "whole family sleeps, eats, cooks, and undertakes all of its daily activities." [46] These statistics help to explain why former UFCO laborers interviewed by the author almost inevitably mentioned the housing *La Frutera* provided as one of the most important benefits — perhaps *the* most important — that they received in conjunction with their employment.

ADDRESSING EDUCATIONAL NEEDS

It is curious that the United Fruit Company's many critics have consistently failed to recognize the important role that the Company played in educating thousands of Guatemalan children. Even the most complete history of education in Guatemala (*Historia de la Educación en Guatemala* by Carlos González Orellana) makes no mention at all of the United Fruit Company's notable contribution to rural education. The author does, however, take the opportunity to write numerous pages denouncing the Company — citing charges which have nothing to do with Guatemala's educational system.

Nevertheless, had it not been for United Fruit Company schools, scores of young Guatemalans probably would not have received any education whatsoever since their parents were farm workers, located in areas where there were no schools. As González Orellana points out, in the early 1900s the law requiring *finca* owners to establish schools on their farms was "frequently violated and converted into a farce." [47]

In fact, *finca* schools were often opened only once or twice a year when government inspectors arrived. In 1925, a mere 182 such schools were functioning (when there were upwards of 2,000 large coffee farms throughout the country) "and by 1932 it was a matter of pride that 367 were actually open and, not, as formerly, working 'only during the examination period.'" [48] That there were so few *finca* schools was due to at least two factors: plantation owners considered the operation of a school as an unnecessary expense more properly borne by the government. Moreover, as Whetten explains, "children of school age may help with the work on the *finca* and one can easily see why it would be to the *finquero's* interest to permit the children to work on the plantation rather than to send them to school." [49]

Compounding the lack of schools on coffee plantations was a critical absence of schools in virtually all of the country's villages. Describing the period between 1871 and 1921, Ernesto Bienvenido Jiménez notes that "it was rare to see schools in the villages; generally they were located in the capitals of each department." [50] The schools that were available, particularly in rural areas, were sadly deficient. Chester Lloyd Jones describes the average rural school in the late 1930s as being "a single-room structure of thatch or adobe furnished with crude benches and often without adequate texts or even a blackboard."[51]

By 1924, when Guatemala's population totaled slightly more than 2 million inhabitants, the government had established only 2,626 primary schools throughout the country — one school for approximately every 80,000 Guatemalans. These schools enrolled less than 93,000 students, which helps to explain why the country's illiteracy rate was upwards of 85 percent.[52] Even when schools were available, the teachers were often poorly prepared. For example, in 1924, only 353 teachers held teaching degrees; 2,824 teachers were classified as *empíricos*, or individuals possessing only three or four years of primary education and no training to become a teacher.

The miserable salaries paid teachers — ranging as low as the equivalent of two to four dollars a month during the Estrada Cabrera regime — was the principal reason so few individuals chose careers in that profession. In fact, during Estrada Cabrera's twenty-two year dictatorship, teachers frequently were not even paid in cash; instead, they were given chits or coupons which they were often forced to sell for prices lower than their face value. Estrada Cabrera's most notable "contribution" to education was the numerous temples he constructed in important towns in honor of Minerva, the Greek goddess of learning.

In many ways, Guatemala's educational system fared even worse under General Ubico. A number of schools and several teacher training institutes were closed; tuition was instated at the previously free secondary schools; and the University of San Carlos lost its autonomy. School inspectors and principals were replaced by army officers, usually at the rank of lieutenant or captain, and the number of students per class was reduced to that of a company, and divided into "sergeants, privates and enlisted men."

González Orellana maintains that under Ubico

> *rural education was completely neglected, with education in that sector limited to the schools maintained by the towns or finca owners. The problem of the Indian was totally ignored, to the extreme that one of the Ministers of Education declared in an international conference that in Guatemala there was no Indian problem.*[53]

During the Ubico regime teachers were no longer paid with coupons, but the salaries for rural teachers were abysmal: the equivalent of seven dollars a month.[54] (Samuel Guy Inman reveals that Ubico's 1943-1944 budget allocated the equivalent of $30 a month toward the upkeep of each of his many fine horses, while the rector of a university received a monthly salary of $85.)[55]

Although numerous improvements were made in Guatemala's educational system after Ubico left office in 1944, the 1950 census revealed that three-fourths of the children of compulsory school age were not attending school; in rural areas, a staggering 84.5 percent of Guatemala's school-age children were not enrolled.[56] As late as 1956, Monteforte Toledo found that out of 700,000 children aged seven to fourteen, only 58,700 youngsters in rural areas attended school. The figure for children located in urban areas was considerably higher (90,400), but revealed how skewed the educational system was since well over 70 percent of the nation's inhabitants lived in rural areas. Nonetheless, both rural and urban groups represented only a minuscule 19.9 percent of the country's primary school-age population — a figure that Monteforte Toledo warns may be too high given "the partial absenteeism of rural students."[57]

Since there were no public schools available in the remote areas where *La Frutera* operated, the Company furnished this service to the children of all its employees. Not surprisingly, the schools, which used the Guatemalan government's curriculum plans, provided a service far superior to anything available in rural areas. As Whetten comments, "it is generally acknowledged by the Ministry of Education in Guatemala, that the private rural schools maintained by the United Fruit Company are among the best in the nation."[58] There were numerous reasons for the Company's outstanding educational system — a system that provided six years of primary schooling to the laborers' children. In the division headquarters of Bananera and Tiquisate, eight years of bilingual schooling was provided.

The bilingual schools have had a significant impact on their students. Staffed by well-qualified U.S. and Guatemalan teachers, the schools taught American children to speak, read and write Spanish. As a result, many of these youths, who were exposed to the Guatemalan government's educational program, not only learned fluent Spanish, they acquired considerable knowledge about the country's history and geography. Equally important, hundreds of Spanish-speaking children learned English — a skill that has helped many of them to obtain important positions within Guatemala's public and private sector.[59] In the numerous interviews the author conducted with individuals who had attended these schools, virtually all of them echoed Aura Marina Meza de Dardón, who attended the Bananera school during the 1950s. "The English I learned has served me enormously," she stated. "I wouldn't have the job I hold now if it weren't for the good English I learned, thanks to the United Fruit Company."[60]

That UFCO's schools far surpassed the government's rural public schools was due primarily to the superior resources the Company invested in this activity. In the first instance, United Fruit paid its Guatemalan teachers salaries that were somewhat higher than those prevailing at the average elementary school. For example, Adán Solís, director of Del Monte's schools in Bananera, recalls that when he began working for the United Fruit Company in 1950, he was paid the equivalent of $88 a month, while public school teachers received about $15 less per month.[61] (Even today the salaries of public school teachers, particularly in rural areas, are not significantly higher than they were forty years ago.) The superior salaries that the Company paid its teachers attracted individuals who were better trained and more experienced than those employed in most of the country's rural schools.

The school houses were also better constructed and designed: class rooms were well-lighted and clean. Unlike many public schools, where children sat on benches, each student was provided with a desk and chair. In addition, all books and other school supplies were furnished free of cost — a benefit not provided at public schools. Also unavailable at government schools was the free medical and dental care provided to each child. At many schools the Company provided a daily pint of milk and bananas as a recess snack for the youngsters. The schooling that UFCO provided was obviously a significant part of the Company's indirect remuneration to its employees; in the 1946-1954 period, United Fruit's annual school subsidies increased markedly: from $50,000 a year to $128,000.[62]

The scope of the United Fruit's educational system is apparent in the figures available for 1950, when the Company employed 11,669 workers. In that year the Bananera division, with eighteen schools, enrolled 787 students and employed twenty-five teachers. On the south coast, the Compañía Agrícola maintained thirty-five schools, which registered 1,900 youngsters, and were staffed by fifty-eight teachers. The total cost of administering the schools was $100,103.[63]

There are no accurate figures on the total number of students who attended UFCO's schools during the sixty-six years that the Company operated in Guatemala. Nevertheless, a conservative estimate, based on 1950 school enrollment figures, is that approximately 118,000 Guatemalans received at least two or three years of elementary schooling at United Fruit Company facilities. There is reason to believe, however, that this estimate should be considerably higher. By 1950, the Company's work force had shrunk considerably: from a high of 14,135 workers in 1941 to slightly more than 11,500 employees in 1950. Moreover, throughout the Company's long tenure in Guatemala, there was undoubtedly a large number of employees who worked only a year or two for United Fruit before moving on to other jobs. Nevertheless, if those employees had school-age children, their youngsters would have attended *La Frutera's* schools.

AN AGRICULTURAL SCHOOL
SERVING THE AMERICAS

It is little known that Guatemala has also benefited from a unique educational facility which the United Fruit Company founded in 1942: the Escuela Agrícola Panamericana. Located in the town of Zamorano, twenty-five miles southeast of the Honduran capital, the school combines a university-level teaching center with a large commercial farming operation. While virtually all Latin American universities offer agricultural degrees based almost exclusively on scholarly, theoretical studies, the Escuela Agrícola Panamericana provides its students with an unusual "hands-on" education.

Imbued with Zemurray's vision of providing Latin American youths with a practical education in agriculture, Zamorano, as the school is popularly known, offers a "learning-by-doing" curriculum that grants two degrees. The *Agrónomo* (agronomist) degree consists of nine trimesters totalling thirty-three months. However, Dr. Simón E. Malo, who ended his fourteen-year tenure as director in 1993, points out that the intense, highly concentrated program of studies represents the equivalent of four and a half years of university study in the United States or Latin America.[64] The *Ingeniero Agrónomo* (agricultural engineer) degree is a forty-four month program that delves deeper into modern agricultural science, with an emphasis on research and individual work. In collaboration with Cornell University, a Master's in tropical agriculture was initiated late in 1992.

What makes the Zamorano curriculum unusual is that while its students take academic courses in subjects such as botany, mathematics, zoology, physics and agricultural economics, they also work in diverse agricultural activities. In fact, the students' course-related work, which generates one-third of the school's financial assets, annually produces an astounding 1.1 million metric tons of fruits, vegetables, basic grains, seeds and meat. Zamorano's livestock also annually accounts for 437,000 liters of milk, and its poultry industry provides nearly 900,000 eggs per year.[65]

With a faculty of nearly 200 academics, many of whom are Zamorano graduates holding advanced degrees from U.S. universities, the school is at the forefront of research projects involving all aspects of tropical agriculture and animal husbandry. Underlying all of the courses and research work is a keen concern for environmental issues, particularly the abuse of pesticides and the use of environmentally harmful fertilizers. Like many university schools of agriculture in the United States, the Escuela Agrícola Panamericana maintains a comprehensive extension program directed, in large part, to small farmers in the area. In addition, Zamorano publishes numerous books, scientific works and guides, many of which fill important needs in the advancement of tropical agriculture in Latin America and elsewhere.

Located on 16,000 acres of land in central Honduras, the school's attractive, colonial-style buildings are valued at $45 million and include classrooms, dormitories, libraries, laboratories, greenhouses, machine shops and administrative offices. In the fifty-four years since the United

Fruit Company founded the school, the Escuela Agrícola Panamericana has graduated more than 3,000 students, 90 percent of them from Central America, but hundreds of youths have also attended from other Latin American countries. Nearly 340 Guatemalans have attended Zamorano, and its graduates include a vice minister of agriculture, a bank president and a college president. In 1992, nearly 100 Guatemalans were included in the 717-member student body. (Only one of every seven applicants was admitted to the school in 1992.) With students enrolled from nearly every country in Latin America, ninety-nine women were included in the class of 1992.

By Latin American standards, tuition at Zamorano is relatively high: the equivalent of $6,500 a year. It includes, however, food and lodging, uniforms, tools and lab supplies during an eleven-month academic year. In fact, the actual cost of a year's study is $13,500; thus the school heavily subsidizes the cost of each student's tuition. Moreover, a generous scholarship program provides grants to 70 percent of the student body. The Escuela Agrícola Panamericana, whose international board of trustees is composed of prominent Latin Americans and Americans (including Mrs. Doris Zemurray Stone, Sam Zemurray's daughter), receives donations from a number of governments, U.S. and other foreign corporations, and individual contributors. In 1992, the school received more that $3.5 million in gifts and grants, which represented nearly 50 percent of its operating revenues.[66]

If the Escuela Agrícola Panamericana is an unusual institution contributing to Latin America's pressing agricultural needs, its founding was also singular. As Malo points out, "no other U.S. corporation, to my knowledge, has founded and for many years supported an institution for tropical development and given it to the tropics of the world. Zamorano is a unique institution, with nothing comparable to its magnitude anywhere in the tropics, or the subtropics or temperate zone, for that matter." The result of Zemurray's interest in the economic development of the region, the school was founded after the United Fruit Company purchased the school's initial 5,000 acres. During the first five years of its operation, UFCO invested more than $6 million in developing the new institution. One of the Company's principal — and continuing — expenses entailed covering the tuition costs for all Zamorano students, a policy that remained in effect until 1960. At the same time, however, no graduate of the school was permitted to work for the United Fruit Company, a procedure established by Zemurray and Dr. Wilson Popenoe, the first director of the school. "This school was not for the benefit of the United Fruit Company," Malo states. "In other words, the Company did not establish Zamorano in order to train its own people." The policy changed, however, in 1962, a year after Zemurray's death. At that time, UFCO determined it would initiate a modest tuition policy and would gradually decrease its contribution to the school. It was hoped that these measures would lead to more financial support from governments, private institutions and individuals. Clearly, these policies have met with considerable success.

HELPING TO PRESERVE GUATEMALA'S HERITAGE

As with many of the other positive contributions that the United Fruit Company made during its nearly seven decades in Guatemala, there has been little recognition of the notable role the Company played in helping to preserve the country's magnificent pre-Columbian past. It is not generally known, for example, that the United Fruit Company established — and for sixty-one years maintained — the archeological park at Quiriguá. Renowned for its nine enormous stelae and six mysterious zoomorphs (elaborately-carved blocks of stone depicting fantastic monsters), the site also contains a group of fine structures known as the Acropolis.

The extraordinary ruins of that river city, which reached its zenith between 731 and 900 AD, first came to public attention after the 1843 publication of *Incidents of Travel in Central America, Chiapas and Yucatan* by John L. Stephens. Accompanied by Frederick Catherwood, a British architect who was also a superb artist, the two-volume study provided numerous pages of text and drawings describing the previously unknown site. In fact, Stephens was so impressed with Quiriguá's awesome stelae that he attempted to purchase two of them from the Guatemalan brothers who owned the site. Apparently he hoped to ship them to New York, where they would be placed on permanent exhibition. Fortunately, however, his audacious plan was never realized.

No effort was made to clear the thick jungle surrounding the ruins until 1881 when Alfred Percival Maudslay, a British explorer and archaeologist, arrived for the first of four visits over a thirteen-year period. Working under primitive conditions, where many of his workers and British colleagues succumbed to malaria, Maudslay partially cleared the jungled area and made hundreds of plaster moldings of the stelae, which he then shipped to London. The site remained untouched until 1909 when the United Fruit Company purchased a large tract of land along the Motagua River, which included the pre-Columbian ruins. UFCO's Cutter, then manager of the Virginia division, set aside, in perpetuity, seventy-five acres surrounding the ruined city, while hundreds of adjacent acres were soon transformed into immense banana plantations.[67] The Company subsequently provided logistical support and, in some instances, equipment and workers to the four U.S. expeditionary teams which began the restoration of Quiriguá in 1910.

As a result of Cutter's actions, the Carnegie Institution of Washington and the Archaeological Institute of America undertook additional excavations and restoration of the ruins between 1919 and 1941. But the restored ruins would soon have reverted back to the primeval jungle had it not been for the United Fruit Company's continuing work to keep the wilderness at bay. The grass surrounding the giant stelae and temples was routinely cut and no weeds or bushes were permitted to invade the cleared area. Armed with machetes, UFCO workers periodically slashed back the nearby jungle when it attempted to encroach on the site. Equally important, drainage ditches, which the Company constructed and which traversed and encircled the ruins, were systematically cleaned.

In addition, the Company provided another vital amenity for visitors who wished to view the splendid ruins: transportation. Until 1959, when the highway to the Atlantic was completed and automobiles were at last able to reach Quiriguá from Guatemala City or Puerto Barrios, the only way to visit the ruins was to travel by rail to the IRCA's Quiriguá station. From there, on a railroad spur constructed by United Fruit, the Company provided motorcars and guides to transport visitors to within a few hundred yards of the archaeological park. Many tourists often stayed at the small hotel the Company operated at the headquarters of its nearby Quiriguá banana farm (where the hospital was also located). Since United Fruit did not operate hotels at any of its other banana farms, it is clear the facility at Quiriguá was established to accommodate the scores of visitors who soon began touring the vanquished city.

The United Fruit Company also played a role in helping to restore the most famous stela at Quiriguá. Measuring twenty-six feet in height (an additional three feet are below the surface of the ground) and weighing sixty-five tons, Stela E is the most gigantic Maya monolith ever discovered. The exquisitely-carved stone shaft, which appears on Guatemala's ten-*centavo* coin, was one of the stelae which Maudslay attempted to reproduce with plaster casts during his 1883 visit. A crack across the base of the nose, however, had so weakened it that the hawked Maya nose fell off at the first touch. Maudslay then carefully cemented the nose back on the stela and bound a rope around it to keep the protuberance in place.

Twenty-seven years later, when the renowned Mayanist, Sylvanus G. Morley, first visited Quiriguá in 1910, the rope had long since rotted, but the nose on Stela E was still intact. Nevertheless, during 1917, when an unusually wet rainy season afflicted the area, Quirigua's most famous monument toppled backwards. When Morley saw the giant stone shaft late that same year, he concluded that "some malicious person" had simply yanked off the classic Maya nose. After an intense search around the stela, however, the archaeologist was fortunate enough to find the stone object. He then gave it to United Fruit's district superintendent of agriculture at Quiriguá for safekeeping. Seventeen years later, in 1934, when the Carnegie Institution undertook major restoration of the stelae, including the raising of Stela E and three others which had also tumbled to the ground, the nose was retrieved from the United Fruit Company safe. Once again, it was cemented onto the face of Stela E, where it remains today.[68]

In an era when U.S. companies were not known for their philanthropy — much less the safeguarding of remote archaeological sites — it is not inconceivable that UFCO's Cutter might have ordered the Quiriguá ruins razed and replaced by banana plantations. At best, he might have left the area untouched, hidden in the dense jungle and unavailable to the public. That he chose to preserve the ancient city, eventually permitting countless tourists to appreciate the unique site, was a rare act of corporate stewardship.

Long before the public was readily able to visit the Maya ruins located in Mexico's Yucatan peninsula or Tikal (the impressive archaeological park in northern Guatemala which many travelers now make a point of visiting), Quiriguá was attracting large numbers of tourists. Indeed, the fact that the remains of the ancient city were located so near to the railroad to the Atlantic made it the country's — and the world's — most accessible Maya ruins at that time.[69] It is not exaggerated, therefore, to credit the United Fruit Company with playing an early and important role in developing a nascent tourist industry that in 1994 is expected to bring more than half a million foreign visitors to Guatemala, providing the nation with nearly $300 million of foreign exchange.[70]

If UFCO's role in establishing and maintaining the archaeological site at Quiriguá has been little recognized, the Company's restoration of the Maya ruins at Zaculeu, in the western highlands of Guatemala, has been frequently criticized. Zaculeu, which means "place of the white earth," was occupied continuously by the Mam Indians from approximately 500 AD until the Spaniards arrived in 1525.

In 1945, responding in part to Zemurray's continuing interest in pre-Columbian cultures, the United Fruit Company sought permission from the Guatemalan government to restore the major structures at Zaculeu.[71] In a richly-illustrated, two-volume study titled *The Ruins of Zaculeu*, which the United Fruit Company published in 1953, John M. Dimick, project director, explained why the site at Zaculeu was chosen. Since the ruins were only a short distance from the city of Huehuetenango, workmen would have little difficulty in reaching the area. In addition, Zaculeu was more accessible to future tourists than were the two other Maya cities that the UFCO-sponsored archaeologists considered. Finally, Dimick states, "we could see that so much of many buildings remained in good condition that restoration could be carried out with confidence."[72]

Once the Guatemalan government had approved United Fruit's plans to restore the ruins, seven American archaeologists and restorative architects, all experienced Mayanists, initiated the laborious work which began in February 1946 and ended after seventy-four weeks of field work spread over a three-year period. The team's decision to cover all of the restored buildings with a combination of lime and cement is the principal reason the work has been criticized. At all other pre-Columbian sites in Guatemala, the restoration of the aged structures stopped once the hewn rocks used by the Maya had been relocated to their original positions.

As a result, those edifices, with rocks and mortar exposed, appear more "original" than the completely intact temples at Zaculeu. As a guidebook to Guatemala states, "the reconstruction work has left the structures looking as if they were erected just a few years ago." [73]

There were two principal reasons for covering the restored buildings with a coat of lime and cement. According to two of the archaeologists who participated in the project, excavations at Zaculeu revealed that there had been four distinct phases of construction during the eight centuries the site was occupied. Even during the earliest period, the experts found that plaster had been "developed into a hard, durable material and was used on floors, terraces and stairways." During three successive phases of construction, the Maya employed a thick lime plaster which was used to coat all of the structures. "In the final building periods a good quality of white lime plaster was used for facing," the archaeologists wrote.[74] Thus, the reconstruction of Zaculeu painstakingly duplicated the structures as they appeared when the Spanish conquistadors arrived.

An equally important factor in finishing the structures with cement was the poor quality of building performed by the Mam Indians. Dr. Edwin M. Shook, a prominent U.S. archaeologist who worked from 1955 to 1964 with the University of Pennsylvania's excavation and consolidation of the Maya ruins at Tikal, served as an advisor to the Zaculeu project. In an interview with the author, Shook explained that it was necessary to place a hard casing of plaster on the Zaculeu structures because

> *the ancient masonry was so poorly built. It was simply earth and stones — not even well-cut stones, but just rough stones — piled up in earth. They did not build the quality of stonework that was customary in such lowland Maya areas as Tikal, Copán or Chichén Itzá. The only thing*

that retained the buildings was a very hard lime coating. The team particularly took pains in studying the original type of plaster used on the buildings, which was basically lime with sand grouting. The closest thing that they could come to that was Portland cement. That was absolutely the quality of the original plaster used by the Maya. You couldn't tell the difference between that and the original plaster, if it were still in good condition . . . Without a question, it was technically the best archeological excavation and repair job that had been done in Guatemala up until that date.[75]

It should also be pointed out that the team's restoration techniques were fully approved by the Guatemalan ministry of public education, which oversaw the work. Dimick explains that "in addition to monthly reports to the sponsor, an annual report was prepared for the minister of education of Guatemala setting forth the accomplishments of the past season and the plans for the ensuing one."[76] Shook adds, "that was a normal procedure. We always made a full, detailed report with drawings, photographs and description of exactly what work was accomplished each season. And that had to be presented to the Guatemalan government. If the government hadn't approved of the work being done, they would have stopped it."

CONCLUSIONS

This chapter has attempted to provide a comprehensive description of the United Fruit Company's human and cultural contributions to Guatemala. Most authors who have written about *La Frutera* have either failed to mention many of the benefits outlined above or have dismissed them as relatively inconsequential. However, the thousands of laborers who received the highest agricultural wages in Guatemala, were furnished with the country's best rural housing and learned new skills would hardly have considered these benefits as irrelevant. Nor would those former employees have criticized the Company commissaries for offering food items at costs well below prevailing market prices. Similarly, the scores of children who were taught at UFCO schools and were routinely provided with free school supplies and medical exams would hardly have characterized the experience as immaterial. The hundreds of Guatemalans exposed to a first-class education at Zamorano would not likely describe their training at that renowned institution as trivial. And the countless men, women and children whose lives were saved because of dedicated physicians like Neil Macphail and many other talented doctors and nurses would scarcely have termed the United Fruit Company's long presence in Guatemala as inconsequential. Finally, there was the intangible pleasure experienced by thousands of appreciative Guatemalans and foreign visitors who toured the Quiriguá ruins during United Fruit's long stewardship of the site. While *Chapter 9* analyzes the notable economic benefits that the United Fruit Company rendered during its sixty-six years in Guatemala, it is nonetheless apparent that UFCO's wide-ranging contributions to the country's human development were also very substantial.

- 6 -

The U.S. and United Fruit Confront the Guatemalan "Time Machine"

By the late 1930s it was apparent that President Jorge Ubico had accomplished most of the major initiatives of his long rule. His frugal economic policies, coupled with rising exports of coffee and bananas, gradually brought the country out of its financial crisis. In the process, however, Guatemalan society had begun to change. The hundreds of miles of new roads that had been constructed not only served to more effectively integrate the small nation, but also made the population more mobile and less regional in outlook. Similarly, Ubico's keen interest in fostering the use of radios allowed Guatemalans, even in remote areas, to be somewhat better informed about national and even international events.

Although the vast majority of the population was still abysmally paid, miserably housed, badly nourished and unable to read and write, Ubico's government had demonstrated the possibility of change. For the Indians, the fact that debt slavery — in practice for 250 years — had been abolished was proof that times were changing. Moreover, a small but growing middle class, particularly in the capital and several larger towns, was beginning to make an appearance. Economic development and expanding commerce had created increasing numbers of middle-level managers, clerks, shopkeepers, bureaucrats and other white-collar positions. But the regime was incapable of broadening its political base to include the growing middle class. With no access to the levers of power, and unable to influence the direction of the country, the middle class had become frustrated, resentful and alienated.

As Ubico's perceptive American biographer remarks,

the transformation of his nation's society was among Ubico's most significant legacies, although one of which he was only partially cognizant. For Ubico focused upon the economic effects of his policies rather than upon the social consequences . . . Eventually, the social changes resulting from Ubico's programs rendered his methods obsolete, and the Caudillo proved unable to change his policies to deal with these new elements and the resulting national circumstances.[1]

In fact, Ubico's inability to undertake new, dynamic initiatives, combined with his cruel, autocratic form of government set the stage for his demise.

While the Ubico regime was stagnating, war-related developments also began to impact on the Guatemalan economy. One of the most important was a sharp drop in the export earnings from bananas. Since the U.S. Navy leased most of the United Fruit Company's Great White Fleet — a total of 113 ships, of which forty-two were lost to enemy action — only a few older ships, most of them without refrigeration, were available to transport bananas from Guatemala and elsewhere in Central America. It is estimated that from 1942 through most of 1944 an average of 75,000 tons of bananas rotted every month on UFCO's isthmian plantations.[2] Thus, Guatemala's exports of the golden fruit dropped precipitously: from 10.3 million stems in 1939 to only 2.5 million in 1943.[3]

On July 1, 1944, after a series of strikes and demonstrations led by university students in Guatemala City, Ubico abruptly tendered his resignation to a hastily selected *junta* of three generals. One of the *junta* members, Brigadier General Federico Ponce Vaides, quickly ordered the *Ubiquista*-dominated Legislative Assembly to name him provisional president. The new strongman then announced that presidential elections would be held in November and that he would be a candidate for that high office. Bowing to public pressure, Ponce also restored constitutional guarantees and permitted the formation of political parties and unions.

The weeks following Ubico's resignation were a heady, euphoric period for Guatemala. As Galich, one of the most articulate and active student leaders, recalls, "it was a country that from one night to the next day, as if it were the owner of a time machine, had burst into the twentieth century after having lived in the darkest of times. Because of that, we felt that we were truly experiencing a revolution." [4]

THE OCTOBER 20 REVOLUTION AND THE "WHITE CANDIDATE"

Even before political organizations were legally allowed, however, a small group of professionals, including several school teachers, had secretly formed a political party they called Renovación Nacional. Their candidate for president would be a self-exiled Guatemalan professor teaching at the National University of Tucumán in Argentina: Dr. Juan José Arévalo Bermejo. Three days after Ubico resigned, Renovación Nacional leaders cabled Arévalo, urging him to accept their candidacy for president. Without hesitation, the thirty-nine-year-old professor immediately replied that he was prepared to "lead the virile resurgence of democracy in Guatemala." [5]

Why had the fledgling new party looked to distant Argentina to select a Ph.D. in the philosophy of education who had been absent from Guatemala for the previous seven years? As K. H. Silvert remarks, these same attributes helped to make Arévalo an attractive candidate. "His civilian status, his social position (modest middle-class rural background), his profession, and the very fact of his lack of well-defined ties to Guatemala appeared to make him an eminently suitable candidate." [6] Moreover, Arévalo, who was the author of several books dealing with education, was relatively well known to many Guatemalan teachers, a group that formed a key element in the revolutionary movement.

Arriving in Guatemala City in early September, Arévalo was given an enormous, tumultuous reception, causing Ponce to have second thoughts about the upcoming elections. Within a few weeks, the provisional president began taking steps to change the constitution — changes that would permit him to remain in office. On October 1, the capital was stunned by the news that the founder and publisher of the country's leading daily had been murdered, presumably because of his paper's strong opposition to Ponce's efforts at *continuismo*. Although the assassination helped to crystallize public opinion against Ubico's successor, Ponce's fate was already sealed. A small group of military officers and civilians had begun to plot the successful overthrow of the general and the effective demise of the Ubico-tainted past that he represented.

The most important individuals involved in the October 20 revolt were the same ones who would compose the three-man revolutionary *junta* which ruled until Arévalo took office five months later. The coup leaders, all in their early thirties, were a somewhat heterogenous group, representing, to some extent, the forces arrayed against Ponce. Jorge Toriello, a prominent businessman, embodied the civilian forces opposed to the Ubico stand-in; Major Javier Arana, an army tank commander attached to the elite Honor Guard, was a line officer; and Captain Jacobo Arbenz Guzmán, a graduate of the Escuela Politécnica, Guatemala's West Point, represented officers who had attended that prestigious institution.

There was, however, a crucial force missing in the composition of the *junta*: there was no representative of the rural masses, particularly the Indians. Given the fact that virtually all of the indigenous community was rural, illiterate and politically-insulated, it is not surprising that no Indian(s) played a role in the coup. Consequently, the indigenous people, who constituted the great majority of the country's population, were never effectively integrated into the power structure of Guatemala's two revolutionary governments — a fact that eventually would have enormous significance for the country.

The revolt began before dawn on October 20 when soldiers from the Honor Guard and approximately 500 carefully selected students and workers moved out of the Guard headquarters and took up positions near the National Palace and two forts loyal to Ponce. Although shelling continued for several hours, the Honor Guard held a clear advantage: it possessed the country's most modern tanks and artillery — equipment that the U.S. government had provided Guatemala the previous year under its Lend Lease program.[7] By 2 PM a white flag was hoisted atop the National Palace. An hour later, the Voice of Guatemala announced Ponce's defeat and divulged the names of the three-man revolutionary *junta* heading up the new government. Arévalo, who had taken asylum in the Mexican Embassy on October 17, when it was feared Ponce's men might assassinate him, appeared in public on the morning of the revolt, soon to renew his successful campaign for the presidency.

A tall, portly man (with an ego to match his size), Arévalo espoused an idealistic, difficult-to-define philosophy that he termed "spiritual socialism." "I decided," he subsequently wrote, "to adopt a scale of values in which the spiritual (morals, justice, etc.) occupied a superior position, leaving material goods on a secondary level. That is why I spoke of 'spiritual socialism.' I did not share the materialistic doctrine preached by the other socialism: Marxism."[8] Nevertheless, the skilled educator, who was also a spell-binding orator, knew that campaign speeches could not dwell on complex political philosophies; his discourses therefore emphasized the need to forge "a new Guatemala," where urgent attention would be given to workers, women, Indians, teachers, youngsters and many other needy elements of society. Early in his campaign, however, it became apparent that Arévalo was no friend of the United Fruit Company.

In his book *El candidato blanco y el huracán* (*The White Candidate and the Hurricane*), which details his campaign, Arévalo recounts having visited Tiquisate in early October 1944. The future president explains that despite his seven-year absence from Guatemala, he was well aware of the situation workers in Tiquisate and Bananera endured because his brother had worked a total of six years in both divisions, where "he heard and saw terrible things."

Before recounting the enthusiastic welcome he received from workers in Tiquisate, Arévalo describes his version of United Fruit's Guatemala operations:

> *typical factories of economic exploitation . . . with methods of work, of discipline, and of pay characterized by a style I later called 'African' . . . the old colonial system . . . Unhealthy housing, without doctors, without medicine. Salaries limited to two or three days a week . . . These were commercial establishments which received the protection*

of the North American government and where workers lived under North American laws . . . islands of the empire, with Guatemalan troops at their disposition.

According to Dr. Arévalo, the most emotional moment of his Tiquisate visit occurred when he told the cheering crowd "if I become president, I will elevate all Guatemalans to the same height where now, on Guatemalan soil, the North Americans stand." He then adds, "the irony was quickly captured by the crowd and my speech was interrupted with shouts of 'even higher, doctor, even higher than them!' and 'down with the *gringo* exploiters!' Their delirium was justified because it was one of the few political promises I made throughout the campaign. And I kept it, without a doubt!" [9]

In November, Arévalo campaigned in Puerto Barrios, where he addressed IRCA railroad workers and UFCO stevedores. In recounting the visit, the future president stated, "I dedicated my speech to the United Fruit . . . a foreign factory inserted into the country like a ganglion of the colonialist commercial system . . . where whiskey was consumed at the social club as if drinking the quintessence of Guatemalan sweat." Admitting he was no longer the "timid orator" who had offered Guatemalans in Tiquisate a status equal to that of the United Fruit Company's foreign employees, Arévalo asserts that his speech was couched "in terms of war." Stimulated by frenetic applause, Arévalo shouted, "the time is past when presidents received Pharaonic gifts and Congressmen accepted checks in order to continue betraying the country. Those foreigners who attempt to corrupt government officials will be pulled out of Guatemala by their ears." [10]

While Arévalo was busy campaigning, the *junta* moved swiftly to enact numerous significant decrees, the first of which dissolved the *Ubiquista* Legislative Assembly and set elections to that body for early November. Within weeks of taking office, the new Congress called for elections for a constituent assembly, charged with drafting a new constitution. In addition, presidential elections were set for three consecutive days in the middle of December. Opposed by three candidates, Arévalo won a predictable victory, garnering a stunning 85 percent of the votes. It is noteworthy, however, that only literate males were allowed to vote.

(The new constitution gave the vote to non-literate males over the age of eighteen and to all literate females.) Guatemala's first democratically elected president took the oath of office on March 15, 1945 — a scant two days after the constitution had been signed and approved by the revolutionary *junta*.

One of the most notable aspects of the new charter was the provision for a Chief of the Armed Forces, with the Legislative Assembly empowered to select the individual who would occupy that key post. The drafters of the constitution obviously instituted the new military position in order to reduce the absolute control Ubico had exerted over the armed forces. Nevertheless, the position clearly undercut the authority of the Minister of Defense, and was bound to cause conflicts between the two incumbents. The probability of such confrontations was made even more likely when the positions were filled by two ambitious men whose political philosophies became increasingly antagonistic. Thus, Arévalo named Captain Jacobo Arbenz to the job of Minister of Defense and the Congress selected Major Francisco Arana as Chief of the Armed Forces.

LABOR UNIONS:
SUSTENANCE OF THE REVOLUTION

Another key provision of the new constitution granted workers the freedom to form unions. Although there had been a flurry of union activities and a few strikes during the 1920s, Ubico had firmly outlawed such activities. Because Ponce had been pressured into permitting unions to organize, several labor groups founded associations months before the new constitution was promulgated. One of the first, established in 1944, was the Sindicato de Acción y Mejoramiento Ferrocarrilero (SAMF), representing the approximately 5,000 workers employed by the International Railways of Central America. Also in July 1944, the 11,000 workers represented by the newly formed Unión de Trabajadores de Tiquisate, later renamed the Sindicato de Empresa de Trabajadores de la Compañía Agrícola de Guatemala (SETCAG), initiated a sixteen-day strike against *La Frutera's* Pacific coast operations. The tense situation and concern for the safety of the Americans in the Tiquisate compound compelled the Ponce government to dispatch troops to the area. The strike ended after the Company agreed to a 15 percent increase in salaries, and a minimum daily wage of 50 to 80 cents.

While long-suppressed trade unions began to make an appearance, another event was also taking place — one that played a major role in the development of the Guatemalan labor movement, and, in fact, would exert strong influence on the overall direction of the revolution. Guatemalan exiles, many of them socialists or Communists, as well as large numbers of leftists from other countries, began descending on the little nation where a vibrant, popular revolution had overthrown one of the hemisphere's most ferocious dictatorships. As Ralph Lee Woodward, Jr., the "dean" of U.S. Central American historians, points out, many of the new arrivals brought with them "a stream of leftist books and pamphlets, mostly by Mexican, French, or Russian authors, with which they sought to develop a Marxist ideology among Guatemalan workers and political leaders." [11] The new arrivals found quick acceptance in the recently established teachers' union, an organization that played a key role in the founding of the powerful Confederación de Trabajadores de Guatemala (CTG).

As one author has stated, "if labor was the key to communism's rise in Guatemala, the teachers' union was the key to its control over labor." [12] In fact, immediately after the CTG was founded in August 1944, it affiliated with the Communist-controlled Confederation of Latin American Workers, led by Mexico's Vicente Lombardo Toledano. According to Woodward, "Communist infiltration of the urban labor movement in Guatemala continued, and by 1950 Communist leaders were well established in organized labor." [13] This was a profound development because Guatemala's labor movement became, in effect, the revolutionary government's most vital source of support. Indeed, it was organized labor that came to Arévalo's defense in 1949 when the president successfully weathered the most serious of innumerable attempts to overthrow his government.

Arévalo's first important piece of labor legislation established a long-overdue social security system, modeled after the U.S. program. The new law provided compensation for injuries, maternity benefits, health care, and guaranteed workers the right to safe working conditions. A new Social Security Institute was charged with building a network of more than fifty hospitals throughout the country. But Arévalo's most historic accomplishment occurred in May 1947, when the bitterly debated Labor Code was promulgated. Addressing issues that had never before been contemplated by Guatemalan employers, the new law set minimum wages, recognized the right to strike and collective bargaining, provided for severance pay and paid vacations, established an eight-hour work day, and regulated the working hours of women and children. In addition, the Code established a system of labor courts — accountable to and under the direct supervision of the president — to adjudicate labor-management disputes.

Parting from the belief that "private interest must give way to the social or collective interest," several provisions of the new law clearly favored labor at the expense of management. In addition, most of the inspectors charged with implementing the law and many of the judges serving on the new labor courts were markedly more sympathetic to labor than to management. Initially, there was also a clear discrimination against rural workers. Thus, urban *sindicatos* (unions) were permitted to organize with a minimum of twenty workers, and only the union's elected officials needed to provide proof of literacy. But *campesino* unions could only be established on farms employing more than 500 workers.

On farms employing less than that number, unions were permitted only when there was a minimum of fifty workers who wanted to establish a *sindicato*. In addition, a full 60 percent of these workers had to provide proof of literacy. In a clear gesture to most of the nation's coffee farmers, strikes were not permitted during the harvesting period except on farms employing more than 500 men. As Richard Adams has noted, "in a country where in 1950, 71.9 percent of the national population over seven years of age was illiterate, the universe for organization in the countryside had been legislated almost out of existence."[14] Because there were only thirty agricultural enterprises that employed more than 500 workers, merely eleven *campesino* unions had been formed a year after the Labor Code was implemented.

The two largest *sindicatos* were those formed by workers of the United Fruit Company and the Compañía Agrícola; six operated on privately owned farms, and three unions were functioning on the national coffee *fincas* that had been expropriated from the Germans during World War II.[15] In 1948, however, the Labor Code was amended, abolishing the discriminatory provisions against agrarian unions and establishing uniform requirements for the organization of all unions. Thus, one year later, forty-six rural unions, with a membership of approximately 12,000, had been legally registered.[16] By 1954, there were 345 such organizations.[17]

Because of the Labor Code's initial, discriminatory requirements for establishing rural unions, the United Fruit Company complained that the thrust of the legislation, as it concerned agricultural enterprises, was directed at the fruit giant. Conceding that the Company's grievances had some validity, Gleijeses remarks that

> *the Arévalo administration was more vigorous in its protection of UFCO's workers than of other rural laborers. It may seem peculiar that a government so timid toward the native elite dared to disturb the American giant. In part, the paradox is explained by the nationalism of the revolutionary leaders. More disturbing than the plight of the peasants was the presence in their midst of an imperial enclave.[18]*

Understandably, *La Frutera* was extremely concerned by the potential implications of the workers' right to strike. Because banana plantations produce throughout the year, and since the highly perishable fruit requires precise harvesting and shipping schedules, strikes of only a few days could cause serious financial losses. As a result, the United Fruit Company considered its control over its own operations seriously jeopardized. When a high-ranking State Department officer subsequently visited Guatemala, he advised Foreign Minister Eugenio Silva Peña that the effect of the law might "seriously interfere with and possibly make impracticable the further operations of the Company," and that "Company officials were studying the matter with great care, taking into account the possibility that they might find it necessary to withdraw from Guatemala." [19]

According to José Aybar de Soto, this "veiled threat" was designed to force the Guatemalan government into exempting the United Fruit

Company from some of the provisions of the Labor Code, particularly the right to strike. That the Company wanted changes made in the new law was confirmed to the author by former President Arévalo. Stating that issues concerning the implementation of the Labor Code constituted the most serious problem he encountered with the United Fruit Company during his six-year term of office, Arévalo admitted that the new law

> *contained obligations that affected UFCO in a serious manner. The Company, displeased, hastened to declare that it was 'unfamiliar' with the law. Soon they requested that various articles of the law be changed. Congress was opposed. There was a crisis of authority. The Company attempted to obtain the support of the chiefs of the army, at that time autonomous. The civilian government was not intimidated. Labor disturbances, based on the new law, occurred. The government supported the workers, disregarding the military. Finally, Boston gave the order for the Company to accept the Labor Code.*[20]

The United Fruit Company did indeed comply with the new labor legislation, but it soon began to suffer numerous costly strikes. One of the first began in Bananera in October 1946, even before the new Labor Code was enacted. Among other things, the workers demanded higher wages, better housing and the "removal of two high employees of the Company who are of American nationality and who treat the workers very badly."[21] Lasting approximately six weeks, the strike was finally settled after President Arévalo personally intervened, with the workers having achieved few of their demands.

A far more damaging strike, enduring nearly six months, took place in 1948-1949 when approximately 2,000 UFCO-employed stevedores in Puerto Barrios called a work stoppage. Unable to export its bananas, the Company ceased operations in both Bananera and Tiquisate. After the labor courts found substantially against UFCO, all workers earning less than the equivalent of $90 a month received a wage increase of 10 percent, and the stevedores won wage increases of 5 *centavos* (the equivalent of 5 cents) per hour, in exchange for an agreement to load at least 2,900 stems of bananas per hour.[22]

U.S.-GUATEMALA RELATIONS DETERIORATE

By 1950, with the Communists in control of China and Soviet containment a growing concern for the Truman administration, the Cold War was at its most frigid stage. Domestically, Senator Joseph D. McCarthy was receiving increasing publicity for his Communist witch hunting within the U.S. government and elsewhere in society. Moreover, as historian Cole Blasier comments,

> *in attempting to mobilize U.S. resources behind the Marshall Plan and containment, the Truman administration focused public attention on the threat of communism to western democracies and to world peace. Fears of Soviet expansionism and of the international Communist movement were confirmed by the Korean War. As a result, such fears continued to be a major concern for many U.S. citizens in the 1950s and early 1960s.*[23]

Against this background, the State Department and the U.S. Congress were becoming increasingly preoccupied by events in Guatemala. Much of the alarm, particularly among Congressmen, was being generated by a growing number of articles that were being published about Guatemala by such prestigious newspapers as the New York *Times* and the now-defunct New York *Herald Tribune*. After *The Nation* published an article in March 1950, reporting the growing strength of Communists in Guatemala, Edward Bernays, United Fruit's "spin doctor," persuaded Zemurray that it was in the United Fruit Company's interest to give the story wide dissemination. Thus, copies of the article were sent to 100,000 key opinion makers throughout the United States. In early 1951, after Iran nationalized British properties, Bernays warned Zemurray that "Guatemala might follow suit." With Zemurray's concurrence, Bernays was thus able to convince several important publications of the need for more reporting on Guatemala.

As a result, an increasing number of articles about Guatemala soon began to appear in such influential magazines as *Time, Newsweek*, the *Atlantic Monthly, U.S. News and World Report*, and the Spanish-language *Visión*.[24] The high visibility being given to Guatemala by the U.S. media pleased Bernays, who "kept emphasizing to the Company the need for continued exposure about events in Guatemala. I had the feeling that Guatemala might respond to pitiless publicity in this country," he later wrote.[25]

Nor did UFCO's adroit public relations counselor overlook the importance of keeping the U.S. Congress informed on what was taking place in Guatemala. As one scholar observes,

> *the United Fruit Company was remarkably successful in conveying its side of the story in the Congress. In 1949 and 1950 leading representatives . . . spoke from the floor opposing discrimination against the United Fruit Company . . . Senator Lodge reported that he was informed that the actions against the Company in Guatemala "can be traced directly to Communist influences." The congressional spokesmen against Guatemala came from both political parties and from conservatives and liberals.*[26]

Although Washington was troubled by the difficulties the United Fruit Company was encountering with Arévalo's Labor Code, it was also displeased that several American businesses — particularly lumber and oil interests hoping to tap into the vast resources of Guatemala's northernmost department — had not been welcomed by the government. Another irritation was Guatemala's independent stance at hemispheric meetings, particularly the 1947 Rio conference on inter-American security and another meeting held in Bogotá the following year which dealt with economic issues.[27] At both these conferences the Guatemalan delegation took positions not always in line with Washington's.

No development more dramatically illustrates the disintegrating relations between the United States and Guatemala than the circumstances surrounding the departure of U.S. Ambassador Richard C. Patterson, Jr. Assigned to Guatemala in 1948, the former chairman of the board of Radio Keith Orpheum had also served as U.S. envoy to Yugoslavia, giving him some perspective on the events unfolding in Guatemala. Nevertheless, Patterson, who made American business interests one of his main concerns, soon became highly unpopular with the Arévalo government. Indeed, Luis Cardoza y Aragón described him as a "violent and vulgar" individual who "tried to put his feet on our table."[28] Guillermo Toriello, who served as President Arbenz's ambassador to Washington and later as his foreign minister, asserts that on at least one occasion Patterson bluntly asked Arévalo to dismiss numerous high-ranking Guatemalan functionaries, and that the envoy attempted several times to bribe government officials.[29] Perhaps the most damning indictment came from Arévalo himself, who asserted in a 1951 presidential report to the Congress that Patterson had conspired with Guatemalans "to overthrow the constitutional system . . . Under these circumstances the immediate recall of this man was requested."[30] Although the State Department categorically rejected the charges, Patterson departed Guatemala early in 1949, and no U.S. ambassador was assigned to replace him for the remaining two years of Arévalo's presidency.

The strained relations between the United States and Guatemala had one particular consequence that would subsequently serve as one of the most critical factors in terminating the nation's "ten years of spring." In 1948, in a move Arévalo correctly perceived as hostile, Washington refused Guatemala's request to purchase arms from the U.S. government — a policy which the Department of State maintained for the next six years. Nor did Washington allow other Western nations to sell arms to Guatemala. In his book *Guatemala, la democracia y el imperio*, Arévalo recounts how an arms deal he personally arranged with a representative of a Danish weapons-manufacturing company in 1948 was thwarted by the U.S. government. "It was then that we began to sense that an official North American sentence weighed upon us," he recalled. "It seems that our crime consisted of having enacted the Labor Code."[31]

ARANA'S MURDER: IMMEDIATE AND LONG-TERM IMPLICATIONS

While the rift with Washington was widening, Arévalo's domestic support was also beginning to splinter. According to Galich, the Labor Code caused a deep rupture in the country, serving as the "meridional line which separated the left from the right" and caused "confrontations, first with words and later with violence."[32]

In fact, violence did erupt in July 1949, following the assassination of Colonel Francisco Arana, the Chief of the Armed Forces, who had announced earlier in the year that he would be a candidate for the 1950 presidential elections. By this time, the military and other elements of society had become notably polarized by many of the controversial measures the Arévalo government had enacted. Arana, whose relations with the president were increasingly strained after 1948, when key amendments were attached to the Labor Code, represented more moderate factions in the country.

As the most influential military officer in Guatemala, Arana had the support of several conservative groups and important elements within the military. Leftists in the powerful Partido de Acción Revolucionaria (PAR) determined that the only individual who could defeat Arana at the polls was another well-regarded military officer who was also a hero of the October revolution: Lieutenant Colonel Jacobo Arbenz. Thus, it was clear by the middle of 1949 that the upcoming presidential elections would be decided between Arana and Arbenz.

Even today Arana's death is shrouded in mystery. Arévalo ordered no official investigation of the murder, and his brief public explanation — that conservatives killed Arana — never rang true. It may be, however, that if Arévalo's memoirs are published posthumously, the former president will provide an accurate account of the historic event. (Arévalo died on October 7, 1990, at the age of eighty-six.) Although many Guatemalans still believe Arbenz masterminded the assassination, his version of the murder makes it clear that Arana's death was an accident. In a 1968 interview with an academic in Switzerland (not published until 1974), Arbenz revealed that President Arévalo had ordered him to apprehend Arana after the latter had demanded that the president fire all of his cabinet ministers and replace them with *Aranistas*.

Dispatching several men to seize Arana as he was returning to the capital from the nearby town of Amatitlán, Arbenz watched the attempted capture from a nearby lookout point. The arrest, which took place on a narrow bridge, turned violent, however, when one of Arana's aides apparently drew his pistol. In the resulting shootout, Arana, his aide and one of the individuals in the group attempting to arrest Arana were all instantly killed. Hearing the gunfire, Arbenz assumed Arana was either dead or wounded, and immediately rushed back to the capital to prepare for the uprising that he knew was inevitable.[33]

When news of Arana's violent death reached Guatemala City, it triggered a furious reaction from those military components who supported Arana, causing them to send tanks rumbling into the streets. Arévalo then took a critical step that would have important repercussions five years later: he ordered army elements loyal to him to provide arms to approximately 2,000 of his civilian supporters — mostly union members and students — who had assembled in front of the National Palace.[34] During the next two days, in which approximately 150 persons were killed, organized labor took an active part in the fierce street battles that swept the capital. In fact, the workers were a critical element in putting down the insurrection.

After the bloody revolt had been squelched, several factors became clear — and they would have notable consequences for the future of the revolution. First, it was more apparent than ever before that there were deep divisions within the armed forces. These divergences were exacerbated by what one Guatemalan historian has termed "an historic error": Arévalo's decision not to court-martial or in any way punish those *Aranista* officers who had risen up against his own government.[35] Moreover, Carlos Manuel Pellecer, a Communist who held a second-echelon position in the Arévalo administration, contends that the president's "strange procedure" displeased many loyal military officers.[36] Thus, while Arana was no longer on the scene, his followers were, and, in fact, his death acted as a catalyst for what one Guatemalan scholar contends was "the beginning of semi-clandestine activities of those who, in conjunction with the church, internally would ally themselves with the old liberal *Ubiquistas* to form a subversive opposition against the democratic regime." [37]

As Dr. Arévalo concluded his period of office, it was obvious that his stewardship of the October revolution had brought about sweeping changes, but there were at least four critical aspects of Guatemala's history that had not been altered. The military was still the key actor on the national scene, with the ability to come to the rescue of a stricken president only if it so chose; the highly inequitable land tenure system had not been touched; and no effort had been made to institute a personal income tax that would have contributed to a more just distribution of the nation's wealth. Finally, a majority of the population, the rural workers and the Indian communities, had not been effectively incorporated into the structure of government. Undeniably, many of the country's agricultural laborers had been positively affected by measures legislated by Arévalo, but they were not represented in the government and did not feel that they were a part of or played a role in "the new Guatemala." It was still a revolution directed by the urban middle class: government emanating from the top down, with no initiatives welling up from the grass-roots.

Furthermore, the Arévalo government undertook too many piecemeal projects too quickly, often resulting in programs that were underfunded and poorly implemented. No detailed studies of Guatemala's essential needs were undertaken, and no comprehensive intra-governmental plan was devised to address the country's development needs. Indeed, each problem which arose was met by the creation of a new department, bureau, agency or private entity, with little centralized coordination evolving among the new organizations. The chaotic situation was compounded by Guatemala's acute lack of trained technicians and administrators. Nor did the country possess the financial resources to fulfill all of the ambitious programs that were attempted.[38]

Ultimately, the most transcendental aspect of Arévalo's six-year presidency helps to explain why Guatemalan Communists assumed increasing influence during President Arbenz's abbreviated term of office. As U.S. historian Ronald M. Schneider observes, "Arévalo opened the doors of Guatemala to Communists and pro-Communist exiles while looking with favor upon their efforts to organize the workers." [39] Schneider, who has written the most detailed study of communism in Guatemala, contends that President Arévalo tolerated Communists as individuals, but was opposed to the formation of an organized Communist Party. In fact, he banned the Communist Party and, early in his administration, deported Communist leaders for illegal activities. But the assassination of Colonel Arana, the strongest anti-Communist in Arévalo's cabinet, made the president increasingly dependent on Arbenz and the left in his final two years in office.

Regardless of whether Arévalo was simply indifferent to the growing strength of the Communists or was acting with expediency, his policies helped the Communists to solidify their influence within the next government. "While their influence in his own administration never became dominant, the end result of Arévalo's tolerance toward the Communists was that they were in a position to strike a more advantageous bargain with his successor," Schneider concludes.[40] And, in fact, the small nucleus of labor leaders and intellectuals that operated clandestinely during the Arévalo government eventually blossomed into a well-organized national party, with a membership possibly as high as 6,000.[41]

Indeed, a significant number of Communists, appointed to key government positions by President Arbenz or other high-ranking officials in his administration, would give the revolution dynamic new directions, implementing policies that would bring the Arbenz government into direct confrontation with the United Fruit Company and, finally, with the U.S. government.

"AN AGRARIAN REFORM IS OF CAPITAL IMPORTANCE"

Our government plans to begin the economic development of Guatemala guided by the following three fundamental objectives: to convert our country from a dependent nation with a semi-colonial economy into a country that is economically independent; to convert Guatemala, a backward country with a predominantly feudal economy, into a modern, capitalistic country . . . An agrarian reform is of capital importance in our program, and will require liquidating latifundos [large estates] and introducing fundamental changes in the primitive methods of work; that is, there will be a better distribution of uncultivated land or that land where feudal customs are practiced.[42]

With those ringing words uttered at his inauguration on March 15, 1951, President Jacobo Arbenz left little doubt as to the direction his presidency would take.[43] Having won the November 1950 elections with 68 percent of the vote, Arbenz apparently possessed a strong mandate for the actions he planned to implement. The elections were not entirely free, however, since a government arrest order forced one of Arbenz's opponents to seek exile in El Salvador four months before the national balloting. The other candidate, fearing for his life, went into hiding shortly before the elections. Nevertheless, Torres Rivas points out that six years earlier, Arévalo had polled 86 percent of the total vote. Attributing declining support for the revolution to "various years of democratic gymnastics which had wearied the small civic tolerance of the agrarian bourgeoisie, landholders and financiers, and had begun to weaken the progressive will of the petit bourgeois," Torres Rivas believes "the 'unity of the Guatemalan family' . . . had been destroyed forever."[44]

Guatemala's new president — at thirty-seven, the youngest chief executive in Latin America — was far different from the genial, charismatic academic who he succeeded. "Mysterious, cold and introverted," Arbenz both appeared and, in many ways, acted more Anglo-Saxon than Latin.[45] His light-colored eyes and fair skin were inherited from his father, a Swiss-German pharmacist who had married a middle-class Guatemalan woman after immigrating in 1901 to Quetzaltenango, the country's second largest city. After Jacobo's father became addicted to morphine, his pharmaceutical business went bankrupt, forcing the family to move to a small farm which a charitable German friend put at their disposal. Unable to afford the costs of attending San Carlos University, Arbenz applied for admission to the Escuela Politécnica, Guatemala's renowned national military academy. After passing the school's entrance examinations, the young man was admitted to the academy in 1932.[46]

A brilliant student and fine athlete, Arbenz graduated in 1935 with the highest scholastic record in the Politécnica's history. As a result, he was soon asked to join the academy's faculty, where he taught such diverse subjects as universal history, military communications, physics, geometry and the mechanics and art of warfare. In 1943, Arbenz was promoted to the rank of captain, but resigned from the army (the only Guatemalan officer to do so) in July 1944 in protest against the Ponce government's excesses.

If Guatemala's West Point played an instrumental role in helping to prepare Arbenz for his nation's highest office, there is little question that his wife, María Cristina Vilanova, was singularly influential in shaping the future president's political ideology. The daughter of a Guatemalan woman and a wealthy Salvadoran coffee and sugar cane *finquero*,

In this 1927 photograph, a surveyor, accompanied by two assistants, squints through a transit as part of the initial engineering required in transforming thousands of swamp-filled acres into north coast banana plantations. In the background is the virtually impenetrable jungle which once covered both coasts. (Courtesy of BANDEGUA.)

A steam-powered dragline scoops mud out of a deep ditch, one of hundreds of canals that the United Fruit Company excavated early in this century in order to drain the water-logged areas skirting the Motagua River. (Courtesy of BANDEGUA.)

In the 1920s, when this photograph was taken, the United Fruit Company housed its north coast farm laborers in well-constructed, four-unit barracks that provided each worker with one room. Although lacking electricity or indoor plumbing, the dwellings were far superior to the palm-thatched, dirt-floor huts furnished to those Guatemalans who worked on the nation's coffee plantations. (Courtesy of BANDEGUA.)

Located many miles from the division headquarters at Bananera, the houses UFCO offered its farm overseers were rustic cottages that provided little compensation for the tedium, hard work and oven-like heat that prevailed throughout the year. (Courtesy of BANDEGUA.)

These clapboard houses, photographed in the late 1920s, were among the first constructed in Bananera. Like most of UFCO's isthmian dwellings, the structures were perched on cement stilts, thus keeping the buildings off the marshy ground and helping to capture prevailing breezes. (Courtesy of BANDEGUA.)

Inaugurated in 1913, an early photograph of the United Fruit Company's hospital at Quiriguá depicts the imposing structure that once accommodated one of the best-staffed and well-equipped medical facilities in Central America. (Courtesy of Nancy Taillon Schaper.)

Dr. Neil P. Macphail joined the United Fruit Company hospital at Dartmouth in 1908 and oversaw construction of the Quiriguá facility.

The seventy-five acres surrounding the archaeological park at Quiriguá were preserved early in this century by UFCO's Victor M. Cutter, then-manager of the Virginia division. As it has been for decades, the pre-Columbian site is completely encircled by hundreds of acres of banana plantations. In the background is the Motagua River. (Photo: Raúl Monzón.)

In 1917, the nose of Quiriguá's Stela E cracked and fell off the largest stela ever crafted by the Maya. Kept in an office safe at the United Fruit Company's Quiriguá banana farm, the nose was cemented back onto the giant face seventeen years later when archaeologists from the Carnegie Institution of Washington began restoring the vanquished city. (Photo: David A. Porter.)

Typical of the single-family houses that the United Fruit Company provided employees living within the Tiquisate and Bananera compounds, the homes were hardly the "palatial mansions" described by some critics. The cemented area under this well-maintained Bananera house has been enclosed by a wooden lattice, providing the occupants with additional privacy and space. (Photo: Raúl Monzón.)

Encased in plastic bags, freshly harvested stems of bananas are hung on aerial tramways and pushed by a tractor-like machine into one of BANDEGUA's many packing stations. (Photo: Raúl Monzón.)

Forty pounds of "branded" bananas are quickly and expertly accommodated into cardboard boxes at a BANDEGUA packing station near Bananera. Approximately 80 percent of the workers in these facilities are women. (Photo: Raúl Monzón.)

1944 photo of the members of the victorious revolutionary triumvirate: Jacobo Arbenz (far left), Guillermo Toriello and Colonel Francisco Javier Arana. (Photo: Colección Fototeca Guatemala, CIRMA.)

President Jacobo Arbenz (lower center) surrounded by a throng of supporters as he heads to the podium to give a Labor Day speech. c. 1952. (Photo: Colección Fototeca Guatemala, CIRMA.)

July 4 reception at the U.S. Embassy during the Arbenz administration. Guatemalan President Jacobo Arbenz (right) shares a toast with U.S. Ambassador Rudolf S. Schoenfeld. c. 1952. (Photo: Colección Fototeca Guatemala, CIRMA.)

President Jacobo Arbenz and his wife at a ribbon-cutting ceremony in 1953, to inaugurate a new highway from Palín to Escuintla. (Photo: Colección Fototeca Guatemala, CIRMA.)

Foreign Minister Guillermo Toriello (center left) greeted by President Jacobo Arbenz on Toriello's triumphant return from Venezuela in March 1954. Toriello successfully thwarted a U.S. attempt to invoke the Rio Treaty against Guatemala. Also present is Miguel Angel Asturias (far right.) (Photo: Colección Fototeca Guatemala, CIRMA.)

Anti-communist demonstration in front of the National Palace, c. 1954. One of the placards reads, "Guatemala is not Communist." (Photo: Colección Fototeca Guatemala, CIRMA.)

The Liberation Army of Castillo Armas in front of the church of Santiago de los Caballeros in Esquipulas, 1954. Coincidentally, the revered Black Christ of Esquipulas had been carried throughout Guatemala for a year and a half prior to the Castillo Armas coup, to ward off the threat of Communism. (Photo: Colección Fototeca Guatemala, CIRMA.)

U.S. Ambassador John Peurifoy and Carlos Castillo Armas, 1954. (Photo: Colección Fototeca Guatemala, CIRMA.)

Demonstration of support for the Castillo Armas junta in August 1954, following an attack on Liberation Army forces camped at the Roosevelt Hospital on August 2. (Photos: Colección Fototeca Guatemala, CIRMA.)

Representatives of the Compañía Agrícola de Guatemala showing President Castillo Armas the location of lands that would be returned to Guatemala through new contracts in 1955. Left to right: UFCO officials Clyde DeLawder and Almyr Bump (background), President Castillo Armas and Major Enrique Taracena Oliva. (Photo: Colección Fototeca Guatemala, CIRMA.)

President Carlos Castillo Armas with Vice-President Richard Nixon during Nixon's visit to Guatemala in February 1955. (Photo: Colección Fototeca Guatemala, CIRMA.)

Guatemalan President Castillo Armas met with U.S. President Eisenhower during a visit to Washington. (Photo: Colección Fototeca Guatemala, CIRMA.)

Vilanova, who was Salvadoran, met Arbenz in 1938 while on a visit to Guatemala. The following year, when Lieutenant Arbenz was earning the equivalent of $90 a month, the couple was married — much to the consternation of Vilanova's family and other Salvadoran elite. Nor were Arbenz and his upper-class wife welcomed by Guatemala's high society. The social rejection that the young couple experienced may have confirmed Señora de Arbenz's growing conviction that Guatemala required a more egalitarian society. In was, therefore, perhaps not surprising that she became an increasingly avid student of Marxism — with a growing interest in local politics. In fact, while her husband was Arévalo's Minister of Defense, Señora de Arbenz became known as the hostess of a leftist salon that attracted numerous prominent Guatemalan Marxists as well as several Latin American Communists resident in the country.[47]

Arbenz's inaugural promise to convert Guatemala into an economically independent country included a four-pronged program designed to break the monopolies that U.S. concerns held on the nation's transportation system, its major Atlantic port and most of the country's electrical system, owned by a subsidiary of Electric Bond and Share. The fourth and boldest aspect of Arbenz's six-year plan was a comprehensive agrarian reform program which would expropriate thousands of acres of fallow land and distribute the holdings to small farmers. According to Handy, much of Arbenz's programs was based on the 1951 report prepared by the International Bank of Reconstruction and Development, elements of which were cited in *Chapter 3*. Regardless of where he sought his inspiration, President Arbenz devised a national program that one Guatemalan scholar has described as "the first in the history of the country which was conceived by a technically organized plan which included the prioritizing of the public works to be undertaken and the financing to accomplish them."[48]

In order to break the IRCA's monopoly on the nation's transportation system, Arbenz undertook the completion of the highway to the Atlantic. The construction of the port at Santo Tomás de Castilla, which went into operation in 1955, effectively destroyed the monopoly that the railroad and the United Fruit Company exerted on the wharf at Puerto Barrios. And the building of a government-owned, 28,000 kilowatt hydroelectric plant demolished the hold that the Empresa Eléctrica exercised on that important utility — a company that provided 100 percent of Guatemala City's electrical needs and 80 percent of the entire country's.[49]

Before Arbenz could promulgate the most significant decree of his administration, however, his government became embroiled in one of *La Frutera's* longest and most bitter strikes.[50] Emboldened by previous gains against the Company and urged on by Communist union leaders who were confident that labor courts would usually rule against United Fruit, the workers in both Bananera and Tiquisate struck in August 1951. (Approximately 4,000 of the Company's workers — or 35 percent of the labor force in both divisions — were unionized.)[51]

This time, however, the unions put nearly 200 demands on the table, requesting, among other things, that fired workers be awarded a severance pay equal to the total of their past earnings; that an entire railroad train should be provided for the exclusive use of union organizers; and that the Company should embalm workers killed during on-the-job accidents, "sending the remains, in a presentable casket, free of charge, to a burial site indicated by survivors, while providing free transportation for the survivors to the site of interment, and assuming the costs of all additional funeral expenses."[52]

In sum, the unions demanded that the Company could not dismiss any worker without proof that there was a cause for his dismissal; that it could not decrease the number of workers it currently employed; nor could it change any working conditions without the previous agreement of the laborers. Finally, the *sindicatos* insisted on an increase in daily minimum wages from the equivalent of $1.36 to $2.50.

While the demands were being negotiated, the strikers agreed to return to work. But in September a hurricane, packing winds of sixty-five miles per hour, roared through the Compañía Agrícola's enormous Tiquisate plantations, flattening 95 percent of its banana plants. The ongoing labor dispute, combined with the ruinous blowdown, caused the Company to suspend all its Pacific coast operations, laying off approximately 4,000 of its more than 7,000 laborers. In an effort to break the deadlock, Zemurray dispatched Walter Turnbull, one of his most trusted lieutenants, to Guatemala in October 1951.

According to Arbenz, who discussed Turnbull's visit in his message to Congress the following March, the UFCO executive sought a three-year extension of its current labor contract, and wanted a promise from Arbenz that United Fruit's taxes would not be raised. Arbenz advised Turnbull that the Company's current labor contract could be extended only if it agreed to respect Guatemala's constitution and, presumably, the Labor Code and other laws relating to workers.

Arbenz then took the occasion to make several demands of his own. He informed the banana executive that the wharf at Puerto Barrios needed improvements; that all previous exemptions granted the Company by former governments would be revised; that there would be government control of the contracts United Fruit executed with independent banana growers; and that IRCA freight rates should be reduced. In a final show of bravura, Arbenz also insisted that UFCO should pay the government for the "exhaustion" of Guatemala's soil.[53]

With the Compañía Agrícola arguing that it could not reinstate its laid-off workers until the wage dispute had been settled, the *sindicato* demanded that the idled workers should be provided their regular wages, regardless of the layoff. In January 1952, a labor court ruled in favor of the workers, ordering the Company to pay the equivalent of $650,000 in back wages. A month later, when the Compañía Agrícola had not complied with the court order, the government announced it would auction off approximately 20,000 acres of the Company's south coast holdings in order to satisfy the union's claims. It is curious that the court equated 21,600 acres of the Company's land with $650,000, or about $30 an acre. Yet, in 1953, after the Arbenz government expropriated more than ten times that amount of land, it offered the Compañía Agrícola considerably less: only $594,572, or about $2.50 an acre.

Although Communist elements in the *sindicato* undoubtedly wanted to see the Company driven out of Guatemala, a growing number of union leaders began to realize the Compañía Agrícola might indeed abandon its Tiquisate operations. By working to convince the rank-and-file of this imminent possibility, the non-Communist leaders were able to persuade a majority of workers that it was in their interest to have the judgement against the Company dropped. Thus, the court order was rescinded and the auction was cancelled. By March, the dispute had been settled: the Compañía Agrícola agreed to pay the equivalent of $650,000 in back pay, while the workers accepted their previous wage levels for a three-year period.[54]

GUATEMALA'S MOST HISTORIC LAW IS PROMULGATED

With Decree 900, the Agrarian Reform Law, issued on June 17, 1952, Cardoza y Aragón maintains that "President Arbenz touched a high tension wire: feudalism and imperialism."[55] The urgent need for a more equitable distribution of Guatemala's arable lands had been clearly revealed in a comprehensive survey undertaken in 1950. It demonstrated that more than 57 percent of the country's rural inhabitants possessed no land whatsoever; 76 percent of those who did own land, held only 10 percent of the tillable land; while 2.2 percent of the population owned 70 percent of the arable land.[56] The United Fruit Company and the Compañía Agrícola, which owned or rented approximately 550,000 acres, were, without a doubt, the largest landholders in the nation, with thousands of acres laying fallow.

It should be noted that several authors have grossly exaggerated the amount of land owned by the United Fruit Company and its Pacific coast subsidiary. For example, Blanche Wiesen Cook asserts in *The Declassified Eisenhower, a Divided Legacy*, that "Ubico extended the UFCO's interests so that it controlled 42 percent of Guatemala's lands." Paraphrasing the same incorrect statement, Walter LaFeber's *Inevitable Revolutions, The United States in Central America* declares that "UFCO had bribed dictators until it owned 42 percent of the nation's land."[57] Were these allegations correct, the Company would have owned a preposterous 11.2 million acres. No doubt Handy's error is typographical; nevertheless, he maintains that the United Fruit Company controlled "over 550 million acres of land;" that is, approximately twenty times the size of Guatemala.[58] Actually, the 550,000 acres that the Company leased or owned represented only 1 percent of the 3.6 million acres that constituted the nation's total crop lands.[59]

The Agrarian Reform Law, undoubtedly the most notable law ever enacted in Guatemala, established that uncultivated land would be expropriated from all *fincas* larger than 672 acres. Farms ranging from 224 to 672 acres would not be affected if less than two-thirds of the land was under cultivation. Holdings smaller than 224 acres were exempt from the law. Owners whose properties were expropriated were to be compensated by interest-bearing government bonds, with the largest landholders being paid at the annual rate of 3 percent over a twenty-five year period.

The new law also hit upon an inexpensive method of indemnifying the owners whose lands were expropriated: the bonds to be issued would be based on the value each owner had declared that his farm was worth — as it appeared in the government's Register of Immovable Property on May 9, 1952. And because Guatemalan *finqueros* had always substantially undervalued their properties for tax purposes, the Arbenz government was able to expropriate thousands of acres of farm land for infinitesimal amounts.

Within six months of its enactment, the Agrarian Reform Law was first implemented on January 5, 1953, when 2,657 acres were expropriated from a large coffee farmer.[60] A month earlier, however, the local agrarian committee in Tiquisate had advised the national agrarian department (Departamento Agrario Nacional or DAN) in Guatemala City that the Compañía Agrícola possessed approximately 549,000 acres (5,000 *caballerías*) of land that were not cultivated and therefore susceptible to expropriation. The DAN then authorized the Tiquisate agrarian committee to undertake a "visual inspection" of the Company's properties, and its members soon confirmed the earlier denouncement.[61] As a result, in early December, the DAN's departmental offices in the town of Escuintla informed Almyr L. Bump, manager of the Tiquisate division, that he had five days in which to "defend himself."

Bump and his Guatemalan attorneys thus began three months of prodigious, but ultimately futile, efforts to avoid a massive expropriation of the Company's south coast properties. They pointed out, for example, that the Tiquisate agrarian committee had vastly exaggerated the size of the Compañía Agrícola's holdings, asserting that instead of 549,000 acres, the Company actually owned 296,460 acres (2,700 *caballerías*). Moreover, as the law required, *La Frutera* made available 1.7 acres of land to each of its approximately 8,000 laborers for their individual use. Therefore, nearly 14,000 acres of Compañía Agrícola land were being cultivated by its own workers. Bump also documented that approximately 100,000 acres were leased to six individuals, most of whom used the land to graze cattle.

The Compañía Agrícola further contended that it was imperative to retain extensive reserve acreage in order to establish new banana plantations to replace farms that became infected by Panama disease.[62] "If the lands destined to replace infected plantations are expropriated, the Company will be obliged to liquidate its operations," Bump argued.[63] In fact, by 1953 the Compañía Agrícola had abandoned over 7,000 acres — approximately 27 percent of its banana plantings — because of Panama disease. Of major concern, however, was the indemnification that the government would pay United Fruit for the 401,849 acres it eventually expropriated on both the Pacific and Atlantic coasts.

Indeed, this subject would become the most contentious issue involving the lands seized from the Tiquisate and Bananera divisions. But few historians have fully detailed the background of the compensation the Arbenz government offered UFCO, thereby failing to explain United Fruit's rationale for its subsequent actions. When dealing with this aspect of the properties expropriated from *La Frutera*, authors fashion comments similar to those found in Stephen Schlesinger and Stephen Kinzer's book, *Bitter Fruit*, one of the most comprehensive accounts of the U.S. government's role in the overthrow of President Arbenz. "United Fruit, like other large landowners," the authors state, "had historically undervalued its property in official declarations in order to reduce its already insignificant tax liability. But now that the declared value was being used to determine compensation, the Company howled in protest."[64]

The Company did indeed protest to the U.S. Department of State after President Arbenz signed a resolution on March 5, 1953, which expropriated 233,973 acres of the Compañía Agrícola's holdings, indemnifying the Company with agrarian bonds worth the equivalent of $594,572.[65] (UFCO's south coast subsidiary was thus left with 62,487 acres.) No author has pointed out, however, that the compensation of $2.54 an acre was based not on the Company's self-declared value of its holdings, but on a tax value fixed by the

Guatemalan government in 1935.

As the State Department noted in an aide-memoire it presented to the Guatemalan ambassador in August 1953,

> *the expropriated lands were purchased from 1928 to 1930. At the time of purchase, the properties were undeveloped and were assessed according to declarations made by the Company's predecessor . . . Although the law authorized the government to rectify the tax values every five years, nothing had been done since 1921 to raise these values. In 1935 the government of Guatemala itself fixed the tax values of the Company's properties.*[66]

Furthermore, the United Fruit Company's many critics have given little attention to the fact that during the previous eight years the Compañía Agrícola had been vainly attempting to increase the declared value of its land. As Bump pointed out in numerous briefs, including a final appeal to President Arbenz on February 26, 1953, the Compañía Agrícola had promptly conformed to a May 1945 government decree which ordered all landholders to "immediately rectify" the value of their properties. Thus, in September 1945 the Company presented documents to authorities in the municipality of Tiquisate which reassessed the value of its Pacific coast holdings at the equivalent of $15 million. The documents, which were presumably sent to the departmental capital of Escuintla, were, however, apparently "lost." As a result, on April 22, 1949, the Company hand-delivered copies of the original documents to the General Directorate of Revenues in Guatemala City.

Since the Guatemalan government required that at least three appraisers physically verify the properties that were being reassessed, the Company subsequently requested the implementation of this procedure, only to be advised that such action would take place when the Directorate of Revenues was able to send inspectors to the Tiquisate area. Nevertheless, if the Compañía Agrícola were willing to pay transportation and per diem for the three inspectors, Bump was informed, the experts could be dispatched sooner. On July 1, 1949, the Company formally agreed to pay these expenses. But it was not until almost two years later, in May 1951 — after repeated requests by the Compañía Agrícola —

that the three appraisers finally arrived in Tiquisate. Two years later, Bump pointed out in one of his innumerable briefs that while the experts completed their work within a few weeks, "the Treasury authorities have refused to rectify the register of the Company's properties in order to adjust them to the assessments undertaken by their own employees."

Not surprisingly, on the Atlantic coast, George D. Munch, manager of the Bananera division, was encountering similar delays in having the value of United Fruit's properties increased to the equivalent of $3.4 million. In early 1949, when he sent a letter to officials in Puerto Barrios enquiring whether the documents he had submitted the previous November had been forwarded to Guatemala City, Munch was advised that the papers had not been sent because "we are waiting for the Office of the Revision of Property Registration to request them." As occurred in Tiquisate, there was also a long delay in sending government appraisers to Bananera. The experts were finally sent only after United Fruit offered to pay their transportation and per diem. Similar to what was occurring with UFCO's Pacific coast operations, the government also failed to increase the value of the Bananera properties. Thus, in February 1954 when the Arbenz administration expropriated 172,532 acres of UFCO's north coast land, the Company was offered the equivalent of only $557,543 in twenty-five year bonds. (The Bananera division was left with approximately 75,000 acres.)

The United Fruit Company's extensive efforts to have their properties revalued effectively ended in August 1952, when Lazarus S. Greenberg, an assistant to UFCO's general manager in Guatemala City, formally requested the government's permission to examine the new property assessments for the Tiquisate and Bananera divisions. The Director General of Income subsequently informed Greenberg that the documents concerning the Company's holdings were in the process of being annulled because of "errors and technical and legal defects." The letter also stated that because the information had not been formally recorded, the files were considered confidential and could not be consulted.

Guatemala's bureaucracy, like most, is notoriously slow and inept. It is difficult to believe, however, that the United Fruit Company's eight-year efforts to revalue its Pacific and Atlantic coast properties were due entirely to bureaucratic inefficiencies. Nor would President Arbenz take into account that his own administration and that of his predecessor had been extraordinarily inefficient in implementing the 1945 decree which ordered all property holders to "immediately rectify" the values of their lands. In his February 28, 1953, response to Bump's final appeal against the proposed expropriation of Compañía Agrícola lands, Arbenz states with some ingenuity

> the fact that the Company began taking measures in 1948 [sic] to rectify the value of its properties does not necessarily imply that the agrarian authorities need to take this point into consideration . . . since the law is extremely clear that indemnifications will be paid in accordance with the fiscal declarations [each landholder's self-declared assessment of the worth of his property] as they existed on May 9, 1952.[67]

Since Decree 900 made the president of the republic — hardly an admirer of the United Fruit Company — the last resort for appeals concerning expropriated lands, the appeals process was clearly prejudiced. Ultimately, by vesting final authority in the president, the Agrarian Reform Law by-passed Guatemala's legal system and, in effect, put the president above the 1945 constitution. That Arbenz was intent upon maintaining his position as the ultimate arbiter of Decree 900 was clearly apparent early in the life of the new law.

In January 1952, after a Guatemalan *finquero*, whose land had been expropriated, appealed the action to the Supreme Court, that body issued an injunction restraining the government from expropriating the property. Arbenz immediately requested Congress to rule on the validity of the high court's action. Not surprisingly, the Legislative Assembly, where Arbenz supporters outnumbered his opponents, censured the Supreme Court's ruling and summarily impeached four of the court's five justices, including the President or Chief Justice, Arturo Herbruger Asturias.

In an interview published in a Guatemala City daily in 1990, Herbruger affirmed

> *Arbenz fired me as president of the Supreme Court because I did not*

accept his point of view, and I maintained that the constitution of the republic should be respected. It all revolved around Decree 900, the Agrarian Reform Law, which was unconstitutional in that it denied the right of appeal against agrarian resolutions. The constitution established the right of appeal against any kind of government action.

Herbruger, then seventy-eight, concluded his comments with an arresting observation: "if the Agrarian Reform Law had been subjected to a legal process of review, it would have functioned with effective justice, avoiding the armed movement of 1954, which overturned both the Arbenz regime and the October 20, 1944, revolution." [68]

As the following chapter details, however, it is clear that Arbenz's expropriation of *La Frutera's* south and north coast holdings did not precipitate the U.S. government's actions against Guatemala's president. While the United Fruit Company had been successful in alerting Washington and the U.S. media about the directions of the Arbenz administration, President Eisenhower's firm conviction that Guatemala represented the Soviet Union's first proxy in Latin America was, in fact, the overriding factor behind the CIA's plot to overthrow Jacobo Arbenz.

DISTRIBUTION OF GUATEMALA'S CROP LANDS (1960)

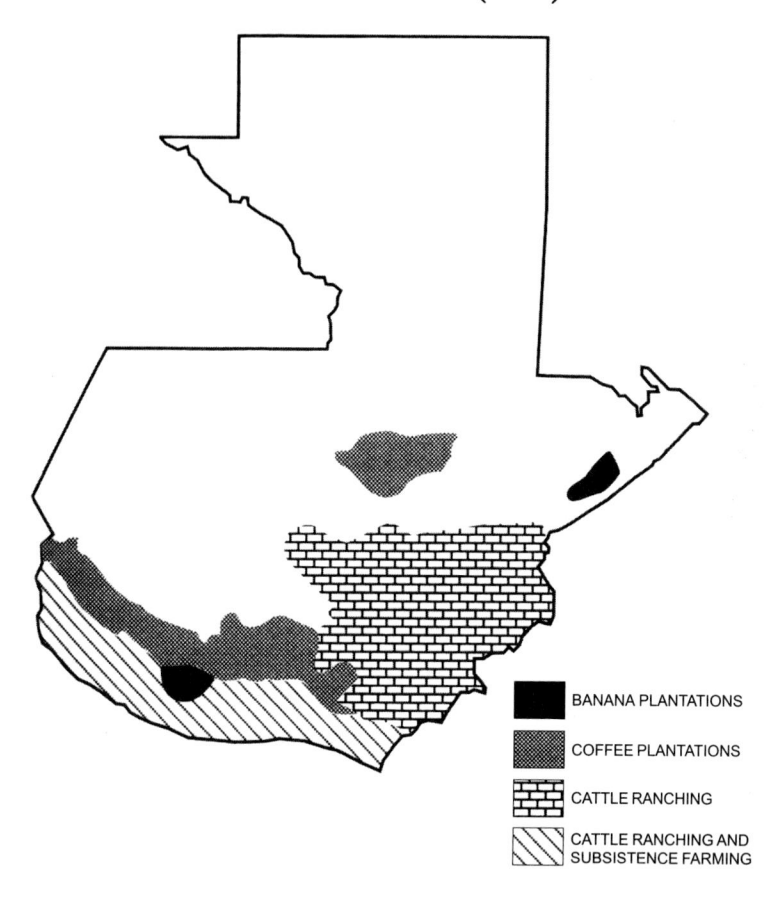

■ BANANA PLANTATIONS
▓ COFFEE PLANTATIONS
▦ CATTLE RANCHING
▧ CATTLE RANCHING AND SUBSISTENCE FARMING

Although many of the United Fruit Company's critics have charged that the Company owned vast areas of Guatemala's most productive farm lands, it is apparent that the 550,000 acres of land that the Company leased or owned constituted only a small portion of the nation's total crop lands. In fact, United Fruit's holdings comprised a scant 1 percent of the country's 3.6 million acres dedicated to agriculture. (Much of the area in white consisted of subsistence farming or virgin forests.)

Protecting UFCO's Interests or Excising a Communist Beachhead?

Once Arbenz had signed the decree expropriating the Compañía Agrícola's Pacific coast holdings, the Company refused to accept the Guatemalan government's agrarian bonds and, instead, requested Washington's intercession.[1] Believing that "it was dealing not with misguided, irresponsible nationalists, but with ruthless agents of international communism," the Eisenhower administration quickly came to UFCO's support.[2] Within three weeks, on March 25, 1953, John Moors Cabot, the Assistant Secretary of State for Inter-American Affairs, handed an aide-memoire to Guillermo Toriello, Guatemala's ambassador to Washington, which advised that the U.S. government did not consider deferred payment in the form of agrarian bonds as constituting prompt and effective compensation for the lands expropriated from the Company. The note also contended that the amount of compensation offered was totally inadequate.

After a three-month delay, Toriello presented the State Department with a memorandum which stressed that the Agrarian Reform Law was an act of "inherent sovereignty;" that the decree was being enforced with no discrimination against foreigners, and that the indemnification to be paid to the United Fruit Company was "entirely just since it was based on the amount which the Company itself had estimated the value of its properties."[3] In a lengthy and sharply worded aide-memoire delivered to Toriello on August 28, 1953, the State Department asserted that

> the obligation of a state imposed by international law to pay just or fair compensation at the time of taking of property of foreigners cannot be abrogated from the international standpoint by local legislation. If the contrary were true, states seeking to avoid the necessity of making payment for property expropriated from foreign nationals could avoid all pecuniary responsibility simply by changing their local laws. Every international obligation could thus be wiped off the books. But international law cannot thus be flouted.

Taking issue with the Guatemalan ambassador's contention that the Agrarian Reform Law was being applied equitably to both foreigners and nationals, Washington noted

> on the basis of data announced by the national agrarian department itself... the total acreage of private land thus far expropriated under the Agrarian Reform Law is some 377,000 acres, against which the total Tiquisate land expropriated is 234,000 acres, or almost two-thirds of the entire amount seized. In addition... the national agrarian council ordered the expropriation of more than 173,000 acres of the United Fruit Company's Atlantic coast plantations... Such a high disproportion raises the very serious question of discrimination, despite assertions to the contrary.

The document also took note of the "studied effort" on the part of Guatemalan officials to refrain from changing the Company's tax evaluations in the tax records, and went on to declare

> the offer of the government of Guatemala to make payment for properties expropriated on the basis of tax value — and that a tax value which Guatemalan officials themselves initially fixed and maintained on the tax records, in spite of the efforts of the Company to have the tax values rectified — represents a mere gesture, certainly not the payment of the just or fair compensation required by international law... Payment in bonds maturing in twenty-five years, with interest at 3 per-

cent per annum, and of uncertain market value is scarcely to be regarded as either prompt or effective payment.

The diplomatic note concluded by proposing that the issue of just compensation could be directly negotiated by the Guatemalan government and the United Fruit Company, or by the two governments. Failing a negotiated settlement, the aide-memoire advised, the U.S. government would submit "a formal claim [on behalf of the Compañía Agrícola] for compensation as required to be paid under international law." [4] With no response forthcoming to its August note, the United States formally suggested in early February 1954 that the dispute be taken to the Permanent Court of Arbitration at The Hague. Once again, however, a stubborn Arbenz chose not to respond to a State Department initiative.

Six weeks later, the Department of State presented Guatemala's chargé d'affaires in Washington with a formal claim, on behalf of the Compañía Agrícola, for $15,854,849. Predictably, the Guatemalan government responded promptly to Washington's multi-million dollar claim. In a memorandum delivered to the American Embassy in Guatemala City on May 24, 1954, the Ministry of Foreign Relations rejected the "absurd, artificial and unjust" claim of "a Company that has caused so much damage to Guatemala," and charged the Department of State with "frank intervention in the internal affairs of Guatemala." [5]

One month and three days later, on June 27, 1954, moments before he resigned the presidency, Jacobo Arbenz addressed his countrymen in a nation-wide radio broadcast:

The United Fruit Company, in collaboration with the governing circles of the United States, is responsible for what is happening to us ... They have used the pretext of anti-communism. The truth is very different. The truth is to be found in the financial interests of the fruit company and the other U.S. monopolies which have invested great amounts of money in Latin America and fear that the example of Guatemala would be followed by other Latin countries. [6]

Arbenz's final remarks as president have helped to sustain the widely accepted belief that the United States conspired to overthrow Arbenz in order to regain the United Fruit Company's expropriated lands. Even as recently as 1989, in a special issue commemorating the forty-fifth anniversary of the October 20 revolution, de León Aragón told *Crónica* magazine that "to save the revolution, it would have been worth paying the $18 million [sic] that the United Fruit Company sought. If Arbenz had paid that amount, Guatemala would have had a different history."[7]

UFCO MOUNTS AN EFFECTIVE MEDIA CAMPAIGN

Believing that the U.S. government covertly overthrew the Arbenz regime because of the expropriation of more than 400,000 acres of United Fruit's banana plantations is a misleadingly facile explanation that fails to take into account the Cold War myopia that had pervaded Washington, personified by Secretary of State John Foster Dulles's unremitting crusade against communism. Nevertheless, it is abundantly clear that the United Fruit Company cleverly utilized the anti-communism hysteria gripping the United States and that the banana company did everything possible to arouse "pitiless publicity" against the Arbenz government.

Indeed, in January 1952, Bernays assumed an even more aggressive role in his attempts to alert the American public to the events unfolding in Guatemala. Assembling a blue ribbon group of ten American journalists, the newsmen toured Central America, including, of course, Guatemala. "After their return, as I had anticipated," Bernays later wrote, "public interest in the Caribbean skyrocketed in this country."[8] The success of Bernays's first fact-finding tour of Central America led him to repeat the effort at least four more times between early 1952 and the spring of 1954. According to McCann, "the trips were ostensibly to gather information, but what the press would hear and see was carefully staged and regulated by the host. The plan represented a serious attempt to compromise objectivity." At the same time, however, the former UFCO executive admits "it was a compromise that was implicit in the invitation . . . It is difficult to make a convincing case for manipulation of the press when the victims proved so eager for the experience."[9] Nor did UFCO rely entirely on press tours to tell the Guatemala story. In 1953 the Company began publishing a confidential weekly newsletter reporting on economic and political events in Guatemala which was distributed to 250 American journalists.

Ultimately, it can be asked why the U.S. press was so receptive to United Fruit's media blitz and so unanimously hostile to the Arbenz government.[10] Part of the answer can be found in the person of Edward Bernays, who "outmaneuvered, outplanned and outspent the Guatemalans. He was far ahead of them in technique, experience and political contacts."[11] And certainly Washington was not adverse to Bernays's efforts. As Immerman points out, the media campaign conducted by United Fruit's public relations counsel "accomplished for the State Department the propaganda component of its own Guatemalan strategy."[12]

In the final analysis, however, Bernays's efforts would not have prospered had it not been for the Cold War mentality that prevailed throughout the United States in the early 1950s. Americans feared an expansionist Communist monolith, as exemplified by the Korean War, while at home the nation was caught up in McCarthy's savage Red baiting. Bernays's timely propaganda campaign took advantage of these developments, and a receptive media proved itself to be both biased and unprofessional.

It is not difficult to understand why Arbenz and others in his government sincerely believed that a vast U.S. media conspiracy had been mounted against his administration. Nor did the president hold any doubts as to the instigators of the adverse reporting on Guatemala. In fact, in December 1953, Arbenz bluntly told the U.S. ambassador that the United Fruit Company "dominated" the press in the United States.[13] Although the nation's most influential newspapers and news magazines would certainly have scoffed at such an exaggerated charge, it is clear that the United Fruit Company's negative views on Guatemala were conclusively and consistently reflected in much of the U.S. media.

JOHN FOSTER DULLES VS. GUATEMALA

If the printed media was slowly transforming the perception of Guatemala held by those Americans interested in Central America, a far more significant change had occurred in Washington — a change that would eventually cause the forced resignation of President Jacobo

Arbenz. Soon after General Dwight Eisenhower took office in January 1953, he dispatched his brother Milton on a fact-finding trip of Latin America. Upon his return, Milton advised his brother that "Guatemala had succumbed to Communist infiltration." Within six months, Undersecretary of State William S. Smith, who, like Milton Eisenhower, enjoyed the president's complete trust, also warned that "the Guatemalan government has abundantly proved its Communist sympathies." [14]

While Smith and Milton Eisenhower's assessment of events in Guatemala undoubtedly had a profound effect on the president, he was also influenced by Secretary of State John Foster Dulles, one of the most powerful individuals ever to hold that key office. Indeed, as Blasier comments,

> *familiarity with John Foster Dulles's personal and political objectives are essential to understanding the Guatemalan intervention of 1954. Dulles's policies toward Guatemala were in part a religious crusade against atheistic communism, in part an ideological struggle on behalf of free enterprise, and in part a political battle with Soviet expansionism . . . If the liberation of Eastern Europe, which he had called for in the 1952 campaign, was too dangerous to undertake, nearby Guatemala provided him a much safer and more convenient country to "save" from communism . . . This background helps explain why he was deaf to arguments that the Arbenz government was not, in fact, a Communist beachhead in the Americas.*[15]

In actuality, however, Dulles heard little within his own Department that contradicted the idea that the Soviet Union had achieved its first foothold in the Western Hemisphere. Indeed, less than a year before the new secretary of state took office, a secret National Intelligence Estimate bluntly began its analysis of the Guatemalan situation by stating "the political situation in Guatemala adversely affects U.S. interests and constitutes a potential threat to U.S. security." [16] Fourteen months later, in May 1953, another National Intelligence Estimate asserted "the Guatemalan Communists exercise a political influence far out of proportion to their small numerical strength. Their influence will probably continue to grow as long as President Arbenz remains in power." [17] Left unsaid, but implicit, was the fact that the United States could not allow the Guatemalan president to retain power.

By August, a draft policy paper prepared in the State Department's Bureau of Inter-American Affairs spelled out another aspect of Guatemala's presumed threat to U.S. national security: "continuation of the present trend in Guatemala would ultimately endanger the unity of the Western Hemisphere against Soviet aggression, and the security of our strategic position in the Caribbean, including the Panama Canal." [18] In fact, the authors of *Bitter Fruit* maintain that the official decision to move against President Arbenz was taken that same month (August 1953) at a meeting of a small committee within the National Security Council. "Eisenhower gave his approval for the plot against Arbenz after Allen Dulles, the director of the CIA and John Foster's brother, told him that the odds of success were better than 40 percent but less than even." [19]

While the CIA and the State Department began to prepare the covert operation that would culminate in the collapse of the Arbenz government in June 1954, Foster Dulles made several key changes in ambassadorial postings throughout Central America. Obviously, the most critical assignment was the chief of mission in Guatemala, and there John E. Peurifoy replaced the mild-mannered Rudolf E. Schoenfeld, a career diplomat who had been named U.S. ambassador to Guatemala in 1951. Flamboyant and hard-driving, Peurifoy, who had served as ambassador to Greece from 1950-1953, was credited with having "jumped into the Greek political fray and rammed together a right-wing coalition government acceptable to the United States and the royal family in the aftermath of the country's bloody civil war." [20]

Less than two months after his arrival in Guatemala, Peurifoy forwarded a secret cable to the secretary of state which soon found its way to President Eisenhower, convincing him of the urgent need to depose Arbenz.[21] The telegram, dated December 17, 1953, detailed a "frank six hour discussion of the Communist problem here" which the ambassador held with President Arbenz during a dinner the latter hosted for Peurifoy and his wife. What is compelling about the cable is the complete dichotomy of views expressed by both men concerning what was actually occurring in Guatemala. Thus, Peurifoy states that he opened the conversation by telling the president that he was interested in learning how relations between the two countries could be improved. Arbenz replied that the problem

> is one between [the] United Fruit Company and his government. He spoke at length and bitterly on [the] fruit company's history since 1904, complaining especially that now [that] his government has a $70 million budget to meet, [it] collects only $150,000 in taxes [from the United Fruit Company]. I interrupted here to say I thought we should put first things first, that as long as Communists exerted their present influence in [the] Guatemalan government, I did not see real hope of better relations.

Although the discussion lasted until 2 AM, it is apparent that neither Arbenz nor Peurifoy gave an inch — each steadfastly maintaining the position he had espoused when the dialogue was joined. "I said I was sorry he had no concrete proposals to make to improve our relations . . . At one point [the] president stated if there were a choice, it would be for Guatemala to live under Communist domination than [to] live for fifty years with [the] fruit company." The ambassador's telegram ended with a terse sentence that undoubtedly made a strong impression on both Eisenhower and Dulles. "I came away definitely convinced that if [the] president is not a Communist, he will certainly do until one comes along, and that normal approaches will not work in Guatemala." [22]

Curiously, much the same discussion, with the principals reversed, was played out a month later when Ambassador Toriello made a farewell call on President Eisenhower (Toriello was returning to Guatemala to take up the post of Minister of Foreign Relations). In a memorandum of conversation drafted by John Moors Cabot, the Assistant Secretary for Inter-American Affairs, who took notes throughout the meeting, he paraphrases President Eisenhower as saying, "We certainly had the impression that the Guatemalan government was infiltrated with Communists, and we couldn't cooperate with a government which openly favored Communists." Just as Arbenz had maintained when he met with Peurifoy, Ambassador Toriello replied that the real question was not that of Communists in the Guatemalan government, but of the monopolistic position of the United Fruit in the country. He went into his usual discreetly distorted indictment of the United Fruit and insisted that this, and not communism in the government, was the source of the difficulties in relations between the United States and Guatemala. He also brought out two scrapbooks of anti-Guatemalan articles published in the U.S. press."

Eisenhower then told Arbenz's personal representative that while the United States

> *wanted no more than justice for any American companies operating in Guatemala, we would be agreeable to having an international tribunal decide what the rights of the controversy were . . . The ambassador continued to harp on the line that the United Fruit Company, and not the few Guatemalan Communists, were the source of our difficulties in relations . . . He particularly mentioned that Sullivan and Cromwell, the secretary of state's former firm, represented the United Fruit . . . The president made a very able and convincing exposition of our thesis that the issue is communism in the Guatemalan government, not the United Fruit question, and that the latter can be decided by international decision.*[23]

Toriello's version of the meeting — at considerable variance with Cabot's memorandum of conversation — clearly illustrates the depth of misunderstanding between the two governments. In his book *La batalla de Guatemala*, the former ambassador contends that Eisenhower was little informed on the reality of Guatemala.

> *All he knew was 'the Communist danger to the continent' and the 'Red menace' that Guatemala represented. He was very surprised when I described the panorama of our economic subjugation caused by the foreign monopolies and their conspiratorial activities to destroy our democratic government, one phase of which was a gigantic propaganda campaign to try to make us appear as Communists . . . The president must have found my reasoning worthy of consideration because he then proposed that an impartial, mixed commission of Guatemalans and North Americans, designated by our respective governments, should be formed to discuss at the highest levels the problem of the monopolistic compa-*

nies, and all other matters that were causing friction between the two countries. I assured him that in principle I was in complete agreement with his proposal and that I was sure my government would welcome it enthusiastically.[24]

Toriello, however, never explains Arbenz's reaction to Eisenhower's proposal nor why the Guatemalan government failed to pursue this consequential overture.

A U.S. POLICY BASED ON VESTED INTERESTS?

Toriello's remark that John Foster Dulles had been associated for many years with Sullivan and Cromwell, a Wall Street law firm which represented the United Fruit Company, is a point that has been frequently cited by Guatemalan and North American authors as evidence that Dulles held a vested interest in the U.S. government's actions against the Arbenz administration. Typical of these comments is Handy's assertion that "the most important tentacle of *El Pulpo* wound its way directly to the heart of the State Department and the CIA."[25] Such charges are based on the fact that both Foster Dulles and his brother Allen had worked for Sullivan and Cromwell.

Although a number of authors have maintained that Foster Dulles served as legal counsel to the United Fruit Company, Gleijeses categorically rejects the allegation.[26] Moreover, Foster Dulles terminated his long relationship with the law firm in 1949 when New York Governor Thomas Dewey selected him to fill a Senate vacancy.[27] Foster Dulles was, however, responsible for the firm's 1926 hiring of his brother Allen, who remained with Sullivan and Cromwell until the early 1940s. One of the Dulles' biographers also reveals that Allen "saw through a complicated case for the United Fruit Company over leases . . . and became a possessor of a block of shares from a grateful United Fruit Company."[28]

The Dulles brothers' former association with UFCO was only one of many links — some professional and others economic — that connected the United Fruit Company with several high-ranking government officials and influential Washington power brokers. John Moors Cabot's family owned United Fruit stock and his brother Thomas had served briefly during 1948-1949 as president of the Company. Heading the U.S. government's mission at the United Nations was Ambassador Henry Cabot Lodge, who was also a United Fruit stockholder. Robert Cutler, presidential Assistant for National Security Affairs and Eisenhower's liaison to the National Security Council, had previously functioned as board chairman of the United Fruit Company. In addition, Anne Whitman, the wife of Edmund S. Whitman, UFCO's director of public relations, was employed as President Eisenhower's personal secretary. Finally, one of the capital's most influential and well-connected attorneys, Thomas ("the Cork") Corcoran, served as the Company's Washington lobbyist and personal counsel to Sam Zemurray.

That the secretary of state, the director of the CIA, the assistant secretary for inter-American affairs and the U.N. ambassador all had previous professional connections or financial interests in the United Fruit Company proved to be a source of grave misunderstanding within the Guatemalan government. President Arbenz, Ambassador Toriello and other high-level officials were convinced that the Dulles brothers and John Moors Cabot maintained interests in the United Fruit Company which clearly conflicted with their official duties. In a thoughtful analysis of this unusual issue, Blasier points out

> *by the nature of their upbringing, associations and private interests, secretaries Dulles and Cabot would tend to give a sympathetic initial hearing to any presentation of the United Fruit Company's point of view . . . In spite of the foregoing, I believe that the Arbenz government greatly misunderstood Dulles and Cabot and the U.S. government in this respect. The Guatemalan properties of the United Fruit Company represented only a fractional part of the Company's total interests . . . Even if the value of United Fruit stock fell sharply as a result of Arbenz's measures — which was not all that likely — it is most improbable that it would have had any substantial effect on the personal fortune of either Dulles or Cabot . . . No doubt, too, they were wiser than to risk their reputations and the verdict of history on behalf of United Fruit profits.*

Nevertheless, by exaggerating the importance of the United Fruit Company's role in the increasingly tense relations between the two countries, Arbenz either discounted or seriously underestimated official American fears about the "Communist beachhead" being established in Guatemala. Moreover, as Blasier remarks, "U.S. policymakers, convinced of the probity of Dulles and Cabot, were offended by the Guatemalan charges which seemed to them preposterous, thereby making it hard to take the Guatemalans seriously on other issues."[29]

"IF THEY GAVE A GOLD PIECE FOR EVERY BANANA"

By February 1954, "Operation Success," the code name for the CIA plot to overthrow Arbenz, was well underway, with two training camps established in Nicaragua, where approximately 300 Guatemalan exiles and mercenaries from other countries were undergoing weapons training and instructions in sabotage and demolition.[30] After being transferred to a camp within Honduras late in the spring, the men would begin the invasion of Guatemala in mid-June.

A month before the invasion, however, an event occurred that effectively sealed the fate of the Arbenz government: the CIA announced that a shipment of nearly two tons of weapons, which had been purchased by the Guatemalan government from Czechoslovakia, had arrived in Puerto Barrios aboard the Swedish freighter *Alfhem*. Terming the news a "development of gravity," the State Department proposed that the Organization of American States condemn Guatemala, and that all ships bound for that country should be detained and inspected. To Dulles's dismay, however, a straw vote revealed that only eleven Latin American countries would vote for the resolution, less than the two-thirds majority necessary for collective action under the Inter-American Treaty of Reciprocal Assistance, known as the Rio Treaty.

But even if the Latin American nations would not vote to invoke the Rio Treaty, Dulles was undeterred. Five days after the world learned of Guatemala's receipt of Czech arms, the secretary of state made a pretentious ceremony of signing a mutual security treaty with Honduras, similar to an agreement that had recently been signed with Nicaragua. Within a few days, the U.S. also announced it was sending Air

Force Globemaster cargo planes with tons of arms and ammunition to Honduras and Nicaragua. The single-minded secretary of state kept up the pressure on Guatemala by calling a news conference on May 25 which may have been designed to help convince "sister republics" of the need to invoke the Rio Treaty or, more probably, was intended to set the stage for the upcoming invasion. Stressing that Guatemala was the only Latin American country to vote against a U.S.-sponsored, anti-communism resolution adopted two months earlier at an inter-American conference in Caracas, Dulles also pointed out that Guatemala, "the heaviest armed of all the Central American states," was "the only American nation to be the recipient of a massive shipment of arms from behind the Iron Curtain."[31]

Within a week after Dulles's news conference and his vague response to questions concerning whether the Rio Treaty might be invoked against Guatemala, Foreign Minister Toriello sought out Ambassador Peurifoy in a last-minute attempt to reconcile U.S.-Guatemalan differences. Recalling President Eisenhower's January offer of a high-level bi-national commission to mediate disputes between the two countries, Toriello told Peurifoy that Guatemala was now ready to accept the offer. Furthermore, he advised that President Arbenz would like to meet with President Eisenhower in Washington, and that the Guatemalan government was even willing to negotiate with the United Fruit Company concerning compensation for its expropriated holdings.[32] Obviously, this was a very major concession. The fact that Washington did not accept Arbenz's offer to arbitrate the United Fruit Company issue provides the most conclusive evidence that the United States did not intervene in Guatemala in order to rescue the banana company.

In fact, Dulles provided a succinct response to Arbenz's offer a week later when he was asked at a June 8 news conference whether President Eisenhower might meet with the Guatemalan president:

There is a persistent effort by the authorities in Guatemala to present the problem there as primarily a problem between Guatemala and the United States relating to the United Fruit Company. That is a totally false presentation of the situation . . . If the United Fruit matter were settled, if they gave a gold piece for every banana, the problem would remain just as it is today as far as the presence of Communist infiltration in Guatemala is concerned. That is the problem, not the United Fruit Company.[33]

Two days later, in a major speech delivered in Seattle, the secretary of state stressed the same point.

It is alleged that the real concern of the United States in Guatemala is not international communism, but the protection of United States investment... However, let me emphasize this. If the problem of United States investors in Guatemala were to be solved tomorrow to the entire satisfaction of all parties, the attitude of the United States government with respect to the dangers of Communist penetration in this hemisphere — and in Guatemala in particular — would remain precisely the same.[34]

MORE THAN A BARRACKS REVOLT

On June 17, a "liberation army," trained by the CIA and under the command of Carlos Castillo Armas, a Guatemalan army colonel who had been involved in the last coup attempt against President Arévalo, led a force of approximately 250 men from Honduras into eastern Guatemala. There is considerable discrepancy on the number of troops Castillo Armas commanded. The figures range from 250 to approximately 1,500 soldiers, although the former figure is more probably correct. Within ten days, President Arbenz would summarily resign and take asylum in the Mexican Embassy, effectively ending Guatemala's "ten years of spring." How could a ragtag assortment of mercenaries defeat an army of 6,000 men, "the heaviest armed of all the Central American states," which had recently received two tons of Czech weapons and ammunition?

The most obvious reason was that the Guatemalan Army remained virtually neutral in the face of the insignificant forces commanded by Castillo Armas. Although one small battle was fought at Gualán, not far from Quiriguá, the army never seriously engaged the invading troops. During the isolated skirmishes that took place, the Guatemalan Army lost fifteen men; twenty-five were wounded and thirty were taken prisoner. Castillo Armas's liberation movement reported that five of its men had been killed.[35] Cardoza y Aragón maintains that "it was not the Guatemalan Army that betrayed Arbenz, but rather a small group of its most important chiefs, placed in key positions by President Arbenz. The majority of the president's general staff was loyal to its leader." [36]

Torres Rivas notes, however, that the "army of the revolution" was, in fact, only a "bourgeois institution, technically trained and ideologically penetrated by North American forces." [37] Blasier argues that it was a "classic Latin American barracks coup," and not Castillo Armas's puny forces that caused Arbenz's downfall.[38] Immerman sees more profound reasons for the coup.

> *The revolution's leadership attempted to overcome Guatemala's historically inequitable social and economic order. In doing so, the government left untouched the 'feudal' elements who benefited from the historic order. The same families owned the land and the same generals ran the army . . . The internal contradictions of the Guatemalan revolution planted the seeds for its defeat; Castillo Armas and the CIA simply reaped the harvest.*[39]

Ultimately, however, Gleijeses provides the most prosaic and compelling analysis of why the army refused to attack Castillo Armas's minuscule forces. Well aware that the "army of liberation" was backed by the U.S. government, Arbenz's officers were paralyzed by the idea of what might happen to them if they crushed Castillo Armas's invasion. "Fear defeated them. They were terrorized by the idea that the United States was looming behind Castillo Armas," a Guatemalan officer subsequently told the historian. The U.S. Army Attaché assigned to the American Embassy at that time later confirmed this observation. "The Guatemalan officers were definitely afraid of U.S. intervention against Arbenz and with good reason. That fear was the stabilizing influence that kept them from coming to Arbenz's support when the chips were down." They were, in fact, officers who "feared the consequences of victory more than defeat." [40]

Although the dread of facing U.S. ground forces and air power was the determining factor in their abject performance, lesser factors contributed to the high command's actions. Basically conservative and middle class, Guatemala's officers had become increasingly preoccupied by the growing influence that Communists were exerting in key government institutions, particularly in the implementation of the agrarian reform program, often plagued by violence. The fact that article thirty-two of the 1945 constitution prohibited "political organizations of an international or foreign character" also concerned the higher echelons of the military who believed that the legally-inscribed Guatemalan Labor Party, an openly Communist organization, was, in fact, illegal. Some officers were also troubled as to the ultimate destination of the recently acquired Czech arms, especially after union leaders began advocating the need for a well-armed civil militia. In a predominantly Roman Catholic country, the church's intensifying and effective campaign against foreign and atheistic communism may also have exerted some influence on military officers, many of whom still suspected that Arbenz had played a leading role in Colonel Arana's 1949 assassination. Still others may have been concerned by Guatemala's growing diplomatic isolation and the U.S. government's increasingly hostile rhetoric.

If the army could not be counted on — a fact that became increasingly obvious to Arbenz during the last days of his government — then how may one explain the seemingly inexplicable passivity of Arbenz's supporters, and the president's own puzzling failure to rally the masses in an overwhelming show of strength? Presumably, the embattled president could have ordered the 100,000 members of the General Confederation of Guatemalan Workers or the National Peasant Confederation — 150,000 strong — to organize huge demonstrations in his support. Why did Arbenz wait until June 25, only two days before he resigned, to command the army to open its weapons caches to civilians? Moreover, it was a command that the army would not obey.

Several scholars have tried to explain why Arbenz made no attempt to rally union members, *campesinos* and *Arbencista* party members in his own support. Torres Rivas believes that the aloof half-European "forgot the masses" because he "did not have confidence in them; in fact, distrusted them."[41] Similarly, Cardoza y Aragón, who terms Arbenz's resignation as a "crass error of extremely grave historical consequences," maintains that Arbenz's military background caused him to rely too heavily on the armed forces, and that he lacked the politician's basic sense of the power inherent in his constituents.[42] Toriello, too, argues that Arbenz's "indisputable error was his blind confidence in the national army," coupled with his failure to recognize that several of the highest ranking army officers were disloyal to him.[43]

Monteforte Toledo provides perhaps the most succinct analysis of the regime's own failure to forge a comprehensive national program that could have produced a united "people power" explosion after Castillo Armas's forces crossed into Guatemala. He notes, for example, that because of the ideological differences within the country's leadership, the government's "campaign of proselytism and propaganda was not effective in awakening the consciousness of the people to the advantages of the revolution." Moreover, the Communist Party was led by individuals who were "inexperienced, ignorant of the national reality, and overestimated their possibilities in the face of the international situation."[44]

The fact that large numbers of Guatemala's *campesinos* and indigenous peoples did not descend on the capital in support of the stricken president is due to a number of complex factors. Gleijeses maintains that "thousands of peasants might have fought . . . but they had no weapons."[45] Nevertheless, Monteforte Toledo points out that despite the fact that tens of thousands of individuals had received land under Arbenz's Agrarian Reform Law, the government had not given the "mass of the Indian population the in-depth attention which it deserved." As a result, a majority of the indigenous peoples, most of whose lives had not improved significantly as a result of the October revolution, felt little or no motivation to come to its rescue. Monteforte Toledo also maintains that because the controversial Agrarian Reform Decree did not, in fact, "develop capitalistic production, nor foment a rational distribution and ownership of the land," a majority of the peasants did not give the law their real support."[46] If Monteforte Toledo is correct, it would follow that the *campesinos* did not give the law's principal champion its undivided support either.

Perhaps more important, however, was the long tradition among the country's poorest citizens — particularly the Indians — of taking little or no part in the struggles for national power sharing. Instead, as they had done for centuries, they simply sat back impassively and waited for the outcome of the invasion to be announced from the capital. It should also be noted, however, that neither did thousands of Guatemalans rush to join Castillo Armas's "army of liberation." Ultimately, the phenomenon that had bedeviled the revolution's leadership from its inception — the absence of grass-roots forces within the structure of government — finally manifested itself in Arbenz's hour of need.

While Decree 900 permitted local agrarian committees to denounce landholders whose properties were not being effectively utilized, Cardoza y Aragón points out that the agrarian movement did not

> *rely on a direct, strong representative of the campesinos, of the plundered Indian: an Emiliano Zapata and his undying, very just slogan of 'land and liberty'... Zapata defended his principles with weapons. He died for those principles. The agrarian leaders in Guatemala did not embody the landless Indian; instead, they represented the middle class, liberal and bureaucratic, without the profound passion born from the knowledge of dispossession and misery.*[47]

In fact, the narrow urban base that defined the leadership of the agrarian reform program was duplicated within the country's labor movement and its political organizations. As Monteforte Toledo has observed,

> *all of the political and union leaders came from within an intellectual sector of the petit bourgeois and, in some cases, because of special interests or ideological confusion, they were incapable of consolidating the labor and political sectors into a union that was authentically based on the support and aspirations of a majority of Guatemalans.*[48]

As the myriad contradictions of the Arbenz government began to coalesce against the president, Ambassador Peurifoy took a leading role in encouraging key officers to force the resignation of their commander-in-chief — an ultimatum several key officers personally delivered to Arbenz on June 27. Hours later, after Arbenz summarily resigned, Peurifoy engineered the formation of a three-man *junta*, led by Colonel

Elfegio Monzón who had served as Arbenz's minister-without-portfolio. Peurifoy then insisted that Monzón meet immediately with Castillo Armas in San Salvador to mediate a cease-fire. When the negotiations broke down, an irate John Foster Dulles immediately ordered Peurifoy to the Salvadoran capital to "crack some heads together."[49]

After arriving in San Salvador on July 1, the ambassador rapidly negotiated an agreement between the two recalcitrant officers. As the authors of *Bitter Fruit* point out, however, "Peurifoy's quick success was not surprising since he held the high cards in the game. Neither Monzón nor Castillo Armas could take power without his blessing."[50] Peurifoy's plan called for a five-man *junta*, composed of Castillo Armas and one of his closest collaborators within the "army of liberation," both of whom would join the already-constituted triumvirate. Two days later, aboard the ambassador's U.S. government aircraft, Monzón and Castillo Armas, accompanied by Peurifoy, touched down at the Guatemala City airport. Within a week, the *junta* elected Castillo Armas provisional president and, on August 31, the last two members of the shrinking *junta* resigned, making Castillo Armas president — the man Washington had selected months earlier to replace Arbenz.

Like hundreds of other Arbenz supporters who immediately sought asylum within the confines of numerous embassies, Arbenz, his wife and three children disappeared into the Mexican Embassy the day after his resignation. It was not until September 9, however, that Castillo Armas finally permitted the former president and his family to leave the country, forcing Arbenz to spend an uncomfortable seventy-three days in the crowded Mexican chancellery which sheltered 380 people, nearly 100 of whom were children under the age of fourteen.[51] A final indignity was thrust upon the deposed leader when he was stripped and searched at the airport before departing the country. The press was allowed to photograph a jut-jawed Arbenz, dressed in shorts, holding open his shirt to expose his naked chest.

Arbenz, whose prosperous cotton *finca* was subsequently confiscated and his attractive Guatemala City home vandalized, was never allowed to return to Guatemala. He and his family spent the next seventeen years in an unhappy, peripatetic exile that included stays in Mexico, Switzerland, France, Czechoslovakia, the Soviet Union, Uruguay and

Cuba. Finally, in 1970, Mexico's President Luis Echeverría permitted Arbenz and his wife to take up residence permanently in Mexico City. In less than a year, however, Arbenz, who was fifty-seven, died of a heart attack on January 27, 1971, at his Mexico City home.

Señora de Arbenz, who now lives quietly in San José, Costa Rica, broke long years of silence in August 1990, when her by-line appeared in an exclusive article entitled "The Conspiracy of Silence," which she wrote for *Siglo Veintiuno*, a Guatemala City daily. The former first lady cites many of her late husband's achievements: an agrarian reform program, the construction of needed highways, a new hydroelectric plant, and attention to the demands of workers. Correctly pointing out that there have been few positive comments on her husband's life and work, Señora de Arbenz also notes with some irony that the little that has been written about the former president has been published "by the foreign press, largely North American, which, paradoxically, previously attacked him." [52]

UNITED FRUIT'S ROLE IN THE COUP

While Schlesinger and Kinzer contend that the United Fruit Company provided important logistical assistance to the CIA, it is evident that any support that UFCO might have furnished the U.S. government was certainly not a determining factor in President Arbenz's abrupt resignation. As noted previously, it was the Guatemalan Army's adamant refusal to confront Castillo Armas's forces that caused the beleaguered commander-in-chief to surrender his office — not the fact that the Company might have "surreptitiously provided to the CIA its Guatemalan railroad system to smuggle in arms; its Atlantic port to land equipment; its telegraph, telephone and radio to relay messages; its Guatemalan properties to give cover to the rebels; and its p.r. men to disseminate photos and bulletins about the advance of Castillo Armas's forces." [53] Aybar de Soto also maintains that supplies for the "army of liberation" were "transported to Honduras aboard the ships of the Great White Fleet and assembled at a Company division in Honduras for distribution." [54] But it is obvious that no amount of UFCO-provided logistical assistance to Castillo Armas's approximately 250 "soldiers" would have defeated the

Guatemalan Army if it had chosen to pit its 6,000 troops against the motley band of invaders.

It has also been alleged that UFCO played a key role in selecting the individual who would lead the "army of liberation." This charge is presumably given credence by a passage in General Miguel Ydígoras Fuentes's autobiography, *My War with Communism*. Asserting that United Fruit's Walter Turnbull paid him a visit during 1953, when he was living in El Salvador, Ydígoras claims that Turnbull was

> *accompanied by two gentlemen whom he introduced as agents of the CIA. They said that I was a popular figure in Guatemala and that they wanted to lend their assistance to overthrow Arbenz. When I asked their conditions for the assistance, I found them unacceptable. Among other things, I was to promise to favor the United Fruit Company and the International Railways of Central America; to destroy the railroad workers' labor union . . . Further, I was to pay back every cent that was invested in the undertaking on the basis of accounts that would be presented to me afterwards.*[55]

Gleijeses, however, convincingly debunks this far-fetched account.

> *As president of Guatemala [1958-1963], Ydígoras was subservient to American companies, undemocratic and corrupt. Why then believe a self-serving statement so out of character with the man? His autobiography — a rambling apologia remarkable only for its distortions and lies — is hardly a reliable source. His entire record indicates that, had he been offered the leadership of the crusade, Ydígoras would have accepted any conditions.*

Indeed, Gleijeses's version of how the leader of the "army of liberation" was selected is far more plausible: in August 1953, the State Department simply asked its embassy in Guatemala to suggest the name of an individual who could lead a movement against President Arbenz. Deputy Chief of Mission William Krieg later confirmed this account: "We decided that among poor starters, Castillo Armas was probably the best."[56] A former classmate of Arbenz's at the Escuela Politécnica, who had resigned as the director of that institution after Arana's murder, Colonel Castillo Armas had undoubtedly come to the embassy's attention following a failed coup attempt against President Arévalo in 1950. Subsequently arrested and imprisoned, Castillo Armas again came to public attention a year later when he tunneled out of Guatemala City's infamous national penitentiary. He was living in self-imposed exile in Honduras when the U.S. government tapped him to lead the forces against Arbenz.

REASONS FOR INTERVENTION STILL IN DISPUTE

From today's vantage it is clear that Arbenz's Guatemala did not represent a national security threat to the United States, nor was it a Communist beachhead manipulated by the Soviet Union. That Guatemala's approximately 6,000 Communists — many of whom worked in strategic ministries and departments — exerted a degree of influence completely out of proportion to their size is obvious. As Immerman argues, however, "for Guatemalan Communists, the vehicle for expanding their power was the electoral process. Of the fifty-six seats in the National Assembly, at no time did members of the Guatemalan Labor Party hold more than four. Most important, Communist influence within the army and police, the key instruments for controlling the country, was negligible." [57]

Nevertheless, many Guatemalan authors who wrote about this period during the 1950s, and were clearly sympathetic to the Arbenz government, have steadfastly maintained that the U.S. intervened in their country in order to regain the United Fruit Company's expropriated properties. Among North American authors, Schlesinger and Kinzer are the leading exponents of this theory, bluntly stating that Arbenz's fate was determined by UFCO's "corps of influential lobbyists and talented publicists." [58] Handy takes a similar tack, arguing that "the country's only crime . . . was to have enacted an agrarian reform that affected the interests of an American-owned fruit company." [59] U.S. historian Susanne Jonas espouses the same line: "the cardinal sin of the Arbenz government had been its implementation of an agrarian reform law in 1952 which affected the (unused) holdings of the United Fruit Company." [60]

The author of *The Declassified Eisenhower* concurs:

> *ultimately, it did not matter whether or not the Arbenz government was Communist, or whether Arbenz considered himself a Communist. His insistence on independent economic development contradicted all normal relations in the Western Hemisphere. The United States judged correctly that the Arbenz government was inimical to its fundamental interests. Communism was used, therefore, both as the tool with which to rally Central American support and as the excuse to overthrow the nationalist, anti-imperialist and naive government of Jacobo Arbenz. Arbenz and his associates apparently believed, sincerely believed, that they could challenge United States business interests and still be considered acceptable by the United States government.[61]*

Arbenz himself apparently remained convinced that his government fell because he dared to expropriate the United Fruit Company's holdings. Three years before he died, in one of the very few post-1954 interviews that he conceded, the former president reiterated that it was his actions against United Fruit that caused the collapse of his administration. Arbenz also admitted, however, that the expropriations of UFCO's land should have been effected in "another manner" and that his policy toward the U.S. company was "bad and imprudent . . . There was a lack of awareness of the possible political implications."[62]

Although there is little question that Arbenz's stubborn, uncompromising stance against United Fruit was imprudent, most U.S. scholars do not believe the Eisenhower administration organized his downfall simply because he affected the interests of the United Fruit Company. Instead, they tend to agree with Britain's Bulmer-Thomas who states that well before the Guatemalan government expropriated the Compañía Agrícola's holdings "the U.S. administration had already decided to overthrow the Arbenz regime. The dispute with UFCO may have reinforced this decision, but it did not precipitate it."[63] Eisenhower biographer Stephen A. Ambrose takes a similar line.

> *What he [Eisenhower] feared was not the loss of American profits in Guatemala, but rather the loss of all Central America . . . In*

Eisenhower's nightmare, the dominoes would fall in both directions, to the south of Guatemala toward Panama, endangering the Canal Zone, and to the north bringing communism to the Rio Grande . . . To prevent the dominoes from falling, he was prepared to, and did, take great risks over tiny Guatemala.[64]

Even Immerman agrees: "the United States did not ultimately intervene in Guatemala to protect United Fruit. It intervened to halt what it believed to be the spread of the international Communist conspiracy."[65] Blasier, however, perceives yet another reason for the intervention. Asserting that U.S. domestic political considerations were the driving force behind Washington's actions, he maintains "under Eisenhower, Dulles sent armed contingents into Guatemala to offset Soviet expansion in Eastern Europe and to strengthen the administration's political position in the elections of 1954 and 1956. He needed and wanted victories against communism."[66]

Perhaps the most profound analysis has been made by Gleijeses, whose richly detailed book on the Guatemalan revolution includes more than sixty interviews with nearly all of the principals, both Guatemalan and American.

UFCO had a motive, and it had the contacts. It is tempting to survey the scene of the crime, find this smoking gun, and arrest the fruit company. There is, however, more evidence. After studying the Guatemalan primary sources and juxtaposing them with U.S. reports, it becomes clearer and clearer that the U.S. Embassy's concern with communism under Arévalo owed much to UFCO's smoke and mirrors; its concerns with communism under Arbenz owed little to the Company . . . In no country in Latin America had the Communists ever been as influential as they were in Guatemala. And no president had ever been as close to the Communists as was Arbenz. It required no manipulations by UFCO minions for U.S. officials to appreciate these truths.

As José Manuel Fortuny, former secretary general of the Guatemalan Communist Party, bitterly told Gleijeses, "They would have overthrown us even if we had grown no bananas."[67]

THE CLOCK TURNS BACK

As expected, the Castillo Armas government lost little time in returning lands that had been expropriated under Decree 900. By the time the Arbenz government fell, nearly 1.5 million acres of land, or 16.3 percent of all of Guatemala's tillable, fallow land held in private hands, had been expropriated. (Among the lands expropriated were 1,700 acres owned by President Arbenz and 1,200 acres belonging to Foreign Minister Toriello.)[68] Agrarian bonds equivalent to $8,345,544 had been issued for the 1,002 plantations affected by the Agrarian Reform Law. These properties, usually in parcels of about ten acres, had been distributed to 138,000 recipients.

Few authors have pointed out, however, that nearly 90 percent of those *campesinos* who received land under the Agrarian Reform Law did not, in fact, obtain titles for the parcels they were awarded. Instead, they merely gained the right of lifetime use of the land, and were required to pay the government a small annual rental fee. As Whetten remarks, "peasants receiving land became state tenants," causing many to criticize the program as "an attempt by the government to gain control of the peasant rather than to help him."[69]

Moreover, the figures for land distribution fail to reveal the chaos and violence that frequently surrounded the expropriation of properties. Acknowledging that the principal defect of the Agrarian Reform Law was its implementation, the Melvilles admit, with some understatement, that "the agrarian committees had trouble controlling the *campesinos*."[70] Indeed, organized raids and illegal seizures of land by peasants, particularly in the department of Escuintla, were not uncommon. Even President Arbenz's Escuintla cotton plantation was attacked by peasants.

More importantly, however, statistics citing how much land was expropriated or how many individuals received properties under the Agrarian Reform Law do not disclose one of the program's most significant flaws: the government's inability to provide adequate credit or technical assistance to a majority of the new landowners. The fact that no Guatemalan government has been willing or able to provide such credit and assistance to the nation's subsistence farmers led LaBarge to expound a provocative thesis. "It is entirely possible, if not indeed probable," he wrote in 1960, "that the unimproved acreage of the United Fruit Company in Guatemala contributes more at present to national economic development as a form of insurance for the multimillion-dollar banana industry than it would were it employed in the small subsistence homesteads of indigenous agriculture."[71] Perceiving ramifications that extended far beyond the United Fruit Company's properties or even Guatemala, another scholar concluded that "the program launched by Arbenz in 1952 was ill-conceived and disastrously executed. The chaotic way in which it was administered almost certainly set back the cause of land reform by many years elsewhere in Central America and was, of course, a major reason for its suppression under Castillo Armas in Guatemala itself."[72]

Indeed, the new president soon began returning lands to many of the individuals or companies whose properties had been expropriated. Through a compromise agreement between the Company and the government, signed on December 27, 1954, the government agreed to return to the Compañía Agrícola all of its expropriated properties. In exchange, the Company voluntarily donated to the government approximately 103,000 acres of its unimproved Pacific coast properties, which *La Frutera* valued in excess of $2 million. The Castillo Armas government subsequently distributed the land to more than 800 *campesinos*.[73]

More significantly, in a contract also signed on December 27, 1954, the Compañía Agrícola agreed to pay an annual tax of 30 percent on its net profits based on a "sworn certificate issued by a firm of public accountants of recognized reputation in the United States of America, which is acceptable to the government of Guatemala and which is authorized to practice before the Treasury of the United States of America."[74] Two years later, in a contract signed December 10, 1956, between the Castillo Armas government and the United Fruit Company's Bananera division, the latter also agreed to pay a 30 percent tax on the annual profits of its north coast properties. Although the government returned 172,532 acres expropriated by the Arbenz regime, United Fruit donated to the nation approximately 110,000 acres of its holdings, valued by the Company at more than $2 million. UFCO also committed itself to investing the equivalent of $5 million over a five-year period to rehabilitate nearly 5,000 acres of the north coast's sterile or swampy land in order to put the area into banana production. It also pledged to keep only 25 percent of its land idle as a reserve against Panama disease.

Since Castillo Armas believed that labor unions and political parties had been key instruments in spreading communism, he promptly disbanded the General Confederation of Guatemalan Workers and the Guatemalan National Peasant Confederation. More than 500 unions were also dissolved for a ninety-day period to permit their reorganization free of Communist influences. While Castillo Armas has been castigated for the actions he took against Guatemala's unions, Edwin W. Bishop points out that many critics "overlooked the fact that the labor movement had become the firm political associate of the Arbenz government, and it was bound to share the fate of that government." [75] Most unions, however, did not reorganize, largely because of government and employer resistance, but also because there were no individuals willing or available to replace the former union leaders. Thus, trade union membership fell from 100,000 to 27,000 between 1954 and 1955; rural labor unions, including the ones at Tiquisate and Bananera, were either proscribed or virtually destroyed. All political parties, except for Castillo Armas's National Liberation Movement, were abolished.

As one historian has observed, "counter-revolutions have a momentum of their own, and Castillo Armas went much further than the relationship with his U.S. mentors strictly demanded." Furthermore, his repressive methods clearly demonstrated that the U.S. government's "ability to control the social and political policies of its proxies was very limited . . . If democracy in Guatemala after 1954 had been given the same priority as communism before 1954, no doubt even Castillo Armas would have been forced to bow to U.S. pressure." [76]

Although there is no question that Castillo Armas reversed many of the progressive measures undertaken by the two previous revolutionary governments, it cannot be said that he totally dismantled all of the reforms of his predecessors. As British historian Franklin D. Parker has pointed out, "the revolution had made too much of an impression to be ruthlessly suppressed." The same author also notes that the 1956 constitution left unchanged the constitutional relationships between the Legislative Assembly, the president and the judiciary, and recognized the social obligations of the government, as had the 1945 constitution. Moreover, several of the institutions that Arévalo created, such as the Guatemalan Institute of Social Security (IGSS), the National Institute for the Development of Production (INFOP), and the Bank of Guatemala remained as "vital government agencies." Labor unions were still recognized, and the voting rights of all adult males and literate women were maintained.[77] The qualifications established for public school teachers, their rankings and salary scales, also remained intact. In addition, Bulmer-Thomas notes that the state's commitment to economic modernization remained even after Arbenz was overthrown.[78] Thus, not all of the significant gains achieved by the "ten years of spring" were completely annulled.

THE ARBENZ LEGACY

As Uruguay's Eduardo Galeano has written, "Arbenz's fall began a conflagration in Guatemala which has never been extinguished." [79] Largely because the agrarian reform program was dramatically reversed, forces were unleashed throughout the small country which still today kill an appalling number of Guatemalans annually. Moreover, no president since Arbenz has dared to effectively address the country's most critical economic problem: an inequitable, centuries-old land tenure system that has changed little from the statistics provided in the previous chapter.

Since Castillo Armas was assassinated in 1957, Guatemala's history has been one of unceasing violence, egregious, continuing human rights violations, corrupt, inefficient, often repressive governments, and frequent coups and counter-coups as military officers fought among themselves for the nation's highest office.[80] In fact, it was not until January 1991 that a democratically-elected civilian president, Vinicio Cerezo Arévalo (no relationship to the former president) turned over the blue and white sash of office to another freely-elected civilian, Jorge Serrano Elías — the first such instance since 1951 when Jacobo Arbenz succeeded Juan José Arévalo.

Military officers abruptly seizing power has hardly been an uncommon phenomenon throughout Latin America during much of the twentieth century, but, unlike most countries, Guatemala has been afflicted for the last thirty-four years with a deadly guerrilla war and with savage government counter-insurgency measures that have killed at least 150,000 Guatemalans, caused 40,000 disappearances, left 250,000 children orphaned, and physically displaced at least 43,000 men, women and children, most of them Indians from the western highlands who have sought exile in southern Mexico.[81]

The origins of Guatemala's guerrilla movement lie in a failed army coup against Castillo Armas's successor, President Ydígoras Fuentes. The leaders of the November 1960 revolt eventually founded a guerrilla movement they called the Rebel Armed Forces (FAR). Twenty-two years later, despite brutal, persistent repression by the Guatemalan Army, the FAR was still intact and joined with three other guerrilla movements to form a united front, the Guatemalan National Revolutionary Unity (URNG).

In April 1991, President Jorge Serrano's government began negotiations with the leaders of the URNG in an effort to convince its members to lay down their arms. The Mexico City talks were disrupted, however, when Serrano abruptly fled Guatemala in June 1993, following his unsuccessful attempt to abolish both the Legislative Assembly and the nation's judicial system. His successor, Ramiro de León Carpio, and the guerrillas agreed early in 1994 to resume the negotiations, but it is likely that the process — if successful — will be as complex and drawn out as the seven years that were required before the government of El Salvador was finally able to sign a peace treaty with the FMLN. In the interim, the approximately 4,000 guerrillas who operate in Guatemala's highlands, on the south coast and in the Petén will probably continue their occasional raids on isolated Indian villages, the periodic destruction of electrical and communications towers and the dynamiting of major bridges on the south coast.

Although some might argue that Guatemala's history would probably have been just as convulsed and violent if President Arbenz had been permitted to finish out his term, the evidence appears otherwise. Had Arbenz been able to complete many of the ambitious and desperately-needed programs he set out to accomplish in 1951, and if the goals of the 1944 revolution had been even partially met, today's Guatemala would probably be a more egalitarian, prosperous and peaceful country.

It is conceivable, however, that even without the intervention of the United States, Arbenz would have been deposed, especially after Communist influence in his government became an increasingly critical concern for many Guatemalans, both in and out of the army. But the U.S. government was not prepared to wait for such an eventuality. Firmly convinced that Guatemala represented communism's first beachhead in Latin America, the Eisenhower administration moved swiftly and successfully to engineer Arbenz's ouster.

- 8 -

New Management Precipitates UFCO's Departure

Exactly five days after the Eisenhower administration engineered the overthrow of President Jacobo Arbenz, the U.S. government administered a staggering blow to the United Fruit Company: the Department of Justice filed a comprehensive law suit against the Company, charging wide-ranging violations of U.S. antitrust laws.

The timing of the Justice Department's action, filed in the U.S. District Court for the Eastern District of Louisiana, led Thomas ("the Cork") Corcoran to charge that Foster Dulles had "begun the antitrust suit against UFCO just to prove he wasn't involved with the Company."[1] Given the fact that Arbenz and his foreign minister had frequently charged that Dulles's previous association with United Fruit influenced the State Department's policies towards Guatemala, it is tempting to concur with Corcoran's statement. Although it may well be that the U.S. government timed its action in order to publicly distance itself from the fruit giant, the Justice Department had, in fact, initiated its complex and lengthy investigation of United Fruit several years earlier.

In 1958, four years after the suit was filed, the case was settled through the entry of a Consent Decree — a legal device which allows the defendant to state that it does not admit to any violation of law, but agrees to cease certain practices and perform whatever remedial action the government requires. This is the only way the defendant can avoid going to trial once this kind of complaint has been filed. Since court records in U.S. vs. the United Fruit Company are still under a protective order and not available to the public, it is not possible to review the government's evidence or the documents submitted by United Fruit.

Examination of the Consent Decree, however, clearly reveals the broad nature of the antitrust violations that the Department of Justice charged in its case against the United Fruit Company. In its complaint, the government charged a plethora of violations concerning the importation and sale of UFCO's bananas within the United States. Accordingly, the United Fruit Company agreed to undertake a series of measures, chief of which was the creation of a competitor capable of importing into the United States approximately nine million stems of bananas annually. In 1955, UFCO imported 29.5 million stems of bananas into North America, thereby cornering 59 percent of the market. The Company's competitors, chiefly the Standard Fruit and Steamship Company, imported a total of 20.4 million stems during the same period.[2]

The court was curiously lenient in the time frame it provided the Company for the implementation of its order. United Fruit was allowed eight years, until June 30, 1966, to submit its plan for the creation of a competing company, and, once the court approved the plan, UFCO was given an additional four years for its execution.[3] The court's three options for compliance provided United Fruit with the possibility of organizing a totally new and independent banana company; alternatively, UFCO could sell to any buyer (other than Standard Fruit) the necessary production and transportation assets to produce annual U.S. imports of nine million stems of bananas. The third option offered the possibility of organizing a new company to which United Fruit could sell part of its production and transportation assets to any individual or company willing to commit not less than $1 million to the new enterprise.

A second specific provision in the Consent Decree ordered the United Fruit Company to divest itself of all its stock "or other proprietary interest" in the International Railways of Central America, which operated in Guatemala and El Salvador. Curiously, neither Guatemala nor any other country where the Company operated was mentioned in the Consent Decree.[4] Instead, the document referred to the "American tropics," which was defined as an area stretching from the Florida Keys to southern Brazil, and spanning an east-west area from the Canary Islands to hundreds of miles off the coast of Guatemala. Moreover, once UFCO divested itself of the stock, the court enjoined and restrained United Fruit and its officers and directors from "acquiring or holding, directly or indirectly, any legal or beneficial interest in any capital stock of International Railways of Central America."[5] On January 26, 1962, the United Fruit Company advised the Department of Justice that it had disposed of all of its IRCA stock.

Many of the United Fruit Company's allegedly unfair practices are revealed in the long list of activities enjoined by the U.S. District Court. Thus, United Fruit was forbidden to engage in any jobbing operations; from maintaining exclusive sales contracts with jobbers, or exclusive purchasing contracts with independent banana suppliers for longer than five years without an escape clause; from acquiring proprietorship, ownership or control of any of its competitors or of any substantial part of their business assets; from entering into collusive agreements with competitors, or using coercive tactics against them; from attempting to control the resale price policies of jobbers or wholesalers; from obtaining preclusive treatment from common carriers; from requiring its customers to use specified transport companies; from refusing to sell in specified markets to any purchaser at its regular terms of sale such bananas as it might have after supplying the needs of regular customers; or from tying up refrigerated space on ships in such a way as to prevent competitors from obtaining space for their shipments.[6]

A NEW TEAM IMPLEMENTS NEEDED CHANGES

The most onerous provision of the Consent Decree was the court's stipulation that United Fruit must either organize a new company or sell a division capable of producing nine million stems of bananas annually. In order to determine how this condition could best be met, and to confront numerous problems in planning, marketing and research that were contributing to sagging sales and earnings, United Fruit's board of directors hired Thomas E. Sunderland, a former vice president of the Standard Oil Company of Indiana.[7] Taking office as the new president, CEO and director of the Company on November 1, 1959, Sunderland and a team of new executives with marketing and managerial skills soon identified four critical issues that required immediate attention.

The major problem confronting the United Fruit Company was the sky-rocketing competition posed by Ecuadorean producers whose low-cost exports had soared from 169,000 metric tons in 1950 to 1,051,700 metric tons in 1959, slightly more than the combined production of Guatemala, Honduras, Costa Rica and Panama.[8] Moreover, as Sunderland subsequently noted, local growers in Ecuador were not required to provide housing, schools, hospitals, access roads, electrical power systems, railroads and port operations — all services or facilities that UFCO usually furnished. In addition, the wages Ecuadorean laborers received were far inferior to those paid by the United Fruit Company. As a result, a stem of Ecuadorean bananas cost approximately $2 to produce, while United Fruit's cost $3.50.[9]

In an effort to lower the Company's production costs, Sunderland began a concerted effort to spin off some of UFCO's tropical assets through selling, leasing, going into partnership with, or contracting to nationals a significant part of United Fruit's banana-producing farms. Not only would such a policy reduce the Company's costly overhead, it would undoubtedly contribute to local entrepreneurship and economic development, while also lowering *El Pulpo's* high profile.[10]

Sunderland was also well aware that Arbenz's expropriation of the Company's Guatemala holdings and Castro's successful nationalization of 271,000 acres of UFCO's Cuban properties had exerted an electrifying effect on United Fruit's stockholders. Clearly, times had changed and it was imperative for the fruit giant to reduce its presence throughout Central America.

Although UFCO management had long resigned itself to absorbing the enormous costs inflicted by Panama disease and annual wind storms, Sunderland concluded that the Company could no longer sustain such heavy losses. Pointing out that UFCO was annually spending approximately $18 million to replace farms ravaged by the fungus, and that blowdowns were causing an estimated $10 million a year in losses, the new president ordered development of the Valery variety of banana. A more compact plant than the Gros Michel, and therefore more resistant to wind damage, the Valery was also completely resistant to Panama disease. Significantly, the Standard Fruit Company, with far fewer resources than UFCO, had begun converting most of its Honduran and Costa Rican plantations from the Gros Michel to a Cavendish variety in 1953.

That United Fruit had not previously converted to the Valery was due to the old line management's steadfast conviction that American consumers would never purchase anything but the Gros Michel variety of banana. (Ironically, UFCO botanists had become aware of the Valery as early as 1928, when specimens were brought from Vietnam to the Company's Lancetilla Experiment Station in Honduras.) When UFCO test marketed the new variety in 1962, however, they discovered that U.S. consumers liked the new type of banana. As a result, Sunderland ordered a massive conversion to the Valery late in 1962. Because the Valery is considerably more delicate than the hardy Gros Michel, however, United Fruit soon began boxing its fruit in order to provide the new variety with maximum protection. This innovation is discussed in more detail in the epilogue.

Yet another issue of concern to Sunderland was how to more effectively market UFCO's bananas. Even if the Company increased its advertising, there was no way for consumers to identify United Fruit's bananas. The solution would be found in a remarkably simple but novel method of "branding" United Fruit's bananas, a development also more fully described in the epilogue.

The fourth area that required Sunderland's immediate attention was the chaotic corporate structure of the sixty-year-old company he had inherited. With operations divided between offices in Boston and New York, the new president discovered that twenty-three executives reported directly to him, most of whom worked in New York and "did not have very clearly defined duties." By merging the New York operations into the Boston headquarters, and significantly reducing personnel, Sunderland forged a more streamlined, coordinated and well-managed organization.

LA FRUTERA ABANDONS
ITS SOUTH COAST PLANTATIONS

The new policies that Sunderland began implementing in 1960 soon impacted on United Fruit's Guatemala operations where, in 1964, the

Compañía Agrícola sold all of its Pacific coast holdings, including the 12,000 acres of banana farms that comprised the Tiquisate division. (The Melvilles erroneously state that the Company sold its south coast plantations in order to comply with the Consent Decree.)[11] Although the sale of UFCO's south coast properties was an integral part of Sunderland's plan to spin off some of its tropical assets, there were two other compelling reasons for abandoning Tiquisate.

According to Ted A. Holcombe, who served as the Compañía Agrícola's last manager in Tiquisate, the continuing wind storms that buffeted Guatemala's south coast, leaving thousands of acres of toppled banana plants in their wake, were a major factor in closing the division. "It took at least a year for a blown down area to come back," he recalled, "and by that time there was usually another wind storm that often destroyed the same areas that had been affected the previous year."[12] Although conversion to the Valery might well have saved the Compañía Agrícola millions of dollars in annual wind losses, it is apparent that UFCO preferred to reduce its presence in Guatemala.

Holcombe also alluded to increasing problems with the long haul rail transportation that was required to ship bananas from Tiquisate to Puerto Barrios. Expanding on this issue, Carlos Haroldo Gomar, another former employee, remembers that "because of the frequent labor problems that the IRCA was experiencing, it often took up to thirty-six hours for bananas to be shipped from Tiquisate to Puerto Barrios. Obviously, the bananas could not withstand such long delays."[13]

In reality, United Fruit's decision to abandon its south coast holdings had been made well before 1964, with the Compañía Agrícola beginning to sell or lease small parcels of land as early as 1960. Because the fertile, flat land on Guatemala's Pacific coast is ideally suited for mechanized agriculture, increasing numbers of Guatemalans were using the area to establish large cotton plantations. In fact, cotton was becoming an ever more important export crop — firmly replacing bananas as the nation's second major foreign exchange earner. By 1970, Guatemala had become the fourth largest cotton producer in Latin America.[14] Obviously, the Compañía Agrícola's banana farms offered superb opportunities for newly-emerging cotton farmers.

Not only was much of the land cleared and largely free of malaria, each banana farm also provided good roads, telephone communications, and housing that was equipped with potable water, electricity and other amenities. The houses in Tiquisate and the overseers' homes on individual farms were sold for a nominal sum: approximately $2,500.[15] The price included domestic appliances, furniture and all other household effects, as well as a large yard. Equally important, the new owners were free to hire the Compañía Agrícola's former laborers, among the most skilled, well-trained and healthy agricultural workers in Guatemala. Nearly every farm also included skilled mechanics, electricians, tractor drivers, carpenters and office clerks.

Clearly, the Compañía Agrícola's well-established farms could have been used to settle thousands of Guatemalan *campesinos* if the government had wanted — or been able — to purchase the land, and to provide the new owners with adequate credit and technical assistance. Among those that might have been settled were the approximately 2,500 laborers the Company dismissed when it closed its Tiquisate operations. It is apparent, however, that President Enrique Peralta Azurdia (1963-1966), the general who overthrew President Ydígoras Fuentes in 1963, was more concerned with eliminating the country's growing guerrilla movement than he was in implementing a significant agrarian program.

According to the Melvilles, all the banana farms were sold to twelve former employees of the Company, including Holcombe, his son and son-in-law.[16] Although Holcombe, who now lives in Texas, acknowledges that he and his family purchased approximately 1,000 acres of the Compañía Agrícola's holdings, he denies that all of the Company's land was sold to a dozen former employees. Instead, he told the author that approximately 90 percent of the land was sold to Guatemalans who had no previous connection with the Company.

Holcombe admits that serious consideration was not given to selling the land to the Company's laborers. "The improved land, that is, land that had been cleared, was selling for the equivalent of $100 an acre, and the workers simply didn't have that kind of money. Nor was the Company prepared to extend any kind of long-term credit," Holcombe recalls. Nevertheless, Silver, who preceded Holcombe as manager in Tiquisate, remembers that a few *campesinos* did purchase small plots of Compañía Agrícola land before 1964. "But they had no money to develop the land and usually only a machete and a hoe to work with. All they could do was grow a few acres of corn. Before long they sold out to people who had more money." [17]

ELI BLACK'S AMK CORPORATION
BUYS OUT UNITED FRUIT

While Thomas Sunderland was restructuring and radically transforming the United Fruit Company, he and his top executives continued to debate how to implement the Consent Decree's divestiture order. Eventually, they decided to establish a new company, called the Sovereign Fruit Company. About the same time, however, an historic event occurred: the United Fruit Company was acquired by Eli M. Black's AMK Corporation. A hard-charging New York conglomerate builder, Black had begun his spectacular career after gaining control of the American Seal Cap Corporation, a small company which annually produced and sold $40 million of liners for bottle caps. In 1967 the forty-six-year-old financier had astounded Wall Street when he acquired John Morrell & Company, a meat packing giant twenty times larger than American Seal Cap, with annual sales of $800 million. Calling his new company the AMK Corporation, Black soon began looking around for other asset-rich companies that he could raid.

Within a year, on September 24, 1968, the man who did not know "a banana tree from a potted palm" bought 733,200 shares of United Fruit's stock at $56 a share — up to that time the third largest block of shares ever traded on the New York Stock Exchange.[18] On the same day, AMK also bought another 7,100 shares on the open market, giving Black more than 9 percent of United Fruit's outstanding stock. To finance most of his $41.7 million purchase, Black borrowed $35 million from a group of banks headed by Morgan Guaranty Trust Company. A little more than two months later, AMK announced a tender offer that 80 percent of the United Fruit Company's stockholders soon accepted: giving up one share of stock that had earned $1.40 the previous year in exchange for a twenty-five-year convertible debenture paying $2.09, and a ten-year warrant to purchase one and a half shares of AMK's common stock. On July 1, 1970, the United Brands Company, as the two newly-merged companies were now called, was admitted to trading on the New York Stock Exchange.

AMK's 80 percent ownership of the United Fruit Company cost the conglomerate $630 million in cash, bonds and stocks. According to McCann, who was well acquainted with AMK's takeover, UFCO's net assets were worth only $286 million, and the remaining $344 million were classified as "goodwill and trademarks." Why was the astute financier willing to pay such an inflated price for the banana giant? There were two principal reasons AMK and numerous other corporations had been interested in acquiring a company "displaying a pair of attractions only a little less prominent than those of that celebrated lady who stopped traffic in New York's financial district." [19] In the first place, the United Fruit Company, which had paid off its outstanding debt in 1922, was one of those rare U.S. corporations with no funded debt. A second, even more important, reason was the reputed $100 million in cash which the United Fruit Company was sitting on. Nevertheless, McCann contends that "most of the legendary $100 million dollars in loose cash that had made United Fruit such an attractive prize ... was simply not there."[20]

In fact, by the mid-sixties Sunderland and his colleagues had recognized the pressing need to diversify the Company's banana operations in order to spread its risks and profit base. Thus, UFCO began acquiring a number of food-related firms which often gave the Company "a case of indigestion that lasted several years." Among the companies acquired were A&W Root Beer Drive-Ins of America, a freeze-dry shrimp processing firm, a catfish farm in Honduras, a Costa Rican margarine-producing company, Baskin-Robbins ice cream, Mexico's Clemente Jacques food company and California's Inter-Harvest Lettuce, the largest lettuce grower in the U.S.

Paradoxically, UFCO's interest in acquiring the Del Monte Corporation eventually led that company to become one of United Brands' major competitors — and the owner of one of UB's Guatemala divisions. When Del Monte's managers learned that United Fruit was planing to buy out their company, they quickly stymied the move by purchasing a small, Miami-based banana operation called the West Indies Fruit Company. And since the Consent Decree prohibited the United Fruit Company from increasing its share of the U.S. banana market, there was no way UFCO could legally acquire another firm that also sold the yellow fruit.

Nonetheless, United Fruit's numerous acquisitions and capital improvements expended on its Central American divisions apparently depleted most of the "loose cash" UFCO was reputed to possess. To restore some of the conglomerate's liquidity and help to pay the enormous debt he assumed in purchasing the banana company, Black soon began selling most of the firms that United Fruit had previously acquired. By firing 400 of UFCO's U.S. employees, he also reduced costs by $10 million. The first year after the takeover, however, the banana component of United Brands showed a net operating loss of $2 million, and reported earnings that were $33 million less than the previous year.

According to McCann, most of the financial difficulties suffered by the previously solvent company were due to Black's management style and his unfamiliarity with the operations of a complex and far-flung organization. "Eli could not run the company, and he was proving it. He could not delegate responsibility, and he wouldn't accept criticism." Moreover, there was another problem that imperious managers often create: many of UFCO's most seasoned veterans at the Boston headquarters "held him in awe, partly because they feared for their jobs. Black got very little backtalk in those days, but he also got very little straight talk. In fact, he was told only what people thought he wanted to hear." [21]

UNITED BRANDS SELLS BANANERA TO DEL MONTE

Black's disastrous management of what had been the United Fruit Company led to copious red ink and stock prices that compared to the depression prices that had brought Sam Zemurray to Boston in 1933. Thus, in 1971 the Company suffered a $24 million loss, the largest in its history, and by 1974 its stock was selling for less than $8 a share. Clearly, the cash-hungry conglomerate was in no position to establish another banana company. Following his policy of marketing former UFCO assets, and to abide by the terms of the Consent Decree, Black decided to sell its Armuelles division, located on Panama's Pacific coast, to Del

Monte. The Panamanian government, however, was adamantly opposed to the sale, perhaps because of the Company's "social responsibility to the country," as McCann explains it. In any event, after Panama threatened to expropriate all of UFCO's plantations, Black backed off and, instead, offered Del Monte its Bananera division.[22]

Like Panama's government, the Guatemalan government, then headed by Colonel Carlos Arana Osorio (1970-1974), was also opposed to the sale, but for a different reason. Because two Guatemalan entrepreneurs were interested in purchasing the Company's holdings, Arana refused to authorize the sale, maintaining that the enclave should revert to nationals. Nevertheless, by November, 1972, Arana had reversed his decision, an action that several authors attribute to an alleged $500,000 bribe that Del Monte made to a close Arana associate.[23] Del Monte paid approximately $20.5 million for United Brands' 58,000 acres of land, nearly 10,000 of which were planted in bananas. In addition, the sale included the contractual rights to purchase bananas produced on 3,200 acres by associate producers, as well as all the buildings, equipment, railroads and other assets previously owned by the United Fruit Company.

Thus, sixty-six years after the United Fruit Company first began operations on Guatemala's steamy, disease-ridden north coast, the much-maligned company quietly departed the country.

- 9 -
Evaluating Sixty-Six Years of Operations

If the U.S. Justice Department charged the United Fruit Company with a lengthy catalog of unfair procedures practiced within the United States, many writers have also accused *La Frutera* of innumerable nefarious practices in Guatemala. Perhaps the most comprehensive — and thoroughly negative — analysis of the Company's operations is Alfonso Bauer Paiz's *Cómo opera el capital Yanqui en Centroamérica (el caso de Guatemala),* published in 1956. Throughout his book, however, Bauer Paiz makes frequent reference to Kepner and Soothill's *The Banana Empire: A Case Study of Economic Imperialism,* published in 1935, and Kepner's *Social Aspects of the Banana Industry,* which was published the following year. Both books treated the United Fruit Company in disparaging terms. Bauer Paiz is not the only author, however, to frequently cite Kepner. As LaBarge noted in 1959, "the seeming unanimity with which Kepner's views were assimilated by students of Latin America was curious, to say the least. Even if one had no criticism of Kepner's methods and conclusions, one had to admit that his studies were out of date."[1]

Perhaps the most frequently repeated criticism against the United Fruit Company is the insignificant export taxes that it paid to the Guatemalan government. As early as 1935, Kepner and Soothill observed that

> *Guatemalan coffee exports, valued at $23,062,533 [in 1928], paid an export tax of $2,016,332, or 8.7 per cent of their total valuation, while banana exports, valued at $3,096,334, paid an export tax of*

$60,856, or 1.97 per cent of their total valuation . . . Of the total governmental revenues during that year, Guatemala received 13 percent from coffee export taxes and 4/10 of 1 per cent from banana export taxes.[2]

There is no question that the export taxes UFCO paid and that were set by the government of Guatemala constituted a minuscule percentage of the total value of the fruit it shipped abroad. It should be pointed out, however, that while the United Fruit Company owned or leased less than 1 percent of the country's total agricultural land, the Company's contribution to export earnings was proportionately far greater than that of any other export crop. In 1955, for example, when Guatemala's agricultural exports (coffee, bananas, cotton and sugar) totaled $108.9 million, the United Fruit Company contributed almost $15 million or 13.7 percent of the country's total exports. Indeed, May and Plaza assert that acre for acre, UFCO's banana plantations were more than three times as productive as Guatemala's coffee farms.[3]

Furthermore, export taxes have never provided the Guatemalan government with its most important source of income. In fact, throughout the period that the United Fruit Company operated in Guatemala, approximately 75 percent of the government's annual revenues were derived from import taxes and consumption levies.[4]

And United Fruit, as described in more detail below, made a substantial annual contribution to the economy through the payment of import taxes which were significantly higher than the export taxes it paid.

While the United Fruit Company has been severely criticized because of the negligible taxes it paid during its long years of operation in Guatemala, far less attention has been given to the insignificant taxes Guatemalans — particularly wealthy Guatemalans — pay on their personal income, businesses and properties. Indeed, it was not until 1963 that the Guatemalan government finally enacted a personal income tax. Even during the Arbenz government, coffee growers paid no income tax, nor were they subject to the business profits tax since income from coffee was treated as accruing to individuals. Moreover, coffee paid only a moderate export tax.[5]

Indeed, the notoriously widespread evasion of export tax payments, particularly on coffee, was one of the principal reasons the Guatemalan government phased out all export taxes in 1990. Willy W. Zapata, former director of the Banco de Guatemala's Department of Economic Studies, and now president of the institution, acknowledges that the government's inability to effectively supervise this aspect of the country's tax collection system was the primary basis for eliminating export taxes.[6] To replace revenues formerly obtained through export taxes, the government hopes to tighten up its collection of corporate taxes and individual incomes taxes.

In fact, appallingly lax enforcement measures and insignificant sanctions for tax evasion have always made a charade of Guatemala's tax system — particularly for its most affluent citizens. For example, in 1990, the approximately 1,500 families who declared incomes of more than $100,000 earned 49.2 percent of all taxable income, but only paid personal taxes amounting to 1.3 percent of their income.[7]

There is also widespread evasion in the payment of corporate income taxes. Taxes on land, assets and inheritance are also extremely low and infrequently paid. Indeed, the insignificant taxes that Guatemalans pay on their properties produce tax revenues, as a percent of the Gross Domestic Product, that are two-and-a-half times less than the Latin American average.[8] As a result of Guatemala's skewed tax system, a full 55 percent of the government's total 1991 revenues were produced by indirect taxes, including the 7 percent Value Added Tax (VAT) which falls most heavily on consumers. Direct taxes contributed only 23 percent of the government's 1991 revenues.[9] (In the United States, personal income taxes provide slightly more than 50 percent of the federal government's total annual revenues.)

Many of Guatemala's most affluent citizens argue — with some justification — that if they paid more taxes, government officials would undoubtedly misappropriate or abscond with the funds, applying little of the increased revenues to improving the welfare of the 80 percent of the population that lives in poverty.[10] Regardless of why many Guatemalans pay virtually no taxes, the fact remains that the country's **wealthiest** citizens still pay fewer taxes than virtually any of their **counterparts** in the Western Hemisphere.

Another frequently cited indictment against the United Fruit is one that former President Juan José Arévalo articulated after the author asked him which single policy or action pursued by the United Fruit Company had been the most detrimental to Guatemala's development. "As concerns economic matters," he responded, "the most damaging effect was the fact that the Company occupied the best land in Guatemala and used it to produce bananas, which are not essential for national consumption. It was a crop raised only for export purposes."[11] Following this line of reasoning, Guatemala presumably should produce only those commodities that can be consumed domestically — obviously an untenable thesis for a small country with no heavy industry. In fact, Arévalo's flawed argument has been effectively refuted in recent years as Guatemala's economy has dramatically diversified, expanded and benefited from its export of new agricultural commodities.

Although traditional exports — coffee, sugar and bananas — still dominate Guatemala's agricultural sector, non-traditional exports are booming. Indeed, in 1991 it became apparent, that for the first time in the country's history, Guatemala's non-traditional exports of $395.4 million had earned $69.5 million more than coffee exports.[12] In comparison, the country's 1991 coffee exports were valued at $325.9 million; sugar at $142.2 million and bananas at $75.6 million.[13] The non-traditional exports, which began making impressive gains after 1986, include the export of large numbers of fresh fruits, vegetables, textiles, cut flowers, rubber, sesame seed, shrimp and tobacco. Furthermore, increasing numbers of the non-traditional agricultural exports (NTAEs) are being produced by small farmers who have abandoned their subsistence farming of corn, beans and other staple crops, and, with technical assistance from the Guatemalan government and foreign donors, are now dedicated to the more lucrative production of export commodities. Moreover, the robust growth of Guatemala's non-traditional exports has also helped to mitigate the continuing decline in export earnings from coffee.[14]

Obviously, there is nothing intrinsically wrong with export-driven economies, as countries such as Japan and Korea have demonstrated. John A. Booth and Thomas W. Walker, however, have pointed out that "the elites of those two more tightly knit societies seem to have a greater sense of social responsibility than the elites of Latin America, and, hence, externally stimulated growth has led to a general rise in the standard of living."[15] Costa Rica, however, is a Latin American exception to their premise. Although smaller and more homogeneous than Guatemala, Costa Rica's economy is also largely dependent on the exports of coffee and several other traditional and non-traditional agricultural products. Nevertheless, the little nation that abolished its army in 1948 has achieved significant improvements in health, education and housing because its elites have been more willing to distribute the income generated from Costa Rican agroexports.

The United Fruit Company is also regularly criticized for the generous concessions that it sought — and obtained — from successive Guatemalan governments. However, May and Plaza justify the contracts the United Fruit Company sought with Central American nations because it was

> *required to risk far more than the normal capital investment when it establishes a new, large-scale enterprise in a wilderness area that can furnish none of the ordinary facilities of industrialized communities. Its risks are compounded when it moves into countries in which no firm tradition of political stability has been established . . . Under such conditions, stockholders and directors are simply unwilling to commit large investments to such areas, and bankers are unwilling to extend loans, without such added assurance as a firm contract with the recognized government of the area can offer . . . The evidence shows that the extraordinary obligations assumed by the United Fruit Company in its agreements are considerably greater than the value of any concessions granted it.*[16]

While conceding that UFCO undoubtedly invested far more in establishing multi-million dollar banana divisions than it received in government concessions, it can be asked why a corporation, with net assets far greater than all of the isthmian nations combined, extracted such avaricious concessions from small, underdeveloped countries. Clearly, the United Fruit Company could readily have afforded to pay duties on all of the equipment that it was permitted to import during the nearly seven decades that it operated in Guatemala. Moreover, because import taxes were a principal source of revenue for the Guatemalan government, United Fruit's failure to pay taxes on many items implied higher tariffs for other importers.

Nor is there any justification for United Fruit's imperious refusal to pay many local taxes. The Company's impressive accumulation of profits stands in stark contrast to the clauses it routinely inserted in its contracts with impoverished Central American countries. The Compañía Agrícola's 1930 contract is a case in point. While obligating itself to pay consular taxes, an export tax of 2 cents per stem of banana, and property taxes, the contract goes on to declare:

> *whatsoever increases in the above-mentioned taxes and contributions, as well as whatsoever other taxes, excise taxes, contributions, charges, or services, now established or to be established, which affect its properties, enterprises, profits and the exportation of its products shall be considered as nonapplicable to the Company, which shall be considered as enjoying these exemptions by virtue of the obligations imposed upon it by this contract.*[17]

The effect of such contracts had two critical consequences for Guatemala: it became more difficult for the government to introduce or increase taxes on Guatemalan companies, and the insignificant taxes that the Company paid on banana exports were used by other exporters (including coffee) to justify low taxes on all exportable commodities.[18]

Several Guatemalan authors have written entire books analyzing in great detail the notoriously ambiguous, long-term contracts that the United Fruit Company signed with successive governments. As Kepner and Soothill remark, the contracts afford "various legal loopholes through which the Company can both evade responsibility and tighten its grip over its competitors or the government. Frequently concessions are so worded that the Company's rights are stated clearly, but those of the national government are merely inferred." [19] Citing the Compañía Agrícola's 1930 contract as a good example of the adroitly-drafted documents that UFCO's attorneys formulated, Kepner and Soothill examine numerous clauses replete with ambiguous phraseology. To illustrate their allegations, the authors discuss those articles dealing with the use of the wharf which the Company committed itself to build. While the contract permitted the Compañía Agrícola to build several wharves, it was actually obliged to construct only one pier destined for public service. Nonetheless, another article in the contract contradicted the requirement for public service by giving United Fruit's ships "preference over whatsoever others when destined to load bananas . . . provided they are berthed at one of the places which the Company reserves for such purposes." [20] Thus, the pier presumably destined solely for public service could be summarily — and legally — appropriated by the Company whenever it chose. The fact that UFCO hired expert attorneys, both in the United States and in the tropics, also meant that few governments or individuals were willing to legally take on the Company's "deep pockets" even when contracts were abrogated.

Defenders of the United Fruit Company point out that it was the Guatemalan government which granted the Company the generous concessions that were incorporated into various contracts. That successive governments did not attempt to rectify the agreements demonstrates the country's perceived need for significant foreign investments — particularly early in the twentieth century when few U.S. companies were investing in Central America — and the desire to diversify Guatemala's monoculture economy. Moreover, if the contracts had been substantially modified, it is likely that the United Fruit Company would have abandoned its Guatemala operations and increased its investments and production elsewhere in Central America. Indeed, the concessions UFCO extracted from Guatemala were not unlike those obtained in Honduras, Costa Rica and Panama, where, as in Guatemala, "both the liberal oligarchic state before the depression and authoritarian *caudillismo* after it accepted the need for foreign direct investment, but were in a weak position to dictate terms." [21]

Yet another oft-repeated charge against the United Fruit Company censures it for bribing government officials to secure concessions or to obtain favorable treatment. Former President Juan José Arévalo told the author that United Fruit bribed "the president, ministers and members of the Legislative Assembly in order to secure laws that were prejudicial to the country and very favorable to the Company. They paid the *jefe político* in Izabal a monthly sum that was larger than his government salary in order to assure that labor disorders were put down."[22] Although there is no way to verify such statements, it is undoubtedly true that the United Fruit Company did suborn government officials, and probably attempted to exert its influence on Guatemalan politics. As Bulmer-Thomas points out, however, "foreign companies were in general pressing for concessions which host governments were often ready to provide even without political influence. Concessions to foreign companies in El Salvador, a country without banana exports, were little different from concessions in Honduras, where the giant fruit companies were dominant."[23]

Moreover, bribing congressmen and government officials has long been a routine aspect of doing business in Guatemala. Even Kepner and Soothill acknowledge that when the United Fruit Company was negotiating a contract with the Guatemalan government during the 1930s, the president of the Congress offered to swing thirty-six votes in favor of the concession if the Company would pay him $80,000 for a piece of south coast land which was worthless for bananas.[24]

Not all of the charges leveled against the United Fruit Company, however, are valid. For example, one of Bauer Paiz's most pernicious charges concerns the "fabulous," unreported profits that *La Frutera* annually extracted from Guatemala. Explaining that his 1950-1953 analysis was based on yearly reports published by United Fruit's Guatemalan operations and other sources, such as the International Monetary Fund's *Balance of Payments Yearbook* and the U.S. Bureau of Labor Statistics, the former Minister of Economy and Labor concluded that *La Frutera* was annually grossing as much as $40 million a year in Guatemala. However, after analyzing the Company's operations during much the same time period (1946-1954), LaBarge determined that the Company was experiencing significant losses in its cash operating returns. For example, in 1952, following the devastating south coast blowdowns of September 1951, LaBarge states that UFCO's Guatemala activities represented a negative cash operating return of $9.1 million.[25]

How could there be such enormous discrepancies in an economic analysis of the same company during the same period of time? It is readily apparent that Bauer Paiz and United Fruit used two very different methods of calculating the value of UFCO's banana exports. The former made his estimates based on a somewhat simplistic calculation: the wholesale price of bananas once the fruit reached U.S. ports. Thus, in 1950, when bananas wholesaled for 8 cents a pound, Bauer Paiz concluded that the Company's 1950 exports of 5.2 million stems grossed United Fruit $33.6 million.[26] In compiling such statistics, however, Bauer Paiz, Cardoza y Aragón and numerous other Guatemalan writers fail to take into account such essential factors as United Fruit's production costs, property investment, net new investments, transportation, insurance and depreciation in all of its tropical divisions.[27]

Obviously, the United Fruit Company did have to consider such factors and arrived at its export figures by a far more complex system than the one used by Bauer Paiz. By using their formula, described in more detail below, the United Fruit Company reported 1950 export sales of its Guatemalan bananas totaling $17.5 million — a whopping $16.1 million less than Bauer Paiz's figure.

Bauer Paiz's analysis of the United Fruit Company's inordinate profits also included numerous activities that the Company did not include in the annual reports of its country-by-country operations. Thus, Bauer Paiz incorporates into UFCO's total annual profits the earnings derived from the Great White Fleet's monopoly of Guatemala's commercial navigation. By doing so, he added an estimated $9 million to United Fruit's yearly profits in Guatemala. Similarly, he believes UFCO's share of income from the International Railways of Central America should have been included in arriving at the United Fruit's yearly profits in Guatemala. In fact, elsewhere in his study Bauer Paiz asserts that the IRCA grossed about $3.6 million annually between 1950 and 1953. The railroad's statistics — audited by Peat, Marwick, Mitchell & Co. — showed annual net earnings that averaged $745,000 for the same period. The author also contends that Tropical Radio's income should have been included in the Company's total annual earnings.[28]

Although it is understandable why Bauer Paiz would contend that all of *El Pulpo's* earnings in Guatemala should have been combined in order to determine the Company's total net earnings, an enterprise as large and diverse as United Fruit enjoyed wide latitude in the methods it used to calculate its profits. As a vertically integrated company, UFCO could transfer earnings or losses from one branch of the Company to another — a practice permitted by the U.S. Internal Revenue Service. For instance, some of the annual losses accruing in banana production might be shifted to earnings realized through its international shipping component.

Moreover, if United Fruit had attempted to break out the earnings of its numerous subsidiaries on a country-by-country basis, the complicated allocation system might well have meant a higher tax bill in each country where it operated. It was therefore in UFCO's interests to maintain separate accounting systems for all of its subsidiaries, consolidating the annual results in Boston in order to ascertain taxes due the U.S. government and dividends to be paid to shareholders. Obviously, Bauer Paiz's argument that the IRCA's profits should have been added to United Fruit's annual earnings is even more contentious since UFCO did not own the railroad.

Examination of the United Fruit Company's earnings record also disputes the frequently made charge that UFCO earned "fabulous" profits throughout Central America. After studying the Company's earnings from 1899 to 1955, May and Plaza found that the average annual net earnings on net assets amounted to just under 13 percent. They noted that this was

> *close to the average for larger U.S. corporations engaged in production and/or sale of commodities . . . The long-term earnings record of the United Fruit Company, measured against net assets, is neither outstandingly better nor worse than the average for representative U.S. corporations, most of which are engaged wholly or largely in domestic operations far less hazardous than any enterprise concerned with foreign-based agricultural operations.*[29]

The study by May and Plaza also belied the oft-repeated myth that the United Fruit Company accumulated millions for a few stockholders. The authors found, in fact, that in 1955 UFCO's 8,775,000 outstanding shares were owned by 72,860 shareholders — approximating the number of Latin Americans then employed by the Company. Moreover, the yearly dividend return to the average shareholder, who owned 120 shares of UFCO stock, was only $360 — considerably less than the average annual wage of $942 that the United Fruit Company paid to each of its tropical employees in 1955. At the opposite end of the scale, the average annual dividend returns for those 141 individuals or trusts that owned 5,000 or more shares was $51,570 — "not of a dimension that would support many racing stables, yachts, or estates on the Riviera," the authors noted."[30]

The frequent charge that the United Fruit Company's subsidiaries remitted profits far in excess of their local expenditures was also studied by May and Plaza. After analyzing the operations of UFCO's subsidiaries in six Latin American countries, the authors found that in 1955, for instance, total receipts for the subsidiaries amounted to $156.8 million ($122 million from exports and $28 million from local sales). Of this $156.8 million, however, approximately 92 percent of the subsidiaries' income ($139 million) remained in the six countries: $103 million in the form of direct expenditures for wages, taxes and local purchases of goods and services, and $36 million expended in duties on imported items. The nearly $18 million that were remitted as dividend income constituted 12 percent of the income of all the subsidiaries and about 11 percent of the depreciated book value of the Company's total investment ($159 million) in its subsidiaries.[31]

May and Plaza's findings were later substantiated in an analysis of United Fruit's Central American operations undertaken in 1969 by economist Benjamín Villanueva T. After analyzing the Company's average annual net profits before taxes in Guatemala, Honduras and Costa Rica, and comparing them with UFCO's new investments during the 1960-1967 period, Villanueva concluded:

> *the average yearly amount of reinvestment for Central America as a whole almost exactly equals the average yearly net profit before taxes obtained by the Company ... If we add the direct and indirect contributions of the Company to Central American development, then the Company has been "putting in" a substantially larger amount that it has been "taking out."*

Villanueva thus determined that the frequent charge that the United

Fruit Company extracted from Central America an amount substantially in excess of what it contributed was "patently false."[32]

Comparison of the United Fruit Company's net assets and gross sales with that of many other American corporations also reveals that the United Fruit Company was not the colossal firm that many Latin Americans believed it to be. For example, UFCO's 1955 net assets of $390 million ranked well below thirty-four other U.S. corporations (excluding banks and insurance companies) with assets in excess of $1 billion. In fact, ten companies had assets ranging from six to thirty-seven times those of the United Fruit Company, and the Company's 1955 gross sales of approximately $288 million, excluding steamship traffic, were exceeded by 120 U.S. industrial corporations and twenty-four merchandising firms.

It is, however, necessary to put these figures into a Central American context. As May and Plaza pointed out,

> *in Costa Rica, Panama, and Honduras central government revenues for 1955 totaled about $47 million, $44 million and $30 million, respectively. In such countries, there is bound to be a perspective different from our own upon a company that showed a consolidated statement listing $330 million of gross revenue, $58 million of earnings before taxes and $33 million of profits after taxes ... The Company is a very large representative of an awesomely large neighbor to the north.*[33]

Bauer Paiz was also the author of another serious charge that has been repeatedly made about UFCO's Guatemala operations. In full-page newspaper advertisements dated October 18, 1951, he accused the Company of significantly undervaluing its banana exports, thereby annually defrauding the Guatemalan government of millions of quetzals in export taxes.[34] Bauer Paiz based his allegations on adjustments in the value of banana exports that the International Monetary Fund (IMF) published in 1951. These adjustments were the result of a new method of estimating the value of banana exports that the IMF had adopted the previous year. As a result of the Fund's revised export figures for Guatemala, Bauer Paiz concludes that in 1946, UFCO concealed nearly 10 million quetzals of banana exports; in 1947, 19 million quetzals; and in

1948, 21 million quetzals.

There are, however, two important aspects of this complicated issue. First, as William L. Taillon, UFCO's general manager in Guatemala, pointed out in an article published in the November 9, 1951, issue of *El Imparcial*, the figures that Bauer Paiz used included all of Guatemala's banana exports.[35] Thus, it was unquestionably erroneous to attribute the entire valuation adjustment to the United Fruit Company's exports. As Taillon noted, during 1946 "other persons or companies" [largely the Standard Fruit Company, which also followed "declared" valuation practices similar to UFCO's] exported 4.2 million stems of bananas, or about 40 percent of Guatemala's total banana exports for that year. The same ratios held true the following year. By 1948, however, United Fruit's competitors exported only 3.6 million stems of bananas, or about 30 percent of the country's total exports of the fruit.[36] As LaBarge remarks, "there has never been any attempt at rejoinder to this article [Taillon's statement]. Instead, the same mistake has been repeated by its originator and by other writers." [37]

A second contentious issue concerned how best to value Guatemala's banana exports. This matter had initially been brought to the IMF's attention by officials at the Banco de Guatemala who claimed that the United Fruit Company's value of its exports was less than 50 percent of that of certain independent producers. Following a review of the Banco's statistics, the IMF decided to change its formula for valuing banana exports from Guatemala and other isthmian countries. Curiously, the IMF adopted one method for Guatemala (based on the formula provided by the Banco de Guatemala) and another method for Costa Rica, Honduras and Panama.

In essence, the Guatemalan formula added the total cost of transportation per ton (maritime charges, insurance expenses, unloading costs and costs of loading the fruit on board trains in New Orleans) and deducted these charges from the wholesale price per ton on bananas once loaded onto trains in New Orleans (FOB). The United Fruit Company, however, had been using a totally different method — approved by the U.S. Internal Revenue Service — for calculating the exports of its bananas from all the countries in which it operated. The Company's formula computed the total value of bananas at the export point (for example, Puerto Barrios) as the quantity of bananas shipped from the port of export, multiplied by the total quantity of UFCO bananas shipped from all tropical ports, and divided by the total profit on all foreign sales, plus the total cost of banana production accumulated for all tropical divisions.

Although LaBarge maintains that "the Banco formula appears to have certain advantages which the Company procedure cannot claim . . . the Banco method was conceived specifically for the purpose of estimating banana values FOB Puerto Barrios; the Company formula was not." Nevertheless, because "the new estimates, with the Fund's prestige behind them, were embroiled almost immediately in Guatemalan politics," UFCO soon proposed that the IMF adopt United Fruit's IRS-approved method for calculating the value of all its banana exports.[38] After some discussion, statisticians at the International Monetary Fund accepted United Fruit's method and discarded the Banco de Guatemala's formula.

Nonetheless, LaBarge points out that, "in view of all this controversy, it is somewhat strange to learn that the two systems apparently yield similar value estimates. For 1950 the Company estimate of the value of its banana exports is 17,597,000 quetzals; the Banco estimate for the same year is 17,828,000 quetzals. The difference of slightly more than 1 percent on either base seems hardly worth the fuss."[39] It is clear, however, that Bauer Paiz misused the results of the Banco's method of calculating the value of Guatemala's banana exports when he attributed 100 percent of the undervaluation to the United Fruit Company. Nor did he or subsequent authors ever bother to rectify the damaging charges made against the Company.

As to the allegations that United Fruit routinely overthrew Central American governments and was responsible for keeping feral dictators in power, there is little evidence to support such indictments. Although it is well known that Zemurray was actively involved in a 1911 coup in Honduras, the event took place many years before his Cuyamel Fruit Company was bought by the United Fruit Company. The assertion that United Fruit bought the Depression-era elections that placed such despots as Guatemala's Ubico and Honduras's Carías Andino in power is also unfounded. Moreover, as Bulmer-Thomas argues, the Carías dictatorship, which ruled Honduras from 1932 to 1949, and "was often said to be within UFCO's sphere of influence," did not differ significantly from the long dictatorship in El Salvador, where UFCO had no banana interests.[40]

Kepner and Soothill also examine at some length "the plight of the private planters," contending that the United Fruit Company often treated unfairly the independent banana producers from whom it purchased fruit. The number of Guatemalan authors who have made similar allegations is sufficient to conclude that inequitable practices probably did occur. The standard contract with independent growers usually covered a five-year period and committed the planter to sell all of his "exportable" bananas to the United Fruit Company at a fixed price. "Exportable" was defined as all stems containing seven, eight and nine hands of fruit, but, as Kepner and Soothill point out, this requirement was subject to interpretation since all the hands had to have at least ten well-developed fingers. Thus, if a seven-hand stem contained one deficient banana, the stem could be down-graded and classified as a six-hand stem, thereby relieving the Company of its obligation to purchase that particular stem of fruit.

The contracts also usually stipulated that the bananas had to be "green and clean, not bruised, stained, dirty, scarred, sun-burned or damaged by any other cause." In addition, each contract contained precise provisions on how much time could elapse between the harvesting of the fruit and its receipt by the Company.[41] As might be expected, such explicit requirements were often arbitrarily applied, especially during periods when the Company wanted to limit the number of bananas it exported to the United States.

UNITED FRUIT'S IMPACT ON THE GUATEMALAN ECONOMY

If UFCO paid negligible taxes on the bananas it exported, much higher taxes were paid on importing many categories of equipment, as well as the goods it sold at Company commissaries. In fact, the import taxes the Company paid the Guatemalan government were sometimes ten times greater than the taxes it paid to export its bananas. (Jonas, among others, erroneously states that the Company was exempt from duties on all imports.)[42] Thus, between 1946 and 1954, *La Frutera* paid the Guatemalan government nearly $7 million in import taxes and slightly more than $1 million in export taxes. Annual import taxes averaged the equivalent of $770,000, while export taxes averaged almost $114,000. In addition, United Fruit annually disbursed approximately $34,000 for government stamps and seals, and spent about $58,000 a year to pay for property taxes and other miscellaneous taxes. It also reimbursed the Ministry of Finance for overtime use of its customs operations, entailing an average annual disbursement of $17,000. By adding the above figures, it can be seen that the United Fruit Company annually paid the government the equivalent of nearly $1 million in taxes and other services during the nine-year period between 1946 and 1954.[43] By 1955, when United Fruit paid the Guatemalan government the equivalent of $1.8 million in taxes, the amount represented 2.5 percent of the central government's total revenues — hardly a negligible amount.[44]

The Company also exerted a positive impact on the country's economy through several programs which affected hundreds of Guatemalan farmers, ranchers and merchants. These individuals benefited from UFCO's annual purchases of tons of corn, beans, rice, sugar, coffee and other staples, as well as dry goods, to sell through its network of commissaries. In the 1946-1954 period, for example, United Fruit annually purchased an average of $2 million worth of food and other consumer items which it retailed to its employees. To increase its dairy herds and provide slaughtered beef to its workers, *La Frutera* bought livestock from Guatemalan ranchers, benefiting them by about $116,000 a year. As mentioned above, the Company also contracted for millions of stems of bananas produced by independent growers, purchasing approximately $590,000 worth of the fruit each year. In addition, United Fruit often loaned these private planters modest sums of capital to assist them in the production of bananas, particularly in the control of sigatoka.

Villanueva's 1969 study of UFCO's Central American operations also examined the multiplier effect of the monies United Fruit annually expended in wages and local purchases. He found that between 1960 and 1966 an average of almost $47 million per year had been injected into the economies of Guatemala, Honduras and Costa Rica as part of the indirect effects of the Company's operations. Villanueva concludes that "the highest indirect contributions of United Fruit have occurred in Guatemala, in which the total payments to nationals averaged about five times the managerial surplus obtained from that country." [45] Villanueva terms "managerial surplus" as total gross income minus wages, salaries and direct production costs, excluding depreciation, taxes and other miscellaneous expenditures.

Utilizing some of the new tools of economic analysis that have become available since the publication more than fifty years ago of Kepner's two highly critical books on the United Fruit Company, LaBarge undertook an extensive and often revealing study of United Fruit's impact on the economic development of Guatemala between 1946 and 1954. His study is undoubtedly the most objective, professional economic analysis that has been conducted on UFCO's Guatemala operations. He found, for example, that "the post-war contribution from United Fruit Company operations in Guatemala has varied from less than 0.5 percent of the Gross National Product, under adverse conditions, to almost 6 percent in favorable periods."

Thus, UFCO's contribution to Guatemala's GNP during a nine-year period averaged 2.5 percent annually, causing LaBarge to conclude:

a product contribution averaging 2.5 percent of the yearly Gross National Product is hardly insignificant; few firms contribute as much to any economic system. With much of this product derived from areas which would otherwise be far less productive [particularly Guatemala's inhospitable north coast], there can be little question that the productive capacity of the country has been considerably enhanced by the Company's operations.[46]

LaBarge is also the first economist to calculate the value of the numerous subsidies UFCO provided its workers. Thus, he computes the benefits provided through the Company's medical program, the value of the housing it provided all workers, low-cost food products available at UFCO's commissaries, tuition-free schooling for dependents, the use of significant acreage to supplement their income, and monies spent for the employees' recreation. LaBarge's "social accounting" method reveals that while United Fruit was paying its approximately 9,000 workers an average annual salary of $916 in 1954, each employee also enjoyed benefits worth approximately $249 in indirect wages.[47] Consequently, the average annual salary of $1,165, which the United Fruit Company directly and indirectly paid its employees forty years ago, was actually a full $100 more than the country's 1992 per capita income of $1,065. (Guatemala's per capita income rose the equivalent of $79 in 1992, but the increase was somewhat leavened by a 13 percent increase in the consumer price index).[48]

In global terms, LaBarge found that during the nine years under review, the United Fruit Company expended approximately $9 million annually in direct wages and $1.6 million in indirect wages. However, because Guatemala did not enact a personal income tax until 1963, the government received no part of the direct wages United Fruit paid its employees during the first fifty-seven years it operated in Guatemala. (By 1944 both Costa Rica and El Salvador had levied direct taxes on personal income; ten years later Honduras and Nicaragua followed suit.)[49]

The foreign exchange earnings that the United Fruit Company annually generated through its sale to Guatemalan banks of dollars for quetzal balances also constituted an important contribution to the economy. Bauer Paiz, however, discounts the approximately $10.8 million which UFCO annually brought into the country, noting that the funds were not "sufficient even to pay for all of the Company's expenses since sums of $10.6 million only cover the wages it pays." Nevertheless, LaBarge maintains that the dollars that UFCO annually brought into Guatemala "stimulates domestic monetary circulation, and the economy acquires dollar balances." [50]

The annual net new investments of a corporation the size of the United Fruit Company would also usually constitute a major contribution to the host country's economy. In fact, during 1946, UFCO actually invested more in Guatemala than it earned there, and for the three-year period 1946-1948, the Company invested a total of $8.4 million in its Guatemala operations.[51] After 1948, however, LaBarge found that several factors "did not make Guatemala attractive for net new investments by the United Fruit Company." Despite the assertion of Bauer Paiz and others that *La Frutera* always earned exorbitant profits in Guatemala, LaBarge's analysis demonstrates a highly uneven performance by the Company's two divisions. One of the principal reasons for United Fruit's irregular production figures concerned factors over which the Company had no control. For example, between 1946 and 1954, blowdowns, floods and plant diseases caused annual losses that fluctuated from a low of 1.5 million stems of bananas to a high of 8 million stems. Thus, the annual average harvest for both divisions was 6 million stems, but each year an average 4.6 million stems were lost.[52]

The widely oscillating production figures that UFCO encountered in Guatemala caused a phenomenal variability in the Company's return to property factor (the property factors utilized by the United Fruit Company were composed of land and ownership capital.)[53] Thus, during the nine-year period described above, LaBarge found that the Company's return to property factors ranged from a gain of approximately 7.4 million quetzals (at par with the dollar) in 1947 to a loss of some 9.7 million quetzals in 1952. As LaBarge states, "such extreme variability means that the Guatemalan operations of the United Fruit Company have been so risky that the Company cannot tell within any reasonable range what the profit or loss from future operations is likely to be." [54]

Indeed, LaBarge found that the cash operating return figures issued by the Company for the period under study reveal an average yearly return of only 137,000 quetzals — less than a 1 percent per annum return on an average aggregate net property investment of nearly 35 million quetzals. Noting that "such rates are abysmally low for returns to the investors in any enterprise, and particularly so in a risky one," the economist concludes that the Company's average yearly rate of return had been insufficient to stimulate the expansion of its investment or even to ensure the replacement of its depreciation.[55] In fact, between 1946 and 1954, there were only four years (1946, 1947, 1948 and 1950) when United Fruit made net new investments in Guatemala, averaging 1.6 million quetzals annually. In the five unprofitable years, UFCO's disinvestments averaged 1.1 million quetzals per year.

During the time that the United Fruit Company was plowing back profits into new investments in Honduras, Costa Rica and Panama, it began heavy disinvestments in Guatemala, where it liquidated $9.5 million of its fixed assets during the 1949-1955 period — or about one-third of the Company's total investment in that country. Although discouraging production figures may have been a factor in *La Frutera's* liquidation, it is clear that the government's increasing hostility toward United Fruit played a significant role in management's decision to make no new investments in Guatemala. By 1956, however, with a far friendlier government in power, profit expectations had improved sufficiently to permit the Bananera division to commit itself to the equivalent of $5 million of new investments.

LA FRUTERA'S LEGACY

Although the United Fruit Company lost its corporate identity more than two decades ago, mention of the Company even today usually elicits a negative reaction from most Americans who are familiar with its history. That there should be such unanimous disapproval is undoubtedly due to the voluminous negative literature on the United Fruit Company's Latin American operations. It is indeed curious that so many North American academics have repeated — or left unchallenged — innumerable false or distorted statements that have been made about the Company. As a result, UFCO's legacy in the United States is that of a corporate pariah that overthrew governments, mercilessly exploited its workers, and extracted millions of dollars of profits while contributing virtually nothing to the impoverished nations in which it operated.

Certainly this is the image held by many Guatemalans who would still today probably agree with Bauer Paiz's searing indictment: "apart from the salaries that it pays its workers — much of which it recoups through its commissary sales — the Company provides no benefit to the economy of Guatemala."[56] A somewhat less radical assertion is made by the Melvilles, who maintain that the benefits the United Fruit Company provided its workers "were indirectly paid many times over by the government because of the taxes which the Company failed to pay."[57]

Such categorical indictments are clearly not merited because *La Frutera* did, in fact, make a significant contribution to Guatemala's development — particularly when juxtaposed against many of the country's current social indicators. Perhaps its most lasting contribution is one that few scholars have addressed: the tens of thousands of rural children who might never have seen the inside of a classroom had it not been for UFCO's excellent educational system. In a country where, in 1988, 71.8 percent of all individuals, fifteen years or older, who lived in rural areas were illiterate, United Fruit's schools represented a major endowment to Guatemala's future. Add to this the dozens of new skills that the Company brought to the nation's largely untrained work force, while simultaneously training a whole managerial and entrepreneurial class in new concepts of management, accounting, and cost control. It is apparent, therefore, that *La Frutera* played a meaningful and long-term role in Guatemala's human development — and this in some of the most isolated, underdeveloped areas of the country.

Another recurring allegation holds that the United Fruit Company ruthlessly exploited its workers. The fact is, the Company paid the best rural wages in Guatemala, causing men and their families to migrate from throughout the country in order to obtain employment with *La Frutera*. For nearly seven decades it thus provided work to tens of thousands of men who would otherwise have been engaged in subsistence agriculture or forced to work for the minuscule wages that most coffee or sugar cane *finqueros* paid their seasonal laborers. (Unlike coffee, cotton, sugar cane and many other crops which are harvested seasonally, the banana industry offered its laborers year-round employment.) The frequently criticized commissaries, which provided most staples at less than prevailing market prices, were also attractive inducements, and meant that UFCO's laborers and their dependents were better nourished than most *campesinos*.

While it is easy for critics to censure the rather primitive housing that United Fruit furnished its laborers, they fail to point out that the dwellings and their sanitary facilities were far superior to the dirt-floor hovels inhabited by most rural workers. Indeed, the trim wooden barracks or single-family houses that the Company offered its workers decades ago contrast sharply with the inadequate huts that 80 percent of Guatemalans are forced to live in today.

Few authors have emphasized that United Fruit operated two of the most modern, well-equipped and staffed hospitals in Guatemala, thereby providing thousands of its employees and their dependents with first rate-medical care. Its comprehensive inoculation programs and extensive sanitation efforts undoubtedly saved the lives of thousands of Guatemalans. Even in the 1990s, Guatemala's overcrowded public hospitals are grossly underfunded, with the media frequently reporting that most facilities lack doctors, medicine, equipment and even adequate food for their patients.

That United Fruit was the first large-scale agricultural enterprise to make productive use of Guatemala's hot, humid jungles was due almost entirely to its pioneering work in eradicating the diseases that had previously prohibited such development. By virtually eliminating such deadly diseases as yellow fever, malaria and typhoid, the Company demonstrated that the country's fertile but disease-ridden coastal areas offered a promising, previously unexploited area for agricultural development. The thousands of acres that it drained and cleared on the north coast are still among the most productive banana farms anywhere in the world, and UFCO's former south coast holdings are today dedicated to some of the nation's most important income-generating exports.

The first truly modernizing foreign corporation to invest in Guatemala, United Fruit's low-cost, efficient methods of clearing and draining jungle lands, and its innovative agricultural techniques brought new farming technologies to the country. Its introduction of Brahman cattle to Guatemala and the establishment of the country's first pure-bred cattle ranch had a lasting effect on the nation's beef industry — today one of the country's major cash exports. Ultimately, by transforming Guatemala into a major banana producer, United Fruit was instrumental in ending Guatemala's unhealthy dependence on coffee as its major source of export revenues.

Contrary to the established view, the United Fruit Company made an important contribution to Guatemala's economy. Although it could certainly have paid import taxes on much of the equipment exonerated by the Guatemalan government and should have paid much higher taxes on its banana exports, the country's economy realized significant benefits from United Fruit's presence. As May and Plaza asserted at the conclusion of their study,

> *the contribution of the United Fruit Company to the economies of the six countries is enormously advantageous when regarded from the view-*

point of their national interest . . . It has been leaving within the production area more than $7 for every dollar in profits withdrawn . . . Its operations in the six countries have yielded a return to their economies several times larger per acre of land and for each agricultural worker employed than any agricultural activity developed through local initiative and capital financing.[58]

In their 1968 study of the banana industry, economists Arthur, Houck and Beckford concurred in this overall conclusion, noting that "the large banana companies contributed more in material terms to rising standards of living and currency viability in the countries where they operated than any other single influence in the pre-World War II period. This is still true today, though relatively less so than before the war." [59]

The approximately ten million quetzals (at par with the dollar) that the United Fruit Company annually paid its workers, combined with the two million quetzals it expended locally to purchase goods for its commissaries created a multiplier effect that exerted a notable impact on Guatemala's economy. In fact, Bauer Paiz, then Minister of Economy and Labor, told the Legislative Assembly in 1949 that no less than 75,000 of Guatemala's 2.7 million citizens were dependent on or influenced by UFCO's operations.[60] In addition, the foreign exchange earnings of approximately $10 million that United Fruit annually generated, and the upwards of one million quetzals it paid yearly in taxes, contributed significantly to the economy.

Although the International Railways of Central America has been much maligned, it is clear that Minor Keith would never have completed the steel line between Puerto Barrios and Guatemala City had it not been for UFCO's assurances that it would soon begin producing millions of stems of bananas for the railroad to transport. Foreign or Guatemalan entrepreneurs, or perhaps even the Guatemalan government, undoubtedly would have eventually completed the line, but in 1904, when Keith took over the building of the final sixty-one miles, the railroad that became such a vital part of Guatemala's infrastructure had been under construction for nearly a quarter of a century. Obviously, Keith's completion of the railroad and the role the IRCA played in sanitizing Puerto Barrios constituted major contributions to the country's economy.

Furthermore, if the United Fruit Company had not purchased a substantial share of the IRCA's stock in 1936, the railroad undoubtedly would have soon declared bankruptcy. Nor is it likely that private investors in Guatemala or the financially-strapped Ubico regime could have acquired and successfully operated the line. With no alternate means of transporting goods imported at Puerto Barrios or conveying coffee, bananas and other export crops to that port, Guatemala's economy would have been critically affected if the United Fruit Company had not bailed out the floundering railroad.

Many authors also maintain that the United States overthrew the democratically elected government of Jacobo Arbenz in order to regain the land he had expropriated from the United Fruit Company. This rudimentary line of reasoning, which fails to take into account the Cold War mentality that permeated Washington during the 1950s, also ignores the fact that American presidents from McKinley through Bush have blatantly intervened in Central America and the Caribbean for reasons that had little to do with protecting American investments, and far more to do with enforcing U.S. hegemony. In ousting Arbenz and later initiating plans to depose Fidel Castro, President Eisenhower was merely following a well-established practice of removing regional heads of state considered inimical to U.S. national security. The secretary general of the Guatemalan Communist Party, who was on the scene in 1954 and closest to the collapse of the Arbenz government, had it right: "They would have overthrown us even if we had grown no bananas."

In the final analysis, the very fact that *La Frutera* made a substantial contribution to Guatemala's development may well have been one of the principal reasons that the fruit giant was both envied and disliked by a large cross-section of the population. Indeed, Frank McNeil, who served as U.S. ambassador to Costa Rica in the early 1980s, made a similar observation about the operations of the United Fruit Company in that country. "The fact that UFCO contributed enormously to the development of transport, public health, elementary schools, and the development of a local managerial class may have even heightened the sense of dependency and resentment," he wrote in 1988.[61]

There were, however, other compelling reasons for resentment against the Boston-based banana company. Understandably, many Guatemalans disliked the fact that a huge, foreign-controlled corporation monopolized the country's largest agricultural enterprise, one that was perceived as annually extracting millions of dollars of profits, while contributing little to the nation's economy. The Company's close relationship with the hated railroad and its control over the docks and shipping facilities in Puerto Barrios and San José were also significant elements in the widespread enmity that United Fruit engendered. That the Company operated its vast enclaves virtually as a state within a state, and was fully capable of intervening in local politics, led Blasier to make a striking statement: "some Guatemalans might have preferred to forego any conceivable economic advantages that association with the United Fruit Company offered in order to avoid what they considered decisive *political* disadvantages." [62]

Since an objective analysis cannot honestly conclude that UFCO provided "no benefit to the economy of Guatemala," Blasier's remark helps to explain Bauer Paiz's negative assessment of the United Fruit Company's operations. Many would undoubtedly argue, however, that because the United Fruit Company's operations encroached on Guatemala's sovereignty and impeded a completely independent economy, the price that the country paid for *La Frutera's* presence was far too high. That there was a vital trade-off caused by United Fruit's long years of operation cannot be denied, but if the U.S. corporation had never functioned in Guatemala, it is doubtful that any private or public entity would have contributed to the innumerable modernizing processes that the United Fruit Company set in motion, particularly early in the twentieth century. Certainly no other institution would have provided the profound and wide-ranging benefits that the United Fruit Company dispensed to the Guatemalan people and its economy during the sixty-six years that it operated in that Central American nation.

Epilogue

Numerous houses in the Tiquisate compound are now virtually hidden from view by a lush growth of tropical trees and bushes that have had little pruning in nearly thirty years. Paint peels off many of the houses that are visible; corrugated iron roofs that have not been painted in decades are rusted and often twisted or loose; cement steps leading to the entrances of most houses are black with mildew. Overgrown by weeds, the previously smooth, gravel roads have been roughly cobblestoned and are replete with potholes. The open spaces, once carefully manicured by dozens of *La Frutera's* yardmen, are covered with six-foot-high weeds and bushes, with cattle grazing in what was previously the airfield.

At the club house, some of the plywood ceiling panels in the former bar have fallen in. The unkempt, decadent appearance of many of the houses in the Tiquisate compound is even more pronounced at the hospital, now administered by the Guatemalan government. In the wards that have been closed, floor boards have rotted; plywood ceilings have fallen in and syringes and other medical refuse are strewn behind the once spotlessly-clean building. In one room, thousands of old medical records have been dumped onto the floor, and a visitor is warned that fleas infest the mildewed papers. At the hospital and throughout the compound there is a melancholy feeling of abandonment and tropical indolence; at the same time, there is a ghostly sense of the vibrant, meticulously-kept community that once housed and provided extensive recreational facilities for dozens of Compañía Agrícola employees.

Many of the Guatemalans who now live in the Tiquisate compound own or administer nearby farms or ranches. Thousands of acres of what once were verdant banana plantations are now incorporated into large *fincas,* providing pastures for cattle or are dedicated to sugar cane, soybeans and sesame. Except for the few distinctive buildings that *La Frutera* built more than fifty years ago and that still dot the area, there is little evidence of the multi-million-dollar agricultural enterprise that once dominated Guatemala's Pacific coast.

On the north coast, the Bananera compound appears frozen in time, little changed from the way the division looked fifty or sixty years ago. The front of each of the approximately eighty houses in the division headquarters bears a small wooden plaque providing the dates of when extensive repairs and needed maintenance were undertaken in both the interior and exterior of the structure. Air conditioning units hum in many windows, where screens have been replaced by air-tight, louvered glass windows. Cable television provides residents with innumerable U.S. and Mexican networks. Workmen prune bushes and trees in the yards and open areas; trash is collected, street lights function, roads and sidewalks are in good condition, and the greens and fairways of the nine-hole golf course are closely cropped. In fact, BANDEGUA (Banana Development Company of Guatemala), the Del Monte Fresh Produce Company's Guatemalan subsidiary, has made only a few changes in Bananera's physical appearance since it bought the division in 1972. There has been, however, a significant change in the nationality of those employees and their families who now live in the compound. No Americans live there, although General Manager Gerald K. Brunelle, who resides in Guatemala City, spends several days each week in Bananera.

The old Quiriguá hospital, which today exudes an overpowering sense of emptiness, was closed in 1960 and replaced by a new facility located directly behind the Bananera compound.[1] Donated by the United Fruit Company to the government of Guatemala, part of the old building is now used by the Ministry of Public Health as a training center for health workers. Like the hospital in Tiquisate, many of the ceiling panels have fallen in; screens are torn and the paint peeling. The elevators have long since ceased to function.

Several hundred yards in front of the former hospital, in a fenced-in area overgrown by weeds, is a tall, white pedestal which serves as a base for a weathered marble bust of the physician who dedicated his life to health care in the Motagua Valley. Commissioned by the United Fruit Company and inaugurated in 1951, Dr. Macphail's bust looks out over the nearby Merendón mountains. A blackened brass plaque provides the only evidence that the United Fruit Company once operated in the area: "Dr. Neil P. Macphail, founder (October 5, 1913) and director (until April 1, 1949) of the hospital at Quiriguá. UFCO."

TRANSFORMATIONS IN THE BANANA INDUSTRY

If time seems to have stood still in Bananera, the production, harvesting and processing of bananas have changed remarkably during the twenty years since United Brands sold its north coast division. One of the major innovations involves the development of several new varieties of Cavandish banana plants, all of which are resistant to Panama disease. Only about twelve feet high, the Grand Naine, produced by Del Monte's Bananera division, is considerably shorter than the Gros Michel, and thus less susceptible to wind damage. Its compact size also makes harvesting the Grand Naine somewhat easier.

Converting to new varieties caused another enormous change in the banana industry — perhaps the most significant innovation since the United Fruit Company began refrigerating its ships early in the twentieth century. Since the Grand Naine and other Cavandish varieties produce fruit that is considerably more delicate and susceptible to bruising than the sturdy Gros Michel, it was necessary to devise a new method of transporting bananas. Thus, in the late 1950s, the Standard Fruit Company (today's Dole Food) began experiments in Honduras, whereby bananas were removed from their stems and shipped in forty-pound cardboard boxes.

The new method of shipping bananas eliminated the rough treatment often given to unwieldy, heavy stems of bananas, greatly improving the appearance of the fruit when it was displayed in supermarket produce departments. Moreover, when bananas had been shipped on the stem, it was often difficult to grade an entire stem because of the unevenness in quality and maturity of the dozens of bananas that comprised a stem. By destemming the fruit into individual hands, however, it was much easier to correctly classify the bananas. The boxes also made it considerably easier for stevedores, banana ripeners and supermarket employees to handle the bananas. Indeed, in a chapter he titles

"A Box Saves an Industry," historian Thomas L. Karnes maintains that "perhaps two dozen steps in the processing, shipping, and handling of the banana were eliminated by the new cartons, for they remained in the container from the Honduran farm to the retail store."[2]

Yet another major development in the shipping of bananas has been the growing use of refrigerated, containerized transportation units. Thus, the approximately 800 boxes of bananas loaded into a container at a packing station are never handled again until they reach their U.S. distributor. The high costs of the units (approximately $40,000 each) and the fact that not all vessels are equipped to handle containers, however, have inhibited the industry's complete conversion to containerized units. In fact, Del Monte does not use containers, and, instead, palletizes all of its boxes.

If Standard Fruit took the lead in converting to a new variety of banana and was the first to begin shipping the fruit in cartons, the United Fruit Company pioneered an ingenious method of "branding" its bananas. Beginning in the early 1960s, every third banana in a hand of eight or more fingers received a small pressure-sensitive sticker that featured United Fruit's registered trademark: a Carmen Miranda-like figure of "Chiquita Banana." (Chiquita took on a life of her own in 1944 after the advertising firm of Batten, Barton, Durstine and Osborn produced one of the most successful and popular radio commercials ever aired. Indeed, the catchy rhumba rhythm and its silly lyrics soon became a hit song across the nation, with popular bands including the banana extolling-tune in their repertoires).[3]

Before United Fruit began branding its bananas, it experimented with various machines that could quickly and lightly attach the stickers to millions of bananas. All of the systems developed, however, were either too complex to operate or were prohibitively expensive. UFCO eventually determined that the easiest, most cost-effective method would be to simply apply the labels by hand, the last step before boxing the fruit.

While the handling and marketing of bananas have undergone enormous transformations during the last twenty years, numerous changes have also been made in the way bananas are grown. For example, young stems of bananas are now fumigated with an insecticide. (According to

Brunelle, myriad tests have shown that the insecticide is not absorbed into the fruit. Moreover, all chemicals used by Del Monte have been approved by the Environmental Protection Agency).[4] After each stem has been fumigated, a worker then encases it in a light weight plastic bag, perforated by small holes. By protecting the bananas against diseases, insects, bats and birds, the bags also reduce sunburning and do not permit the insecticide to be washed away by rain. Furthermore, by providing the stem with its own "micro climate," the fruit matures one to two weeks more quickly than bananas that have not been bagged.

At the same time that the plastic jacket is slipped over the immature stem, a worker places a colored, plastic ribbon around the stem — above the jacket and readily visible from the ground. Thirteen colors are used, corresponding to the approximately thirteen weeks that it will take for the bananas to mature. Each color represents seven days. Thus, the fruit cutters can immediately ascertain the age of each stem. In addition, the ribbons are essential in calculating, within precise time frames, the amount of fruit that will be available for harvesting.

Although Cavendish varieties of bananas are resistant to Panama disease, sigatoka continues to plague banana plantations throughout the isthmus. In fact, black sigatoka, first identified in Honduras in 1972, is considerably more difficult to control than was yellow sigatoka, which invaded Central America earlier in the twentieth century. Since black sigatoka did not respond to the Bordeaux mixture that United Fruit pioneered, intense research was initiated to discover a pesticide that would combat the new and hardy fungus. The spores of black sigatoka, which will soon develop a resistance to any one particular pesticide, now requires the alternate application of at least six different pesticides to the banana plants. But black sigatoka is still today devastating millions of banana plants throughout the isthmus.

There is now a far more sophisticated method of applying the pesticides used to control sigatoka. The thousands of workers who once painstakingly hand sprayed the Bordeaux mixture on UFCO's banana plants and the giant risers that automatically showered the mix have been replaced by low-flying airplanes which spray the pesticides on the plants. Moreover, BANDEGUA is now experimenting with computer-based methods of forecasting the growth periods of the disease and then attacking those specific areas of sigatoka development. If this technology can be perfected, it will preclude the current, costly method of periodically spraying an entire farm. (In its unrelenting fight against sigatoka, BANDEGUA annually spends approximately $275 on every acre of banana-producing land).

Del Monte also continually monitors the soil contents of its fields and systematically fertilizes its plants in order to maintain the soil composition that banana plants thrive on. While the fertilizers — urea and potassium — apparently do not contribute to larger bananas, they do prevent the soil from becoming depleted of needed minerals. As a result, the problems of soil exhaustion that United Fruit once faced, and which necessitated periodically establishing new farms, is no longer an ongoing concern.

In addition, Cavendish varieties, particularly the Grand Naine, produce far more bananas per acre than did the Gros Michel. While the Gros Michel annually yielded approximately 1,100 boxes of bananas per hectare, (2.47 acres) the Grand Naine can produce up to 3,000 boxes per hectare — or an astounding fifty-five tons annually.[5] One of the reasons the Grand Naine is so productive is precisely because of its small size: approximately 650 of its rhizomes can be planted to an acre, whereas only 250 of the much larger Gros Michel variety were planted per acre.[6]

As a result of the new varieties of bananas and improved technologies, nearly all of BANDEGUA's land is in production. Of the approximately 15,000 acres of Motagua Valley land that the company owns, a full 11,500 acres are planted in bananas. "Most of the land we're not using is not good for bananas," Brunelle explains. "But some of the fallow land, which does contain soil appropriate for bananas, will probably eventually go into production."[7]

Another innovation in the banana industry are the miles of aerial tramways that are now used to transport harvested stems from the fields directly into packing stations. Thus, after approximately seventy to ninety stems of bananas are cut and hung on the tramways, a tractor pulls the "train" directly into a packing station. There, the stems are debagged and individual hands of bananas are removed from each stem and placed in tanks of water. Immersing the fruit in two different tanks of water permits the latex which seeps out of the crown of each hand to coagulate; it also removes any traces of the insecticide sprayed on the bananas three months earlier. At this point the green fruit is submitted to a rigorous selection process. Ideally, the "perfect banana" will be eight to nine inches long; a little more than an inch in thickness, with no visible imperfections. Hands that are accepted are placed on conveyor belts and are trimmed, culled, separated and labelled as they move toward the boxing facilities. One of the last steps involves placing each box on a scale to assure that at least forty-one pounds of bananas are packed into the carton.

Throughout BANDEGUA's packing process, a random, ongoing inspection system is utilized to assure that the most exacting handling standards are being observed — and that the highest quality of bananas has been selected. Random quality checks are also conducted alongside the vessel once the fruit has reached the port of Santo Tomás; a final random inspection is undertaken after the bananas are loaded into the refrigerated hold of the ship, which usually accommodates approximately 110,000 boxes of bananas — more than 4.5 million pounds.

Clearly, the new methods of raising, harvesting and processing bananas have caused profound transformations in the number of employees that are required in today's banana industry. Undoubtedly one of the most notable changes has been the increased number of laborers required to operate the packing stations. Another new development has been the employment of large numbers of women who work in these packing facilities. In the Bananera division, approximately 80 percent of the workers in the packing stations are women, thus comprising from 15 to 20 percent of BANDEGUA's total work force.

Just as the United Fruit Company once did, Del Monte makes a notable contribution to Guatemala's economy.[8] In addition to paying its 6,000 employees the equivalent of $7 million annually, approximately 35,000 Guatemalans are directly affected by the banana company's operations.[9] The most vital benefit that Del Monte provides the Guatemalan economy, however, is the hard currency that it generates. In 1991, for example, the figure totalled nearly $51 million. (After BANDEGUA sells its fruit, it is required to repatriate approximately $4.50 for every box of premium, Class One bananas that it has exported. About 93 percent of the company's bananas are classified as premium).

While BANDEGUA provides the Guatemalan treasury with far more hard currency than United Fruit did, there is also another noteworthy difference between the operations of the two companies: Del Monte enjoys no exclusive concessions. As Brunelle explains, "our operations in Guatemala are premised on what is known as the banana law, which provides for certain tax exemptions, such as tax-free status for items brought in specifically for bananas: fertilizers or specific machinery used for the production of bananas. It's very much a development-oriented law, and certainly not exclusive to Del Monte. If you're in the banana business, you qualify."

CHIQUITA BANANA RETURNS TO GUATEMALA

It is little known in Guatemala that the successor to the United Fruit Company, Chiquita Brands International, Inc. is once again purchasing large quantities of bananas raised on land previously leased by UFCO. And much of the fruit is shipped from a remodeled wharf that *La Frutera* formerly used in Puerto Barrios. Founded in 1988, the Compañía Bananera Guatemalteca Independiente (COBIGUA) consists of six independent growers, all Guatemalans, who in 1991 produced an estimated 8.5 million boxes of bananas — 80 percent of which were sold to Chiquita Brands. With 10,000 acres under cultivation, COBIGUA's plantations are located north and east of Del Monte's banana farms — the same land that the United Fruit Company first leased from the Guatemalan government in 1924. The largest producer and general manager of the company is Mario Mena, who was raised in Tiquisate where his father, a thirty-year veteran of the Compañía Agrícola, was employed as an irrigation pumping stations supervisor. Before founding COBIGUA, Mena spent eleven years as the general manager of Del Monte's Bananera division.

Employing 3,000 workers (15 percent of whom are women), COBIGUA spends the equivalent of $6 million a year in wages, paying salaries that are considerably higher than most agricultural enterprises in Guatemala. Just as the United Fruit Company once did, Mena's company allocates a substantial part of its operating costs ($1.2 million annually) to providing its employees with free housing, medical care and six years of primary education for dependent children. When these benefits are added to COBIGUA's minimum hourly wage, even the lowest paid laborer earns the equivalent of $140 a month — at least twice as much as most of Guatemala's rural workers earn.

Mena's company is also responsible for rehabilitating the old wharf at Puerto Barrios, which the government took over in 1969 after it nationalized the International Railways of Central America. Badly damaged during the devastating earthquake of 1976, the wharf was little used until the Cerezo administration turned over the facility to COBIGUA in 1990. After the company invested approximately $11 million to repair the wharf and to upgrade offices and other related shipping facilities, the pier was inaugurated in October 1990. According to Mena, his company, which also uses the facilities at Santo Tomás, undertook the refurbishing of the Puerto Barrios wharf in order to expand its banana operations and provide COBIGUA with a second point of embarkation. The only privately-administered government facility in Guatemala, Puerto Barrios accommodates about four ships weekly, one of which is owned or leased by Chiquita Brands. Each vessel departs with nearly 200,000 boxes of bananas.

The monies COBIGUA annually expends in repatriated dollars for its bananas, the direct and indirect wages that it disburses, and its payment of property taxes, social security payments, consular fees, and other expenses total approximately $50 million.[10] Viewed another way, every acre of COBIGUA's banana-producing farms annually provides the Guatemalan economy with an estimated $5,000 — one of the highest rates of return for any of the country's agroexports.

CHIQUITA BRANDS INTERNATIONAL TODAY

The former United Brands, which changed its name to Chiquita Brands International in March 1990, has undergone numerous changes since Eli Black purchased the company in 1969. Perhaps one of the company's most highly-publicized events concerned Black's 1975 suicide when he leaped from the forty-fourth floor of his mid-town Manhattan office. United Brands's declining profits and the dwindling price of its stocks, Black's continuing problems with UB's board of directors, and the enormous corporate debt that the flamboyant executive confronted after purchasing United Fruit undoubtedly all contributed to his suicide. After Black's death, however, it became apparent that he had been involved in allegedly illegal actions in Honduras and Italy that might also have been factors in his dramatic suicide.

Shortly after Black's suicide, United Brands was purchased by Max M. Fisher and Seymor Milstein and family. They, in turn, sold their majority interests in the company in 1984 to Carl H. Lindner's American Financial Corporation, which currently owns 46 percent of the corporation. It is apparent, however, that the Lindner family would like to distance Chiquita Brands as much as possible from its UFCO past. When the author wrote several Chiquita executives seeking information on the United Fruit Company, her letters were never answered; nor were telephone calls returned. Similarly, Chiquita Brands would not permit the author to consult several boxes of United Fruit Company files still in the possession of a former employee in Guatemala.

With 1992 net sales of $2.7 billion, Chiquita Brands, which ranks 115 among *Fortune's* Five Hundred, is today a far more diversified company than was the United Fruit Company.[11] It now markets bananas, pineapples, mangos, papayas, melons, citrus, lettuce, potatoes and other vegetables. Until 1992, the company also marketed a wide variety of prepared foods, particularly meat products (John Morrell, Nathan's Famous, Rath Black Hawk, etc.), but the income from these products were often ten times less than those of Chiquita's fresh foods. (In 1991, for example, its prepared foods component yielded only $40.9 million in operating income, while its fresh foods division generated $198.3 million.) Late in 1992, therefore, Chiquita's management began the sale of all of its meat division operations. In other words, Chiquita's recent reorganization, with an increased emphasis on the sale of fresh fruits — particularly bananas — appears to represent a return to the United Fruit Company's emphasis on the sale of the world's most popular and widely-sold fruit.

Approximately three-quarters of Chiquita's net sales are generated by bananas. Thus, the company's 1992 net loss of $284 million from continuing operations was due, in large part, to a sharp decline in the sales of its bananas. The Lindners attributed this unprecedented loss to "the extraordinary outbreak of disease [black sigatoka] and unusual weather patterns (El Niño) affecting banana industry cultivation." [12] Nevertheless, Chiquita Brands still commands about 25 percent of the U.S. market, where it sells it bananas under the Chiquita, Consul, Chico and Amigo brand names. Dole, with approximately 30 percent of the U.S. market, ranks first in sales, but Chiquita outsells Dole three to one in Western Europe — the world's largest market for the golden fruit.

Although Chiquita Brands attributes part of its competitive edge to the geographic diversity of its banana sourcing, more than half of the bananas it sells are produced by subsidiaries operating on former United Fruit Company divisions located in Panama and Honduras. In fact, a third of all the bananas the company sold in 1990 were produced in Panama; about 20 percent originated in Honduras. To hedge against floods, blowdowns, banana diseases and "political changes," however, the company also purchases fruit from independent planters in Colombia, the Philippines, Ecuador, Costa Rica and Guatemala. These nations produced from 6 to 14 percent of the bananas Chiquita sold during 1990.

With a total labor force of 46,000, Chiquita Brands employs 38,000 persons in Central and South America. The company owns 125,000 acres of land and leases approximately 45,000 acres of improved land, principally in Costa Rica, Panama and Honduras. Although no longer operating under the name of the Great White Fleet, Chiquita Brands boasts the world's largest fleet of refrigerated ships. By the end of 1994, the company will own thirty ships, and currently has long-term freighting arrangements utilizing another twenty refrigerated vessels. By 1990, all ships serving North America were equipped for pallets or containers.

Like many U.S. corporations, Chiquita Brands and its competitors are hoping for a substantial expansion of their markets in Eastern Europe and the republics that comprised the former Soviet Union, where per capita banana consumption is less than 10 percent of Western European levels. Undoubtedly U.S. banana companies would like to foment an annual per capita consumption in Eastern Europe that would rival Sweden's thirty-six pounds — approximately eleven pounds more than per capita consumption in North America.[13]

Of greater concern, however, is the current standoff between the Council of the European Communities and Latin America's principal banana producers. Eight Latin American countries currently sell Western Europe approximately 2.6 million tons of bananas each year, paying a 20 percent tariff ($117 a ton) on the yellow fruit. However, led by Great Britain and France, which purchase bananas from their former colonies in Africa, the Caribbean and the Pacific, (known as the APC countries), the European Community has recently negotiated an agreement which will permit only 2.2 million tons of Latin American bananas to be imported during 1994. If imports increase beyond this figure, the EC plans to impose an additional tariff (a whopping $995 a ton) effective July 1994. Meanwhile, the APC countries will be permitted to continue selling their bananas duty-free. Threatened with measures that could cost the hemisphere's banana-producing nations approximately $1 billion a year, severely affecting the approximately 250,000 workers employed in the industry, Latin American leaders are negotiating the issue in the Uruguay Round of the General Agreement on Tariffs and Trade (GATT).[14]

THE RAILROAD: OBSOLETE, INEFFICIENT AND SUBSIDIZED

In the nearly twenty-five years since the Guatemalan government nationalized the International Railways of Central America, the Ferrocarriles de Guatemala (FEGUA) has become the country's most ineffective and deteriorated public utility. Although most of its rolling stock, which has not been replaced or given virtually any maintenance during a quarter-century, is in calamitous conditions, the railroad's most critical problem is the dangerous state of its road bed. Particularly in the Motagua Valley, where thousands of wooden ties have rotted or been weakened by floods, the railroad's trains suffer an average of 300 derailments annually.

In fact, the precarious state of FEGUA's road bed now requires an interminable eighteen hours for its locomotives to make the 191-mile trip from Guatemala City to Puerto Barrios. If a derailment occurs, the trip can take upwards of twenty-four hours. (While FEGUA charges the equivalent of only $1.40 for the trip, bus companies exact a fare of $6, but make the run in six hours). Although the IRCA's trains, which also stopped at dozens of villages, were hardly rapid, the trip from the capital to the Atlantic port was accomplished in approximately ten hours. Moreover, there were daily passenger and freight trains scheduled between the two cities. Today, FEGUA usually provides only three trains a week to and from the capital to Puerto Barrios, and a similar number to and from Tecún Umán on the Mexican border.[15] The service that used to operate between Zacapa and Anguiatú, on the border with El Salvador, was eliminated after the 1976 earthquake. Although the Ferrocarril Nacional de El Salvador, nationalized by that government in 1974, continues to operate from the Guatemalan border to the Gulf of Fonseca, it, too, is a money-losing enterprise, requiring state subsidies.[16]

The railroad that once employed approximately 5,000 workers is now using attrition to gradually reduce a labor force which numbers approximately 1,400. Nevertheless, the utility continues to be a drain on the Guatemalan government. In 1991, for example, the government provided the equivalent of $800,000 to FEGUA's annual $3.8 million budget. As it has since it nationalized the IRCA in 1968, the government is also forced to provide additional yearly subsidies. In 1991, the sum totalled approximately $2 million and was used to help pay salaries, purchase diesel and furnish a minimum of maintenance to its rolling stock. As J. Rodolfo Bendfeldt, advisor to FEGUA's manager, points out, "the critical problem for the company is that the government has never really preoccupied itself with the railroad. It has provided palliatives, but not solutions."[17]

In an era when Mexico, Argentina and other Latin American countries are beginning to sell off many inefficient, publicly-owned companies, the Guatemalan government has expressed interest in privatizing a number of state-owned organizations. In fact, President Ramiro de León Carpio plans to permit the country's private sector to assume ownership of the railroad sometime during 1994. It is conceivable, therefore, that one of Minor Keith's proudest achievements will once again provide Guatemalans with an efficient, coast-to-coast railroad system.

Notes

Chapter 1: The Historical Setting

1. Guatemalans term their country's Atlantic seaboard the "north coast." The area that borders the Pacific Ocean is called the *costa sur* or "south coast."
2. Nathan L. Whetten, *Guatemala, The Land and the People*, (New Haven: Yale University Press, 1961), 5.
3. Frederick Upham Adams, *Conquest of the Tropics*, (New York: Doubleday, Page & Company, 1914), 199.
4. William J. Griffith, *Empires in the Wilderness, Foreign Colonization and Development in Guatemala, 1834-1844*, (Chapel Hill: University of North Carolina Press, 1965), 141-42.
5. Valentín Solórzano F., *Evolución económica de Guatemala*, 4th ed. rev., (Guatemala: Editorial José de Pineda Ibarra, 1977), 293-94.
6. Edelberto Torres Rivas, *Centroamerica hoy*, (Mexico: Siglo XXI, 1976), 52.
7. Bananas, which are not native to the Western Hemisphere, probably originated in South Asia and were transported by traders to the Middle East and Africa. Friar Tomás de Berlanga, who later became bishop of Panama, is generally credited with having introduced bananas to the New World in 1516, when he brought banana rhizomes from the Canary Islands to Santo Domingo. The earliest date available for the export of bananas from Guatemala is 1881, when 10,044 stems were shipped to the United States. In 1902, after the United Fruit Company began purchasing bananas on Guatemala's north coast, almost 240,000 stems were exported.

    Charles Morrow Wilson, *Empire in Green and Gold, The Story of the American Banana Trade*, (New York: Henry Holt and Company, 1947), 13-14; Rafael Piedra-Santa Arandi, *Introducción a los problemas económicos de Guatemala*, 2nd ed., (Guatemala: Ediciones Superiores, 1977), 119.
8. David J. McCreery, "Coffee and Class in Liberal Guatemala," *The Hispanic American Historical Review*, Vol. 56, No. 3, (1976), 456.
9. Regina Wagner, "Empresarios alemanes en Guatemala," *(Mesoamérica*, 13, 1987), 96-97.
10. Ibid., 102; 107.
11. Ibid., 102.
12. *Central America as an Export Field*, (Washington, D.C.: Department of Commerce, Special Agents Series, No. 113, 1916), 24.
13. Wagner, "Empresarios alemanes en Guatemala," 106.
14. Torres Rivas, *Centroamérica hoy*, 87.
15. Entrusting the management of large coffee *fincas* to hired administrators continues today. In fact, the conditions prevailing on many large coffee planta-

tions have not changed markedly from the observations made forty years ago by a team of experts from the International Bank for Reconstruction and Development. "Many large [coffee] landowners have the traditional attitudes of absentee landlords, content with one yearly inspection of their farms and interested only in the total amount of immediate cash income, however ruinous the production methods used. On many coffee farms the lack of care of the land and trees, as well as outmoded planting practices, have kept output far below the potential maximum."

International Bank for Reconstruction and Development, *The Economic Development of Guatemala*, (Washington, D.C., 1951), 26.

16. José M. Aybar de Soto, *Dependency and Intervention: The Case of Guatemala in 1954*, (Boulder, Colorado: Westview Press, 1978), 84-85.

17. J.C. Cambranes, "Los empresarios agrarios modernos y el estado en Guatemala," *(Mesoamérica*, 10, 1985), 288.

18. Alfonso Bauer Paiz, *Catalogación de leyes y disposiciones de trabajo de Guatemala del período 1872 a 1930*, (Guatemala: Instituto de Investigaciones Económicas y Sociales, Universidad de San Carlos, 1965), 91-92.

19. J.C. Cambranes, *Desarrollo económico y social de Guatemala: 1868-85* (Guatemala: Instituto de Investigaciones Económicas y Sociales de la Universidad de San Carlos de Guatemala, 1975), 104.

20. Chester Lloyd Jones, *Guatemala Past and Present*, (Minneapolis: University of Minnesota, 1940), 154-55.

21. No one has articulated this argument more eloquently than Miguel Angel Asturias, Guatemala's Nobel literature laureate, who contended that "new blood" could counterbalance the Indians' "functional deficiencies, moral vices and biological exhaustion . . . To improve cattle, it was necessary to bring in new breeds . . . Why not bring in other vigorous and more capable races to improve our Indians?" Asturias asked in a thesis he presented for a university degree in 1923.

Miguel Angel Asturias, *El problema social del indio*, 2nd ed. rev. (Paris: Centre de Recherches de L'Institut D'Etudes Hispanics, 1971), 107.

22. Francis Polo Sifontes, *Historia de Guatemala*, (León, Spain: Editorial Evergráficas, S.A., 1988), 242.

23. Michael McClintock, *The American Connection, State Terror and Popular Resistance in Guatemala*, Vol. 2, (London: Zed Books, 1985), 8.

24. Sanford A. Mosk, "Economía cafetalera de Guatemala durante el período 1850-1918," translated from *Inter-American Economic Affairs*, v. 9, No. 3, 1955. Quoted in Jorge Luján Muñoz, *Economía de Guatemala, 1750-1940, antología de lecturas y materiales*, Vol. 1, (Guatemala: Universidad de San Carlos, 1980), 353.

25. Ibid., 355.

26. Edelberto Torres Rivas, *Desarrollo social Centroamericano*, 5th ed., (San José, Costa Rica: EDUCA, 1977), 62.

27. McCreery, "Coffee and Class in Liberal Guatemala," 443.

28. Ibid., 445.

29. Jones, *Guatemala Past and Present*, 251.
30. Herman E. Krooss and Charles Gilbert, *American Business History*, (Englewood Cliffs, New Jersey: Prentice Hall Inc., 1972), 166.
31. Oscar de León Aragón, *Los contratos de la United Fruit Company y las compañías muelleras en Guatemala*, (Guatemala: Editorial del Ministerio de Educación Pública, 1950), 42.
32. Solórzano, *Evolución económica de Guatemala*, 354.
33. Jones, *Guatemala Past and Present*, 251-52.
34. McCreery, "Coffee and Class in Liberal Guatemala," 451.
35. Ibid., 449.
36. J. Fred Rippy, *Latin America and the Industrial Age*, 2nd ed., (New York: G. P. Putnam's Sons, 1947), 138.
37. Ibid., 139.

Chapter 2: A Major Merger and a Major Railroad

1. Miguel Angel Asturias, *Viento fuerte* (Guatemala: Editorial del Ministerio de Educación Pública, 1950), 20.
2. The gross sales, excluding steamship traffic, of approximately $288 million represented banana production in six countries: Guatemala, Honduras, Costa Rica, Panama, Colombia and Ecuador.

    Stacy May and Galo Plaza, *The United Fruit Company in Latin America*, (New York: National Planning Association, 1958), 115.
3. Bananas began to be regularly imported into the United States in 1866 after Carl B. Frank, an American, initiated shipments of the fruit from Colón, Panama to New York City.

    Ibid., 4.
4. Samuel Crowther, *The Romance and Rise of the American Tropics*, (Garden City, New York: Doubleday, Doran & Company, 1929), 170.
5. Wilson, *Empire in Green and Gold*, 71-72.
6. The United Fruit Company began refrigerating the holds of its banana ships in 1903, the first U.S. company to undertake such procedures.
7. Wilson, *Empire in Green and Gold*, 73-74.
8. Ibid., 73.
9. Ibid., 76-77.
10. At a time when Americans were substantially increasing their consumption of coffee, their demand for bananas was also sharply on the rise. In 1890, approximately 12,582,000 stems of the yellow fruit were imported into the U.S., almost a fourth as many as the previous year. Ranking as the country's number one banana port was the city of New Orleans, where 3,668,000 stems were unloaded. Next in importance was New York, and then Boston, where

1,602,000 stems were imported. About half of the Massachusetts produce was handled by the Boston Fruit Company. Considering the total number of bananas brought into the United States in 1890, it is clear the Boston-based company was still only a small player on the national scene.

Ibid., 83.

11. Ibid., 80.
12. Ibid., 99.
13. Ibid., 42-43.
14. During the first three years and twenty miles, at least 4,000 deaths from malaria, yellow fever, and other diseases were recorded.

Ibid., 52.

15. Ralph Lee Woodward, Jr., *Central America: A Nation Divided*, (New York: Oxford University Press, 1976), 178.
16. *Unifruitco*, (New York: United Fruit Company, June-July, 1949), 1.
17. Wilson, *Empire in Green and Gold*, 107-08.
18. May and Plaza, *The United Fruit Company in Latin America*, 6-7.
19. By 1899, the three middle-aged men had enjoyed widely different and unusual careers, but they all had two things in common. They had been poor boys who began working at an early age: Lorenzo Baker as an apprentice sailor at fourteen; Minor Keith as a lumberyard helper at thirteen; and Andrew Preston as a produce-dealer's handyman at eighteen. Moreover, none of them had more than five years of schooling.

Wilson, *Empire in Green and Gold*, 69.

20. Guatemalan historian Mario Monteforte Toledo, who claims that all of the privileges that the United Fruit Company gained were related to the inception and perpetuation of illegal and dictatorial regimes, states that Estrada Cabrera assumed the presidency in a "very suspicious manner" — the implication being that the United Fruit Company either plotted Reyna Barrios's murder or engineered Estrada Cabrera's election. The author's statement is apparently based on the fact that a full three years after Estrada Cabrera became president, he signed Guatemala's first contract with United Fruit. Apart from the fact that the first designate to the presidency was almost invariably elected president if the president died or was incapacitated, the United Fruit Company had not even been founded when Estrada Cabrera became president.

Mario Monteforte Toledo, *Guatemala — monografía sociológica*, 2d ed., (Mexico: Universidad Autónoma de Mexico, 1965), 537.

21. Thomas P. McCann, *An American Company, The Tragedy of United Fruit*, (New York: Crown Publishers, Inc., 1976), 45.
22. Dana G. Munro, *The Five Republics of Central America*, (New York: Oxford University Press, 1918), 53.
23. Estrada Cabrera's dictatorship and the United Fruit Company's first years in Guatemala coincided with an era in which the United States government began intervening in Central America and the Caribbean with increasing impu-

nity. The same year that Estrada Cabrera was elected, the U.S. went to war with Spain over Cuba, subsequently occupying the new republic for three years. During the next fifteen years, U.S. troops were deployed in Nicaragua, Cuba, Haiti and the Dominican Republic — often more than once, and frequently occupying one or more of the small nations for many years. Understandably, Latin Americans, and particularly those in Central America and the Caribbean, soon came to resent and fear the "big stick" that successive American presidents wielded. As the largest and most visible symbol of U.S. economic dominance in the area, the United Fruit Company quickly became linked — in the minds of many Latin Americans — with Washington's imperialistic actions.

24. Solórzano, *Evolución económica de Guatemala*, 348.

25. Prologue to *Los contratos de la United Fruit Company y las compañías muelleras en Guatemala* by Manuel Galich, 10.

26. Alfonso Bauer Paiz, *Cómo opera el capital Yanqui en Centroamérica (el caso de Guatemala)*, (Mexico: Editorial Ibero-Mexicana, 1956), 205.

27. De León Aragón, *Los contratos de la United Fruit Company*, 45-46.

28. Rafael Piedra-Santa Arandi, *Introducción a los problemas económicos de Guatemala*, 2nd edition, (Guatemala: Ediciones Superiores, 1977), 117.

29. Monteforte Toledo also overlooks the fact that by 1904 Guatemala's desperately needed railroad to the Atlantic had been under construction for twenty-one years, with successive governments having invested more than $8 million in the project. Of critical importance to Guatemala's continuing economic development, the railroad was Estrada Cabrera's highest priority. Indeed, when he was asked why he sought re-election in 1904, the dictator reportedly replied that he wanted to see the railroad to the Atlantic completed — "the strongest yearning of his existence."

    Monteforte Toledo, *Guatemala — monografía sociológica*, 537; Rafael Arévalo Martínez, *Ecce Pericles*, 2d ed. (San José, Costa Rica: EDUCA, 1982), 117.

30. Regina Wagner, *Los alemanes en Guatemala, 1828-1944*, (Guatemala: Editorial Idea, 1991), 228-29; 244.

31. It is not generally known that while President Justo Rufino Barrios was visiting the United States in the fall of 1882, he signed a contract with General Ulysses S. Grant which committed the Civil War hero to build 250 miles of railroad in Guatemala. At the time, Grant had already obtained a concession from the Mexican government to construct a railroad in that country, and he and his associates envisioned a steel line that eventually would traverse Central America. Grant soon suffered severe financial reverses, however, and was unable to carry out his ambitious plan.

    Rippy, *Latin America and the Industrial Age*, 134.

32. Crowther, *The Romance and Rise of the American Tropics*, 158.

33. De León Aragón, *Los Contratos de la United Fruit Company*, 46-47.

34. Charles David Kepner, Jr. and Jay Henry Soothill, *The Banana Empire: A Case Study of Economic Imperialism*, (New York: The Vanguard Press, 1935), 158.

35. Louis S. Sisto to Joseph W. Montgomery, correspondence, 21 June 1955, in Richard Allen LaBarge, "Impact of the United Fruit Company on the Economic Development of Guatemala, 1946-1954," *Studies in Middle American Economics*, (New Orleans: Tulane University, 1968), 14-15.
36. Secretaría de Fomento, *Ferrocarril a El Salvador, documentos relativos a la caducidad del contrato Méndez-Williamson*, (Guatemala: Imprenta Nacional La Instrucción, 1921), 32.
37. May and Plaza, *The United Fruit Company in Latin America*, 166.
38. Jones, *Guatemala Past and Present*, 253.
39. Solórzano, *Evolución económica de Guatemala*, 355-56.
40. Jim Handy, *Gift of the Devil, A History of Guatemala*, (Toronto: Between the Lines, 1984), 79-80.
41. Secretaría de Fomento, *Ferrocarril a El Salvador*, 15.
42. César Solís G., *Los ferrocarriles en Guatemala*, (Guatemala: Tipografía Nacional, 1952), 425.
43. Secretaría de Fomento, *Ferrocarril a El Salvador*, 52.
44. Solís, *Los ferrocarriles en Guatemala*, 462-63; 449-50.
45. As late as 1953, only three major ports in Central America were owned by nationals; all the others were in the hands of U.S. companies.

    Piero Gleijeses, *Shattered Hope, The Guatemalan Revolution and the United States, 1944-1954*, (Princeton: Princeton University Press, 1991), 87.
46. De León Aragón, *Los contratos de la United Fruit Company*, 195-96.
47. Solís, *Los ferrocarriles en Guatemala*, 408.
48. Estrada Cabrera's apologist, Héctor Gálvez E., recounts that a friend of the dictator reproached him for having awarded Minor Keith a ninety-nine-year concession. "Don't you know that there are now carriages which move by themselves and are called automobiles?" the strongman reputedly asked. "The future is in those vehicles, and you will see that before ninety-nine years, railroads won't exist."

    Solís, *Los ferrocarriles en Guatemala*, 423; Héctor Gálvez E., *Conozca a Estrada Cabrera*, (Guatemala: Editorial Prensa Libre, 1976), 221.
49. Secretaría de Fomento, *Ferrocarril a El Salvador*, 30.
50. Ibid., 29.
51. Rafael Piedra-Santa Arandi, "La construcción de ferrocarriles en Guatemala y los problemas financieros de la IRCA," *Economía*, January-March, 1968), 22.
52. Secretaría de Fomento, *Ferrocarril a El Salvador*, 29.
53. Joseph A. Pitti, *"Jorge Ubico and Guatemalan Politics in the 1920's"* (Ph.D. diss., University of New Mexico, 1975), 62-63.
54. Secretaría de fomento, *Ferrocarril a El Salvador*, 49.
55. Piedra-Santa Arandi, "La construcción de ferrocarriles en Guatemala," 22.
56. Solís, *Los Ferrocarriles en Guatemala*, 107-108.

57. Handy, *Gift of the Devil*, 95.
58. Solís, *Los ferrocarriles en Guatemala*, 111-24.
59. Jones, *Guatemala Past and Present*, 228.
60. *Memoria de las labores del ejecutivo en el ramo de hacienda y crédito público, 1936*, (Guatemala: Tipografía Nacional, 1937), 26-27.
61. Bauer Paiz, *Cómo opera el capital Yanqui en Centroamérica*, 152-53.
62. Ibid., 130-31.
63. Virtually no U.S. or Guatemalan scholars have noted the impact of the Zacapa line on the economy of El Salvador, the only country in Central America without an Atlantic seaboard. Until 1930, all of the country's exports and imports either traversed the Panama Canal or were handled via the west coast of the United States. Before the inauguration of the IRCA's line to El Salvador and the use of the pier at Puerto Barrios, coffee shipments to Hamburg, for example, required thirty to forty-five days' transit time — and cost considerably more than Guatemalan or Costa Rican coffee which did not have to transit the Panama Canal. The railroad, however, made it possible for Salvadoran coffee to arrive in Germany within three weeks. Exports to the U.S. were also significantly expedited: goods dispatched from eastern or southern ports in the United States, which previously required nearly one month before delivery at the port of Cutuco, arrived in El Salvador within six days.

E.J. Daly, "Through Barrios to Salvador," *(Unifruito*, April 30, 1930), 523-25.

Chapter 3: The Origins of United Fruit's "Black Legend"

1. Victor M. Cutter, "Foreign Trade's Golden Rule: You can't Exploit your Markets and have them too," *(Unifruitco*, February, 1929), 390-94.
2. Adams, *Conquest of the Tropics*, 197.
3. Ibid., 198.
4. Manuel Galich, *Por qué lucha Guatemala, Arévalo y Arbenz: dos hombres contra un imperio*, (Buenos Aires: Elmer Editor, 1956), 37.
5. *English Translation of Basic Operating Contracts between the United Fruit Company and its Respective Subsidiary*, internal document of the United Fruit Company, 105-06.
6. Richard Allen LaBarge, "A Study of United Fruit Company Operations in Isthmian America, 1946-1954," (Ph.D. diss, Duke University, 1959), 51 and 39.
7. Ibid., 52-56.
8. May and Plaza, *The United Fruit Company in Latin America*, 86.
9. De León Aragón, *Los contratos de la United Fruit Company*, 252-57.
10. Richard H. Immerman, *The CIA in Guatemala: The Foreign Policy of Intervention*, (Austin: University of Texas Press, 1982), 70.
11. De León Aragón, *Los contratos de la United Fruit Company*, 253.

12. LaBarge, "Impact of the United Fruit Company on the Economic Development of Guatemala, 1946-1954," 10-11.
13. Victor Bulmer-Thomas, *The Political Economy of Central America since 1920*, (Cambridge, England: Cambridge University Press, 1987), 287-88.
14. Zemurray's initial activities in Honduras were often unprincipled, but his philanthropic work is less known. Through his intercession, the United Fruit Company established in Honduras one of the world's outstanding schools of tropical agriculture. (The Escuela Agrícola Panamericana is more fully discussed in Chapter 5). Also in Honduras, Zemurray founded the Lancetilla Experiment Station, now called the Dr. Wilson Popenoe Botanical Garden, which was once the best arboretum of tropical fruit and forest trees in the hemisphere. During the forty-nine years that UFCO administered the gardens, (1925-1974) its staff introduced to Latin America a large variety of new plant species, including the African oil palm, now grown extensively in Honduras and Costa Rica. Fascinated by Mayan culture, Zemurray provided more than $1 million to establish a center for the study of Mayan art and Middle American research at Tulane University. The magnate also helped back the founding of *The Nation*.

McCann, *An American Company*, 23; Frederic Rosengarten, Jr., *Wilson Popenoe, Agricultural Explorer, Educator, and Friend of Latin America*, (Lawai, Kauai, Hawaii: National Tropical Botanical Garden, 1991), 102-09).

15. Virgilio Rodríguez Beteta, *No es guerra de hermanos sino de bananos*, (Guatemala: Imprenta Universitaria, Universidad de San Carlos, 1969), 29.
16. Ibid., 31.
17. May and Plaza, *The United Fruit Company in Latin America*, 17.
18. Wilson, *Empire in Green and Gold*, 246.
19. Pitti, "Jorge Ubico and Guatemalan Politics in the 1920's" 178.
20. Mario R. Argueta, *Bananos y política: Samuel Zemurray y la Cuyamel Fruit Company en Honduras*, (Tegucigalpa: Universidad Nacional Autónoma de Honduras, 1989), 100.
21. De León Aragón, *Los Contratos de la United Fruit Company*, 158.
22. Kenneth Grieb, *Guatemalan Caudillo, The Regime of Jorge Ubico*, (Athens, Ohio: Ohio University Press, 1967), 186; May and Plaza, *The United Fruit Company in Latin America*, 166.
23. Pitti, "Jorge Ubico and Guatemalan Politics in the 1920's", 360.
24. Ibid., 361; 390; 388.
25. Immerman, *The CIA in Guatemala*, 71.
26. Grieb, *Guatemalan Caudillo*, 283.
27. Handy, *Gift of the Devil*, 90.
28. Pitti, "Jorge Ubico and Guatemalan Politics in the 1920's," 458.
29. Grieb, "American Involvement in the Rise of Jorge Ubico," *Caribbean Studies*, Vol. 10, Number 1, 20-21.
30. De León Aragón, *Los contratos de la United Fruit*, 12.

CHAPTER 3 NOTES

31. Gleijeses, *Shattered Hope*, 21.
32. *English Translation of Basic Operating Contracts*, 129.
33. Pitti, "Jorge Ubico and Guatemalan Politics in the 1920's," 457-58.
34. IBRD, *The Economic Development of Guatemala*, 3.
35. De León Aragón, *Los contratos de la United Fruit Company*, 85.
36. Guillermo Toriello, *La batalla de Guatemala*, (Mexico: Ediciones Cuadernos Americanos, 1955), 50.
37. LaBarge, *A Study of United Fruit Company Operations*, 19.
38. Kepner and Soothill, *The Banana Empire*, 264.
39. Wilson, *Empire in Green and Gold*, 267.
40. Kepner and Soothill, *The Banana Empire*, 152.
41. Bulmer-Thomas, *The Political Economy of Central America since 1920*, 51.
42. Kepner and Soothill, *The Banana Empire*, 264-65 and 383.
43. The new technology used to treat sigatoka required training thousands of farm workers as pipe fitters, maintenance men and spray teams. Millions of feet of galvanized piping were purchased for all isthmian divisions and thousands of pumps and motors were installed in order to provide every plantation with a means of combating the dreaded leaf blight. By 1937, approximately 75,000 acres of bananas were being regularly sprayed with the UFCO-developed Bordeaux mixture. In addition, the Company advanced loans and materials to private planters whose fields had also been invaded by the virulent fungus. It has been little recognized that the United Fruit Company's conquest of sigatoka not only saved Central America's banana industry, but also constitutes one of the most successful struggles against a major tropical fungus.

    Wilson, *Empire in Green and Gold*, 274-75.
44. Grieb, *Guatemala Caudillo*, 185.
45. Bulmer-Thomas, *The Political Economy of Central America since 1920*, 326; 328.
46. International Railways of Central America, *1963 Annual Report*, 15.
47. The collapse of world coffee prices caused Guatemala's coffee exports to plunge from 1,200,000 quintals in 1926 to only 789,041 in 1931, with a corresponding drop in prices from $26 a quintal in 1927 to $7.50 in 1932. Government receipts from coffee exports therefore plummeted from a high of $28,568,560 in 1927 to $7,385,524 in 1932. Receipts for banana exports declined from $3,212,317 in 1929 to $2,437,000 the following year.

    Grieb, *Guatemalan Caudillo*, 52-53.
48. Bauer Paiz, *Cómo opera el capital Yanqui en Centroamérica*, 248.
49. Immerman, *The CIA in Guatemala*, 72.
50. *English Translation of Basic Operating Contracts*, 130-31.
51. Piero Gleijeses, "La aldea de Ubico: Guatemala, 1931-1944," *Mesoamérica* 17 (1989), 45-46.

247

52. Indeed, Grieb maintains that the Ubico regime "acted with considerable skill to utilize the corporation's inability to construct the port to obtain needed financial relief that contributed to the stabilization of the economy without the loss of the Company's continued investment." He also notes that, "United Fruit made a significant financial commitment in Guatemala the very year the accords were signed, materially increasing the rolling stock of the International Railways of Central America."

    Grieb, *Guatemalan Caudillo*, 187. 53. Bauer Paiz, *Cómo opera el capital Yanqui en Centroamérica*, 254.

54. Grieb, *Guatemalan Caudillo*, 187.
55. Ibid., 122-25.
56. Ibid., 185.
57. Ibid., 185; 183-84.
58. United Fruit Company, *Datos Estadísticos 1950*, 7.
59. May and Plaza, *The United Fruit Company in Latin America*, 165.
60. LaBarge, "A Study of United Fruit Company Operations," 20.
61. Munro, *The Five Republics of Central America*, 69.
62. Kepner and Soothill, *The Banana Empire*, 163.
63. Carlos Wyld Ospina, *El autócrata*, 2d ed., (Guatemala: Editorial José de Piñeda Ibarra, 1967), 235.
64. IBRD, *The Economic Development of Guatemala*, 172.
65. Ibid., 169.
66. "Central America as an Export Field," (Washington, D.C.: U.S. Department of Commerce, Special Agents Series, No. 113, 1916), 25.
67. IBRD, *The Economic Development of Guatemala*, 172.
68. Bulmer-Thomas, *The Political Economy of Central America since 1920*, 77.
69. Daniel James, *Red Design for the Americas: Guatemalan Prelude*, (New York: The John Day Company, 1954), 16.
70. LaBarge, "Impact of the United Fruit Company on the Economic Development of Guatemala, 1946-1954," 15.
71. International Railways of Central America, *1959 Annual Report*, 16.
72. *English Translation of Basic Operating Contracts*, 113.
73. Ibid., 137.
74. De León Aragón, *Los contratos de la United Fruit Company*, 199.
75. Written interview with former President Juan José Arévalo, April, 1989.
76. Monteforte Toledo, *Guatemala — monografía social*, 521.
77. LaBarge, "Impact of the United Fruit Company on the Economic Development of Guatemala, 1946-1954," 16-17.
78. Monteforte Toledo, *Guatemala — monografía social*, 540.
79. IBRD, *The Economic Development of Guatemala*, 175.

80. Interview with Rolando Erales, Comisión Portuaria Nacional, February 8, 1991, Guatemala City.
81. "Comparative statement of income for the years 1912 to 1963," International Railways of Central America, *1963 Annual Report*, 15.
82. In 1991, Puerto Quetzal provided employment for approximately 1,000 stevedores and 400 administrative personnel.

Chapter 4: Banana Production and its Personnel

1. In their 1958 book, May and Plaza state that establishing a modern banana division of approximately 20,000 producing acres can cost between $20 million to $25 million in initial capital investment. Depending on the amount of hydraulic engineering required, it will cost from $1,000 to $1,500 to develop each banana-producing acre. The costs today, of course, are significantly higher. May and Plaza, *The United Fruit Company in Latin America*, 90.
2. Crowther, *The Romance and Rise of the American Tropics*, 229.
3. In 1926, William L. Taillon, a timekeeper on a United Fruit Company farm in Tela, Honduras, vividly described a day-long exploration through the Honduran jungles in search of potential new banana lands. In a letter to his parents in North Dakota, Taillon, who was accompanied by five machete-armed Hondurans and two pistol-packing Americans, describes conditions similar to those on the nearby north coast of Guatemala. "Slash here, slash there, the natives began downing prickly vines, grasses, bushes that reach out and grab your clothing like a lot of animated fish hooks. Comes noon and 110 degrees, we are now walking in high swamp grass on peat beds made up of generations of dead grasses. This peat is stove-like in the heat it puts out, 100 degrees from below, 110 degrees from above, not a breath of air. Dante's inferno for an American who dared to leave North Dakota . . . You enter areas where the men had made a tunnel through the underbrush, a reeking, damp tunnel, somewhat terrifying because you pictured yourself suddenly writhing in agony from the fatal bite of some unknown insect that likely had bitten you."

   If the jungle was a sweltering, virtually impenetrable "vegetable hell," the tropical wildlife that Taillon observed was remarkably varied and exotic: ant bears, deer, possums, coons and "grinning noisy white-faced monkeys, thousands of colorful lizards that change their coloring to suit their surroundings, hundreds of little slimy creatures that one does not recognize, and snakes, the boa sliding away, giving out halo-like a beautiful blue sheen, the dangerous *barba amarilla* [fer-de-lance] the superbly colored coral, all of these in their own homes. Gorgeous macaws call raucously as they fly overhead. High above this uncanny harmony of the jungle booms the bull baboon, presiding over a meeting of his colleagues, sitting high up in a massive *ceiba* tree."

   From personal papers provided to the author by Taillon's daughter, Nancy Schaper.
4. Clyde S. Stephens, *Bananeros in Central America*, (Fort Myers, Florida: Press Printing Company, 1989), 107-109.

FOR THE RECORD

5. Ibid., 111.
6. In 1944, A.A. Pollan, executive vice president of the United Fruit Company, estimated that his Company had "caused hundreds of thousands of acres of lowland swamps and jungles [in Central America, Colombia and the Caribbean] to be cleared, drained and planted. The drainage alone of these areas has involved the removal in the last ten years of over fifty million cubic yards, or more than one-fifth of the total dirt excavated from the Panama Canal."

   A.A. Pollan, "The United Fruit Company and Middle America," in a speech delivered at the New School for Social Research, New York City, January 1944, 14.
7. UFCO's costly irrigation system required approximately one ton of metal pipe to be installed in each acre of banana land.
8. LaBarge, "A Study of United Fruit Company Operations," 50.
9. Ike M. Smith, who began a forty-four year career with United Fruit in Honduras in 1927 and was employed as chief engineer in Bananera from 1947-1952, recollects that each farm was provided with an enormous pump that distributed the Bordeaux mixture through a high pressure pipe system that crisscrossed every farm. Two-man teams would attach long hoses to the pipes and then laboriously spray the solution on the tallest leaves of each plant. A team could usually cover about five acres a day. The pump, however, was sufficiently large to permit sixteen two-man teams to simultaneously spray the pesticide on thousands of banana plants. "Hence, 80 gallons per minute of Bordeaux were sprayed on at the same time."

   Letter from Ike M. Smith, February 5, 1991.
10. Edmund S. Whitman, *Those Wild West Indies*, (New York: The American Book Bindery-Stratford Press, Inc., 1938), 129.
11. Crowther, *The Romance and Rise of the American Tropics*, 229.
12. May and Plaza, *The United Fruit Company in Latin America*, 90.
13. Eventually, every root system contains three generations of plants: the mature one which soon produces a stem of fruit; the "daughter" or younger plant which will flower shortly after the mature fruit is harvested and one small sucker that will ultimately succeed the "daughter" — when the whole cycle begins again. In fact, with proper fertilization, it is now possible for banana plants to produce fruit for upwards of twenty years, if not longer. Nevertheless, because of the plant's method of reproduction, the once-straight lines of plants soon disappear, causing one banana executive to describe his plantations as a "moveable population."

    Interview with Gerald K. Brunelle, November 23, 1990, Bananera.
14. Although there are approximately thirty species or sub-species of bananas, the Gros Michel once accounted for 99 percent of the banana imports into the United States. According to Wilson, the Gros Michel originated about 1836 in Jamaica, the product of a graft from parent stocks of Old World origin implanted onto a variety of banana grown on the West Indian island of Martinique. Francois Pouyat, a French botanist who performed the initial graft, named the new variety "Banana-Pouyat." It was later renamed the

"Martinique," and still later the "Gros Michel," or "Big Mike," as many United Fruit employees termed the species.

Wilson, *Empire in Green and Gold*, 14-15.

15. In the 1920s it required from twelve to fifteen hours of uninterrupted work to load approximately 75,000 stems of bananas into the hold of a United Fruit Company ship.

Crowther, *The Romance and Rise of the American Tropics*, 237.

16. Before the fruit appears in supermarkets, however, the green bananas are handled by banana ripeners who purchase the fruit from various importers at shipside. They complete the ripening process under controlled conditions and then sell or transfer the bananas to retailers or to regional wholesalers. Although the banana ripeners only have about ten days to hold the fruit before it must be displayed in super markets, today's technology permits a somewhat limited speeding up or retarding of the ripening process. That is, by introducing ethylene gas into the ripening rooms, the ripening process is speeded up. (Ethylene is a chemical naturally produced by ripening bananas and other fruits.) Ripening can be retarded, however, by withholding additional ethylene and maintaining lower temperatures and humidity.

Henry B. Arthur, James P. Houck, George L. Beckford, *Tropical Structures and Adjustments — Bananas*, (Boston: Harvard University, 1968), 37.

17. Adams, *Conquest of the Tropics*, 200.

18. John R. Silver letter to the author, November 28, 1990.

19. Gomar began as a time keeper on one of UFCO's north coast banana farms and assumed increasingly important positions within the United Fruit structure. When the Company sold its holdings to Del Monte in 1972, he continued with the new company, retiring in 1990 as superintendent of agriculture.

Interview with Carlos Haroldo Gomar, November 21, 1990, Bananera.

20. Letter from Ike M. Smith, February 5, 1991.

21. Gabriel García Márquez, Colombia's Nobel Prize-winning author, describes the sudden, almost magical appearance of a United Fruit Company town in his masterful novel *One Hundred Years of Solitude*. "The suspicious inhabitants of Macondo barely began to wonder what the devil was going on when the town had already become transformed into an encampment of wooden houses with zinc roofs inhabited by foreigners who arrived on the train from halfway around the world." Letting his imagination take flight, the master of magic realism writes, "The gringos, who later on brought their languid wives in muslin dresses and large veiled hats, built a separate town across the railroad tracks with streets lined with palm trees, houses with screened windows, small white tables on the terraces and fans mounted on the ceilings, and extensive blue lawns with peacocks and quails."

Gabriel García Márquez, *One Hundred Years of Solitude*, (New York: Avon Books, 1970), 214.

22. "The Division: The Little World of Gros Michel," *United Fruit Report*, November 3, 1953, in LaBarge, "Impact of the United Fruit Company on the Economic Development of Guatemala, 1946-1954," 8.

23. During World War II, when it became impossible for the United Fruit Company to purchase Collins machetes in the United States, Henry T. Heyl, general manager in Guatemala, ordered the Tiquisate machine shop to produce the urgently-needed items. Wilson Stanley, chief of the mechanical department, and his brother-in-law, Max P. Campbell, designed an ingenious "factory" that soon began producing thousands of machetes for all eight of UFCO's Central American divisions. The last step in the "manufacturing process" required a worker to test the machete by slamming it against a mahogany log. Paid the equivalent of 50 cents for every blade he could snap, the worker usually succeeded in breaking only about ten machetes out of the approximately 200 he tested each day.

    In a letter from Max P. Campbell to the author, November 26, 1990.

24. United Fruit Company, *Datos Estadísticos 1950*, 7.
25. LaBarge, "A Study of United Fruit Company Operations," 210.
26. Ibid., 210.
27. Ibid., 235.
28. Ibid., 220.
29. Dirección general de estadística, ministerio de economía, *Anuario estadístico, 1971*, 127.
30. Campbell's contract are among personal papers owned by the author.
31. Whitman, *Those Wild West Indies*, 131-32.
32. Wilson, *Empire in Green and Gold*, 212.
33. May and Plaza, *The United Fruit Company in Latin America*, 240-41.
34. Eugene Cunningham, *Gypsying through Central America*, (New York: E.P. Dutton & Company, 1922), 146; 232.
35. LaBarge, "A Study of United Fruit Company Operations," 213.
36. Ibid., 276.
37. Immerman, *The CIA in Guatemala*, 74; Stephen Schlesinger and Stephen Kinzer, *Bitter Fruit, The Untold Story of the American Coup in Guatemala*, (Garden City, New York: Anchor Press/Doubleday, 1983), 71.
38. John L. Williams, "The Rise of the Banana Industry and its Influence on Caribbean Countries," Master's Thesis, Clark University, Worcester, Massachusetts, 1925, 124.
39. Ibid., 119.
40. Letter from John R. Silver to the author, July 13, 1991.
41. Kepner, *Social Aspects of the Banana Industry*, 170.
42. This theme was exploited by Monteforte Toledo in an inept play titled "Los gringos," which was staged in Guatemala City in 1989. Set in Bananera at the time of the 1954 invasion of Guatemala, it featured a Guatemalan employee whose sentiments were more American than Guatemalan. Similarly, in the most famous book written about the United Fruit Company by a Honduran, Ramón Amaya Amador's *Prisión verde (Green Prison)*, the novelist creates a swag-

gering, murderous "black gringo" who supervises his own countrymen with appalling cruelty.

Ramón Amaya Amador, *Prisión verde*, 5th ed. (Tegucigalpa: Editorial Universitaria, 1988).

43. LaBarge, "A Study of United Fruit Company Operations," 216.
44. Kepner, *Social Aspects of the Banana Industry*, 177.
45. LaBarge, "A Study of United Fruit Company Operations," 205-06.
46. Ibid., 218.
47. Wilson, *Empire in Green and Gold*, 287.
48. In *Biography of an Idea*, Bernays recounts his first meeting with Zemurray who, in discussing Central Americans, told Bernays, "We can't get them to love us. Maybe they will learn to tolerate us." Bernays commented that the public, presumably both in Latin America and the United States, "thought of the Company in its old role of colonial exploiter, and those days were over in the early forties." The perceptive nephew of Sigmund Freud also correctly pointed out to Zemurray that UFCO's image had suffered because "the Company had not told the public about itself, believing in the privacy of a privately-owned business."

Edward Bernays, *Biography of an Idea*, (New York: Simon and Shuster, 1965), 749.

49. Ibid., 754-55.
50. At 54, Bump, who joined United Fruit's Honduras division in 1925 as an engineer, had spent most of his life in the tropics. A graduate of the South Dakota State School of Mines, he was assigned to Tiquisate in 1945, after serving in Colombia and Panama. Seven years later he was advanced to the position of general manager for the Guatemala operations. When he was transferred to Boston in 1955, the United Fruit Company rewarded him with one of its most important positions: vice president of tropical operations. LaBarge notes that both administrative employees and common workers in Guatemala characterized Bump's managerial style as *"lo mejor que ha venido"* (the best that has come along).
51. LaBarge, "A Study of United Fruit Company Operations," 277.

Chapter 5: Social Live and Social Concerns

1. Interview with César A. Castillo Barrajas, UFCO paymaster at Bananera from 1958-72; July 24, 1990, Bananera.
2. LaBarge, "Impact of the United Fruit Company on the Economic Development of Guatemala, 1946-1954," 47.
3. In its 1951 report, the International Bank for Reconstruction and Development noted "the Guatemalan worker is greatly handicapped. His general level of health is poor. Malaria and intestinal disorders in some regions reduce his capacity and ambition. His nutrition often is not such to permit him to do

intensive work for long hours. Although inherently able to learn special skills, the local worker frequently lacks even a good elementary school education. Without this background his vocational training is made more difficult."

IBRD, *The Economic Development of Guatemala*, 95.

4. The section titled "The States" included news of personnel at UFCO's operations in the Boston headquarters, the Freight Traffic Department, Pier Operations, Freight Terminal, the New York accounting department, the Fruit Dispatch Company, etc.

5. In its first twenty years, *Unifruitco* published numerous articles, written by employees, that readily illustrate some of the diverse subjects that confronted individuals working on banana plantations: poisonous anthropods, banana varieties, how to care for farm mules, banana root systems, training a timekeeper, how to keep fit in the tropics, locusts, tropical paints, and recent developments in the control of malaria. Many issues also published recipes for countless culinary uses of the banana.

6. Stephens, *Bananeros in Central America*, 170.

7. Ibid., 171-74.

For twenty-six years, retired UFCO employees, their spouses and often one or more of their children, have staged an annual "homecoming" in Punta Gorda or Sebring, Florida. The two-day reunion is always held on a weekend near the *Quince de Septiembre*, Central America's September 15 independence day. Approximately 100 persons, most of them now Florida residents, usually attend the "Quince Reunion." In Guatemala, former employees and their children also periodically organize "banana family" reunions. The last *Fiesta Bananera*, which was staged on July 4, 1992 at a Guatemala City hotel, brought together more than 100 ex-*Fruteros* and their families, nearly all of whom were Guatemalans.

8. Interview with Laura de la Vega, Del Monte assistant administrator in Bananera, July 25, 1990.

9. Indeed, many coffee *finqueros* and independent banana growers resented the higher wages that the United Fruit Company paid its laborers. In the 1930s, when UFCO sought to pay its workers the equivalent of one dollar a day, President Ubico insisted that the wage be reduced to a daily 50 cents, so that a "bad" example might not be set for other employers. Even so, 50 cents a day was well over twice the prevailing agricultural wage, and general conditions on *La Frutera's* farms were far superior to most other plantations in Guatemala.

James, *Red Design for the Americas*, 162.

10. Written interview with former President Juan José Arévalo, April, 1989.

11. Luis Cardoza y Aragón, "Land for the Many," *Nation*, CLXXVI (March 14, 1953) in LaBarge, *A Study of United Fruit Company Operations*, 230.

12. José E. Pinzón Salazar, "Entre la satisfacción técnica gubernamental y la incertidumbre de las mayorías," *Siglo Veintiuno*, December 28, 1991.

13. LaBarge, "Impact of the United Fruit Company on the Economic Development of Guatemala, 1946-54," 44-45.

14. Kepner, *Social Aspects of the Banana Industry*, 189.

15. Handy, *Gift of the Devil*, 83.
16. On pay days, many workers often spent a good portion of their salaries at local *cantinas* (bars) which were frequently the scene of violent fights.
17. In a letter from John R. Silver to the author, March 28, 1991.
18. Monteforte Toledo, *Guatemala — monografía social*, 543.
19. LaBarge, "Impact of the United Fruit Company on the Economic Development of Guatemala, 1946-1954," 44.
20. Victor M. Cutter, "Trade Relations with Latin America," (Boston: United Fruit Company, 1929) 45.
21. Adams, *Conquest of the Tropics*, 274.
22. Ibid., 276.
23. Aldous Huxley, *Beyond the Mexique Bay* 2nd rev. ed., (New York: Vantage Books, Inc., 1960), 34.
24. The author is indebted to Dr. E. Croft Long, a physician and long-time resident of Guatemala, for providing little-known information about Macphail. Having extensively researched Macphail's medical accomplishments, Long notes that the resourceful Scot was among the first to treat large numbers of malaria-infected patients through the use of intramuscular injections of quinine. There were at least three significant advantages to this method of treating the illness: health dispensers, located on remote banana farms, could be trained to give the injections, therefore avoiding the need to hospitalize hundreds of malaria-infected individuals. In acute stages of the illness, when the patient was comatose and unable to ingest liquid quinine, intramuscular injections could be administered. Moreover, because malaria often causes frequent vomiting, the beneficial effects of the bitter-tasting liquid quinine could be lost, with no such loss occurring when the fluid was injected.

    Interview with Dr. E. Croft Long, April 12, 1991, Antigua.
25. George Cheever Shattuck, *A Medical Survey of the Republic of Guatemala*, (Washington, D.C.: Carnegie Institution of Washington, 1938), 36.
26. Ibid., 27.
27. United Fruit Company, *Datos Estadísticos 1950*, 9.
28. LaBarge, "Impact of the United Fruit Company on the Economic Development of Guatemala, 1946-1954," 32.
29. George E. Britnell, "Economic and Social Change in Guatemala," *The Canadian Journal of Economics and Political Science*, Vol. 17, No.4, November, 1951, 474.
30. LaBarge, "Impact of the United Fruit Company on the Economic Development of Guatemala, 1946-1954," 32.
31. Kepner, *Social Aspects of the Banana Industry*, 214-15.
32. Interview with Benjamín Carol Cardoza, November 21, 1990, Bananera.
33. The barbed-wire fences and guarded entrance gates that the Company maintained at Bananera and Tiquisate were criticized by some Guatemalans who claimed the "colonial islands" typified the aloof, imperious attitude of UFCO's

foreign employees. Although the fences may well have been offensive to many Guatemalans, they served two functions: they helped to reduce the number of burglaries, and they kept stray animals out of the compound. That such security measures were necessary is apparent today in Tiquisate, where the United Fruit sold its houses to individual home owners in 1964. The fence surrounding the town was removed and the entrance gates were left unguarded. Many of the town's residents now complain about constant burglaries.

34. May and Plaza, *The United Fruit Company in Latin America*, 187.
35. McCann describes a United Fruit division this way: "The Company owns it all, lock, stock and barrel. It owns the clubs and offices, the sheds, the land, every piece of equipment, the golf course and tennis courts, the sewer lines and streetlights and fire hydrants . . . every house from the division manager's right down to the lowest worker's, along with every stick of furniture and even the plates they eat from and the knives and forks on the tables. Even the water in the faucets and electricity in the walls are supplied by the Company."

McCann, *An American Company*, 141.
36. Handy, *Gift of the Devil*, 83.
37. Kepner, *Social Aspects of the Banana Industry*, 114.
38. Ibid., 115.
39. Mira Wilkins, *The Maturing of Multinational Enterprise: American Business Abroad from 1914 to 1970*, (Cambridge: Harvard University Press, 1974), 124.
40. Whetten, *Guatemala, The Land and the People*, 177-78.
41. James, *Red Design for the Americas*, 164.
42. In the 1940s, after the United Fruit Company contracted a professor from Iowa State College to study the psychological effects on new employees who came from rural homes and were subsequently provided UFCO quarters, it was found that "the native workers were slow in appreciating flush toilets and garbage cans, but they gave a high significance to the virtues of privacy in housing and of plants and flowers around the house. In those respects, the Company housing was of a lower standard than that to which they were accustomed."

Samuel Guy Inman, *A New Day in Guatemala*, (Wilton, Connecticut: Worldover Press, 1950), 56-57.
43. May and Plaza, *The United Fruit Company in Latin America*, 184-86.
44. USAID Mission, "Plantation health-care in Guatemala: Aspects of the Problem," (Guatemala, 1980), 20; 18-19.
45. *Siglo Veintiuno*, July 9, 1990.
46. Ibid., August 19, 1990.
47. Carlos González Orellana, *Historia de la educación en Guatemala*, (Guatemala: Editorial Universitaria 1980), 333.
48. Jones, *Guatemala Past and Present*, 334.
49. Whetten, *Guatemala, The Land and the People*, 276.

CHAPTER 5 NOTES

50. Ernesto Bienvenido Jiménez, *La Educación Rural en Guatemala*, (Guatemala: Editorial José de Pineda Ibarra, 1966), 43.
51. Jones, *Guatemala Past and Present*, 334.
52. Dirección general de estadística, *Cuarto censo de la población de la república*, (Guatemala: Talleres Gutenberg, 1924), 67.
53. González Orellana, *Historia de la educación en Guatemala*, 360.
54. Luis Cardoza y Aragón, *Guatemala, las líneas de su mano*, 2d ed., (Mexico: Fondo de Cultura Económica, 1965), 337.
55. Inman, *A New Day in Guatemala*, 7.
56. Cardoza y Aragón, *Guatemala, las líneas de su mano*, 265-66.
57. Monteforte Toledo, *Guatemala — monografía social*, 611.
58. Whetten, *Guatemala, The Land and the People*, 267.
59. Among them are Claudia Arenas Bianchi whose father worked for many years for the Compañía Agrícola. After serving as spokesperson for President Vinicio Cerezo, she was named the director of the country's national institute of tourism (INGUAT) in 1992. Beatriz Zúñiga Seigné, who also grew up in Tiquisate, served as INGUAT director from 1987 to 1989. One of the country's leading architects is José Jorge Iturbide, whose father worked as a physician in both Tiquisate and Bananera, and Mario Mena is the general manager of the country's second-largest banana company.
60. Interview with Aura Marina Meza de Dardón, secretary in the office of the manager at Del Monte's Bananera headquarters, July 25, 1990, Bananera.
61. Interview with Adán Solís, November 21, 1990, Bananera.
62. LaBarge, "Impact of the United Fruit Company on the Economic Development of Guatemala, 1946-1954," 47.
63. United Fruit Company, *Datos Estadísticos 1950*, 13.
64. Interview with Dr. Simón E. Malo, director of the Escuela Agrícola Panamericana, January 8, 1991, Zamorano, Honduras. Malo currently serves as a member of Zamorano's board of trustees. Dr. Keith Andrews assumed the position of director early in 1993.
65. *Zamorano*, Annual Report, 1992-1993, 17.
66. Ibid., 32.
67. Sylvanus G. Morley, *Guide Book to the Ruins of Quirigua*, (Washington, D.C.: Carnegie Institution of Washington, 1935), 9.
68. Ibid., 86.
    The Instituto de Antropología e Historia de Guatemala took possession of the archaeological park in 1970.
69. William R. Coe and Robert J. Sharer, "The Quirigua Project, 1975 Season," *Quirigua Reports*, Vol. I, Papers 1-5, (Philadelphia: University Museum, University of Pennsylvania, 1979), 5.
70. "Buenas Perspectivas," *Crónica*, January 7, 1994, 32.
71. Zemurray's abiding interest in the Maya was responsible for the 1946 discov-

ery of Bonampak, deep in the jungles of southern Mexico, not far from the Guatemalan border. On assignment from Zemurray to prepare a documentary film on Maya civilization, Giles Healey, an archaeologist and motion picture photographer, discovered the site, which contains three rooms of magnificent, brightly-painted murals — the most well-preserved Maya frescoes known.

Unifruitco, February, 1948, 4-8.

72. John M. Dimick, "Introduction," in *The Ruins of Zaculeu, Guatemala* by Richard B. Woodbury and Aubrey S. Trik, (Boston: United Fruit Company, Vol. 1, 1953), 3.

73. Paul Glassman, *Guatemala Guide*, (Champlain, New York: Passport Press, 1990), 193-94.

74. Richard B. Woodbury and Aubrey S. Trik, "Summary of Important Traits" in *The Ruins of Zaculeu, Guatemala*, 284-87.

75. Interview with Dr. Edwin M. Shook, September 28, 1990, Antigua.

76. Dimick, "Introduction" in *The Ruins of Zaculeu, Guatemala*, 7.

Chapter 6: The U.S. and United Fruit Confront the Guatemalan "Time Machine"

1. Grieb, *Guatemalan Caudillo*, 283.
2. Wilson, *Empire in Green and Gold*, 289.
3. Ellis, *Las transnacionales del banano en Centroamérica*, 56.
4. Manuel Galich, "Diez años de primavera (1944-1954) en el país de la eterna tiranía (1838-1974)" *Alero* 8, September-October, 1974, 60.
5. Juan José Arévalo, *El candidato blanco y el huracán, 1944-1945*, (Guatemala: Editorial Académico Centroamérica, S.A., 1984), 9-10.
6. K. H. Silvert, *A Study in Government: Guatemala, Part 1, National and Local Government since 1944*, (New Orleans: Tulane University, 1954), 7-8.
7. Colonel Carlos Paz Tejada, who took part in the revolt, recalled in a 1991 newspaper interview that, prior to the U.S. donations, the Guatemalan Army used machine guns that dated to World War I, and its artillery was similar to what the French used in the Battle of the Marne. "The *gringos* gave us a few airplanes for training purposes and about a dozen tanks, which at that time were a great novelty."

   Colonel Carlos Paz Tejada, "Pasajes de la revolución de octubre," *Siglo Veintiuno*, January 30, 1991.
8. Juan José Arévalo, *Escritos complementarios*, (Guatemala: CENALTEX, ministerio de educación, 1988), 384.
9. Arévalo, *El candidato blanco y el huracán*, 239-41.
10. Ibid., 430-32.
11. Ralph Lee Woodward, Jr., *Central America: A Nation Divided*, (New York: Oxford University Press, 1976), 174.

12. James, *Red Design for the Americas*, 111.
13. Woodward, *Central America: A Nation Divided*, 229.
14. Richard Adams, *Crucifixion by Power*, (Austin: University of Texas Press, 1970), 444.
15. Ibid., 444.
16. James, *Red Design for the Americas*, 155.
17. Adams, *Crucifixion by Power*, 446.
18. Gleijeses, *Shattered Hope*, 93.
19. Aybar de Soto, *Dependency and Intervention*, 120.
20. Written interview with former President Juan José Arévalo, April, 1989.
21. LeBarge, "Impact of the United Fruit Company on the Economic Development of Guatemala, 1946-1954,: 49.
22. Ibid., 49.
23. Cole Blasier, *The Hovering Giant, U.S. Responses to Revolutionary Change in Latin America 1910-1985*, rev. ed. (Pittsburgh: University of Pittsburgh Press, 1985), 231.
24. Gleijeses points out that much of the reporting on the Arévalo government was "yellow journalism in the style of the 1890s . . . Cold War paranoia and sheer ignorance were more powerful than all the manipulations of Edward Bernays and other skillful minions in the pay of United Fruit."

    Gleijeses, *Shattered Hope*, 130-31.
25. Bernays, *Biography of an Idea*, 761.
26. Blasier, *The Hovering Giant*, 61-62.
27. As if presaging the arguments the Arbenz government would use in 1953 after it expropriated more than 400,000 acres of the United Fruit Company's holdings in Guatemala, the Arévalo-instructed delegation at Bogotá argued that prompt, adequate and effective compensation for expropriated land should be subject to each country's constitution, and that articles concerning the protection of foreign investors should be interpreted to make clear that foreigners were subject to the laws of the country concerned.
28. Luis Cardoza y Aragón, *La revolución guatemalteca*, (Mexico: Cuadernos Americanos, 1955), 65.
29. Toriello, *La batalla de Guatemala*, 64.
30. Blasier, *The Hovering Giant*, 60.
31. Juan José Arévalo, *Guatemala, la democracia y el imperio*, (Santiago: Editora Juventus, 1954), 38.
32. Galich, "Diez años de primavera," 60.
33. Marta Cehelsky, "Habla Arbenz," *Alero* 8, September-October, 1974, 120-21.
34. Carlos Manuel Pellecer, *Dos Yanquis más contra Guatemala*, (Guatemala: Edinter-Artemis, 1986), 51.
35. Fernando González Davison, *Guatemala 1500-1970, reflexiones sobre su desarrollo*

histórico, (Guatemala: Editorial Universitaria de Guatemala, 1987), 75.

36. Pellecer, *Dos Yanquis*, 58.
37. González Davison, *Guatemala 1500-1970*, 75.
38. Leo O. Suslow, *Aspects of Social Reform in Guatemala 1944-1949*, (Hamilton, New York: Colgate University, 1949), 119-20.
39. Ronald M. Schneider, *Communism in Guatemala 1944-1954*, (New York: Octagon Books, 1979), 23.
40. Ibid., 23.
41. Although most historians and the U.S. Department of State maintain that Guatemala's Communist Party (Partido Guatemalteco del Trabajo) included nearly 4,000 members, two knowledgeable party officials have disputed this figure. José Manuel Fortuny, former secretary general of the PGT, told Gleijeses that in August, 1953, the party numbered close to 5,000 members. Alfredo Guerra Borges, who was a member of the party's secretariat, placed the membership at nearly 6,000.

    Gleijeses, *Shattered Hope*, 195.

42. "Discurso del Teniente Coronel Jacobo Arbenz Guzmán, 15 de marzo de 1951," (Guatemala: Tipografía Nacional, 1951), 12-13.

    While Arbenz's inaugural address was imbued with optimism, Arévalo's last speech as president, delivered at the same ceremony, expressed deep bitterness toward the U.S. government and the United Fruit Company.

    I believed that Guatemala could govern herself . . . without submission to foreigners . . . The banana magnates, compatriots of Roosevelt's, rebelled against the audacity of a Central American president who placed the honorable families of the exporters on the same legal basis as their compatriots . . . I came to confirm that, according to certain international norms . . . small countries do not have a right to sovereignty . . . The arms of the Third Reich were broken and conquered . . . but in the ideological dialogue . . . Roosevelt lost the war. The real winner was Hitler.

    Blasier, *The Hovering Giant*, 63.

43. Arbenz's speech should have alerted the country's largest landowner that an agrarian reform was imminent. Had the United Fruit Company and its Pacific coast subsidiary voluntarily ceded a portion of the thousands of acres of virgin land that they possessed, the Arbenz government might have found it more difficult to expropriate all of the land that it eventually took from *La Frutera*.
44. Edelberto Torres Rivas, "Crisis y conyuntura crítica: la caída de Arbenz y los contratiempos de la revolución burguesa," *Revista Mexicana de Sociología*, Vol. XLI, No. 1, January-March, 1979, 300.
45. Carlos Samayoa Chinchilla, *El quetzal no es rojo*, (Mexico: Arana Hermanos, 1956), 162.
46. Arbenz's first significant contact with an American may have occurred at the Escuela Politécnica, where President Ubico had seconded Major John A. Considine, previously assigned to the U.S. Legation, as director of the acad-

emy in 1931. Ordered by Ubico "to make the place as near like West Point as possible," Considine's assignment to Guatemala was extended in 1934, at Ubico's request. Thus a U.S. Army major served as the director of the academy throughout the three years that Arbenz was enrolled there.

Grieb, *Guatemalan Caudillo*, 75-76.

47. It is not known whether Arbenz's spouse was a "card-carrying Communist." Woodward asserts she was indeed an "active member of the party," and that because of her, "Communists had easy access to the president." According to Gleijeses, Arbenz did not become a member of the Communist Partido Guatemalteco del Trabajo until 1957, three years after he was overthrown. "Had he joined while president, he would have had to submit to party discipline. This could have created unnecessary conflict and disturbed the close cooperation between him and the party. But in the last two years of his administration he considered himself a Communist, and with his few confidants, he spoke like one."

Woodward, *Central America: A Nation Divided*, 234; Gleijeses, *Shattered Hope*, 147.

48. Mario Monteforte Toledo, "La revolución de Guatemala 1944-1945," *Organismo Judicial*, Vol. 1, No. 9, October, 1987, 8.

49. Historians Blanche Wiesen Cook and Walter LaFeber both incorrectly assert that the United Fruit Company owned the Empresa Eléctrica.

Blanche Wiesen Cook, *The Declassified Eisenhower, A Divided Legacy*, (New York: Doubleday and Company, Inc., 1981) 221; Walter LaFeber, *Inevitable Revolutions, The United States in Central America*, (New York: W. W. Norton & Company, 1984), 118.

50. Edwin W. Bishop, who conducted an extensive study of the Guatemalan labor movement during the 1944-1959 period, perceives complex motives behind the continuing strikes that the United Fruit Company suffered during the Arévalo and Arbenz years. Labor leaders, he contends, feared the U.S. companies not as employers, but as political antagonists who they believed would use their financial resources and influence to bring down the revolutionary government. The primary frame of reference for Guatemalan unionism, therefore, was not the economic struggle for improvement of wages and working conditions. This was the ultimate goal, but to achieve this end, Guatemala's economic and political structure had to be modernized and the revolution safeguarded.

Edwin Warren Bishop, "The Guatemalan Labor Movement 1944-1959," Ph.D. diss., University of Wisconsin, 1959, 109.

51. Ellis, *Las transnacionales del banano en Centroamérica*, 240.

52. Alfonso Bauer Paiz and Julio Valladares Castillo, *La Frutera ante la ley (los conflictos laborales de Izabal y Tiquisate)*, (Guatemala: ministerio de economía y trabajo, 1949) 83-90.

53. Thomas and Marjorie Melville, *Tierra y poder en Guatemala*, 2nd ed. (San José, Costa Rica: EDUCA, 1982), 69-70.

54. Handy's version of the settlement is somewhat different. "When the Com-

pany refused [to pay the $650,000], the government called its bluff and made preparations to auction off some Company land for the back wages. The Company, temporarily bested, settled with the workers." But Bernays puts a different slant on the same event: "in March, in a surprise move, Guatemala offered United Fruit the labor contract it wanted. United Fruit thought it had won a great victory and accepted it." The U.S. State Department also perceived another important element in the settlement of the strike. "The basic weakness of Guatemalan Communist labor leadership is that it is imposed from above through top control of the machinery of labor organization and cannot be sure of rank-and-file support in all circumstances."

Handy, *Gift of the Devil*, 138; Bernays, *Biography of an Idea*, 762; Department of State, *Foreign Relations, 1952-1954*, IV, 1065-66.

55. Cardoza y Aragón, *La revolución guatemalteca*, 87.
56. Ibid., 98.
57. Cook, *The Declassified Eisenhower*, 221; LaFeber, *Inevitable Revolutions*, 118.
58. Handy, *Gift of the Devil*, 142.
59. May and Plaza, *The United Fruit Company*, 81.
60. Melvilles, *Tierra y poder en Guatemala*, 76.
61. Presidencia de la República, publicaciones del Departamento Agrario Nacional, *Expediente de expropiación seguido contra la Compañía Agrícola de Guatemala con la ley de reforma agraria*, (Guatemala: Tipografía Nacional, 1954), 5.
62. McCann charges that one of the most important reasons the Company retained hundreds of acres in reserve was to "guarantee that they would not become farm land for our competition — whoever that might prove to be." Nevertheless, Ted A. Holcombe, who worked in Tiquisate from 1936 until 1965, when he retired as manager of the division, refutes the allegation. "Good land was available if companies or individuals were prepared to spend a lot of money to produce bananas," he told the author. And since the Compañía Agrícola annually purchased millions of stems of bananas from independent south coast producers, it was in the Company's interest to encourage Guatemalan *finqueros* to go into the banana business.

McCann, *An American Company*, 39-40; interview with Ted A. Holcombe, March 11, 1991, Guatemala City.

63. Presidencia de la República, *Expediente de expropiación*, 78.
64. Schlesinger and Kinzer, *Bitter Fruit*, 76.
65. Presidencia de la República, *Expediente de expropiación*, 100-04.
66. Department of State *Bulletin*, September 14, 1953, 359.

Numerous authors, among them the Melvilles, point out that the compensation offered by the Guatemalan government was more than adequate since United Fruit had paid only $1.48 per acre when they purchased the land in 1928. Even if no improvements had been made to the properties the Compañía Agrícola had purchased twenty-five years earlier, it is obvious that holdings on the Pacific coast, Guatemala's most valuable farm land, would have appreciated considerably more than $1.19 per acre during the ensuing quarter of a

century. Indeed, when the Company sold its holdings in 1964, it offered its "improved land," those areas that had been cleared and were in production, for approximately $100 an acre.
67. Presidencia de la República, *Expediente de expropriación*, 34; 51-52; 97; 222; 223.
68. Arturo Herbruger, "Mi conciencia está límpia," *Siglo Veintiuno*, September 5, 1990. In the confused events following President Jorge Serrano Elías's abrupt flight from Guatemala in June, 1993, Herbruger was soon elected by the Legislative Assembly as President Ramiro de León Carpio's vice president.

Chapter 7: Protecting UFCO's Interests or Excising a Communist Beachhead?

1. Although the Compañía Agrícola's 1936 contract with the government of Guatemala stated that both parties agreed that "in no case will they resort to diplomatic intervention to resolve any differences arising from this contract," the United Fruit Company maintained that its dispute with the Arbenz administration did not arise from the contract. Such a stance was technically correct since the contract did not provide government land concessions for banana production.
2. Stephen G. Rabe, *Eisenhower and Latin America*, (Chapel Hill: University of North Carolina Press, 1988), 46.
3. Toriello, *La batalla de Guatemala*, 249-53.
4. Department of State *Bulletin*, September 14, 1953; 357-60.
5. Toriello, *La batalla de Guatemala*, 255-58.
6. Schlesinger and Kinzer, *Bitter Fruit*, 199.
7. "El gobierno de Jacobo Arbenz," *Crónica*, October 20, 1989, 44.
8. Bernays, *Biography of an Idea*, 761.
9. McCann, *An American Company*, 47.
10. James disagrees on the extent of U.S. media coverage provided to events in Guatemala.

    "Arbenz's frequent charges that our 'information monopolies' were waging a campaign against him were, to say the least, ironic, in view of the fact that only a handful of U.S. publications were printing anything at all about Guatemala . . . The author remembers the blank look he received from editors and writers with whom he discussed Guatemala at the beginning of 1953, and the comment of one editor: 'We'll wait until there's a revolution.' The phrase summed up the attitude of nearly every North American editor toward Guatemala until the very moment when revolution did, in fact, break out."

    James, *Red Design for the Americas*, 296.
11. Schlesinger and Kinzer, *Bitter Fruit*, 90.
12. Immerman, *The CIA in Guatemala*, 111.
13. Department of State, *Foreign Relations of the United States*, 1091-93.

14. Stephen E. Ambrose, *Eisenhower, The President*, Vol. 2, (New York: Simon and Schuster, 1984), 192.
15. Blasier, *The Hovering Giant*, 229, 163.
16. "Present Political Situation in Guatemala and Possible Developments during 1952," March 11, 1952, Department of State, *Foreign Relations of the United States, the American Republics, 1952-1954*, 1031.
17. Ibid., 1061.
18. Ibid., 1074.
19. Schlesinger and Kinzer, *Bitter Fruit*, 108.
20. Ibid., 132.
21. Dwight Eisenhower, *The White House Years: Mandate for Change*, Vol. 1, (Garden City, New York: Doubleday, 1963), 422-23.
22. Department of State, *Foreign Relations of the United States*, 1091-93.
23. Ibid., 1095-97.
24. Toriello, *La batalla de Guatemala*, 82-84.
25. Handy, *Gift of the Devil*, 139.
26. Gleijeses, *Shattered Hope*, 230.
27. Michael A. Guhen, *John Foster Dulles, A Statesman and his Times*, (New York: Columbia University Press, 1972), 55.
28. Leonard Mosley, *Dulles: A Biography of Eleanor, Allen and John Foster Dulles and their Family Network*, (New York: The Dial Press/James Wade, 1978), 77.
29. Blasier, *The Hovering Giant*, 165-66.
30. Schlesinger and Kinzer, *Bitter Fruit*, 114.
31. Department of State, *American Foreign Policy, 1950-1955*, 1308-09.
32. Gleijeses cites a May 29 New York *Times* dispatch quoting Toriello as saying that while the Guatemalan government was willing to hold talks with United Fruit Company officials, the Agrarian Reform Law "is not a subject for negotiation or discussion." However, the authors of *Bitter Fruit* maintain that Peurifoy sent the Department of State several telegrams between June 1 and June 5 that confirmed Arbenz's willingness to negotiate the issue of UFCO's expropriated lands.
    Gleijeses, *Shattered Hope*, 312; Schlesinger and Kinzer, *Bitter Fruit*, 164.
33. Department of State *Bulletin*, June 21, 1954, 950-51.
34. Speech made by Secretary of State John Foster Dulles to the forty-fifth annual convention of Rotary International, Seattle, Washington, June 10, 1954, Ibid., 938-39.
35. Blasier, *The Hovering Giant*, 172-73.
36. Cardoza y Aragón, *La revolución guatemalteca*, 173.
37. Torres Rivas, "Crisis y conyuntura crítica," 303.
38. Blasier, *The Hovering Giant*, 206.

39. Immerman, *The CIA in Guatemala*, 186.
40. Gleijeses, *Shattered Hope*, 338.
41. Torres Rivas, "Crisis y conyuntura crítica," 311.
42. Cardoza y Aragón, *La revolución guatemalteca*, 183.
43. Toriello, *Tras la cortina de banano*, 225.
44. Monteforte Toledo, "La revolución de Guatemala," 9.
45. Gleijeses, *Shattered Hope*, 343.
46. Monteforte Toledo, "La revolución de Guatemala," 9.
47. Cardoza y Aragón, *La revolución guatemalteca*, 164-65.
48. Monteforte Toledo, "La revolución de Guatemala," 9.
49. Schlesinger and Kinzer, *Bitter Fruit*, 213.
50. Ibid., 213.
51. Eduardo Weymann Fuentes, "Jacobo Arbenz, las motivaciones del discutido ex-presidente de Guatemala," V parte, *Siglo Veintiuno*, August 8, 1990.
52. María Vilanova de Arbenz, "La conspiración del silencio," *Siglo Veintiuno*, August 31, 1990.
53. Schlesinger and Kinzer, *Bitter Fruit*, 170-71.
54. Aybar de Soto, *Dependency and Intervention*, 250.
55. Miguel Ydígoras Fuentes, *My War with Communism*, (Englewood Cliffs, New Jersey: Prentice-Hall, 1963), 49-50.
56. Gleijeses, *Shattered Hope*, 249-50.
57. Immerman, *The CIA in Guatemala*, 184.
58. Schlesinger and Kinzer, *Bitter Fruit*, 77.
59. Handy, *Gift of the Devil*, 147.
60. Susanne Jonas, "Contradictions of Revolution and Intervention in Central America in the Transnational Era: The Case of Guatemala" in *Revolution and Intervention in Central America*, edited by Marlene Dixon and Susanne Jonas (San Francisco: Synthesis Press, 1983), 285.
61. Cook, *The Declassified Eisenhower*, 231.
62. Cehelsky, "Habla Arbenz," *Alero* 8, 118.
63. Bulmer-Thomas, *The Political Economy of Central America since 1920*, 148.
64. Ambrose, *Eisenhower*, 197.
65. Immerman, *The CIA in Guatemala*, 82.
66. Indeed, the U.S. government's "victory" over communism in Guatemala helped convince the Eisenhower administration that the same successful strategies used in 1954 could be duplicated in 1961 against Fidel Castro. Plans for the "liberation of Cuba" began early in 1960 and were well underway when President John F. Kennedy was inaugurated in January, 1961. By that time approximately 1,400 Cuban exiles — no match for Castro's 200,000-man army — had

been recruited and trained at a secret site on the Pacific coast of Guatemala. Innumerable books and articles have analyzed why the Bay of Pigs exercise failed, but Blasier makes a compelling observation: "The Bay of Pigs fiasco emboldened Castro and the Soviet Union to establish nuclear missiles in Cuba, an effort which led directly to the Cuban missile crisis of 1963 . . . U.S. policies in Guatemala in 1954 led to the Bay of Pigs in 1961, and the latter to the missile crisis, one of the single most dangerous armed confrontations in human history."

Blasier, *The Hovering Giant*, 298; 202.

67. Gleijeses, *Shattered Hope*, 362; 366.
68. *Guatemala in Rebellion: Unfinished History*, edited by Johnathan L. Fried, Marvin E. Gettleman, Deborah T. Levenson and Nancy Peckenham, (New York: Grove Press, Inc., 1983), 52.
69. Whetten, *Guatemala, The Land and the People*, 160.
70. Melvilles, *Tierra y poder en Guatemala*, 86.
71. LaBarge, "Impact of the United Fruit Company on the Economic Development of Guatemala," 42.
72. Bulmer-Thomas, *The Political Economy of Central America since 1920*, 128.
73. Melvilles, *Tierra y poder en Guatemala*, 130-31.
74. United Fruit Company, *Basic Operating Contracts*, 176.

    It is puzzling that neither the Arévalo or Arbenz administrations instituted a tax on United Fruit's profits, particularly since the governments of Honduras and Costa Rica established a 15 percent tax on UFCO's profits in 1949, the year before Arbenz was elected president. The Panamanian government followed with a similar tax in 1950. Five years later, both Honduras and Costa Rica had increased the tax on Company profits to 30 percent.

    Ellis, *Las trasnacionales del banano en Centroamérica*, 72.

75. Bishop, "The Guatemalan Labor Movement, 1944-1959," 162-63.
76. Bulmer-Thomas, *The Political Economy of Central America since 1920*, 146.
77. Franklin D. Parker, *The Central American Republics*, (London: Oxford University Press, 1964), 105.
78. Bulmer-Thomas, *The Political Economy of Central America since 1920*, 165.
79. Eduardo Galeano, *Open Veins of Latin America, Five Centuries of the Pillage of a Continent*, (New York: Monthly Review Press, 1973), 128.
80. Like the death of Colonel Francisco Arana eight years earlier, Castillo Armas's assassination has never been adequately explained. Gunned down in his living quarters, the president was apparently shot by a palace guard. The assassin's body was found nearby, presumably having taken his own life after killing Castillo Armas. It is generally assumed, however, that the guard was not the intellectual author of the crime.
81. Ramiro de León Carpio, Guatemala's former attorney for human rights, and now president of the country, made public these statistics at a conference held in Mexico City in November, 1991.

"Guerra e impunidad en Guatemala afectan a los derechos humanos," *Prensa Libre*, November 18, 1991.

Chapter 8: New Management Precipitates UFCO's Departure

1. Schlesinger and Kinzer, *Bitter Fruit*, 221.
2. May and Plaza, *The United Fruit Company*, 38.
3. According to Patricia Price Bailey, a Washington attorney and former Federal Trade commissioner, current enforcement policy would more likely allow six months to establish a competitor and two years to accomplish viability. Moreover, a Consent Decree filed today would almost certainly detail the consequences of failure to comply with all the provisions of the decree, while the document signed by the United Fruit Company provided no such sanctions.

   Telephone interview with Patricia Price Bailey, June 10, 1991, Washington, D.C.
4. Schlesinger and Kinzer erroneously state that the Consent Decree forced the United Fruit Company to "curtail its business in Guatemala by surrendering some of its trade to local companies and some of its land to local businessmen." It is true that United Brands, which acquired the United Fruit Company in 1969, sold its Atlantic coast holdings to Del Monte in 1972 in order to comply with the Consent Decree, but the decision to sell the Bananera division was made by UB's management, and was not specifically mandated by the Consent Decree.

   Schlesinger and Kinzer, *Bitter Fruit*, 229.
5. *Trade Cases, 1958*, (Chicago: Commerce Clearing House, Inc., 1959), 73,799.
6. May and Plaza, *The United Fruit Company in Latin America*, 252-53.
7. Between 1955 and 1969, UFCO's sales plummeted from $333 million to $304 million; its after tax profits fell from $33.5 million to a scant $2.2 million.
8. Arthur, et al., *Tropical Agribusiness Structures and Adjustments — Bananas*, 174.
9. Ibid., 67.
10. Even before Sunderland began selling or leasing large areas of UFCO's tropical holdings, the Company had already initiated a similar program, although far more modest in scope. Thus, between 1951 and 1971, the United Fruit Company sold or leased more than one million acres of its properties in Guatemala, Honduras, Costa Rica, Panama and Ecuador. During this twenty-year period, the Company reduced its isthmian holdings from 1,726,000 acres to 672,000 acres.
11. Melvilles, *Tierra y poder en Guatemala*, 190.
12. Interview with Ted A. Holcombe, March 11, 1991, Guatemala City.
13. Interview with Carlos Haroldo Gomar, November 21, 1990, Bananera.
14. James Painter, *Guatemala, False Hope, False Freedom*, (London: Catholic Institute for International Relations, 1987), 38.

15. Interview with Jean Palmer de Tabush, April 11, 1992, Guatemala City.
16. Melvilles, *Tierra y poder en Guatemala*, 189.
17. Telephone interview with John R. Silver, July 3, 1991, Brevard, North Carolina.
18. Stanley H. Brown, "United Fruit's Shotgun Marriage," *Fortune*, April 1969, 133-34.
19. Ibid., 132.
20. McCann, *An American Company*, 182.
21. Ibid., 185-86.
22. McCann puts a different slant on Black's decision to sell the Guatemala holdings. "I felt the reasons we went back to Guatemala to satisfy the conditions of the Consent Decree were the same reasons we had gone there in the first place: it had a weak, permissive and corrupt government, and the Company's social responsibility to the country was not likely to be made the issue that it had been in Panama." Like the peculiar comments McCann made about Estrada Cabrera, it is difficult to understand how President Carlos Arana Osorio could be described as "weak" or "permissive." Before his election, his brutal suppression of guerrillas in northeastern Guatemala had earned him the nickname "the butcher of Zacapa." Once in power, the tough, law-and-order leader declared a state of siege, sent troops into three university campuses and disrupted the activities of opposition parties.

    Ibid., 188.
23. Roger Burbach and Patricia Flynn provide the most detailed account of the alleged bribe, claiming that a Cuban-born Guatemalan businessman, hired by Del Monte as a consultant, paid a "good-sized chunk" of his $500,000 fee to President Arana.

    Fried, et al. *Guatemala in Rebellion*, 107; James Painter, *Guatemala, False Hope, False Freedom*, 51; Handy, *Gift of the Devil*, 198: Roger Burbach and Patricia Flynn, *Agribusiness in the Americas*, (New York: Monthly Review Press, 1980), 209-10.

Chapter 9: Evaluating Sixty-Six Years of Operations

1. LaBarge, "A Study of United Fruit Company Operations," vi.
2. Kepner and Soothill, *The Banana Empire*, 213.
3. May and Plaza, *The United Fruit Company*, 169.
4. John H. Adler, Eugene R. Schlesinger and Ernest C. Olson, *Public Finance and Economic Development in Guatemala*, (Stanford: Stanford University Press, 1952), 48.
5. Bulmer-Thomas, *The Political Economy of Central America since 1920*, 126, 357.
6. Interview with Willy W. Zapata, December 9, 1991, Guatemala City.
7. *Análisis evaluativo del sistema tributario de Guatemala*, Policy Economics Group,

KPMG Peat Marwick and College of Business Administration, Georgia State University, July 5, 1990, 7.
8. Ibid., 26.
9. Banco de Guatemala, "Situación financiera del gobierno central, años 1991-92," November 29, 1991.
10. In a hard-hitting article titled "What the Cerezo Government Cost Us and Will Continue to Cost Us," the weekly news magazine *Crónica* revealed in June, 1991, that during President Vinicio Cerezo's five years in office (1986-1991) his unvouchered "confidential expenses" rocketed from the equivalent of $1.3 million in 1986 to $22.6 million in 1990. Moreover, while the total expenditures of the office of the presidency increased to approximately $51.1 million in 1990, or 6 percent of the national budget, the Ministry of Public Health received a scant 0.32 percent of the government's revenues. The Ministry of Education fared little better, reduced to distributing chalk and mops to the nation's public schools during the last two years of the Cerezo government.

"Lo que nos costó, y nos seguirá costando, el gobierno de Cerezo," *Crónica*, June 14-20, 1991, 15-18.
11. Written interview with President Juan José Arévalo, April, 1989.

Many of the United Fruit Company's Guatemalan critics have also maintained that the Company utilized the country's "best land." It was *La Frutera*, however, that transformed impenetrable jungles into productive farm lands. Moreover, as previously noted, United Fruit occupied only 1 percent of Guatemala's crop lands.
12. Irene Solares S. "Aumenta la importancia de los productos no tradicionales," *Siglo Veintiuno*, January 7, 1992.
13. Interview with Willy W. Zapata, former director of the department of economic studies, Banco de Guatemala, December 9, 1991, Guatemala City.
14. Agricultural Attaché Office, U.S. Embassy, *Guatemala — Agricultural Annual Situation Report*, September 30, 1993.
15. John A. Booth and Thomas W. Walker, *Understanding Central America*, (Boulder, Colorado: Westview Press, 1989), 12.
16. May and Plaza, *The United Fruit Company*, 248-49.
17. United Fruit Company, *Basic Operating Contracts*, 126.
18. Bulmer-Thomas, *The Political Economy of Central America since 1920*, 286.
19. Kepner and Soothill, *The Banana Empire*, 229.
20. United Fruit Company, *Basic Operating Contracts*, 121.
21. Bulmer-Thomas, *The Political Economy of Central America since 1920*, 287.
22. Written interview with former President Juan José Arévalo, April, 1989.
23. Bulmer-Thomas, *The Political Economy of Central America since 1920*, 287.
24. Kepner and Soothill, *The Banana Empire*, 221.
25. LaBarge, "Impact of the United Fruit Company on the Economic Development of Guatemala," 35.

26. Bauer Paiz, *Cómo opera el capital Yanqui*, 326.
27. As economists Arthur, Houck and Beckford point out,

    "one of the characteristics of the vertically integrated company is that fixed costs represent a very high proportion of total costs. Depending upon definition of terms and the time period in view, this figure could reach extremes as high as two-thirds to three-quarters of total charges, even assuming a 'normal' volume of movement . . . With such high fixed costs, the management problem is predominantly one of maximizing the volume of exportable supplies in order to keep unit costs at a minimum."

    Arthur, et al, *Tropical Agribusiness Structures and Adjustments — Bananas*, 68.
28. Bauer Paiz, *Cómo opera el capital Yanqui*, 329-30.
29. In the years before the Depression, however, United Fruit Company stock paid significantly higher returns. Kepner found that because of several stock splits early in the Company's history and attractive annual dividends, an individual who had purchased $10,000 worth of UFCO stock in 1900 would have received, by 1933, a total of $58,959 in dividends — an average annual return of almost 18 percent.

    May and Plaza, *The United Fruit Company in Latin America*, 112; Kepner, *Social Aspects of the Banana Industry*, 23.
30. May and Plaza, *The United Fruit Company in Latin America*, 117.
31. Ibid., 227.
32. Benjamín Villanueva T., *An Approach to the Study of the Industrial Surplus: The Case of the United Fruit Company in Central America*, (Madison: University of Wisconsin, 1969), 53; 58.
33. May and Plaza, *The United Fruit Company in Latin America*, 117, 22.
34. "Hacia la independencia económica de la nación," *El Imparcial*, October 18, 1951.
35. "Hechos en que se basa la compañía para responder a asertos del FPL," *El Imparcial*, November 9, 1951.
36. Ibid.
37. LaBarge, "A Study of United Fruit Company Operations," 378.
38. Ibid., 379.
39. LaBarge, "Impact of the United Fruit Company on the Economic Development of Guatemala," 59.
40. Bulmer-Thomas, *The Political Economy of Central America since 1920*, 287.
41. Kepner and Soothill, *The Banana Empire*, 266.
42. Susanne Jonas, *The Battle for Guatemala, Rebels, Death Squads and U.S. Power*, (Boulder, Colorado: Westview Press, 1991), 19.
43. LaBarge, "Impact of the United Fruit Company on the Economic Development of Guatemala," 60-68.
44. May and Plaza, *The United Fruit Company*, 169.

45. Villanueva, *An Approach to the Study of the Industrial Surplus*, 37.
46. LaBarge, "Impact of the United Fruit Company on the Economic Development of Guatemala," 24-25.
47. Ibid., 44.
48. U.S. Embassy, *Agricultural Annual Situation Report, September 30, 1993*, 22.
49. Bulmer-Thomas, *The Political Economy of Central America since 1920*, 122.
50. LaBarge, "Impact of the United Fruit Company on the Economic Development of Guatemala," 29-30.
51. LaBarge, "A Study of United Fruit Company Operations," 138.
52. LaBarge, "Impact of the United Fruit Company on the Economic Development of Guatemala," 33.
53. Like Monteforte Toledo, Cardoza y Aragón contends that since high winds periodically destroyed thousands of acres of banana lands in Guatemala, United Fruit had "perfectly calculated" the extent of such damages. As a result, he came to the astounding conclusion that, "the 'losses' due to high winds or torrential rains that are so common in the tropics, do not in reality exist."

    Luis Cardoza y Aragón, "Guatemala y el imperio bananero," *Cuadernos Americanos*, LXXIV, No. 2 (1954), 28.
54. LaBarge, "Impact of the United Fruit Company on the Economic Development of Guatemala," 33-34.
55. Ibid., 35.
56. Bauer Paiz, *Cómo opera el capital Yanqui*, 331-32.
57. Melvilles, *Tierra y poder en Guatemala*, 72.
58. May and Plaza, *The United Fruit Company*, 229-30.
59. Arthur, et al., *Tropical Agribusiness Structures and Adjustments, Bananas*, 140.
60. United Fruit estimated that between 32,000 to 37,000 Guatemalans depended on the activities of the Company.

    LaBarge, "Impact of the United Fruit Company on the Economic Development of Guatemala," 43.
61. Frank McNeil, *War and Peace in Central America*, (New York: Charles Scribner's Sons, 1988), 51-52.
62. Blasier, *The Hovering Giant*, 57.

Epilogue

1. The 150-bed facility, one of the best-equipped hospitals in Guatemala, employs ten physicians, two surgeons and various other specialists. BANDEGUA annually spends the equivalent of approximately $1.5 million to administer the facility, thus providing a level of funding that "even the best public hospitals in Guatemala City do not receive," notes Dr. Francisco Alvarez, chief of

FOR THE RECORD

medical services.

Interview with Dr. Francisco Alvarez, November 21, 1990, Quiriguá Hospital, Bananera.

2. Thomas L. Karnes, *Tropical Enterprise: The Standard Fruit and Steamship Company*, (Baton Rouge: Louisiana State Press, 1978), 285.
3. According to McCann, however, one line of the jingle was to cost the banana industry millions of dollars. Since the authors of the commercial wanted to emphasize that bananas are an exotic, tropical fruit, they included the line "bananas like the climate of the very, very tropical equator." In order to find a word to rhyme with "equator," the ditty ended by advising "so you should never put bananas in the refrigerator." The fact is, bananas can be refrigerated for a few days even after they have been displayed in produce departments. Nevertheless, many Americans still believe the Chiquita jingle and purchase just a few bananas in order to consume them — unrefrigerated — within a day or two.
4. Interview with Gerald K. Brunelle, November 23, 1990, Bananera.
5. R. H. Stover and N.W. Simmonds, *Bananas*, (London: Longmans, 3rd ed., 1987), 426; 429.
6. Interview with Roberto Turnbull, January 14, 1992, La Lima, Honduras.
7. That production costs for the banana industry are significantly higher than any of Guatemala's leading export crops is apparent in the following table prepared by the Bank of Guatemala for the 1990-1991 crop year. It provides a ratio of dollar costs per hectare. (One hectare equals 2.47 acres).

	Labor costs*	Inputs**	Indirect costs***	Total direct & indirect costs	Average yield per hec.****
Bananas	$260	210	201	819	38.92
Coffee	91	72	61	253	0.52
Cotton	127	155	77	421	0.99
Sugar	103	37	80	351	60.3

*Includes land preparation/planting, fertilizer application, cleaning/weeding/pruning, pest control, irrigation, harvesting, post-harvest handling, and bonus.

**Includes seed, fertilizers, pesticides, herbicides, fungicides, fuel, lubricants, and implements.

***Includes administrative costs, social security quota, finance costs, legal costs associated with credit, and stamps/seals.

****Metric tons

U.S. Embassy, "Guatemala — Agricultural Annual Situation Report," March 3, 1991; 43.

8. BANDEGUA and the country's two other major banana companies produced 26.2 million boxes of the yellow fruit in 1992, generating $102.4 in export earnings. Guatemala's most important export was coffee, providng $248.9

million in earnings. Sugar ranked second, with export earnings of $158.1. U.S. Embassy, *Agricultural Annual Situation Report, 1993*, 5; 26.

9. Without including the substantial fringe benefits that BANDEGUA provides all its workers, the lowest-paid laborers received an annual salary equivalent to $1,896 during 1991, "higher than the salaries of many office workers in Guatemala City," César Castillo Barrajas, BANDEGUA's paymaster, points out.

10. Interview with Mario Mena, general manager of COBIGUA, November 26, 1991, Guatemala City.

11. Chiquita Brands International, *1992 Annual Report*.

12. Ibid.

13. By breaking down the North American consumption of bananas into seven age groups, Chiquita Brands's researchers have found that the biggest consumers of the fruit are persons sixty and over who annually purchase a remarkable fifty pounds of bananas. Individuals between the ages of fifty-one and sixty are the next largest group of consumers (thirty-five pounds annually), followed by youngsters from one to ten, who eat 21.5 pounds a year. The eleven to twenty-year-old group consumes the least: only 13.3 pounds per year.

    Chiquita Brands International, *1990 Annual Report*. 14. Quoted in an interview with Honduran President Rafael Leonardo Callejas, *Siglo Veintiuno*, February 18, 1993.

15. María Olga Paiz, "El tren que se detuvo en el tiempo," *Crónica,* January 24, 1992, 45.

16. Telephone interview with Luis Guzmán, statistician, Ferrocarril Nacional de El Salvador, April 23, 1992, San Salvador.

17. Interview with J. Rodolfo Bendfeldt A., advisor to the manager of FEGUA, February 5, 1992, Guatemala City.

BIBLIOGRAPHY

BOOKS AND MANUSCRIPTS

Acker, Alison, *Honduras, the Making of a Banana Republic*. Toronto: Between the Lines, 1988.

Adams, Frederick Upham, *Conquest of the Tropics*. New York: Doubleday, Page & Company, 1914.

Adams, Richard Newbold, *Crucifixion by Power: Essays on Guatemalan National Social Structure, 1944-1966*. Austin: University of Texas Press, 1970.

Adler, John H., Eugene R. Schlesinger, Ernest C. Olson, *Public Finance and Economic Development in Guatemala*. Stanford: Stanford University Press, 1952.

Amaya Amador, Ramón, *Prisión verde*, 5th ed. Tegucigalpa: Editorial Universitaria, 1988.

Ambrose, Stephen A., *Eisenhower, The President*, Volume 2. New York: Simon and Schuster, 1984.

Arévalo Bermejo, Juan José, *El candidato blanco y el huracán, 1944-1945*. Guatemala: Editorial Académico Centroamérica, S.A., 1984.

——— *Escritos complementarios*. Guatemala: CENALTEX, Ministerio de Educación, 1988.

——— *Guatemala, la democracia y el imperio*. Santiago: Editorial Juventus, 1954.

Arévalo Martínez, Rafael, *Ecce Perícles*, 2nd ed. San José, Costa Rica: EDUCA, 1982.

Argueta, Mario R., *Bananos y política: Samuel Zemurray y la Cuyamel Fruit Company en Honduras*. Tegucigalpa: Universidad Nacional Autónoma de Honduras, 1989.

Arthur, Henry B., James P. Houck, George L. Beckford, *Tropical Agribusiness Structures and Adjustments — Bananas*. Boston: Harvard University, 1968.

Asturias, Miguel Angel, *El papa verde*, 3rd. rev. Madrid: Alianza Editorial, S.A., 1988.

——— *Viento fuerte*. Guatemala: Editorial del Ministerio de Educación Pública, 1950.

——— *El problema social del indio*, 2nd ed. rev. Paris: Centre de Recherches de L'Institut D'Etudes Hispanics, 1971.

Barry, Tom, *Roots of Rebellion, Land & Hunger in Central America*. Boston: South End Press, 1987.

Bauer Paiz, Alfonso, *Cómo opera el capital Yanqui en Centroamérica (el caso de Guatemala)*. Mexico: Editorial Ibero-Mexicano, 1956.

——— *Catalogación de leyes y disposiciones del trabajo de Guatemala del periódo 1872 a 1930*. Guatemala: Universidad de San Carlos, 1965.

Bauer Paiz, Alfonso and Julio Valladares Castillo, *La Frutera ante la ley (los conflictos laborales de Izabal y Tiquisate).* Guatemala: Ministerio de Economía y Trabajo, 1949.

Bernays, Edward, *Biography of an Idea.* New York: Simon and Shuster, 1965.

Bishop, Edwin Warren, "The Guatemalan Labor Movement, 1944-1959," Ph.D. diss., University of Wisconsin, 1959.

Blasier, Cole, *The Hovering Giant, U.S. Responses to Revolutionary Change in Latin America 1910-1985*, rev. ed. Pittsburgh: University of Pittsburgh Press, 1985.

Booth, John A. and Thomas W. Walker, *Understanding Central America.* Boulder, Colorado: Westview Press, 1989.

Braden, Spruille, *Diplomats and Demagogues.* New Rochelle, New York: Arlington House, 1971.

Brigham, William T., *Guatemala, The Land of the Quetzal.* New York: Charles Scribner's Sons, 1887.

Bulmer-Thomas, Victor, *The Political Economy of Central America since 1920.* Cambridge, England: Cambridge University Press, 1987.

Burbach, Roger and Patricia Flynn, *Agribusiness in the Americas.* New York: Monthly Review Press, 1980.

Cambranes, J.C. *Coffee and Peasants in Guatemala.* Stockholm: Tryckop, 1985.

Cardoza y Aragón, Luis, *Guatemala, las líneas de su mano*, 2d ed. Mexico: Fondo de Cultural Económica, 1965.

——— *La revolución guatemalteca.* Mexico: Ediciones Cuadernos Americanos, 1955.

Chinchilla Aguilar, Ernesto, *Blasones y heredades.* Guatemala: Editorial José de Pineda Ibarra, 1975.

Commerce Clearing House, Inc., *Trade Cases 1958.* Chicago: 1959.

Cook, Blanche Wiesen, *The Declassified Eisenhower, a Divided Legacy.* New York: Doubleday and Company, Inc. 1981.

Crowther, Samuel, *The Romance and Rise of the American Tropics.* Garden City, New York: Doubleday, Doran & Company, 1929.

Cunningham, Eugene, *Gypsying through Central America.* New York: E.P. Dutton & Company, 1922.

De León Aragón, Oscar, *Los contratos de la United Fruit Company y las compañias muelleras en Guatemala.* Guatemala: Editorial del Ministerio de Educación Pública, 1950.

Dixon, Marlene and Susanne Jonas, eds., *Revolution and Intervention in Central America.* San Francisco: Synthesis Press, 1983.

Domínguez, Mauricio T., "The Development of the Technological and Scientific Coffee Industry in Guatemala, 1830-1930." Ph.D. diss., Tulane University, 1970.

Eisenhower, Dwight, *The White House Years: Mandate for Change*, Vol. 1. Garden City, New York: Doubleday, 1963.

Ellis, Frank, *Las transnacionales del banano en Centroamérica.* San José, Costa Rica: EDUCA, 1983.

Flores Valeriano, Enrique, *La explotación bananera en Honduras*, rev. ed. Tegucigalpa: Universidad Nacional Autónoma de Honduras, 1987.

Fried, Johnathan L., Marvin E. Gettleman, Deborah T. Levenson and Nancy Peckenham, *Guatemala in Rebellion: Unfinished History*. New York: Grove Press, Inc., 1983.

Galeano, Eduardo, *Open Veins of Latin America, Five Centuries of the Pillage of a Continent*. New York: Monthly Review Press, 1973.

Galich, Manuel, "Prólogo." Oscar de León Aragón, *Los contratos de La United Fruit Company y las compañías muelleras en Guatemala*. Guatemala: Editorial del Ministerio de Educación Pública, 1950.

———*Por qué lucha Guatemala, Arévalo y Arbenz: dos hombres contra un imperio*. Buenos Aires: Elmer Editor, 1956.

Galvez E, Héctor, *Conozca a Estrada Cabrera*. Guatemala: Editorial Prensa Libre, 1976.

García Márquez, Gabriel, *One Hundred Years of Solitude*. New York: Avon Books, 1970.

Glassman, Paul, *Guatemala Guide*. Champlain, New York: Passport Press, 1990.

Gleijeses, Piero, *Shattered Hope, The Guatemalan Revolution and the United States, 1944-1954*. Princeton: Princeton University Press, 1991.

González Davison, Fernando, *Guatemala 1500-1970, reflexiones sobre su desarrollo histórico*. Guatemala: Editorial Universitaria de Guatemala, 1987.

González Orellana, Carlos, *Historia de la educación en Guatemala*. Guatemala: Editorial Universitaria, 1980.

Grieb, Kenneth, *Guatemalan Caudillo, The Regime of Jorge Ubico*. Athens, Ohio: Ohio University Press, 1967.

Griffith, William J., *Empires in the Wilderness, Foreign Colonization and Development in Guatemala 1834-1844*. Chapel Hill: University of North Carolina Press, 1965.

Guhen, Michael A., *John Foster Dulles, A Statesman and his Times*. New York: Columbia University Press, 1972.

Handy, Jim, *Gift of the Devil, A History of Guatemala*. Toronto: Between the Lines, 1984.

Healy, David, *Drive to Hegemony, the United States in the Caribbean, 1898-1917*. Madison: University of Wisconsin Press, 1988.

Huxley, Aldous *Beyond the Mexique Bay*, 2nd ed. rev. New York: Vantage Books, Inc. 1960.

Immerman, Richard H., *The CIA in Guatemala, The Foreign Policy of Intervention*. Austin: University of Texas Press, 1982.

Inman, Samuel Guy, *A New Day in Guatemala*. Wilton, Connecticut: Worldover Press, 1950.

International Bank for Reconstruction and Development, *The Economic Development of Guatemala*. Washington, D.C.: 1951.

James, Daniel, *Red Design for the Americas: Guatemalan Prelude*. New York: The John

Day Company, 1954.

Jiménez, Ernesto Bienvenido, *La educación rural en Guatemala*. Guatemala: Editorial José de Pineda Ibarra, 1966.

Jonas, Susanne, *The Battle for Guatemala, Rebels, Death Squads and U.S. Power*. Boulder, Colorado: Westview Press, 1991.

Jones, Chester Lloyd, *Guatemala Past and Present*. Minneapolis: University of Minnesota, 1940.

Karnes, Thomas L., *Tropical Enterprise: The Standard Fruit and Steamship Company*. Baton Rouge: Louisiana State University Press, 1978.

Kepner, Charles David, Jr., *Social Aspects of the Banana Industry*. New York: Columbia University Press, 1936.

Kepner, Charles David, Jr., and Jay Henry Soothill, *The Banana Empire: a Case Study of Economic Imperialism*. New York: The Vanguard Press, 1935.

Krauss, *Inside Central America: Its People, Politics and History*. New York: Summit Books, 1991.

Krehm, William, *Democracia y tiranías en el Caribe*. Mexico: Unión Democrática Centroamericana, 1949.

Krooss, Herman E., and Charles Gilbert, *American Business History*. Englewood Cliffs, New Jersey: Prentice Hall Inc., 1972.

LaBarge, Richard Allen, "A Study of United Fruit Company Operations in Isthmian America, 1946-1954." Ph.D. diss., Duke University, 1959.

LaFeber, Walter, *Inevitable Revolutions: The United States in Central America*. New York: W.W. Norton & Company, 1984.

Maudslay, Anne Cary, and Alfred Percival Maudslay, *A Glimpse of Guatemala*. London: John Murray, 1899.

May, Stacy, and Galo Plaza, *The United Fruit Company in Latin America*. New York: National Planning Association, 1958.

McCann, Thomas P., *An American Company, The Tragedy of United Fruit*. New York: Crown Publishers, Inc. 1976.

McClintock, Michael, *The American Connection, State Terror and Popular Resistance in Guatemala*, Vol. 2. London: Zed Books, 1985.

McNeil, Frank, *War and Peace in Central America*. New York: Charles Scribner's Sons, 1988.

Melville, Thomas and Marjorie, *Tierra y poder en Guatemala*, 2nd ed. San José, Costa Rica: EDUCA, 1982.

Monteforte Toledo, Mario, *Guatemala — monografía sociológica*, 2nd ed. Mexico: Universidad Autónoma de Mexico, 1965.

Morley, Sylvanus G., *Guide Book to the Ruins of Quirigua*. Washington, D.C.: Carnegie Institution of Washington, 1935.

Mosley, Leonard, *Dulles: A Biography of Eleanor, Allen and John Foster Dulles and Their Family Network*. New York: The Dial Press/James Wade, 1978.

Munro, Dana G., *The Five Republics of Central America*. New York: Oxford University Press, 1918.

———*Intervention and Dollar Diplomacy in the Caribbean, 1900-1921*. Princeton: Princeton University Press, 1964.

Nájara Fanfán, Mario, *Los estafadores de la democracia (hombres y hechos en Guatemala)*. Buenos Aires: Editorial Glem, 1956.

Painter, James, *Guatemala, False Hope, False Freedom*. London: Catholic Institute for International Relations, 1987.

Parker, Franklin D., *The Central American Republics*. London: Oxford University Press, 1964.

Pellecer, Carlos Manuel, *Dos Yanquis más contra Guatemala*. Guatemala: Edinter-Artemis, 1986.

Piedra-Santa Arandi, Rafael, *Introducción a los problemas económicos de Guatemala*, 2nd ed. Guatemala: Ediciones Superiores, 1977.

Pitti, Joseph A., "Jorge Ubico and Guatemalan Politics in the 1920s." Ph.D. diss., University of New Mexico, 1975.

Phillips, David Atlee, *The Night Watch*. New York: Atheneum, 1977.

Polo Sifontes, Francis, *Historia de Guatemala*. León, Spain: Editorial Evergráficas, S.A., 1988.

Rippy, J. Fred, *Latin America and the Industrial Age*, 2nd ed. New York: G.P. Putnam's Sons, 1947.

Rabe, Stephen G., *Eisenhower and Latin America*. Chapel Hill: University of North Carolina Press, 1988.

Rodríguez Beteta, Virgilio, *No es guerra de hermanos sino de bananos*. Guatemala: Universidad de San Carlos, 1969.

Rosengarten, Frederic, Jr., *Wilson Popenoe, Agricultural Explorer, Educator, and Friend of Latin America*. Lawai, Kauai, Hawaii: National Tropical Botanical Garden, 1991.

Rosenthal, Mario, *Guatemala, The Story of an Emergent Latin American Democracy*. New York: Twayne Publishers, Inc. 1962.

Samayoa Chinchilla, Carlos, *El dictador y yo*, 2nd ed., Guatemala: Editorial José de Pineda Ibarra, 1967.

———*El quetzal no es rojo*. Mexico: Arana Hermanos, 1956.

Sapper, Karl, *Sobre la geografía física*, 2nd ed. rev., Guatemala: Ministerio de Educación Pública, 1958.

Schlesinger, Stephen, and Stephen Kinzer, *Bitter Fruit, The Untold Story of the American Coup in Guatemala*. Garden City, New York: Anchor Press/Doubleday, 1983.

Schneider, Ronald M., *Communism in Guatemala 1944-1954*. New York: Octagon Books, 1979.

Shattuck, George Cheever, *A Medical Survey of the Republic of Guatemala*. Washington, D.C.: Carnegie Institution of Washington, 1938.

Silvert, K.H., *A Study in Government: Guatemala, Part 1, National and Local Government since 1944*. New Orleans: Tulane University, 1954.

——*The Conflict Society*. New York: Harper & Row, 1966.

Skinner-Klee, Jorge, *Legislación indigenista de Guatemala*. Mexico: Instituto Indigenista Interamericano, 1954.

Solís, César G., *Los ferrocarriles en Guatemala*. Guatemala: Tipografía Nacional, 1952.

Smith, Carol A., ed. *Guatemalan Indians and the State, 1540 to 1988*. Austin: University of Texas Press, 1990.

Solórzano, Valentín F., *Evolución económica de Guatemala*, 4th ed.rev. Guatemala: Editorial José de Pineda Ibarra, 1977.

Stephens, Clyde S., *Bananeros in Central America*. Fort Myers, Florida: Press Printing Company, 1989.

Stephens, John L., *Incidents of Travel in Central America, Chiapas and Yucatan*, Vol. 2, 12th ed. New York: Harper & Brothers, 1858.

Stover, R. H. and N.W. Simmonds, *Bananas*, 3rd ed., London: Longmans, 1987.

Suslow, Leo O., *Aspects of Social Reform in Guatemala 1944-1949*. Hamilton, New York: Colgate University, 1949.

Taylor, Frank J., Earl M. Welty and David W. Eyre, *From Land and Sea, the Story of Castle & Cooke of Hawaii*. San Francisco: Chronicle Books, 1976.

Toriello, Guillermo, *La batalla de Guatemala*. Mexico: Ediciones Cuadernos Americanos, 1955.

——*Tras la cortina de banano*. Mexico: Fondo de Cultura Económica, 1976.

Torres Rivas, Edelberto, *Centroamérica hoy*. Mexico: Siglo XXI, 1976.

——*Desarrollo social Centroamericano*, 5th ed. San José, Costa Rica: EDUCA, 1977.

——*Interpretación del desarrollo Centroamericano, procesos y estructuras de una sociedad independiente*, 3rd ed. San José, Costa Rica: EDUCA, 1973.

Villanueva T., Benjamin, *An Approach to the Study of the Industrial Surplus: The Case of the United Fruit Company in Central America*. Madison: University of Wisconsin, 1969.

Wagner, Regina, *Los alemanes en Guatemala 1828-1944*. Guatemala: Editorial Idea, 1992.

Whetten, Nathan L., *Guatemala the Land and the People*. New Haven: Yale University Press, 1961.

Whitman, Edmund S., *Those Wild West Indies*. New York: The American Book Bindery-Stratford Press, Inc., 1938.

Wilkins, Mira, *The Maturing of Multinational Enterprise: American Business Abroad from 1914 to 1970*. Cambridge: Harvard University Press, 1974.

Williams, John L., "The Rise of the Banana Industry and its Influence on Caribbean Countries." Master's Thesis, Clark University, 1925.

Wilson, Charles Morrow, *Empire in Green and Gold the Story of the American Banana Trade*. New York: Henry Holt and Company, 1947.

Wise, David and Thomas B. Ross, *The Invisible Government.* New York: Random House, 1964.

Woodbury, Richard B. and Aubrey S. Trik, *The Ruins of Zaculeu, Guatemala,* Vol. 1. Boston: The United Fruit Company, 1953.

Woodward, Ralph Lee, Jr., *Central America: A Nation Divided.* New York: Oxford University Press, 19

Wyld Ospina, Carlos, *El autócrata.* Guatemala: Editorial José de Pineda Ibarra, 1967.

Ydígoras Fuentes, Miguel, *My War with Communism.* Englewood Cliffs, New Jersey: Prentice-Hall, 1963.

ARTICLES, REPORTS AND SURVEYS

Banco de Guatemala, "Situación financiera del gobierno central años 1991-92," November, 1991.

Balsells Tojo, Edgar Alfredo, "La revolución necesaria," *Crónica,* October 20, 1989.

Britnell, George E., "Economic and Social Change in Guatemala," *The Canadian Journal of Economics and Political Science,* 17 (1951).

Brown, Stanley H., "United Fruit's Shotgun Marriage," *Fortune* 79, no.4 (1969).

Cambranes, J.C., "Los empresarios agrarios modernos y el estado en Guatemala," *Mesoamérica,* 10 (1985):243-91.

—— "El desarrollo socio-económico de Guatemala: 1868-85." *Economía de Guatemala 1750-1940, lecturas y materiales,* Tomo 1, edited by Jorge Luján Muñoz. Guatemala: Universidad de San Carlos, 1980.

Cardoza y Aragón, Luis, "Guatemala y el imperio bananero," *Cuadernos Americanos,* LXXIV 2 (1954):19-45.

Castle & Cooke, *1990 Annual Report.*

Cehelsky, Marta, "Habla Arbenz, *Alero* 8 (1974):116-24.

Chiquita Brands International, Inc. "Prospectus," July 11, 1991; *1990 Annual Report.*

Coe, William R. and Robert J. Sharer, "The Quirigua Project 1975 Season," *Quirigua Reports,* Vol. I, Papers 1-5. Philadelphia: University of Pennsylvania, 1979.

Crónica, "El gobierno de Jacobo Arbenz," October 20, 1989.

Cutter, Victor M., "Foreign Trade's Golden Rule: You Can't Exploit your Markets and Have Them Too." United Fruit Company, *Unifruitco,* February, 1929.

—— "Trade Relations with Latin America," United Fruit Company, 1929.

Daly, E.J. "Through Barrios to Salvador," United Fruit Company, *Unifruitco,* April 30, 1930.

Dirección General de Estadística, Ministerio de Economía, *Anuario estadístico 1971.*

——*Cuarto censo de la población de la república, 1924.*

"Discurso del Teniente Coronel Jacobo Arbenz, 15 de Marzo de 1951." Guatemala: Tipografía Nacional, 1951.

El Imparcial, "Hacia la independencia económica de la nación," October 18, 1951.

——— "Hechos en que se basa la compañia para responder a asertos del FPL," November 9, 1951.

——— "Ferrocarriles de Guatemala: júbilo trenero," December 28, 1968.

——— "IRCA inició entrega de bienes," January 3, 1969.

English Translation of Basic Operating Contracts between United Fruit Company or its Respective Subsidiary and the Governments of Colombia, Costa Rica, Ecuador, Guatemala, Honduras and Panama Respectively. Internal Document of the United Fruit Company.

Fresse, Ana, "Decentralización más urgente que simple," *Siglo Veintiuno*, November 15, 1991.

——— "FEGUA: tras el éxito?" *Siglo Veintiuno*, November 20, 1991.

Galich, Manuel, "Diez años de primavera (1944-54) en el país de la eterna tiranía (1838-1974)" *Alero* 8 (1974):53-71.

Gleijeses, Piero, "La aldea de Ubico: Guatemala, 1931-1944," *Mesoamérica* 17 (1989):25-59.

Grieb, Kenneth, "American Involvement in the Rise of Jorge Ubico," *Caribbean Studies*, 10, no.1 (1970):5-21.

Herbruger, Arturo, "Mi conciencia está limpia," *Siglo Veintiuno*, September 5, 1990.

International Monetary Fund, *Balance of Payments Yearbook*, V, 1947-53. Washington, D.C., 1954.

International Railways of Central America, *Annual Report*, 1959; 1963.

Instituto Nacional de Estadística, *Encuesta nacional sociodemográfica.* Guatemala, 1990.

———*Estadística de transporte de Guatemala, 1988.* Guatemala, 1990.

———*Algunos indicadores estadísticos, 1989.*

Jonas, Susanne, "Contradictions of Revolution and Intervention in Central America in the Transnational Era: The Case of Guatemala" in *Revolution and Intervention in Central America*, edited by Marlene Dixon and Susanne Jonas. San Francisco: Synthesis Press, 1983.

LaBarge, Richard Allen, "Impact of the United Fruit Company on the Economic Development of Guatemala, 1946-1954," *Studies in Middle American Economics*, 29 (1968):3-72.

McCreery, David J., "Coffee and Class in Liberal Guatemala," *The Hispanic American Historical Review*, 56, no.3 (1976):438-60.

Memoria de las labores del ejecutivo en el ramo de hacienda y crédito público. Guatemala: Tipografía Nacional, 1937.

Monteforte Toledo, Mario, "La revolución de Guatemala," *Organismo Judicial* 1, no. 8 (1987):3-10.

Mosk, Sanford A., "Economía cafetalera de Guatemala durante el período 1850-

1918." *Economía de Guatemala 1750-1840, antología de lecturas y materiales, Tomo 1*, edited by Jorge Luján Muñoz. Guatemala: Universidad de San Carlos, 1980.

North American Congress on Latin America (NACLA) "United Fruit is not Chiquita." Berkeley: Waller Press, 1974.

Organization of American States, Executive Secretariat for Economic and Social Affairs, "Sectoral Study of Transnational Enterprises in Latin America: The Banana Industry." Washington, D.C., 1975.

Paz Tejada, Carlos, "Pasajes de la revolución de octubre," *Siglo Veintiuno*, January 30, 1991.

Paiz, María Olga, "El tren que se detuvo en el tiempo," *Crónica*, (January 24, 1992).

Piedra-Santa Arandi, Rafael, "La construcción de ferrocarriles en Guatemala y los problemas financieros de la IRCA," *Economía* 15 (1968):5-48.

Pinzón Salazar, José, "Entre la satisfacción técnica gubernamental y la incertidumbre de las mayorías," *Siglo Veintiuno*, December 28, 1991.

Policy Economics Group, KPMG Peat Marwick and College of Business Administration, Georgia State University, *Análisis Evaluativo del Sistema Tributario de Guatemala*. Guatemala, 1990.

Pollan, A.A., "The United Fruit Company and Middle America." Speech delivered at the New School for Social Research, New York City, January, 1944.

PPI Del Monte Tropical Fruit Company, *Fresh Press*. Miami, November 1991.

Prensa Libre, "FEGUA quedará en poder de empresarios Guatemaltecos," October 20, 1991.

—— "Guerra e impunidad en Guatemala afectan a los derechos humanos," November 18, 1991.

Presidencia de la República, Publicaciones del Departamento Agrario Nacional, *Expediente de expropriación seguido contra la Compañía Agrícola de Guatemala con la ley de reforma agraria*. Guatemala: Tipografía Nacional, 1954.

Secretaría de Fomento, *Ferrocarril a El Salvador, documentos relativos a la caducidad del contrato Méndez-Williamson*. Guatemala: Imprenta Nacional La Instrucción, 1921

Silvert, K.H., "Guatemala after Revolution," *The Conflict Society*, rev. ed. New York: Harper & Row, 1966.

Skavroneck, Drew, "Hey, So What is a Banana?" PPI Del Monte Tropical Fruit Company, *Fresh Press*, November, 1990.

Solares S., Irene, "Aumenta la importancia de los productos no tradicionales," *Siglo Veintiuno*, January 7, 1992.

Toriello, Jorge, "Puntualización a un artículo del licenciado Rolz Bennett," *Siglo Veintiuno*, October 5, 1991.

Torres Rivas, Edelberto, "Crisis y conyuntura crítica: la caída de Arbenz y los contratiempos de la revolución burguesa," *Revista Mexicana de Sociología*, 41, no.1 (1979):297-323.

United Fruit Company, *Datos Estadísticos 1950*.

USAID Mission: "Plantation Health-care in Guatemala: Aspects of the Problem." Guatemala, 1980.

U.S. Department of Commerce, *Central America as an Export Field.* Special Agents Series, No. 113; 1916.

U.S. Department of State *Bulletin,* September 14, 1953; May 3, 1954; June 21, 1954.

——*Foreign Relations of the United States, the American Republics, 1952-1954.*

U.S. Embassy, *Guatemala — Agricultural Annual Situation Report,* March 1, 1991.

——*Foreign Economic Trends, Guatemala,* March, 1991.

——*Program Assistance Approval Document, FY 91,* August, 1991.

Velásquez M., Diego, C.S. Brenes, Gustavo Berganza and E. Blanck, "Lo que nos costó, y nos seguirá costando, el gobierno de Cerezo," *Crónica* (June 14, 1991):15-18.

Vilanova de Arbenz, María, "La conspiración del silencio," *Siglo Veintiuno,* August 31, 1990.

Wagner, Regina, "Empresarios alemanes en Guatemala." *Mesoamérica* 13 (1987):87-123.

Wasserstrom, Robert, "Revolution in Guatemala: Peasant and Politics under the Arbenz Government," *Comparative Studies in Society and History,* 17, no. 4 (1975):443-78.

Weymann Fuentes, Eduardo, "Jacobo Arbenz: Las motivaciones del discutido ex-presidente de Guatemala," *Siglo Veintiuno,* August 5 and 8, 1990.

Woodward, Ralph Lee, Jr., "Changes in the Nineteenth Century Guatemalan State and its Indian Policies." *Guatemalan Indians and the State, 1540 to 1988,* edited by Carol A. Smith. Austin: University of Texas Press, 1990.

Zamorano, Annual Report, 1992-1993.

INTERVIEWS AND CORRESPONDENCE

Alvarez, Dr. Francisco, November 21, 1990, Quiriguá Hospital.

Arbenz, María Vilanova de, letter to Stanley, October 26, 1990.

Arévalo Bermejo, Dr. Juan José, letter to Stanley, April, 1989.

Bailey, Patricia Price, June 10, 1991, Washington, D.C.

Benfeldt A., J. Rodolfo, February 5, 1992, Guatemala City.

Brunelle, Gerald K., November 23, 1990, Bananera; January 24, 1991, Guatemala City.

Campbell, Max P., letter to Stanley, November 26, 1990.

Carol Cardoza, Benjamín, November 21, 1993, Bananera.

Castillo Barajas, César S., July 24, 1990, Bananera.

De la Vega, Laura, July 25, 1990, Bananera.
Erales, Rolando, February 8, 1991, Guatemala City.
Gomar, Carlos Haroldo, November 21, 1990, Bananera.
Guzmán, Luis, telephone interview, April 23, 1992, San Salvador, El Salvador.
Greenberg, Lazarus, S., March 3, 1992, Guatemala City.
Holcombe, Ted A., March 11, 1991, Guatemala City.
Jablon, Stuart, January 14, 1992, La Ceiba, Honduras.
Long, Dr. E. Croft, April 12, 1991, Antigua.
Malo, Dr. Simón E., January 8, 1991, Zamorano, Honduras.
Mena, Mario, November 26, 1991, Guatemala City.
Meza de Dardón, Aura Marina, July 25, 1990, Bananera.
Palacios Porta, José María, February 4, 1992, Guatemala City.
Palmer de Tabush, Jean, April 11, 1992, Guatemala City.
Pocasangre, Ana Vilma, January 16, 1992, Guatemala City.
Russell, Chad R., November 13, 1991, Guatemala City.
Shook, Dr. Edwin M., September 28, 1990, Antigua.
Silver, John R., letter to Stanley, November 28, 1990; March 28, 1991; July 13, 1991.
Smith, Ike M., letter to Stanley, February 5, 1991.
Solís, Adán, November 21, 1990, Bananera.
Swinford, William S., January 14, 1992 La Ceiba, Honduras.
Taillon, William L., personal papers provided to Stanley by Taillon's daughter, Nancy Taillon Schaper.
Turnbull, Roberto, January 14, 1992, La Lima, Honduras.
Wagner, Regina, April 13, 1992, Guatemala City.
Zapata, Willy W., December 9, 1991, Guatemala City.

Index

A
A & W Root Beer Drive Ins of America, 198
Abbotsville, 4
Adams, Frederick Upham, 3, 77, 105, 106
Adams, Richard, 138
Agrarian Reform Law, 152, 158, 161, 176
   need for, 152
   description of, 152-53
   expropriation of Compañía Agrícola's holdings, 154-55
   Compañía Agrícola's efforts against expropriation, 153-54
   expropriation of Bananera holdings, 156-57
   assessment of, 184-85
   See Arbenz
   See Castillo Armas
   See U.S. Department of State
Alfem, 171
Alta Verapaz, 6, 50
Amatitlán, 144
Ambrose, Stephen A., 182
AMK Corporation, 197-98
American Financial Corporation, 235
American Seal Cap Corporation, 197
An American Company, The Tragedy of United Fruit (McCann), 27
Anguiatú, 35-36, 38, 238
Antitrust suit, 63, 190-92, 3n267, 4n267 22n268
Arana, Francisco, Javier, 133, 136, 143-47, 175
Arana Osorio, Carlos, 200
Arbenz, Guzmán, Jacobo, 28, 133, 136, 142, 146, 154, 157, 158, 190, 46n260
   on Arana's death, 144-45
   principal goals of his administration, 149
   demands changes in UFCO's operations, 151
   denies appeal on expropriation, 157
   resigns presidency, 162, 177
   reasons for resignation, 174-77, 182
   in exile, 178-79
   member of Communist Party, 47n261
Archaeological Institute of America, 124
Arévalo Bermejo, Juan José, 132-36, 137-39, 143-47, 173
   on Great White Fleet, 64
   on UFCO salaries, 102
   campaign rhetoric against UFCO, 134-35
   on Labor Code problems with UFCO, 139-40
   on UFCO's impact on Guatemala's development, 204, 11n269
   on UFCO-paid bribes, 207
   U.S. relations, 142-43
   evaluation of his administration, 145-46
   tolerance of Communists, 146-47
   farewell speech, 42n260
Argentina, 132, 238
Argueta, Mario R., 47
Asturias, Miguel Angel, 27, 41, 21n240
Arthur, Henry B., James P. Houck, George L. Beckford, 223
Atlantic Monthly, 141
Aviateca, 98
Aybar de Soto, José, 139, 179

B
Baker, Lorenzo Dow, 20-24, 26
Banana Empire: A Case Study of Economic Imperialism, The (Kepner and Soothill), 30, 201
Bananas:
   origins of, 7n239
   first sales in U.S., 20-22, 3n241, 10n241
   soil and climate requirements, 40, 13n250
   considerations in harvesting, 76
   preparing plantations, 70-75, 6n250
   varieties of, 14n250
Banana production:
   developing Guatemala's north coast plantations, 40-41

costs of, 1n249, 27n270, 7n272
requirements of, 44, 74-75
organization of division, 79-80, 33n255, 35n256
role of overseers, 86-89
and Depression, 54
and World War II, 131
Guatemalans employed by UFCO in 1931 and 1941, 59
Guatemalans dependent on UFCO's operations in 1946 and 1956, 59, Bauer Paiz's estimate in 1949, 223, 60n271
innovations, 228-33, 16n251
Bananera, 70, 78-82, 87, 97, 99, 100, 101, 102, 104, 109, 110, 111, 112, 119, 120, 134, 140, 150, 156, 200
contemporary description of, 227
BANDEGUA. *See* Del Monte Tropical Produce Company
Banes, Cuba, 23
Bank of Guatemala, 64, 238, 250-51
Barrios, Justo Rufino, 6, 11, 12, 15, 18, 21, 31n243, 50
role in fomenting coffee industry, 6, 11, 12
construction of railroads, 13-16
Baskin Robbins, 198
Batalla de Guatemala, La (Toriello), 168
Batten, Barton, Durstine and Osborn, 229
Bauer Paiz, Alfonso, 28, 36, 38, 39, 56, 57, 201, 208, 209, 210, 212, 213, 214, 218, 220, 223, 225
Benfeldt, J. Rodolfo, 238
Bernays, Edward, 94-95, 141, 163-64
Bishop, Edwin W., 186
Bitter Fruit: The Untold Story of the American Coup in Guatemala (Schlesinger and Kinzer), 154, 166, 178
Black, Eli M., 197-99, 234-35
"Black legend," analysis of, 66-69
Blasier, Cole, 141, 165, 170, 174, 183, 225
Blowdowns, 76, 150, 193, 219, 53n271
Bocas de Toro, Panama, 52
Bonds of the Republic of 1927, 39
Booth, John A., 204
Bordeaux mixture, 54, 73, 9n250

Border dispute between Guatemala and Honduras, 45-47
Boston, 20, 21, 23, 87, 95, 194, 199
Boston Fruit Company, 21-24, 10n241
Brahman cattle, 222
Bribes, 208
See Arévalo
Britnell, George E., 109
Brunelle, Gerald K., 227, 230, 231, 233
Bulmer-Thomas, Victor, 45, 54, 62, 182, 187
Bunting, D. P., 14
Bump, Almyr L., 96, 153-56, 50n253
Bush, George Herbert Walker, 224

C
Caballo Blanco, 14
Cabot, John Moors, 160, 167-68, 170-71
Cabot, Thomas, 170
California Guatemala Fruit Corporation, 53
Cambranes, J.C., 9
Campbell, Kathryn, 82
Candidato blanco y el huracán, El (Arévalo), 134
Cardoza y Aragón, Luis, 103, 142, 152, 174, 175, 209
Carnegie Institution of Washington, 124-25
Carías Andino, Tiburcio, ??
Carol Cardoza, Benjamín, 111
Carrera, Rafael, 5
Castillo Armas, Carlos, 173, 177, 178, 181
leads "army of liberation," 173-74
becomes president, 178
reforms undertaken, 184-87
assassination, 187, 80n266
Castro, Fidel, 193, 224
Catherwood, Frederick, 123
Caudillo. See Ubico
Central American Improvement Company, 17, 29
Cerezo Arévalo, Vinicio, 187, 234
Chacón, Lázaro, 39, 48-49
attempts to obtain legislative approval for port-building contract, 48-49

INDEX

role in Guatemala-Honduras border dispute, 46
Champerico, 14, 60, 64, 67
Chile, 24
"Chiquita Banana," 229, 3n272
Chiquita Brands International, 232-37
CIA in Guatemala, The Foreign Policy of Intervention, The (Immerman), 43
Clemente Jacques food company, 198
Coatepeque, 14, 34
Cobán, 3, 6
COBIGUA. *See* Compañía Bananera Guatemalteca Indepediente
Coffee:
  as emerging export crop, 4-5
  land made available for, 5-7
  and German predominance, 7-11
  and Depression, 55
Colombia, 25, 41, 105, 236
Colonization efforts, 3-4
Commissaries:
  as fringe benefit, 103
  targets of criticism, 103-04
  domestic items purchased for, 216
Cómo opera el capital Yanqui en Centroamérica (el caso de Guatemala) (Bauer Paiz), 201
Compañía Agrícola de Guatemala, 2, 43, 48, 52, 53, 56, 68
  purchases south coast properties, 52
  becomes majority stock holder in IRCA, 59
  sells holdings, 194-97
  See Agrarian Reform Law
  See Arbenz
  See Communists
  See contracts
  See strikes
Compañía Bananera Guatemalteca Independiente (COBIGUA), 233-34
Communists, 90, 137, 141-43, 145-51, 167-68, 171, 173, 175, 181, 182-83, 189, 41n260
  See Arbenz
  See Arévalo
  See Castillo Armas
  See U.S. Department of State
  See U.S. media

Concessions:
  of land by governments to railroad builders, 14
  to Keith for railroad to the Atlantic, 32-34
  of land for all railroad construction, 32
  granted to UFCO by government, 205, 207
  See contracts
Confederación de Trabajadores de Guatemala (CTG), 137
Confederation of Latin American Workers, 137
Consent Decree. *See* antitrust suit
Contracts:
  for construction of first railroads, 13-17
  government and UFCO (1901), 27
  government and Keith (1904), 28-35, 38, 44
  government and Keith for railroad to El Salvador (1908, also known as Méndez-Williamson contract), 35, 36, (1923), 37-39
  government and UFCO to rent north coast land (1924), 41-46
  government and Compañía Agrícola to construct Pacific port (1930), 47-57, 66-67, 206-07
  government and Compañía Agrícola (1936), 56-57
  government and UFCO/Bananera (1936), 57-58
  government and Tropical Radio Telegraph Company (1926), 63-64
  UFCO and its foreign employees, 82-85
  Castillo Armas and La Frutera, 185
  private banana planters, 214
Cook, Blanche Wiesen, 152
Corcoran, Thomas, 170, 190
Cornie & Company, 16
Costa Rica, 24, 25, 29, 41, 42, 82, 91, 105, 179, 193, 194, 198, 205, 207, 211, 212, 213, 216, 218, 219, 224, 236
Council of the European Communities, 237

287

Crónica, 163
Cuba, 23, 24, 82, 105, 179, 193
Cunningham, Eugene, 88
Cutler, Robert, 170
Cutter, Victor M., 40, 105, 124, 125
Cuyamel Fruit Company, 45-47, 214
Czechoslovakia, 171, 178

D
Dartmouth, 106
Davis, George W., 36, 38
De la Vega, Laura, 103
De León Aragón, Oscar, 30, 36, 38, 43, 48, 52, 53, 57, 163
De León Carpio, Ramiro, 188, 238
Del Monte Corporation, 198-99, 23n268
Del Monte Tropical Produce Company, 111, 119, 199, 227, 229, 230, 231, 232, 233, 8n272
Declassified Eisenhower, A Divided Legacy, The (Cook), 152, 182
Decree 900. *See* Agrarian Reform Law
Departamento Agrario Nacional (DAN), 153
Dieseldorff, Erwin Paul, 9
Dimick, John M., 126, 128
Director General of Income, 156
Division headquarters, 71-72
Dole Fresh Fruit Company, 228, 236
Dulles, Allen, 166, 169
Dulles, John Foster, 163, 164-66, 169-72, 178, 190

E
Echeverría, Luis, 179
Ecuador, 193, 236
Education:
 provided by government and/or *finqueros* in early 1900s, 116-17
 under Estrada Cabrera, 117
 under Ubico, 117-18
 school attendance in rural areas (1956), 118
 importance of UFCO's bi-lingual schools, 118-19, 59n267
 description of UFCO schools, 119
 estimate of Guatemalans who attended UFCO's schools, 120

See Escuela Agrícola Panamericana
Eisenhower, Dwight D., 159, 165, 166, 167, 168, 169, 170, 172, 182, 183, 189, 224, 66n265
Eisenhower, Milton, 165
El Imparcial, 231
El Pulpo. *See* United Fruit Company/Boston
El Rancho, 17, 18, 33
El Reformador. *See* Justo Rufino Barrios
El Salvador, 2, 29, 35, 36, 38, 39, 147, 178, 191, 208, 215, 218, 238
Electric Bond and Share Company, 37, 149
Empresa Eléctrica, 150
Escuela Agrícola Panamericana, 120-23
Escuela Politécnica, 133, 148, 180, 46n260
Escuintla, 3, 14, 62, 108, 155, 184
Estrada Cabrera, Manuel, 17, 26, 27, 46, 50, 52, 117, 20n242, 48n244
 efforts to interest Germans in rail road to Atlantic, 29
 See contracts
Exports:
 during 19th century, 4
 coffee, 12, 13, 60
 cotton, 195
 sugar, 204
 bananas, 204, 208, 212
 effects of Depression, 55, 47n247
 effects of World War II, 131
 UFCO's contribution to export earnings in 1955, 202
 alleged undervaluing of banana exports, 212
 differing methods of valuing banana exports, 212-14

F
FAR. *See* Rebel Armed Forces
Farquhar, Percival, 28
FEGUA. *See* Ferrocarriles de Guatemala
Fenner, D. P., 14
Ferrocarril Nacional de El Salvador, 238
Ferrocarriles de Guatemala (FEGUA), 237-38

Fisher, Max M., 235
Flood fallowing, 42
FLMN (Farabundo Martí National Liberation Front), 188
Foreign exchange earnings, 218, 223
Fortune's Five Hundred, 235
Fortuny, José Manuel, 183
Fringe benefits:
  free land to cultivate crops, 104, 154-55
  total annual costs during 1946-1954, 217-18
  See commissaries
  See education
  See housing
  See medical care
Fruit Dispatch Company, 23

G
Galeano, Eduardo, 187
Galich, Manuel, 28, 41, 132, 143
Gálvez, Mariano, 3, 5
General Confederation of Guatemalan Workers, 175, 186
Germans:
  as early immigrants, 5, 6
  as productive coffee planters, 7-8
  ownership of agricultural and commercial enterprises, 6-7
  majority owners of railroad and shipping company, 6
  economic/political influence, 9
  interest in completing railroad to Atlantic, 29
Gleijeses, Piero, 51, 57, 139, 169, 174, 176, 180, 183
Gomar, Carlos Haroldo, 78, 195
González Orellana, Carlos, 116, 117
Grand Naine, 228, 231
Great White Fleet, 64, 69, 107, 131, 179, 209, 236
Greenberg, Lazarus S., 156
Grieb, Kenneth, 48, 50, 51, 55, 57, 58
Gros Michel, 42, 75, 193, 194, 228, 231, 14n250
Gross Domestic Product, 203, 217
Gualán, 173
Guardia, Tomás, 24
Guatemala:
  description of, 2-3
Guatemala City, 14, 15, 33, 37, 61, 67, 69, 81, 97, 98, 99, 124, 145, 150, 155, 156, 178, 223, 237
Guatemala, la democracia y el imperio (Arévalo), 143
Guatemala Plantation Limited, 52
Guatemala Railway Company, 30, 32
Guatemala Institute of Social Security (IGSS), 187
Guatemala Labor Party (Partido Guatemalteco del Trabajo), 175
Guatemala National Revolutionary Unity (URNG), 188
Guerrillas, 188, 196

H
Hague, The, Permanent Court of Arbitration, 162
Handy, Jim, 32, 38, 50, 104, 112, 149, 152, 169, 181
Health dispensers. *See* medical care
Herbruger Asturias, Arturo, 156-57, 68n263
Herrera, Carlos, 34, 36-38
Heyl, Henry T., 53
Highway to the Atlantic, 97
  recommended by IBRD mission, 67
  See Arbenz
  See IRCA
Historia de la educación en Guatemala (González Orellana), 116
Holcombe, Ted A., 195-96
Honduras, 29, 42, 45-47, 68, 94, 110, 120, 171, 172, 173, 179, 193, 198, 207, 208, 211, 212, 213, 214, 216, 218, 229, 236
Housing:
  provided laborers and white collar workers, 110-12
  criticisms of, 112-14, 42n256
  provided by other U.S. companies in Latin America, 113
  provided by plantation owners, 11
  compared to majority of population (1960s and 1990s), 113-15
  new design of UFCO housing for laborers, 114-15
Hubbard, Thomas H., 30, 31
Hubbard-Zemurray Company, 45
Huehuetenango, 126
Huxley, Aldous, 107

I
Illiteracy rates, in 1924, 117, in 1950, 138, in 1988, 221
Immerman, Richard H., 43, 49, 56, 90, 164, 174
Incidents of Travel in Central America, Chiapas and Yucatan (Stephens), 123
Indians, 3, 7, 16, 117, 133, 134, 146, 176, 177
  as laborers on coffee plantations, 11-12
  as regarded by Guatemalan elite, 1, 2, 16, 89, 21n240
Inevitable Revolutions, The United States in Central America (LaFeber), 152
Inman, Samuel Guy, 118
Inter-American Treaty of Reciprocal Assistance (Rio Treaty), 171, 172
Inter-Harvest Lettuce, 198
International Bank for Reconstruction and Development (IBRD), 52, 64-67
  on management practices of coffee planters, 15n239
  on reasons for IRCA's high freight rates, 60-62
  on management of Puerto Barrios port facilities, 65-66
  on Compañía Agrícola reduction of malaria, 109-11
  on Guatemalan laborers, 3n253
International Monetary Fund (IMF), 208, 212, 213
International Railways of Central America (IRCA), 30, 31, 32, 36, 38, 51, 55, 56, 71, 78, 209, 210, 223-24, 234, 238
  impact of spur from Zacapa on Salvadoran economy, 63n245
  financial effects of the Depression, 55
  freight rates, 60-62
  preferential rates to UFCO, 62
  U.S. government orders UFCO's divestiture of IRCA stock, 191
  nationalized by government, 67, 237
  See contracts
  See highway to the Atlantic
Investments in Guatemala by UFCO, 41, 218-20

Italy, 235
Izabal, 3, 4, 14, 108, 208

J
Jamaica, 20, 21, 22, 23, 105
Jamaican blacks, 91, 113
James, Daniel, 114
Jiménez, Ernesto Bienvenido, 116
John Morell & Company, 197, 235
Jonas, Susanne, 181
Jones, Chester Lloyd, 116

K
Karnes, Thomas L., 229
Keith, Minor C., 17, 24-33, 37, 38, 41, 43, 67, 105, 238
  construction of Costa Rica's Atlantic railroad, 24-25
  begins exporting bananas from Costa Rica, 25
  sells his holdings to Boston Fruit, 25-26
  dream of trans-isthmian railroad, 29, 39
  See contracts
Kepner, Charles David, Jr., 90, 92, 103, 110, 113, 201
  and Jay Henry Soothill, 30, 201, 206, 215
Korea, 204
Korean War, 141, 164
Krieg, William, 180

L
La Barge, Richard Allen, 30, 44, 62, 64, 81, 89, 92-93, 110, 184-85, 201, 213, 214, 217, 218
La Frutera. *See* United Fruit Company/Bananera and/or Compañia Agrícola de Guatemala
Labor Code, 138-40, 142, 143, 144
  See Arévalo
Labor courts, 138, 150, 151
Labor relations:
  See Arévalo
  See Arbenz
  See labor unions
  See strikes
Labor unions, 89-90, 96, 132, 186, 187, 54n261
  See Arévalo

See Arbenz
See Castillo Armas
See Communists
LaFeber, Walter, 152
Lake Izabal, 3, 6
Lancetilla Experiment Station, 194
Land:
  sold or granted for coffee plantations, 12
  awarded for railroad construction, 14
  extent of UFCO's holdings in 1913, 41, in 1930, 51, in 1953, 153
  UFCO's ownership of country's total crop lands, 152
  value placed on holdings by government during 1952 strike, 154
  returned by Keith, 38
  returned by Compañía Agrícola, 57, 185
  returned by UFCO/Bananera, 185
  sold or leased throughout the isthmus between 1951-1971, 10n267
  See Agrarian Reform Law
  See contracts
Liberals, 6, 13, 15, 16
Lindner, Carl H., 235
Living conditions:
  See housing
  See personnel policies
Livingston, 6, 13
Lodge, Henry Cabot, 170
Lombardo Toledano, Vicente, 137
Los Amates, 67
Lyman, J. H., 14

M
McCann, Thomas P., 27, 163, 198, 199
McCarthy, Joseph R., 141, 164
McKinley, William, 224
McMillin, Benton, 37
McNeil, Frank, 224
Macphail, Neil P., 1, 106-07, 24n255, 129, 228
Malaria, 3, 34, 44, 108, 109, 110, 195
  See IBRD
  See medical care
Malo, Simón E., 121, 122
Marxism, 134, 137, 149

Maudslay, Alfred Percivel, 124, 125
May, Stacy and Galo Plaza, 48, 59, 74, 88, 115, 205, 210, 211, 222-23
Mayas, 1, 3, 6, 10-11, 125-28
Medical care:
  need for, 105, 109-10
  establishment of Quiriguá hospital, 106
  effectiveness of health dispensers, 108-10
  charity cases, 107, 109
Meiggs, Henry, 24, 29
Melville, Thomas and Marjorie, 184, 195, 196, 220
Mena, Mario, 234
Méndez-Williamson contract. *See* contracts (1908)
Mexico, 29, 36, 47, 126, 178, 188, 198, 238
Meza de Dardón, Aura Marina, 119
Miller, Sylvanus, 17
Milstein, Seymour, 235
Monopoly:
  of maritime trade, 64-65, 69
  of banana industry, 48
  of transportation system, 48, 68, 69
Monteforte Toledo, Mario, 29, 36, 37, 49, 65, 104, 118, 176, 177
Monzón, Elfegio, 178
Morales, 78
Morgan Guarantee Trust Company, 197
Morley, Sylvanus G., 125
Motagua River, 2, 15, 28, 31, 41, 45, 46, 124
Motagua Valley, 28, 40, 41, 47, 70, 106, 227, 231, 237
Multiplier effect of UFCO's operations, 59, 216
Munch, George D., 156
Munro, Dana G., 27, 60
My War with Communism (Ydígoras Fuentes), 180

N
Nagualate Land Company, 53
Nanne, William, 14
Nathan's Famous, 235
Nation, The, 141
National Institute for the Development of Production (INFOP), 187

291

National Liberation Movement, 186
National Peasant Confederation, 175, 186
New Liverpool, 3
New Orleans, 22, 25, 28, 76, 213
New York *Herald Tribune*, 141
New York Stock Exchange, 197
New York State Supreme Court, 62-63
New York *Times*, 141
Newsweek, 141
Nicaragua, 25, 29, 46, 171, 172, 218
Non-traditional exports, 204-05

O
Ocós, 34
October revolution, 133-34, 144, 145, 158, 163, 176, 188, 7n258
"Octopus." *See* United Fruit Company
Office of the Revision of Property Registration, 156
"Operation Success," 171
Orellana, José María, 37, 43, 47
Orellana, Manuel, 50
Organization of American States, 171

P
Palmer, Bradley W., 30
Panama, 25, 29, 39, 41, 82, 91, 101, 105, 193, 199, 200
Panama Canal, 60, 166, 183
Panama disease, 32, 47, 154, 193, 230
  description of, 42
  forces United Fruit to abandon banana lands, 42-43
  flood fallowing to combat, 42
  reason for holding reserve land, 43, 62n262
Parker, Franklin D., 186
Partido Guatemalteco del Trabajo (PGT), 175
Partido de Acción Revolucionaria (PAR), 144
Patterson, Richard C., Jr., 142-43
Peat, Marwick, Mitchell & Co., 209
Pellecer, Carlos Manuel, 145
Peralta Azurdia, Enríque, 196
Per capita income, in 1956, 82, in 1992, 218

Personnel:
  categories of Guatemalan employees, 80-82
  UFCO's declining ability to attract American employees, 81
  employed by La Frutera, (1931, 1941, 1950), 59
  Anglo-Saxon feelings of superiority, 88-89
  See contracts
Personnel policies:
  providing boredom-fighting recreational facilities, 97-99
  treatment of laborers, 89-90
  alleged racism, 90-91
  salary discrimination based on nationality, 92
  failure to teach foreign employees Spanish, 93-94
  Bernays's evaluation of, 94-95
  new policy on labor relations (1956), 95-96
Peru, 24
Peurifoy, John E., 166-67, 172, 177
Philippines, 236
Piedra Santa-Arandi, Rafael, 28, 36
Pitti, Joseph A., 37, 47, 48, 50, 52
Polochic River, 3, 6
Ponce Vaides, Federico, 131, 136, 137, 148
Popenoe, Wilson, 123
Port Antonio, Jamaica, 20
Preston, Andrew W., 21-22, 26, 30
Profits:
  charges of UFCO's unreported, 208-12
  UFCO's method of calculating, 209-10
  compared to other U.S. corporations, 210, 212
  dividends to stockholders, 210-11, 29n270
  remission of, 211, 222-23
  reasons for wide oscillations of, 219
Pueblo Nuevo, 114
Puerto Barrios, 4, 15, 16, 17, 28, 31, 33, 44, 53, 60, 61, 62, 63, 64, 66, 67, 69, 107, 124, 135, 151, 171, 195, 214, 223, 224, 225, 233, 234, 237

Puerto Cortés, Honduras, 46, 47
Puerto Quetzal, 67, 68

Q
Quiriguá, 1, 2, 3, 40, 67, 71, 78, 102, 106, 107, 124, 125, 126, 173
Quiriguá archaeological park, 123-26, 129
Quiriguá hospital, 106-10, 227
See medical care
Quetzaltenango, 148

R
Railroads:
  constructed with German capital, 6
  first segments on south coast, 14
  in Costa Rica, 24-25
  See contracts
  See Keith
Rath Black Hawk, 235
Rebel Armed Forces (FAR), 188
Register of Immovable Property, 153
Reglamento de Servicio de Trabajadores Agrícolas, 10
Reina Andrade, José María, 50
Renovación Nacional, 132
Retalhuleu, 14, 50
Reyna Barrios, José María, 10, 17, 27
Río Bravo, 62, 71
Rippy, J. Fred, 17
"Rise of the Banana Industry and its Influence on Caribbean Countries, The" (Williams), 90
Roberts, Martin, 17
Rodríguez Beteta, Virgilio, 46
Roman Catholic Church, 6, 145, 175
Ruins of Zaculeu, Guatemala, The (Woodbury and Trik), 126

S
Salaries:
  averages paid by *finqueros* at turn of century, 11
  paid by UFCO in 1930s, 9n254, in 1949, 102-03, in 1954, 218, in 1956, 81
  total expended annually during 1946-1954, 218
  paid to teachers, 119
  paid by banana companies in the 1990s, 233-34, 9n273
  paid to Guatemalan farm laborers in the 1990s, 103
  See fringe benefits
  See personnel policies
Sanitation programs, 44, 109, 111-12
San Jerónimo, El Salvador, 36
San José, 14, 34, 52, 60, 64, 67
Santo Domingo, 24
Santo Tomás de Castilla, 4, 67, 149, 234
Schlesinger, Louis, 14
Schlesinger, Stephen and Stephen Kinzer, 154, 179, 181
Schneider, Ronald M., 146
Schoenfeld, Rudolph E., 166
Schroeder, Henry and Company, 30
Señor Presidente, El (Asturias), 27
Serrano Elías, Jorge, 188
Shook, Edwin M., 127-28
Sigatoka:
  invades isthmian banana plantations, 54-55
  method of controlling, 54-55, 43n247
  black sigatoka in the 1990s, 230-31, 236
Siglo Veintiuno, 179
Silva Peña, Eugenio, 139
Silver, John R., 77-78, 91, 196-97
Silvert, K. H., 132
Sindicato de Acción y Mejoramiento Ferrocarrilero (SAMF), 136
Sindicato de Empresa de Trabajadores de la Compañía Agrícola de Guatemala (SETCAG), 136
Smith, William S., 165
Snyder Banana Company, 26
Social Aspects of the Banana Industry (Kepner), 103, 201
Social security system, 137-38, 187
Solís, Adán, 119
Solórzano, Valentín F., 5, 32
Solovan, Jean, 100-02
Soothill, Jay Henry, 91
Sovereign Fruit Company, 197
Soviet Union, 158, 165, 181, 236
Spaniards, 3, 11, 126, 127
Standard Fruit and Steamship Company (now Dole Fresh Fruit Company), 62, 191, 193, 213, 229

Standard Oil Company of Indiana, 192
Stephens, John L., 123
Strikes, 140, 150, 50n261, 54n261
Sullivan and Cromwell, 168, 169
Sunderland, Thomas E., 192-94, 196, 198
Sweden, 236
Switzerland, 178

T
Taxes:
  paid by UFCO on exports, 43, 52, 57-58, 59, 201-02, 215
  on imports, 202, 215-16
  total annual taxes paid by UFCO between 1946-1954, 216
  on land holdings, 216
  on coffee exports, 202-03
  on UFCO profits, 185, 74n266
  as sources of government revenues, 202, 206
  paid by Guatemalans, 202-03, 10n269
  export taxes eliminated by Guatemalan government, 203
Taillon, William L., 213, 3n249
Tecún Umán, 14, 238
Tenedores, 17
Tikal, 126, 127
Tiquisate, 1, 51, 52, 56, 71, 73, 80, 81, 87, 96, 97, 98, 99, 100, 102, 104, 107, 111, 112, 114, 115, 118, 134, 135, 136, 150, 153, 155, 156, 161, 195, 196, 227, 233
  established as headquarters for south coast operations, 53
  sold in 1964, 194-97
  current description of, 226-27
  See medical care
Toriello, Guillermo, 143, 160, 167-69, 172, 176, 184
Toriello, Jorge, 133
Torres Rivas, Edelberto, 12, 28, 148, 174, 175
Tourism, 23, 107, 126
Trafton, Mark, Jr., 72
Tropical Radio Telegraph Company, 63-64
Tropical Trading and Export Company, 25, 26

Truman administration, 141
Turnbull, Walter, 150, 151, 180

U
Ubico, Jorge, 38, 48, 49-51, 56, 70, 103, 117, 118, 130, 133, 136
  U.S. role in his election, 49-51
  changes under, 130-31
  tenders resignation, 131-32
  See contracts
Unifruitco, 100, 103, 5n254
United Brands Company, 197-200, 234
United Fruit Company/Boston, 2, 18, 20, 31, 45, 53, 123, 160, 162, 163, 167, 170, 171, 172, 180, 182
  founding, 25-26
  extent of initial holdings, 26
  role in Arbenz's resignation, 179-80
  sold to AMK Corporation, 197-98
  interference in domestic politics, 214
  See antitrust suit
  See Arévalo
  See bribes
  See Castillo Armas
  See contracts
  See IRCA
  See Sunderland
  See Zemurray
United Fruit Company/Bananera, 2, 46, 124
  sold to Del Monte Corporation, 200
  current description of, 227
  See Agrarian Reform Law
  See Castillo Armas
  See contracts
  See strikes
United States government:
  wields "big stick," 23n242
  on Herrera's resignation, 37
  demands on Orellana, 37
  "vested interests" in policy toward Guatemala, 170-71
  See Arévalo
  See Arbenz
  Agency for International Development (USAID), 115
  Bureau of Labor Statistics, 208

Central Intelligence Agency (CIA), 166, 170, 171, 174, 179
Department of Commerce, 8, 61
Department of Justice, 63, 190, 201
Department of State, 141, 143, 154, 162, 171, 190
  attempts to mediate Guatemala-Honduras border dispute, 46
  aids Ubico's election, 50-51
  refuses to sell arms to Arévalo administration, 143
  on Compañía Agrícola's valuation of its properties, 155
  protests expropriation of Company's holdings,160-62
Environmental Protection Agency, 230
Internal Revenue Service, 210, 213
National Intelligence Estimate, 165
U.S. media, 141-42, 163-64, 24n259, 10n263
U.S. News and World Report, 141
University of San Carlos, 117, 148
URNG. *See* Guatemalan National Revolutionary Unity
Uruguay, 178

V
Vagrancy laws, 10-11
Valery, 193, 194, 195
Van Horne, Sir William, 30, 31
Vietnam, 194
Vilanova de Arbenz, María Cristina, 148-49, 179, 47n261
Villaneuva T., Benjamin, 211, 216
Virginia, 71, 76, 77, 82, 106, 124
Visión, 141
Von Bergen, Werner, 7

W
Wagner, Regina, 8, 29
Walker, Thomas W., 204
Wallenberg, Arthur E., 52
West Indies Fruit Company, 198
Whetten, Nathan L., 113-14, 116, 118, 184
Whitehouse, Sheldon, 49, 50
Whitman, Anne, 170
Whitman, Edmund S., 86-87, 170
Wild West Indies, The (Whitman), 86

Williams, John L., 90-91
Williamson, Frederick, 35
Wilkins, Mira, 113
Wilson, Charles Morrow, 22, 87, 93
Woodward, Ralph Lee, Jr., 137
Wyld Ospina, Oscar, 60

Y
Ydígoras Fuentes, Miguel, 180, 188, 196

Z
Zacapa, 15, 17, 35, 38, 238
Zaculeu, 126-28
Zamorano. *See* Escuela Agrícola Panamericana
Zapata, Emiliano, 177
Zemurray, Samuel, 45-47, 49, 54, 94, 95, 141, 150, 170, 199, 214, 14n246, 48n253, 71n257
  founds Cuyamel Fruit Company, 45
  becomes UFCO's largest stockholder, 47
  becomes UFCO's managing director, 54
  See Escuela Agrícola Panamericana